SOCIOCULTURAL CONTEXTS OF LANGUAGE AND LITERACY

Second Edition

SOCIOCULTURAL CONTEXTS OF LANGUAGE AND LITERACY

Second Edition

Edited by

BERTHA PÉREZ
The University of Texas at San Antonio

With
Teresa L. McCarty
Lucille J. Watahomigie
María E. Torres-Guzmán
To thi Dien
Ji-Mei Chang
Howard L. Smith
Aurelia Dávila de Silva
Amy Nordlander

2004

LAWRENCE ERLBAUM ASSOCIATES, PUBLISHERS
Mahwah, New Jersey   London

Lawrence Erlbaum Associates, Inc., Publishers
10 Industrial Avenue
Mahwah, New Jersey 07430

Cover design by Kathryn Houghtaling Lacey

Library of Congress Cataloging-in-Publication Data

Socialcultural contexts of language and literacy / edited by
    Bertha Pérez with Teresa L. McCarty ... [et al.].—2nd ed.
p. cm.

Includes bibliographical references and index.
ISBN 0-8058-4341-8 (alk. paper)
1. Language and languages—Study and teaching—Social aspects.
    2. Literacy. I. Pérez, Bertha, 1945–   II. McCarty, T. L.
P53.8.S628   2004
418'.0071—dc22   2003060793
                                                          CIP

Books published by Lawrence Erlbaum Associates are printed
on acid-free paper, and their bindings are chosen for strength
and durability.

Printed in the United States of America
10 9 8 7 6 5 4 3 2

Dedicated to the memory of To thi Dien,
scholar/teacher whose life was dedicated
to improving education for all children.

Contents

Preface

This book shares with prospective and in-service teachers information about learning and teaching reading, writing, and thinking in linguistically and culturally diverse classrooms and communities. The underlying and recurrent thread throughout the book is the necessity for teachers to examine every instructional practice from the perspective of the culturally and linguistically diverse learner. This is a difficult task because prospective teachers and in-service teachers must "let go" of many concepts and practices they themselves experienced as students. Thus, the goal of this book is to inform and challenge English-speaking teachers who will be teaching English literacy to linguistically and culturally diverse students. However, the focus on English literacy development does not imply advocacy for "English only" or even English as a second language (ESL) as the primary mode of literacy instruction. I have written elsewhere about the importance and benefits of first or native literacy development. In this book, I and the contributing authors assume a position that learners need to develop literacy in their native language and that the concepts and skills learned in developing the native language create a foundation of strength from which students can develop English literacy.

In this book, the contributing authors assume a view of literacy acquisition that can be characterized as constructive within a sociocultural context. *Constructivism* views the learner as an active participant in "meaning making" and "reality construction" within their environment and purpose (Bruner, 1996). *Socioculturalism* views the learner and learning as situated in a social plane where learning emerges within cultural practice (Vygotsky, 1978). Students learn as they interact with and interpret their world within their culture and in their social group. The student's environment and purpose provide the sociocultural context within which they construct or make meaning.

The book contains current research and theory that integrate constructivist and sociocultural concepts and perspectives. I also describe instructional practices that I have observed teachers using that have improved the school literacy learning of students from diverse cultural backgrounds. Together with the contributing authors, we relate concepts introduced in one chapter from one culture group to another group in subsequent chapters, and we discuss unique concerns and approaches related to using the native language and literacy for each group. Knowledge and understanding of the diversity of students, their experiences, and their sociocultural contexts are the beginning. Based on this understanding, prospective teachers will be guided to develop strategies that break out of traditional instructional patterns currently used in schools, and to begin using these new patterns of literacy instruction. The reader is encouraged to further explore the themes, concepts, and suggested practices by examining the recommended readings at the end of each chapter.

Part I presents information concerning research and language-learning theories of linguistically and culturally diverse students. The first three chapters examine definitions, concepts, models, and theories that provide a foundation for understanding first- and second-language literacy development or literacy in bilingual settings; they also examine new perspectives on literacy, the role of text and context, and, above all, the role of sociocultural experience in creating meaning. You, as teachers and future teachers, will also be challenged to investigate schools, programs, and public policies and the effects that these have on the education of linguistically and culturally diverse student populations. Programs such as bilingual education, English as a second language, and new immigrant centers need to be understood within the context of language policy and the sociopolitical context of the times.

Part II reviews research studies and presents information about literacy learning within Native American, Puerto Rican, Chinese, Vietnamese, African American, and Mexican American communities. Many members of these groups have developed literacy in their native languages and are developing English school literacy within a second-language context. How can we build on the students' background knowledge of their world and their developing literacy in school literacy experiences? Information that will assist you in examining and developing answers to the foregoing question is discussed from the perspectives of educators/researchers who are actively engaged in constructing new alternative responses. Teresa McCarty and Lucille Watahomigie, in their exquisitely crafted chapter, give us a historical and contemporary perspective of the language and literacy experiences of American Indians and Alaska Natives. María Torres-Guzmán discusses key cultural and linguistic concepts relevant to literacy learning of Puerto Ricans and reviews programs where students are experiencing success. To thi Dien introduces us to the variations in language, literacy, and cultures found in the Southeast Asian communities, and especially the attitudes of students and parents to schooling and English literacy. Ji-Mei Chang challenges our thinking about the Chinese American student in her discussion of inner-city Chinese American limited English proficient students. Howard Smith critically discusses the historical and contemporary literacy and schooling experiences of African Americans and suggests ways teachers can create literacy opportunities for all students. This section ends with a chapter by Aurelia de Silva, who demonstrates a process for conducting case studies with her case study of a Mexican American child's literacy experiences.

The combined information from Part I and the specific information in the various chapters in Part II form a framework for teachers to analyze, understand, and accommodate the multiple social, intellectual, cultural, and language differences or "ways of knowing" and "ways of doing" that children bring to the classroom. Within one classroom, children with different culture and language backgrounds and prior experiences interact with one another and with texts to create new and different ways of interpreting and learning.

The chapters in Part III will challenge the reader to view differences as an opportunity for learning and building on the diversity among students. Strategies that teachers may use to promote two-way communication, social integration, and collaboration within the linguistically diverse classroom and school are discussed. Instructional practices and the key roles teachers play in facilitating or thwarting literacy development for linguistically diverse students are examined and alternative collaborative practices suggested. The reader is guided to evaluate literacy curriculum frameworks within the specific cultural and linguistic knowledge previously developed in Part II of the book. Processes for adapting and developing literacy curriculum for multicultural and multilingual contexts are recommended. A sociocultural constructivist framework for the development of literacy curriculum that focuses on collaborative theme-based inquiry within a community setting is illustrated.

Assessment processes must also be examined for their cultural and linguistic appropriateness. Therefore, some literacy assessment strategies (e.g., observations, home/community informants, journals, portfolios) that can be used within multilevel literacy contexts are examined. The chapters in this section illustrate the manner in which a sociocultural perspective and a constructivist approach to literacy instruction provide a framework for making school literacy accessible to culturally diverse students.

Our intent is for the book to assist you in creating a sociocultural context for literacy learning within your classroom community of learners. The activities and suggested readings at the end of each chapter will permit you to "make meaning," observe, reflect, and construct application processes for your new understandings. In other words, we recommend that you read and interact with this text in much the same way that we are suggesting you encourage your students or future students to interact with "text" or "print" during literacy development. A constructivist view of learning is encouraged for the readers of this book. The reader is expected to:

- Reflect on the content based on the reader's background.
- Observe in elementary schools and communities the contexts in which children are developing literacy.
- Develop an understanding of how literacy is viewed by people from diverse speech communities.
- Test teaching strategies and learning opportunities that can assist the literacy development of diverse learners.
- Investigate and reflect on existing institutional responses to the literacy needs of linguistically and culturally diverse learners.
- Formulate the reader's own meaning of literacy and literacy instruction within diverse sociocultural contexts.

As you and your current or future students learn multiple ways of interacting and making meaning, the acquisition of higher literacies is possible. That is, you and your students will develop the ability to construct meanings from different perspectives and to understand how one's meanings may differ from those of others. More important, being able to construct meanings from different perspectives will necessitate the use of varied literacy discourses. As students learn to manipulate a variety of discourses, they can use their knowledge of discourse to analyze the very functions and uses of literacy within a society thus leading to the obtainment of levels of literacy that may be empowering. In this sense, learning about literacy in a diverse classroom can be seen as a preparation for using literacy in a diverse world society or the world as a "global village."

NEW IN THE SECOND EDITION

In this edition we have updated the research related to second-language literacy and have focused on the interpretation of these research findings to make them useful for teachers and teacher educators. With the current intense attention on research and reading, teachers and prospective teachers will find this second edition useful in understanding and articulating the research bases for literacy practices. In addition to updating the research and theories on multilingual and second-language literacy, we have included new activities that will assist you in discussing, reflecting, and putting into practice these new findings. The new suggested readings at the end of each chapter encourage the reader to further explore the topics.

ACKNOWLEDGMENTS

While preparing revisions for the second edition we suffered the loss of one of our valued and loved contributors, Dien thi To. Dr. To's untimely death has left a void that will be deeply felt by those of us involved in improving educational opportunity for culturally and linguistically diverse students. I have dedicated the second editions of this book to the memory of Dien, in appreciation for her lifetime work.

There are many people to whom I am indebted for helping with the writing and editing of the first and second editions of this book. I am indebted first of all to my colleagues and friends who contributed chapters, Ji-Mei Chang, To thi Dien, Aurelia de Silva, Teresa McCarthy, Lucille Watahomigie, and Amy Nordlander; and especially to Howard Smith and María Torres-Guzmán for their special effort and words of encouragement. The experience of working with and struggling to understand the diverse viewpoints of the contributors was a very special privilege for me.

This volume would not have been possible without the faith and support of my friend and husband Xavier King. He listened, and made suggestions and arguments that challenged and helped clarify my ideas. He also read multiple versions of many chapters and suggested changes and corrections. Most important, he has been ever cheerful, positive, and encouraging; I am grateful for his patience and his friendship.

A special debt of gratitude is owed to Naomi Silverman, who believed in the project and supported its development through some difficult times. Finally, I am indebted to colleagues who reviewed, critiqued, and gave invaluable feedback on earlier versions of the manuscript, including two reviewers for Lawrence Erlbaum Associations, Inc., Michael D. Guerrero, University of Texas at Austin, and John Hedgcock, Monterery Institute of International Studies.

—*Bertha Pérez*

REFERENCES

Bruner, J. (1996). *The culture of education*. Cambridge, MA: Harvard University Press.
Vygotsky, L. S. (1978). *Mind and society*. Cambridge, MA: Harvard University Press.

I

THEORETICAL PERSPECTIVES ON LANGUAGE AND LITERACY

1

Literacy, Diversity, and Programmatic Responses

Bertha Pérez

A teacher who grew up in Kentucky and moved to northern California, where she is teaching sixth-grade language arts, reading, and social studies, describes the diversity of her classroom:

> Samoan, Tongan, Hispanic students from Central America and Latin America; we have Russian children, and a lot from Fiji, Japan, of course, many from Hong Kong, Taiwan and Indonesia. Did I say Vietnamese? We have a lot of Vietnamese, and quite a few from the Philippines. And, we have people migrating from the east coast, from the south. We have all colors and languages and nations here. (Olsen & Mullen, 1990, p. 59)

Since the 1990s, when this northern California teacher described her classroom, the diversity has continued to dramatically increase. A visit to almost any urban public school will illustrate the linguistic and cultural diversity found in our schools and communities. In some schools, linguistically diverse students may share one common home language, such as Spanish; however, in many other schools students may come from homes that speak a number of other languages. Regardless of language and level of bilingualism and biliteracy, children's knowledge of their home language, literacy, and culture will influence how they perceive, negotiate, and process school literacy and learning.

The growing number of speakers of languages other than English and the current hostile political climate toward immigrants have created a dilemma for teachers. Not only must teachers provide the best instruction for increasingly diverse English language learners (ELLs), but also they must do so in an increasingly restrictive political climate that is openly dismissive of native-language instructional support. Teachers also find themselves under tremendous pressure to prepare children to use their nascent English literacy to perform on state tests in the name of accountability. Nonetheless, teachers must focus on making the right ethical decisions that will assist all children to learn and become literate.

In order for teachers to provide all linguistically diverse students with the most effective instruction, it is important that they have an understanding of the past efforts and relevant research. The lessons learned from previous instructional improvement efforts create a context for current practices, and they can inform educators and policymakers about future efforts.

This chapter begins by examining some of the literacy assumptions and programs. It discusses a sociocultural theory of literacy; cultural and linguistic diversity in the United States; additive and subtractive approaches and bilingualism; and programmatic responses, such as bilingual education, ESL (English as a second language) instruction, newcomer centers, and foreign-language education.

A SOCIOCULTURAL THEORY OF LITERACY

Current research and perspectives define literacy within a sociocultural context. *Literacy* is defined not just as the multifaceted act of reading, writing, and thinking, but as constructing meaning from printed text within a sociocultural context (Barton & Hamilton, 1998; Erickson, 1984; Gee, 1992, 2000; Heath, 1983; Scollon & Scollon, 1981; Street, 1995). The sociocultural context organizes literacy and what counts for literacy. A view of literacy from a sociocultural theory of learning considers and seeks to understand the cultural context within which children have grown and developed. It seeks to understand how children interpret who they are in relation to others, and how children have learned to process, interpret, and encode their world. The sociocultural theory is derived from Vygotskian (Vygotsky, 1978) views that emphasize the social world where learning and literacy emerge. A central tenet of Vygotsky's theory was that more knowledgeable members of a group engage in social mediation to bring others into the cultural practices. Wertsch (1998) extended this notion to posit that how one comes to know something cannot be separated for the cultural tools that mediate and transform the very act of knowing.

Ferdman (1991) examined the relationship between literacy and culture: "Each of us maintains an image of the behaviours, beliefs, values, and norms—in short, of the culture—appropriate to members of the ethnic group(s) to which we belong. This is what I call *cultural identity*. Cultural identity, I argue, both derives from and modulates the symbolic and practical significance of literacy for individuals as well as groups" (p. 348). All literacy users are members of a defined culture with a cultural identity, and the degree to which they engage in learning or using literacy is a function of this cultural identity. Literacy cannot be considered to be content free or context free, for it is always used in service of or filtered through the culture. The struggle for making meaning of a text on one's own terms, which may or may not be the "official" or "standard" interpretations—that is, the reader's or writer's "agency"—is central to any act of literacy (Barton & Hamilton, 1998). Thus, literacy is always socially and culturally situated. We grow, develop, and learn as we interact with and interpret our world within our culture and in our social group. The ways in which literacy users interpret and encode information about the world and their experience are determined by their cultural identity (Ferdman, 1991; Purcell-Gates, 1995).

Understanding literacy as the construction of meaning within a sociocultural context attempts to account for aim, purpose, audience, text, and the context in which reading and writing occur. The framing of literacy within the sociocultural constructivist view is informed partially by the theories of constructivist psychologists such as Jerome Bruner. According to Bruner's (1996) *constructivism tenet*, the learner uses the cultural tools, the symbols, texts, and ways of thinking, in an active process of "meaning making and reality construction" (p. 20). Thus one brings the experiences with the world, the ways of interacting with text learned in the culture group, the knowledge and skills with letters, words, and text organization as they interpret a written text. The construction of reality is also situated within the cultural context where the environment and purpose help shape the meaning (Au, 1998). For example, the construction of meaning and literacy for food shopping might require knowledge of foods, organizations of food markets, as well as the ability to interpret print in numerous typefaces on a variety of packages. In contrast, the need to write a letter will require construction of the literacy task in a totally different way; the person will need some ability to handle writing instruments, the cultural form for letters, and so forth (Ferdman, 1991). The environment and purpose provide the sociocultural context within which meaning is constructed.

A sociocultural constructivist's framework of literacy rejects the view that literacy consists of decontextualized linguistic skills (sounds of letters, knowledge of words, etc.) and that becoming literate requires the learning of discrete skills. The notion of literacy as a set of autonomous, transferable, basic reading and writing skills gives way within a sociocultural framework to a more functional, constructivist, and culturally relative view of literacy as situated social practice. Literacy is contextualized into everyday life and sustained by talk, time, and place (Street, 1995). Being literate is defined not only as being able to read and write the symbols, but also as the ability to do so in a culturally appropriate manner. In an increasingly pluralistic society, it is important to recognize that literacy is not an autonomous cognitive practice, but is an interactive process where talk plays a significant role in defining and negotiating meaning as readers and writers transact with text in sociocultural environment.

CULTURAL AND LINGUISTIC DIVERSITY IN THE UNITED STATES

Many cultures are represented in the classrooms of today, and major linguistic diversity concerns and issues faced by schools and teachers will persist and become more political as we proceed into this new century. The term *linguistically diverse* is used to refer to students whose first language or home language is either a language other than English or a language other than the middle-class, mainstream English used in schools. For example, many Hispanic students speak Spanish as their first language, and some African American students may speak and use English differently from English used in schools and classrooms (Delpit & Dowdy, 2002; Lippi-Green, 2000). Many linguistically diverse students are bilingual, or able to speak two languages: their home language and English. Other terms used to describe linguistically diverse students are English language learners (ELLs), second-language learners, language-minority students, or limited English proficient (LEP) students. Speaking in a home language other than English is not in itself a barrier to student success in school; in fact, there are studies that show some advantage to knowing more than one language (Ben-Zeev, 1977; Bialystok, 1986; Cook, 1997; Díaz, 1983; Hakuta, Ferdman, & Díaz, 1987; Náñez, Padilla, & Máez, 1992). What is essential is for teachers to allow students to use strengths in their home language as the basis for learning to read and write in English (Snow, 1990).

The term *culturally diverse* refers to students who may be distinguished by ethnicity, social class, and/or language. Ethnicity is determined by national origin or one's ancestors and a "sense of people-hood" (Au, 1993, p.1), reflected in shared history, values, and ways of and for behaving. For example, many culturally diverse students are grouped or labeled African American, Asian American, Hispanic American, and Native American, although these may not be the terms students and their families might use to describe their ethnicity. Rather, individuals are likely to speak of themselves as Haitian, Chinese American, Mexican American, or Navajo. The background knowledge and experiences that culturally diverse students bring to reading and writing have been shaped by their cultural and social group.

These concepts of linguistic and cultural diversity and the role they play in literacy development are discussed further in later chapters. Here we discuss the cultural and linguistic changes that have occurred and are occurring as a result of population trends and what that means for teachers and students.

Historical Diversity

Public education, following the social and political mood of the times, has a long history of inclusion and exclusion of languages other than English for instruction. During the colonial period the United States attempted to obliterate American Indian linguistic communities while showing tolerance to European immigrants, who were allowed to maintain and use their native languages for public and private education. The European immigrant languages were also used and supported by social and religious organizations, newspapers, and community governments. During most of the 18th and 19th centuries, many immigrant groups, whether German, Dutch, French, Norwegian, Polish, or Swiss, were able to incorporate native-language instruction into community schools as separate subjects or as languages of instruction (Heath, 1981; Leibowitz, 1982). During this time, schools were controlled by and reflective of their communities and were staffed by bilingual or native-language teachers from the local community (Perlmann, 1990). It was not until the late 19th and early 20th centuries that legal, social, and political forces began to oppose the maintenance of native languages. According to Heath (1981), the lack of competition between public and private schools contributed to the lack of support for native languages. In the early 19th century, public schools had to compete with private academies where instruction was often given in the native languages. By the end of the century, the number of new immigrants increased and public schools filled up their classrooms. The need to make accommodations for immigrant children or to compete with private academies became less important (Heath, 1981).

Increases in immigration and specifically the changing source countries of immigrants from Northern and Western Europe to Southern and Eastern Europe as well as China gave rise to fears of the "foreign element" and to the resurgence of nativism. The Nationality Act, passed in 1906, became the first legislation to require aliens to speak English in order to become naturalized (Leibowitz, 1982). This set the stage for the use of language as a mode of exclusion or discrimination for many culturally and linguistically diverse populations. During this period, the use of languages other than English was prohibited in schools. Throughout the Southwest, language was used as the rationale for the segregation of Mexican American and American Indian students, and many students were subjected to punishment when they used their native language to communicate in schools (Casanova & Arias, 1993).

The Struggle for Language Rights

As a result of the civil rights movements of the 1960s and the arrival of large numbers of Cuban refugees in Florida, educational programs using native language for instruction began to be implemented (Faltis, 1993). In 1968, the U.S. Congress passed the Bilingual Education Act; several states (California, Florida, Illinois, Massachusetts, Texas, New York, and others) followed with passage of state statutes. A number of court cases were filed on behalf of language-minority students concerning language and students' rights to education. Perhaps the most significant of these cases was *Lau v. Nichols* (1974).

In 1970, Kinney Knmon Lau and the parents of 12 other Chinese American students filed a class action suit on behalf of Chinese-speaking students in the San Francisco Unified School District, claiming that the children were being denied equal educational opportunity. The primary issue was whether non-English-speaking children in English-only classrooms were receiving an equal education and whether the school district had a legal obligation to provide special instructional programs. In 1974, the U.S. Supreme Court affirmed in *Lau v. Nichols* the right of the students and their parents to a meaningful education and that some instructional remedy was required. The court recommended that school districts implement appropriate remedies taking into account the number of non-English-speaking students in the district. School districts were free to design the type of instructional response that they assessed as most appropriate for their population and context.

The *Lau* decision had a powerful impact on the education of linguistically diverse students. National, state, and local policymakers were challenged to design and implement programs that would respond to the special needs of non-English-speaking students. Through the late 1970s, the federal government pressured many states and local districts to implement special programs, including bilingual and English as a second language (ESL) programs. The *Lau* decision and remedies remain in effect today, and continue to be a major force in supporting the educational rights of linguistically diverse students. During the 1980s, a period of language conservatism resurfaced, with federal officials relinquishing their proactive role and recommending more decision making be shifted to local control. The 1980s also saw the rise of the official English or English-only movement, which fueled the contemporary debate surrounding language and which created new tensions for educators working with linguistically diverse students (Crawford, 1992; McGroarty, 1992). In the 1990s, the sociopolitical climate became overtly antagonistic toward the linguistic rights of non-English speakers with the passage of California Proposition 227 (García, 2000). The California proposition specified that all children be placed in English-language classrooms, regardless of English-language ability. New immigrant non-English-speaking children were allowed to participate in ESL classes for 1 year (180 school days). The proposition's intent was to do away with bilingual education for linguistically diverse children (Lindholm-Leary, 2001). Skutnabb-Kangas (1988, 2000) coined the term *linguicism* to refer to language discrimination and the cacophonous debate over official language. She defined linguicism as "ideologies and structures that are used to legitimate, effectuate and reproduce an unequal division of power and resources between groups which are defined on the basis of language" (Skutnabb-Kangas, 1988, p. 13). Although today linguicism is more generally associated with racially and economically oppressed groups, since the turn of this century, linguicism has been practiced against all languages other than English. For example, in the early history of this country, German was a language almost on a par with English and was used in bilingual programs during past centuries, but because of the xenophobic policies immediately prior to, during, and after World War I, German-language instruction languished in the United States (Nieto, 1992, 1993).

Linguicism also affects African American children who may speak *Black English Vernacular (BEV)*, also called Ebonics (see Smith, chap. 8, this volume) or what is increasingly being called *African American Language*. These children "must cope with the burden of the negative stigma attached to the language they speak" (Nieto, 1992, p. 155). Ladson-Billings (1994) stated that "the language they bring with them serves as a tool that helps them with additional language learning, just as speakers of Standard English use English to help them acquire new languages" (p. 84). She further related how one teacher helps her students to see the connections between African American language and Standard English:

> I don't want them to be ashamed of what they know but I also want them to know and be comfortable with what school and the rest of the society requires. When I put it in the context of "translation" they get excited. They see it is possible to go from one to the other. It's not that they are not familiar with Standard English .... They hear Standard English all the time on TV. It's certainly what I use in the classroom. But there is rarely any connection made between the way they speak and Standard English. I think that when they can see the connections and know that they can make the shifts, they become better at both. They're bilingual! (p. 84)

Purcell-Gates (1995) described how the negative stigma of linguicism is also applied to White Appalachian English speakers: "Language is a highly visible marker of culture ... that can be used by schools to discount the speaker as ... unable and unwilling to learn. It was used as a wall to exclude her [Jenny] from access to an effective education" (pp. 164–165). Purcell-Gates went on to explain that the school's and society's "reaction to it [dialect] was governed by political and social factors" (p. 165). The reaction of the schools to the use of language by White Appalachian dialect speakers today reads like the many stories about the schools' reaction to speakers of other dialects and languages.

When the roles of official language, ideology, and political structures within society and in particular schools are not examined and addressed, the resultant literacy programs that develop are described by Devine (1994) as being based on the *muted group theory*. That is, the literacy programs hearten the lopsided power relationship within a society. Devine suggested that the dominant group's relative privileged position gives it power over other groups as it gets to determine the model of language and literacy. Other groups, by virtue of their class, race, ethnic origin, or gender, are muted. Thus, the muted group theory suggests "that constant reference to the dominant model as a way of validating experiences threatens to undermine the non-dominant groups' ability to separate their attitudes and experiences from those of the group in power, perhaps even to articulate their own attitudes and values other than in relation to the powerful group" (Devine, 1994, p. 231). The social tensions that shape the policy context of programs for language-minority students today are always referenced against the majority group's experiences with schooling.

> Learning to read and write ought to be an opportunity for men to know what *speaking the word* really means: a human act implying reflection and action. As such it is a primordial human right and not the privilege of the few. Speaking the word is not a true act if it is not at the same time associ-

> ated with the right of self-expression and world-expression, of creating
> and re-creating, of deciding and choosing and ultimately participating in
> society's historical process. (Freire, 1991, p. 253)

In examining the practices of the past and the existence of linguicism, it is also important to remember that in becoming Americans, all
people have enriched the national language and culture. The language
reflects cultural patterns, refined and strengthened through association and social status. Pederson (1993) described the role the middle
class has played in the absorption of immigrant groups and the contributions to the language that some of these groups have made:

> In America, the middle classes have generated great changes. These in-
> clude the absorption of immigrant cultures at the lower level and influ-
> ence upon the dominant culture at the higher level. As the linguistic and
> cultural forms are traditionally conservative in both aristocratic and folk
> groups, however different their social styles, middle-class society and
> speech alter those conventional patterns from below and from above ....
> In the process of Americanization, Europeans, Africans, and Asians gave
> the language some of its most familiar words: Chop suey, hamburger, hill-
> billy, juke box, pizza, prairie, rodeo, Santa Claus, smorgasbord, and ty-
> coon .... Through common-law customs of speech and writing the
> national language develops words and records social facts. (pp. 21–22)

Current Diversity

The 2000 Census estimated that over 46 million or 17.9% of people 5
years old and over spoke a language other than English at home (U.S.
Bureau of the Census, 2001). Although Spanish was the predominant
language after English, more than 25 other languages have significant
numbers of speakers concentrated within specific communities.

According to Kindler (2002), "LEP [limited English proficient stu-
dent] enrollment levels in the U.S. continued to increase in 2000–2001,
both in absolute numbers and as a percentage of the total student enrollment" (p. 3). Of the 4.6 million school-age students whose native
language was other than English, 79% reported Spanish was the primary language of communication in the home. The other four most
common home languages were Vietnamese, Hmong, Cantonese (Chinese), and Korean. Figure 1.1 illustrates the diversity of native languages that linguistically diverse students bring to the classroom.

Linguistically diverse students live in all areas of the United States.
The 2000 Census reported an increase in the number of school-age
language-minority population in all states. The largest numbers of
LEP students were enrolled in California, Puerto Rico, Texas, Florida,
New York, Illinois, and Arizona. Some states, like Georgia, with a

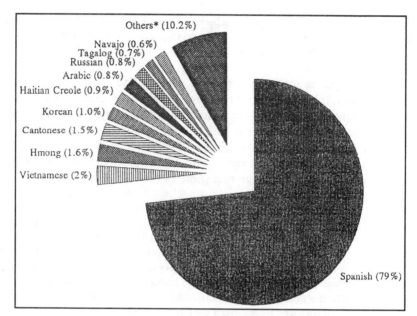

FIG. 1.1.   Native languages of language-minority students.

113% increase of LEP students, have seen significant changes in the diversity of their school population. Many of the LEP students are children of fairly new or recent immigrants that have come to this county for economic reasons. A large number are children of war or political refugees from the Middle East, Southeast Asia, Eastern Europe, Central America, and Africa. Others were born in the United States of U.S. citizens, as is the case with some Puerto Ricans and Mexican Americans. Also, the Native American or American Indian children have a heritage in the United States that goes back for countless generations.

Twenty million African American school-age students come to school speaking English as a native language; however, for many of these children the sociocultural context in which they learned language is significantly different from (a) the context in which European Americans learned English and (b) the context of school learning. Although in 1980 three of four school-age children were of Euro-American origin (Pallas, Natriello, & McDill, 1989), by 2020, only one of two or half of school-age children will be of Euro-American ancestry. The concern is for children who are marked both by the linguistic and cultural differences between their homes/communities and schools, and by the low status of their parents in comparison with the mainstream society.

PROGRAMS FOR LINGUISTICALLY DIVERSE STUDENTS

Teachers are expected to provide all students with the most effective programs and best instructional practices while meeting their individual linguistic and educational needs. An examination of the responses to linguistic diversity of the past can provide a context for current and future efforts.

Additive Versus Subtractive Approaches and Bilingualism

The sociopolitical context of language learning in the United States has created an environment where learning or maintaining a language other than English for minority groups is considered a disadvantage. Thus, many of the bilingual programs are driven by subtractive bilingualism approaches, with less than a fourth of the programs providing for continued development of the student's native language (Kindler, 2002). *Subtractive bilingualism* encourages the children to supplant their first language with the second language. When one language is valued over the other, a conflict or a competitive context is created, resulting in subtractive bilingualism. Subtractive bilingualism is the social context found in many language-minority communities within the United States, where ethno-minority languages are not only not valued but there is also a strong societal expectation and pressure for the native language to be abandoned in favor of English (Hakuta, 1990). For some children the perception that learning English involves betrayal of one's cultural group makes it difficult for them to acquire a high level of English proficiency (Náñez et al., 1992; Scollon & Scollon, 1981). By contrast, in some middle-class homes and schools children are encouraged to maintain and develop all their linguistic skills in the first language while acquiring a second language; here, *additive bilingualism* is being supported. Additive bilingualism refers to situations where both the native language and the second language are supported and developed (Díaz & Klingler, 1991). Social contexts that promote additive bilingualism are found in societies that value both languages and perceive the acquisition of multiple languages as a positive achievement, for example, Finland, where learning both Finnish and Swedish languages and cultures are valued.

Effects of bilinguality on cognition or mental functioning have long been used as an argument for or against bilingual education in the

United States and elsewhere. Research conducted in the last 30 years has shown, with some degree of consistency, that the early learning of a second language, either by simultaneous acquisition at home or in bilingual education programs, is associated with positive cognitive gains (Ben-Zeev, 1977; Bialystok, 1986; Díaz & Klingler, 1991; Peal & Lambert, 1962). However, findings from research conducted prior to the 1960s continue to "haunt current perceptions of the effects of bilingual education or bilingual upbringing, even among otherwise knowledgeable educators and scholars" (Casanova & Arias, 1993, p. 20).

Náñez et al. (1992) attributed findings of research studies conducted prior to the 1960s to the political agenda, which "influenced psychometric researchers of the period to produce a steady flow of studies indicating that bilinguality hinders cognitive processes" (p. 45). Later studies conducted in Canada (Lambert & Anisfeld, 1969; Peal & Lambert, 1962) found no negative effects and in fact found "enhancement of intelligence and cognitive flexibility" (Náñez et al., 1992, p. 48). Since the first Peal and Lambert study, research findings documented advantages on "different types of tasks, including psychometric and experimenter-made tests of both verbal and non-verbal abilities" (Díaz & Klingler, 1991, p. 172). The positive results have appeared in studies comparing bilingual children including children who are learning both languages in bilingual education programs (additive bilingual). However, negative results were found when the second language is "both the dominant and prestigious language ... [and] the devaluation and dismantling of L1 [first language] coupled with a lack of command of L2 [second language] is seen as having subtractive (negative) effects on the individual's cognitive abilities" (Náñez et al., 1992, p. 48). Educators have to learn how to interpret the knowledge gained from the research studies on bilingualism and cognition into strategies that can be used by students as they work to become bilingual and biliterate.

The educational programs that linguistically diverse children are experiencing in schools may vary vastly with respect to the attention to language and literacy development in their first language. The most frequently occurring programs can be grouped into the following major categories: bilingual education, English as a second language, newcomer or new immigrant centers, and foreign-language education. In this section, these types of programs and issues related to these programs are discussed.

Bilingual Programs in Multilingual Communities

Within multilingual communities, and even within communities that may be primarily bilingual, the existence of educational programs that are designed to address the needs of the communities varies. Given the diversity of language-minority students, local circumstances, and program alternatives, there is no single bilingual education model. The term *bilingual education* implies using two languages for instruction; however, in schools the interpretation of the term can mean a wide range of programs primarily reflecting sociopolitical or ideological orientations. This results in much confusion about the instructional practices and effectiveness of the program, as well as continued conflict within policy circles and in the popular media (Gutiérrez, Baquedano-López, & Asato, 2000).

Bilingual programs can be vastly different with respect to the use and the development of literacy in the native language; "ranging from total absence to benign neglect to active development; and from mainstream with pull-out ESOL [English for speakers of other languages] to transitional bilingual education to two-way maintenance bilingual education" (Hornberger, 1994, p. 104). In 2000–2001, only "22.7% [of limited English proficient students] were receiving instruction that incorporated the student's native language" (Kindler, 2002, p. 14). Most bilingual education is offered in the early elementary grades within a context based on the primacy of English literacy. The *No Child Left Behind Act of 2001*, also known as H.R. 1 (U.S. Department of Education, 2002), states:

> H.R. 1 consolidates the US Department of Education's bilingual and immigrant education programs ... focuses support on enabling all limited English proficient (LEP) students to learn English as quickly and effectively as possible .... Under H.R. 1, all LEP students will be tested for reading and language arts in English after they have attended school in the United States for three consecutive years. (p. 3)

The *transitional* bilingual programs emphasize relatively rapid transition from an instructional program in the first language accompanied by English-language development into the all-English classroom. Most transitional bilingual programs reflect subtractive bilingualism approaches. According to Freeman (1998), "The transitional model encompasses all of those bilingual education programs that encourage language minority students to shift to the majority language, assimilate to mainstream cultural norms, and be incorporated into the national society" (p. 3). *The maintenance* bilingual programs stress preservation of the child's first language, with a more gradual development of English and a continuation of first-language instruction throughout the upper elementary grades. Maintenance programs encourage additive bilingualism and biculturalism.

Other distinctions that exist in bilingual programs are between *one-way* bilingual programs, where only the limited English proficient members of minority groups are provided bilingual instruction, and *two-way* bilingual programs, where both minority-group members and English-dominant speakers (minority- and majority-culture students) are provided bilingual instruction. Researchers (Christian, Monotone, Lindholm, & Carranza, 1997; Lindholm, 1992; Lindholm-Leary, 2001; McEachern, 2000; Pérez, 2004; Thomas & Collier, 1997) reported that dual-language or two-way bilingual programs can promote high levels of language and academic achievement. Lindholm (1992) found that

> the bilingual individual must develop full academic language proficiency in both languages in order for the cognitive and academic advantages to accrue. This means that a bilingual/immersion program needs a full maintenance model that completely develops both languages over an extended period of time to reap the cognitive and academic advantages. (Lindholm, 1992, p. 215)

Two-way bilingual programs also have the potential for transforming what Cummins (1994) termed "coercive relations of power into collaborative relations" (p. 319) as both majority and minority students develop bilingualism and biliteracy. Both majority and minority parent and community groups should see the developing of linguistic assets as a potential that might result in future educational, social, and economic benefits.

Although there is continuing controversy about the effectiveness of bilingual education, much of this controversy is really about political power, cultural identity, and social status (Crawford, 1992) rather than about the academic performance of bilingual children who have participated in bilingual education. Arias and Casanova (1993) assessed the status of bilingual research, saying:

> Research has been used through the years to alternatively support and attack bilingual education programs. From the negative finding of Baker and de Kanter in 1973 to the increasingly positive findings of Willig in 1985 and Ramírez, Yuen, Ramey, and Pasta in 1991, the thoroughness and frequency of federally commissioned research has been unprecedented. It is interesting that assiduous attention has been bestowed on bilingual education while similarly funded programs for the gifted and talented have remained largely unquestioned .... Investigations with bilingual populations during the last thirty years have enhanced our understanding of language and cognitive development and of the cognitive and social implications of the pedagogical strategies used in bilingual instruction. (p. xi)

In general, most research (Collier, 1989; Ramírez, Yuen, & Ramey, 1991; Thomas & Collier, 1997; Willig, 1985) has defined effectiveness of bilingual programs primarily on measures of English language and reading and ability to do mathematics in English. Ramírez (1992) found that bilingual programs were effective not only in teaching students content area knowledge in their native language but also in teaching them English. An important result of the Ramírez study is that

> LEP [limited English proficient] students can be provided with substantial amounts of primary language instruction without impeding their acquisition of English language and reading skills.
>
> LEP students who are provided with substantial instruction in their primary language (40%) successfully continue to increase their achievement in content areas such as mathematics, while they are acquiring their skills in English; in contrast, students who are quickly transitioned into E-O [English only] instruction tend to grow slower than the norming population. (p. 43)

According to Hakuta (1990) and Willig (1985), there are also some secondary benefits of bilingual education, such as motivating students to remain in school rather than drop out and reinforcing important family relationships as children maintain their ability to communicate with their parents and elders.

English as a Second Language (ESL) and Literacy

English as a second language (ESL) either can be a component of a bilingual education program or can be a stand-alone program. Some schools opt for ESL programs over offering bilingual education programs for sociopolitical reasons (Ovando, Collier, & Combs, 2003). However, most opt for ESL because of low incidence of populations that speak any given language or because of the school's inability to find a credentialed bilingual teacher. Where schools need to serve many language groups, students may receive ESL instruction through "pullout classes" either daily or a few times a week. Although the methodologies vary widely, ESL teachers generally focus their instruction on the development of listening, speaking, reading, and writing skills in English by creating low-stress learning environments, what Krashen (1995) called reducing the affective filter and providing for comprehensible input. The student's native language may be used to clarify meaning and enhance understanding when the ESL teacher or aide speaks the child's native language. Several studies (Toohey, 2000; Valdés, 2001) have demonstrated how social practices, student identity, and ESL instructional practices that do not recognize and value students' native language may hinder second-language learners' acquisition of English.

Newcomer Centers for New Immigrants

In districts with high numbers of new immigrant students, a central location may be set up to process these students. The students may undergo screening in a variety of areas, including language assessment in both English and their native language. Orientation classes are conducted to acquaint the students with information on topics related to their new school setting, for example, health and nutrition information and expected school behavior. Some newcomer centers are designed to provide intensive English-language development lessons that provide students with the communication skills necessary to function socially in the school setting.

A number of factors influence the type of newcomer centers or programs available to immigrant students. Ferdman and Weber (1994) delineated these factors to include (a) the availability of resources in the native language(s), (b) the status of the language(s) in the United States and within the sociocultural group, (c) the relationship of the native language to English, (d) the existence of prior literacy skills in the native language, and (e) the perceived need for developing English literacy. These factors describe the needs of new immigrants in relation to their previous experience with schooling: "Immigrant children who have been in school in their native country can be expected to be different in terms of literacy acquisition than children without prior schooling ... immigrants' experiences will vary depending on their motivations for coming to and staying in the United States ... and on their current and previous social roles" (Ferdman & Weber, 1994, p. 11).

In a California study, Valdés (2001) followed four Latino students over 2 years in three middle schools. Valdés examined the instructional programs offered through ESL and newcomer classes and she summarized her findings:

> Sequestering English-language learners for all or most of the day to "study" English may not result in the outcomes that the children themselves, their families, and the public are expecting. Contrary to what proponents of Proposition 227 in California have claimed, *English cannot be learned in a single year.* (Valdés, 2001, p. 147, italics in the original)

Foreign-Language Education: Enrichment Versus Remediation

Few critics of education programs for culturally and linguistically diverse students recognize that the goals of foreign- or modern-language education, second-language education, and bilingual education are compatible. All three are educational processes that develop second-language skills and cross-cultural competencies among American students.

Minority-language students bring a language other than English to school; in contrast, the students who study "foreign" languages are for the most part English monolinguals. Typically, foreign-language education begins at the secondary level, whereas bilingual education more often starts at the elementary level. Exceptions to this distinction are the foreign-language programs for "gifted" monolingual English students that begin at the elementary level. Perhaps one of the most interesting contradictions in the public's perception of second-language learning is that the study of a foreign language is viewed as enrichment for English monolingual students, yet minority-language students who speak that same foreign language and learn English as a second language are viewed as needing "remedial" education (Saravia-Shore & Arvizu, 1992, pp. 492–493).

The linguistic capital found in this country, although sometimes unrecognized, is truly incredible. The cultural and linguistic diversity could be a valuable resource that would help us to understand and work with people from other countries and also to compete with them in the global marketplace.

SUMMARY

As the society of the United States continues to become more linguistically and culturally diverse, it is important to develop an understanding of the interplay of social, cultural, political, and geographic forces contribution to literacy attainment. A view of literacy that is founded on a sociocultural theory of learning recognizes that meaning can be constructed from multiple perspectives. It permits learners to bring all their knowledge to the task of interpreting or encoding texts, including the frames of references from their culture and experience for comprehending the contents. Accounting for the context of literacy recognizes the "agency" of readers and writers.

As teachers prepare to work with linguistically diverse students and as they struggle with instructional issues, it is important that they have an understanding of the past efforts. Knowledge that a number of alternative approaches can be effective in the education of linguistically diverse students provides those responsible for decision making with choices. Programmatic choices can be made within the sociocultural and linguistic context of their communities. However, for communities that have large numbers of children who speak a given language, it would be an inexcusable error not to maintain and develop the diverse linguistic resources of the community.

■ ACTIVITIES

1. In a group, brainstorm questions that you might ask classroom teachers about their attitudes toward special programs, such as bilingual education, ESL, and other programs, for culturally and linguistically diverse students. Use the questions to interview two teachers. Bring the data collected to class and summarize the results for discussion.
2. Observe in a classroom that has culturally and linguistically diverse students. Analyze the power messages implicitly or explicitly conveyed by the language and literacy opportunities provided in this classroom.
3. In small groups, discuss your own cultural and linguistic background. Because the United States is a nation of immigrants, who was the last member of your family to speak a native language other than English? How do you think your linguistic and cultural background might affect your teaching of students from diverse backgrounds?
4. In small groups, describe how you learned to read and write. Categorize the approaches to reading and writing described in your group. Does any member of your group come from a culturally or linguistically diverse background? Discuss how you think your own experience learning to read and write will influence the way you will teach literacy to linguistically and culturally diverse students.

SUGGESTED READINGS

Escamilla, K. (1994). The sociolinguistic environment of a bilingual school: A case study introduction. *Bilingual Research Journal, 18*, 21–48.

Gutiérrez, K. D., Baquedano-López, P., & Asato, J. (2000). "English for the Children": The new literacy of the old world order, language policy and educational reform. *Bilingual Research Journal, 24*(1), 87–112.

McLaughlin, D. (1995). Strategies for enabling bilingual program development in American Indian schools. *Bilingual Research Journal, 19*, 169–178.

Montero-Sieburth, M., & Peterson, L. (1991). Immigrants and schooling: An ethnohistorical account of political and family perspectives in an urban community. *Anthropology and Education Quarterly, 22*, 300–325.

Phillips, D. C. (1995). The good, the bad, and the ugly: The many faces of constructivism. *Educational Researcher, 24*, 5–12.

Schiller, L. (1996). Coming to America: Community from diversity. *Language Arts, 73*, 46–51.

REFERENCES

Au, K. H. (1993). *Literacy instruction in multicultural settings*. Fort Worth, TX: Harcourt Brace.

Au, K. H. (1998). Social constructivism and the school literacy learning of students of diverse backgrounds. *Journal of Literacy Research, 30*, 297–319.

Arias, M., & Casanova, U. (Eds.). (1993). *Bilingual education: Politics, practice, and research*. Chicago: University of Chicago Press.

Barton, D., & Hamilton, M. (1998). *Local literacies: Reading and writing in one community*. London: Routledge.

Ben-Zeev, S. (1977). The influence of bilingualism on cognitive strategy and cognitive development. *Child Development, 48*, 1009–1018.

Bialystok, E. (1986). Factors in the growth of linguistic awareness. *Child Development, 57*, 498–510.

Bruner, J. (1996). *The culture of education*. Cambridge, MA: Harvard University Press.

Casanova, U., & Arias, M. B. (1993). Contextualizing bilingual education. In M. B. Arias & U. Casanova (Eds.), *Bilingual education: Politics, practice, and research* (pp. 1–35). Chicago: University of Chicago Press.

Christian, D., Montone, C. L., Lindholm, K. L., & Carranza, I. (1997). *Profiles in two-way immersion education*. Washington, DC: Center for Applied Linguistics and Delta Systems.

Collier, V. (1989). How long? A synthesis of research on academic achievement in a second language. *TESOL Quarterly, 23*(3), 509–532.

Cook, V. (1997). The consequences of bilingualism for cognitive processing. In A. M. B. de Groot & J. F. Kroll (Eds.), *Tutorials in bilingualism* (pp. 279–299). Mahwah, NJ: Lawrence Erlbaum Associates.

Crawford, J. (Ed.). (1992). *Language loyalties: A source book on the official English controversy*. Chicago: University of Chicago Press.

Cummins, J. (1994). From coercive to collaborative relations of power in the teaching of literacy. In B. M. Ferdman, R. M. Weber, & A. G. Ramírez (Eds.), *Literacy across languages and cultures* (pp. 295–330). Albany: State University of New York Press.

Delpit, L., & Dowdy, J. K. (2002). *The skin that we speak: Thoughts on language and culture in the classroom*. New York: New Press.

Devine, J. (1994). Literacy and social power. In B. M. Ferdman, R. M. Weber, & A. G. Ramírez (Eds.), *Literacy across languages and cultures* (pp. 221–237). Albany: State University of New York Press.

Díaz, R. M. (1983). Thought and two languages: The impact of bilingualism on cognitive development. In E. W. Gordon (Ed.), *Review of research in education* (Vol. X, pp. 23–54). Washington, DC: American Education Research Association.

Díaz, R. M., & Klingler, C. (1991). Towards an explanatory model of the interaction between bilingualism and cognitive development. In E. Bialystok (Ed.), *Language processing in bilingual children* (pp. 167–192). Cambridge, England: Cambridge University Press.

Erickson, F. (1984). School literacy, reasoning and civility: An anthropologist's perspective. *Review of Educational Research, 54*, 525–544.

Faltis, C. J. (1993). *Joinfostering: Adapting teaching strategies for the multilingual classroom*. New York: Merrill.

Ferdman, B. M. (1991). Literacy and cultural identity. In. M. Minami & B. P. Kennedy (Eds.), *Language issues in literacy and bilingual/multicultural education* (pp. 347–390). Cambridge, MA: Harvard Educational Review.

Ferdman, B. M., & Weber, R. M. (1994). Literacy across languages and cultures. In B. M. Ferdman, R. M. Weber, & A. G. Ramírez (Eds.), *Literacy across languages and cultures* (pp. 3–29). Albany: State University of New York Press.

Freeman, R. D. (1998). *Bilingual education and social change*. Clevedon, England: Multilingual Matters.

Freire, P. (1991). The adult literacy process. In M. Minami & B. P. Kennedy (Eds.), *Language issues in literacy and bilingual/multicultural education* (pp. 248–265). Cambridge, MA: Harvard Educational Review.

García, E. E. (2000). Implementation of California's Proposition 227: 1998–2000. *Bilingual Research Journal, 24*, 1–15.

Gee, J. (1992). Socio-cultural approaches to literacy (literacies). *Annual Review of Applied Linguistics, 12*, 31–48.

Gee, J. (2000). Discourse and sociocultural studies in reading. In M. L. Kamil, P. B. Mosenthal, P. D. Pearson, & R. Barr (Eds.), *Handbook of reading research* (Vol. III, pp. 195–207). Mahwah, NJ: Lawrence Erlbaum Associates.

Gutiérrez, K. D., Baquedano-López, P., & Asato, J. (2002). "English for the children": The new literacy of the old world order, language policy and educational reform. *Bilingual Research Journal, 24*(1), 87–112.

Hakuta, K. (1990). *Bilingualism and bilingual education: A research perspective, No. 1*. Washington, DC: National Clearinghouse for Bilingual Education.

Hakuta, K., Ferdman, B. M., & Díaz, R. M. (1987). Bilingualism and cognitive development: Three perspectives. In S. Rosenberg (Ed.), *Advances in applied psycholinguistics: Reading, writing and language learning* (Vol. II, pp. 284–319). New York: Cambridge University Press.

Heath, S. B. (1981). English in our language history. In C. A. Ferguson & S. B. Heath (Eds.), *Language in the USA* (pp. 6–20). Cambridge, England: Cambridge University Press.

Heath, S. B. (1983). *Ways with words*. Cambridge, England: Cambridge University Press.

Hornberger, N. H. (1994). Continua of biliteracy. In B. M. Ferdman, R. M. Weber, & A. G. Ramírez (Eds.), *Literacy across languages and cultures* (pp. 103–139). Albany: State University of New York Press.

Kindler, A. L. (2002). *Survey of the states limited English proficient students and available educational programs and services 2000–2001 summary report*. Washington, DC: National Clearinghouse for English Language Acquisition & Language Instruction Educational Programs.

Krashen, S. D. (1995). Bilingual education and second language acquisition theory. In D. B. Durkin (Ed.), *Language issues: Readings for teachers* (pp. 90–116). New York: Longman.

Ladson-Billings, G. (1994). *The dreamkeepers: Successful teachers of African American children*. San Francisco: Jossey-Bass.

Lambert, W. E., & Anisfeld, E. (1969). A note on the relation of bilingualism and intelligence. *Canadian Journal of Behavioral Science, 1*, 123–128.

Lau v. Nichols, 414 U.S. 563 (1974).

Leibowitz, A. H. (1982). *Federal recognition of the rights of language minority groups*. Roslyn, VA: National Clearinghouse on Bilingual Education & Inter-America Research Associates.

Lindholm, K. J. (1992). Two-way bilingual/immersion education: Theory, conceptual issues, and pedagogical implications. In R. V. Padilla & A. H. Benavides (Eds.), *Critical perspectives on bilingual education research* (pp. 195–220). Tempe, AZ: Bilingual Press/Editorial Bilingüe.

Lindholm-Leary, K. J. (2001). *Dual language education*. Clevedon, England: Multilingual Matters.

Lippi-Green, R. (2000). That's not my language: The struggle to (re)define African American English. In R. Dueñas González & I. Melis (Eds.), *Language ideologies: Critical perspectives on the official English movement: Vol 1. Education and the social implications of official language* (pp. 230–247). Mahwah, NJ: Lawrence Erlbaum Associates.

McEachern, F. L. W. (2000). The influence of bilingualism on English reading scores. *Reading Improvement, 37*(2), 87–91.

McGroarty, M. (1992). The societal context of bilingual education. *Educational Researcher, 21*, 7–9.

Náñez, J. E., Padilla, R. V., & Máez, B. L. (1992). Bilinguality, intelligence, and cognitive information processing. In R. V. Padilla & A. H. Benavides (Eds.), *Critical perspectives on bilingual education research* (pp. 42–69). Tempe, AZ: Bilingual Press/Editorial Bilingüe.

Nieto, S. (1992). *Affirming diversity: The sociopolitical context of multicultural education.* New York: Longman.

Nieto, S. (1993). We speak in many tongues: Language diversity and multicultural education. In J. V. Tinajero & A. F. Ada (Eds.), *The power of two languages: Literacy and biliteracy for Spanish-speaking students* (pp. 37–48). New York: Macmillan/McGraw-Hill.

Olsen, L., & Mullen, N. A. (1990). *Embracing diversity: Teachers' voices from California's classrooms.* San Francisco: California Tomorrow.

Ovando, C. J., Collier, V. P., & Combs, M. C. (2003). *Bilingual and ESL classrooms: Teaching in multicultural contexts.* New York: McGraw-Hill.

Pallas, A. M., Natriello, G., & McDill, E. L. (1989). Changing nature of the disadvantaged population: Current dimensions and future trends. *Education Researcher, 18*, 16–22.

Peal, E., & Lambert, W. E. (1962). The relation of bilingualism to intelligence. *Psychological Monographs: General and Applied, 76*, 1–23.

Pederson, L. (1993). Language, culture, and the American heritage. In L. M. Cleary & M. D. Linn (Eds.), *Linguistics for teachers* (pp. 4–22). New York: McGraw-Hill.

Perlmann, J. (1990). Historical legacies: 1840–1920. *Annals of the American Academy of Political and Social Science, 5*, 27–37.

Pérez, B. (2004). *Becoming biliterate: A study of two-way bilingual immersion education.* Mahwah, NJ: Lawrence Erlbaum Associates.

Purcell-Gates, V. (1995). *Other people's words: The cycle of low literacy.* Cambridge, MA: Harvard University Press.

Ramírez, J. D. (1992). Executive summary. *Bilingual Research Journal, 16*, 1–62.

Ramírez, J. D., Yuen, S. D., & Ramey, D. R. (1991). *Final report: Longitudinal study of structured English immersion strategy, early-exit and late-exit programs for language-minority children. Report submitted to the U.S. Department of Education.* San Mateo, CA: Aguirre Internacional.

Saravia-Shore, M., & Arvizu, S. F. (1992). Implications for policy and practice. In M. Saravia-Shore & S. F. Arvizu (Eds.), *Cross-cultural literacy: Ethnographies of communication in multiethnic classrooms* (pp. 491–510). New York: Garland.

Scollon, R., & Scollon, S. (1981). *Narrative, literacy, and face in interethnic communication.* Norwood, NJ: Ablex.

Skutnabb-Kangas, T. (1988). Multilingualism and the education of minority children. In T. Skutnabb-Kangas & J. Cummins (Eds.), *Minority education: From shame to struggle* (pp. 12–20). Clevedon, England: Multilingual Matters.

Skutnabb-Kangas, T. (2000). *Linguistic genocide in education—Or worldwide diversity and human rights?* Mahwah, NJ: Lawrence Erlbaum Associates.

Snow, C. E. (1990). Rationales for native language instruction: Evidence from research. In A. M. Padilla, H. H. Fairchild, & C. M. Valadez (Eds.), *Bilingual education: Issues and strategies* (pp. 60–74). Newbury Park, CA: Sage.

Street, B. (1995). *Social literacies: Critical approaches to literacy development, ethnography, and education*. London: Longman.

Thomas, W. P., & Collier, V. (1997). *School effectiveness for language minority students*. Washington, DC: National Clearinghouse for Bilingual Education.

Toohey, K. (2000). *Learning English at school: Identity, social relations and classroom practice*. Clevedon, England: Multilingual Matters.

U.S. Bureau of the Census. (2001). *Census 2000: Profile of selected social characteristics*. Washington, DC: Author.

U.S. Department of Education. (2002). *No Child Left Behind Act of 2001*, H.R. 1. Washington, DC: Author.

Valdés, G. (2001). *Learning and not learning English*. New York: Teachers College Press.

Vygotsky, L. S. (1978). *Mind and society*. Cambridge, MA: Harvard University Press.

Wertsch, J. V. (1998). *Mind as action*. Oxford, England: Oxford University Press.

Willig, A. C. (1985). A meta-analysis of selected studies on the effectiveness of bilingual education. *Review of Educational Research, 55*, 269–317.

2

Language, Literacy, and Biliteracy

Bertha Pérez

There is always a sense of wanting to hide a part of myself that other people feel is different or foreign. But lately, I feel I can be more open about my language and culture. (Alice, Chinese American, as quoted in Igoa, 1995, p. 108)

Language and literacy are highly visible markers of culture and social group (Igoa, 1995; Purcell-Gates, 1995; Sánchez, 1993; Valenzuela, 1999). The way one talks, conducts interpersonal relationships and communications, and the ways of doing the everyday business of one's life are acquired within specific cultural and social settings. Generally, within these everyday cultural and social settings, children encounter literate behaviors used by more capable members of the family or culture group. However, some children are born into homes where reading and writing are seldom observed. Unless children observe literate behaviors and have experiences with literate others around print, they cannot fully develop literacy. Still other children are expected to acquire literacy in a second language, English, without having fully acquired literacy in their native language. Both of these groups of children may have a more difficult task becoming literate. Learning to read and write is not as natural a process of acquisition when you are confronted with these tasks in a language you have

25

not fully mastered. The process requires much more attention, effort, and mediation. Children from culturally and linguistically diverse homes may have had limited experiences with English literacy prior to schooling (Snow, Burns, & Griffin, 1998). As they enter school, primarily designed for children from middle-class English-literate homes, they experience lower levels of English literacy attainment (Gersten & Woodward, 1995; Goldenberg & Gallimore, 1991; National Center for Education Statistics [NAEP], 1995, 1999).

We find that children born into a rich and varied literate world where important others in their lives use print regularly do acquire reading and writing with relative ease. They understand reading and writing as part of the cultural and social practices needed to live. They acquire literacy implicitly as they develop knowledge about the "ways of meaning" and "ways of saying" of print, texts, and written language in general. These children learn to give meaning to texts in a familiar language, about which they already know quite a bit. In turn, they develop as literate individuals, learning new concepts and accompanying language as they read and write to learn and to communicate at increasingly more complex levels.

Numerous research studies document how culturally and linguistically diverse children and adults from different communities experience learning to read and write. In this chapter, we discuss the theoretical and research bases for the current perspectives and definitions of literacy and biliteracy; the role of the child's native language and literacy in English literacy development; the social nature of literacy learning; the research of community-centered and family literacy; and school-based literacy and biliteracy research.

SOCIOCULTURAL PERSPECTIVES TO LITERACY

Perspectives on what constitutes literacy have changed dramatically. Each new literacy definition increases expectations of what it means to be literate. Until recently the term *literacy* was defined within the literacy–illiteracy dichotomy. In this context, many perceived literacy to be a rather simple notion—the ability to read and write, and most often, in the standard national language. Current positions on definitions of literacy tend to cluster around two major dimensions, "the *individual* dimension and the *social* dimension" (Green & Dixon, 1996, p. 292). From the individual dimension, literacy is defined as a person's ability to read and write. Literacy becomes a personal mental attribute to be used for individual purposes and for individual benefit (Ferdman, 1991). In contrast, the social dimension sees literacy as a social practice and a cultural phenomenon. Literacy is defined in more complex terms as a set of social activities involving written language in terms of its function and context, that is, the ways that people use literacy to achieve their goals in a variety of sociocultural contexts (Cazden, 1988; Cook-Gumperz, 1986a; Gee, 1992, 2000; Heath, 1983; Street, 1984).

The literacy research of the last 20 years has given us new understanding of how students learn to read and write. From this body of research some findings emerged that are of vital significance to literacy instruction of culturally and linguistically diverse students. These major findings are:

- Children acquire the foundations of literacy within their native language and culture (Bialystok, 1997; Cummins, 1989; Purcell-Gates, 1993, 1995; Wells, 1986; Wong Fillmore, 1991).
- There is a social nature to literacy learning (Au & Mason, 1981; Ballenger, 1999; Heath, 1983; Scribner & Cole, 1981; Pérez, 2004; Street, 1995; Vygotsky, 1978; Wertsch, 1998).
- Background knowledge plays a significant role in meaning making (Bruner, 1996; K. S. Goodman, 1992; Hudson, 1982, 1991; Langer, 1984; Pritchard, 1990).
- Reading and writing are interrelated (Clay, 1979; Edelsky, 1986; Harste, Woodward, & Burke, 1984; Vernon & Ferreiro, 1999).
- Becoming literate in a second language requires time, from 5 to 7 years, depending on the individual, strength of native literacy, type of second-language instruction, and status of second language (Cummins, 1989; Ramirez, Yuen, Ramey, & Pasta, 1991; Tucker, 1986, Verhoeven, 1994).

Sociocultural perspectives (Barton & Hamilton, 1998; Gee, 2000; Heath, 1986; McLaughlin, 1989; Moll, 1992; Street, 1995) of literacy argue that writing, reading, and language are not isolated and decontextualized; nor are they generalized skills separate from specific contents, contexts, and social-communicative purposes; rather, there are *multiple literacies* (Barton & Hamilton, 1998; Scribner & Cole, 1981; Street, 1984, 1995), and reading, writing, and language are embedded in and inextricable from *discourses* (the way the communicative systems are organized within social practices).

Let us examine the plurality of literacy first. In this evolving notion of multiple literacies and literacy practices (Erickson, 1984; Scribner & Cole, 1981; Street, 1984), literacy necessarily varies from context to context and group to group. Scribner and Cole studied the multiple literacies of the Vai people in West Africa. The Vai are exposed to three kinds of literacy: They learn English in school, they learn Arabic as they are led by the local Iman in morning prayers from the Quran, and they also learn the Vai script that has been used for community life since the 19th century. In all of these tasks, the uses of literacy or performance reflected a skill involved in the very acquisition or process of the literacy task itself. Scribner and Cole found that where a literacy skill was part of only one literacy, performance of that particular skill was promoted by engaging in similar tasks in that literacy alone. Where the literacy skill was part of literacy in general, performance on similar tasks was fostered by all three literacies. Though each literacy did not have a distinct set of functions, there were some literacy practices used in specific languages. For example, people used English and Vai for letter writing; Arabic was generally not used for letter writing.

Within the functional multiple literacies definition, literacy is a technology or a tool that is culturally determined and used for specific purposes. As the specific purposes and contexts for literacy use change, that is, as the elements of the specific environment (the tools, symbols—words or numbers—social relationships) are altered, a person's ability to perform literacy tasks or to learn at optimum levels also changes. Thus, literacy practices are culture-specific ways of knowing. Regardless of educational background, most people in the United States have "some knowledge of literacy and live in cultural settings where various kinds of literacy are valued" (Street, 1995, p. ii).

Knowledge of a specific function of literacy, such as the use of literacy to gain services, will vary according to culture group and to the context of social (family, doctor, store, etc.) relationships. For example, culturally and linguistically diverse children may have observed and participated in using literacy for reading and writing about or to their home country (Delgado-Gaitan & Trueba, 1991) or for seeking information on employment or medical services (Moll, 1992). Multiple literacies develop to meet the broad spectrum of functions required within diverse social contexts, and they begin in the home and community, before children enter school.

According to the sociocultural perspective, these multiple literacies are embedded within discourses or social practices. The discourses acquired to deal with everyday life within sociocultural contexts that center around print or written text are literacy practices that Gee (1992) argued are much more than reading and writing but rather are a part of a larger communicative societal system or sociopolitical entity. Gee argued that one never learns simply to read or write, but to read and write within certain Discourse or Discourses, "with a capital 'D'" (p. 32). He further defined *Discourse* as "a socioculturally distinctive and integrated way of thinking, acting, interacting, talking, and valuing connected with a particular social identity or role, with its own unique history, and often with its own distinctive 'props' (buildings, objects, spaces, schedules, books, etc.)" (p. 33).

For Gee, a Discourse is an "identity kit," that is, ways of acting, talking, writing, that communicate a particular role that others will recognize. Some examples of Discourse might be the Discourse of doctors, the Discourse of factory workers, the Discourse of a working-class home, or the Discourse of a political science student. Gee asserted that primary Discourses (home based) cannot be "overtly" taught, but are acquired by enculturation in the home by social practices. He argued that not all Discourses are equal in status, and that the status of individuals born into a particular Discourse tends to be maintained because some primary Discourses are linked with secondary Discourses (public oriented) and given similar status in our society, for example, middle-class home Discourse to school Discourse. To gain access and to learn the rules required to master a secondary Discourse, for example, the middle-class English classroom discourse, individuals must already have access to the social institutions connected to that Discourse.

Delpit (1993) and others were concerned and troubled by this Discourse theory.

> Gee's argument suggests a dangerous kind of determinism as flagrant as that espoused by the geneticists: Instead of being locked into "your place" by your genes, you are now locked hopelessly into a lower-class status by your Discourse. Clearly, such a stance can leave a teacher feeling powerless to effect change, and a student feeling hopeless that change can occur. (Delpit, 1993, p. 286)

Numerous studies documented the conflict created by these primary and dominant discourses (Heath, 1983; López, 1999; Purcell-Gates, 1995; Rosaldo, 1989). Some of these same studies and others also showed how teachers work to provide access to the secondary Discourses for culturally diverse students (Ballenger, 1999; Ladson-Billings, 1994; McCarty & Watahomigie, chap. 4, this volume; Moll & González, 1994; Torres-Guzmán, 1992). The hopelessness of Discourse status was also challenged by Smitherman (1994). In an analysis of African American students' use of discernable Black discourse style in the NAEP 1984 and 1988 persuasive essays, Smitherman found that "students who employed a black expressive discourse style received higher NAEP scores than those who did not" (p. 94). Although the different Discourses may embody conflicting values, Smitherman, Delpit, and others believed that there are "many individuals, who have faced and overcome the problems that such a conflict might cause" (Delpit, 1993, p. 287).

Within an overall sociocultural approach to literacy, learning to read and learning to write are constituted as acts of knowing or multiple literacies, and are situated within a given cultural and social context (including Discourse). Learners assume an active role of creative participation. The very act of participation transforms aspects of the social practices or the meaning of literacy.

The Child's Native Language and Literacy

Developing literacy in the native language and culture gives children opportunities to learn or construct notions about the purposes, functions, and processes involved in reading, writing, and thinking. When children acquire literacy in their native language with the cultural referents for which they have background knowledge, they have certain meaning-making advantages that will help them to later explore English literacy.

The native or home language is the tool through which the child develops a sense of self-identity and cultural identity (Delpit & Dowdy, 2002; Ferdman, 1991; Solsken, 1993; Valenzuela, 1999); acquires cultural knowledge and values (Ballenger, 1999; Mulhern, 1994, 1997); and develops the cognitive skills for learning (Heath, 1983, 1986; Merino, Trueba, & Samaniego, 1993; Wong Fillmore, 1991). It is through language that children understand different situations and settings, different interaction and participation patterns, the various usages and purposes of language, different functions, forms, and genres of communication, and the norms of communication associated with the various forms and usages (Trueba, 1993). Children learn their native language by engaging in meaningful acts of communication with those around them in social interactions and by constructing their own ideas or theories about the principles of language (Pinker, 1994; Wells, 1986). Children develop theories about the how, what, and when of speaking through their interactions and communications with others.

In the home or community where children see adult or older members of their social groups reading and writing, young children will acquire their native literacy in much the same way as they learn to speak, with little formal instruction (Anderson & Stokes, 1984; Ferreiro & Teberosky, 1982; Hartle-Schutte, 1993; Heath, 1983; Taylor & Dorsey-Gaines, 1988; Teale, 1987). The process of becoming literate is facilitated by children engaging in the interpretation of print (such as household product labels) or in the production of writing (such as writing lists and notes) during acts of communication with parents, caregivers, and older siblings. Literacy is thus socially constructed as children form their ideas or theories about the principles of reading and writing; these principles are reinforced or rejected in acts of communication with text (or the authors of the text) and with others around text.

Whether the children have developed fluency in their native literacy or not, encouraging and allowing children to access their cultural and linguistic knowledge and skills in school literacy tasks will facilitate the process of becoming literate in English (Au, 1993; Jiménez, 2000; Lanauze & Snow, 1989; Pérez & Torres-Guzmán, 2002).

Social Interaction and Literacy Development

Language and literacy are *socially constructed;* that is, language and literacy users construct and interpret the meaning of language within social interactions (Wells, 1986). Social interaction has always been considered central to oral communication, while literacy was considered to be decontextualized. Reading or writing a text was considered apart from the physical social context.

In the 1920s, Vygotsky (1978), a Soviet psychologist, theorized that sociocultural changes formed the basis for the development of higher memory and thinking processes, and that at the center of learning was the social interaction or cooperation between the child and the parent/teacher. This conception of learning suggests that the cultural practices and ways of understanding them depend on the social conditions and culture in which they are learned. Vygotsky described the process as follows: "Human learning presupposes a specific social nature and a process by which children grow into the intellectual life of those around them" (p. 88). The skills, concepts, and ways of thinking that an individual develops reflect the uses and approaches that permeate the community or social group of which that person is a member.

Vygotsky (1978) also suggested that the focus or object of learning was on the use of the cultural tools (literacy, mathematics, etc.). He stated: "Any function in the child's cultural development appears ... in two planes. First, it appears in the social plane, and then on the psychological plane. First, it appears between people, as an inter-psychological category, and then within the child as an intra-psychological category" (p. 90).

Thus, in a Vygotskian perspective, children learn literacy as a set of particular social-interactional practices as they engage in interactions with adults or more capable peers in the interpsychological category. The practices emphasized most depend on the dominant values of the community and the relative needs of individuals to be a part of that community. It is only after learning in social interaction with others that the child begins to internalize that learning in his or her mind and in more abstract forms in the intrapsychological category. Viewed from a Vygotskian perspective, "literacy was an important intellectual

tool with the power of transforming the higher psychological processes" (Greenfield, 1991, p. 334).

The Vygotskian perspective has been central to the discussion of issues affecting linguistically diverse students in mainstream educational
contexts (Au, 1993; Díaz & Klingler, 1991; Moll, Vélez-Ibáñez, &
Greenberg, 1990). Many linguistically diverse students have developed
sets of particular literacy skills and practices unique to their community
that may be not only different but oftentimes at odds with school-based
literacy practices. As Scribner and Cole (1981) pointed out, "literacy is
not simply learning how to read and write a particular script but applying this knowledge for specific purposes in specific contexts of use" (p.
236). The interpretations of texts and applications of literacy made by
members of linguistically diverse groups reflect their cultural experience and context but may not meet with the expectations and interpretations of the schools' literacy context and practices.

The research on *emergent literacy*, children's development of
reading and writing before schooling without direct instruction, documents the central role social interaction plays in literacy development (Ferreiro & Teberosky, 1982; Y. M. Goodman, 1990; Harste et al.,
1984; McGee & Purcell-Gates, 1997; Sulzby & Teale, 1991; Teberosky,
1990). Individual children's interactions with print and talk with
more capable literacy users refine their understandings of written language. Children in social interactions with either adults or other children participate in these *literacy events* (Anderson, Teale, & Estrada,
1980; Heath, 1983) where they ask about or observe some aspect of
print. For example, they discuss reading or writing with a more experienced literacy user, or take part in some activity that requires reading or writing. Heath suggested "that literacy events have social
interactional rules which regulate the type and amount of *talk* about
what is written, and define ways in which *oral language* reinforces,
denies, extends, or sets aside the written material" (p. 386). Thus social interaction is in fact just as crucial in literacy development as in
oral language. Children, especially culturally and linguistically diverse students, need to talk about what they are doing as they acquire
literacy, and they need to talk with their teachers and peers, and indeed with themselves, as they work their way through reading and
writing tasks (Dyson, 1984, 1993).

Some aspects of the role of social interaction, as well as the theory
of emergent literacy and more recently the family/home literacy
movement, have been criticized for comparing and even measuring
children's literacy development against a school-like or middle-class
standard (Solsken, 1993). Where home literacy environments and social interactions around books are not as "rich" or the same as those
described in the bulk of the literature, they are viewed as deficient.

Low-income and culturally diverse families have often been blamed because their children enter school with different kinds of experiences than those of their "average" middle-class peers (Delgado-Gaitan & Trueba, 1991; Flores, Cousin, & Díaz, 1991; López, 1999; Teale, 1987; Valdés, 1996). A national policy example of this lack of understanding of cultural differences in social interactions and literacy can be deduced from the implications of the first National Educational Goal of 1996, that "all American children will start school ready to learn." As stated, the goal implied that some children are not "ready to learn" if they have not been prepared for school in the same way as middle-class children. Furthermore, the burden of preparedness for some preconceived notion of schooling seems to rest on individual children and their families, rather than schools preparing to receive and lead all children to learning (Prince & Lawrence, 1993).

Schools can create environments where the children can find social interaction patterns and literacy tasks that build on their prior knowledge. Literacy instruction from a social interaction perspective builds on the strengths of students so that they can acquire literacy levels required for full participation in a complex and diverse society. A study that illustrates the role of social interaction in literacy development is Au and Mason's (1981) study of the Hawaiian community and school's differing ways of interacting.

At the Kamehameha Elementary Education Program (KEEP), studied by Au and Mason, two culturally differing ways of teaching reading were conducted with native Hawaiian first graders. A control group followed the mainstream patterns found in most U.S. schools of turn taking when discussing reading stories. Those patterns often require children to raise their hand and only one child can speak at a time. The other group incorporated the community cultural norms for conversation into the reading discussion. Children were allowed to comment and build on each other's comments in overlapping talk. The overlapping talk had characteristics of "talk-story," a way of retelling events and narratives that students had experienced in family and community life. The students in the group that organized reading lessons in a talk-story-like way manifested more enthusiastic discussion and understanding of the reading texts. This group also performed better as measured by reading tests given to both groups.

This example of a school accepting and adjusting the teaching practices to the cultural style the children had experienced in community life may have been perceived, even by young children, as a "symbolic affirmation of themselves and their community" (Erickson, 1993, p. 31). Allowing students to concentrate on the discussion of the sense of the story, repeating and adding to each other's ideas, also provided *scaffolding* (Bruner, 1983) for each other. Teachers and peers can

shape literacy discussions through scaffolding, those informal conversations, questions, and comments that provide frameworks for the
cognitive processes to be used with the reading or writing activity
(Cazden, 1988; Tharp, 1994).

Classrooms as social environments for literacy learning have been
examined by researchers, who have found that the purposes, values,
and meanings of literacy in these classrooms were constructed by
both the teacher and students (Bloome, 1989; Dyson, 1984; Kantor,
Miller, & Fernie, 1992; Tharp, 1994). Dyson described how through
social interactions the teacher and learners constructed a "culture"
and through their ways of using and valuing reading and writing a
"literacy culture." Other studies of the social construction of literacy
have led to insights into how children's development of school literacy strategies and knowledge comes to reflect the social learning situations they face at school (Alton-Lee, Nuthall, & Patrick, 1993;
McIntyre, 1992).

Wong Fillmore (1976) studied the role of sustained student–student interaction in the second-language acquisition of five children.
The study illustrated that second-language learners benefited from interactions with English-speaking children who provided them with
useful linguistic input for acquisition. The most successful of the five
learners studied were those who were able to establish and maintain
social contact with peers and adults who gave them the type of input
they needed for language learning. The successful students used social interaction and cognitive strategies to learn English.

Solsken (1993) studied the social context of the classroom and the
broader social relations of individual children and the relationship of
gender to literacy. Children made decisions about what they would
read or write and whom they would work with; in this process they defined themselves as literate persons and gendered persons. "In learning to read and write, children ... construct definitions of themselves
and their relations with parents, siblings, teachers, and peers ...
[they] strive both to be counted as members of social groups and to be
recognized as unique individuals" (Solsken, 1993, p. 9).

Literacy Learning Contexts

We have learned much about the contexts of literacy use from the increasing numbers of ethnographic studies that incorporate sociolinguistic and anthropological perspectives to study literacy
development, literacy events, and literacy environments (e.g.,
Bloome, 1989; Cook-Gumperz, 1986a; Heath, 1983, 1986; Langer,
1991; Moll et al., 1990; Pérez, in press).

These studies suggest that language and literacy are contextualized interactive processes, integrating individual learners' cognitive and linguistic abilities with the need to communicate meaningfully with others in social environments (Heath, 1983; Wells, 1986; Wong Fill-more, 1979). They reveal that, in different contexts, users engage in different literacy practices, using oral communication, computation, problem solving, and decision making, as well as written communication skills (Cook-Gumperz, 1986b; Erickson, 1977; Heath, 1983; Ogbu, 1983; Scribner & Cole, 1981), and an individual's need for literacy is also constrained by community or group practices (Scribner & Cole, 1981; Weinstein-Shr, 1990). Ferdman (1991) suggested that "in a culturally heterogeneous society, literacy … becomes an interactive process that is constantly redefined and renegotiated, as the individual transacts with the socioculturally fluid surroundings" (p. 353).

Many ethnographic studies have looked at literacy learning in a variety of contexts and they often provide a commentary on the educational contexts of literacy. Some studies describe how linguistically diverse students from different social groups perform literacy tasks differently from teacher/school expectations; and how school-based literacy tasks create inequalities (Heath, 1983; Moll et al., 1990; Mulhern, 1997). What has emerged from these studies is that ways of speaking greatly influence literacy instruction and learning (Au, 1993; Gee, 1990, 2000). Literacy and education are viewed as social and cultural practices and actions (Bloome & Green, 1992; Street, 1984, 1995) that vary across cultures and communities (Gibson, 1993; Heath, 1983, 1986) and across situations within the same setting. Underlying much of this work is the belief that use of cultural tools, such as literacy, shapes thinking and learning, and that the contribution of context and culture cannot be overstated in what is learned and how.

Thinking and Literacy

Literacy requires different means of thinking, expression, and meaning making from those used in oral production. Although thinking is not the result of literacy (Scribner & Cole, 1981; Traugott, 1987), thinking reflects the particular oral and written ways of solving problems (Bialystok, 1986; Ungerer & Schmid, 1996), organizing knowledge (Díaz, 1983; Hakuta, Ferdman, & Díaz, 1987), and communicating (Olson, 1986) that are learned early and have enormous consequences for the use of literacy and knowledge throughout life. Literacy is constructed by an individual's or group's view of the world (Freire, 1970). Literacy is a significant instrument in the culture's tool kit of ways of thought; thinking reflects the particular oral and written ways of solving problems.

Additionally, because of the abstract and decontextualized nature of the written text, literacy requires the reader to use background knowledge to contextualize and give meaning to the text. To give meaning to what is read, the reader draws on cultural models (Shore, 1996; Strauss & Quinn, 1998) or culturally constructed mental *schemata*. Schemata are the cognitive representations or referents for words, consisting of relevant knowledge about the meaning of individual words and expressions, the context or situation they are being used in, and other contexts in which one has experienced their use or that have been similar in terms of sensory, emotive, or other experience. The meaning of a word is not inherent in the object or event it represents; its meaning is understood within a context (Lakoff, 1987; Ungerer & Schmid, 1996). For example, most cultures and peoples have rice or bread of some kind; however, embedded into the word "rice" for an individual person are all his or her specific cultural ways of using, preparing, sharing, and eating of rice, including the experiential and emotional contexts. We generalize experiences into schemata from very early in our lives and have a tremendous number of them by the time we come to formal literacy instruction. Events, activities, and objects become schematized very quickly, and repeated experiences extend and develop our schemata (Mayher, 1993).

Scinto (1986) pointed out that literacy involves learning language in abstraction. He argued that the use of written language and the process of schooling are interfunctional in our society. One is learned in the context of the other, and both together determine how learning and literacy will be used. However, when the literacy of the classroom and the literacy of community differ, as is the case for linguistically and culturally diverse students, students cannot bring to literacy and learning tasks all of their acquired knowledge and experiences.

RESEARCH ON LITERACY AND BILITERACY

Hornberger (1994, 2003) put forth a framework for understanding the continuum of biliteracy in order to situate research and teaching practices. The continuum of biliteracy attempts to account for the complex dimensions of monolingualism versus bilingualism and oral versus literate behaviors in terms of a continuum rather than bipolar conditions. Studies of some successful literacy practices from various points on this continuum of biliteracy development of linguistically diverse students can provide prospective teachers with understandings and insights about the sociocultural situatedness of literacy.

Some studies also suggest ways that students acquire literacy and how school literacy practices can improve or impede literacy development along this continuum to full biliteracy.

Community Literacy

The community and the school often encompass different social relationships that create varying contexts for the development of literacy. Paulo Freire (1970; Freire & Macedo, 1987) stressed the importance of reading the world before reading the word; within the social contexts of community literacy, children learn to read the world and learn to read the word in service to reading the world. Community literacy is focused on meaning and function (Barton & Hamilton, 1998). For children, community literacy is often associated with sharing and group interactions, and has short-term goals or gratification (Fagan, 1995; Pérez, 1994). Examples include a child answering a phone and writing a message, parent and child reading street signs and bus stops, parents reading and sharing stories from the community newspaper, parent and child reading and interpreting school communications, and so on. From activities such as these that are situated within a child's world where children can call on and use their world knowledge and social relationships, children learn to attend to print and give it meaning. Fagan (1995) pointed out that within home and community literacy practices,

> Children have many opportunities to apply their literacy knowledge and to develop additional concepts of the meaning and functions of literacy and the importance of prior or world knowledge. Children learn that their involvement with literacy extends to and includes many people and many goals. Literacy often occurs for the sake of others rather than for the sake of developing literacy competency as a skill in itself. (p. 261)

Dissonance between children's home and school literacy experiences has been reported for African American children by Heath (1983), Taylor and Dorsey-Gaines (1988), among Hawaiian children (Au & Mason, 1981), among Latino children (Battle, 1993; Delgado-Gaitan, 1990; Delgado-Gaitan & Trueba, 1991; Moll et al., 1990), and among Cantonese Chinese students (Guthrie & Guthrie, 1987). Some of these studies also give us insights to community literacy practices of particular groups. For example, Heath studied the use of language and literacy in the Trackton and Roadville communities, and Moll et al. studied community sources of knowledge and literacy in a Hispanic community.

Heath (1983) described the nature of language and literacy use in two culturally diverse communities, Trackton and Roadville. Both working-class communities are within a few miles of each other in the Piedmont Carolinas. She examined how children learned to use language and literacy in their social group. For both groups, the development of literacy evolved from the oral or spoken word to the written use of language. The African American children from Trackton developed literacy before entering school; reading was done aloud as a performance, with multiple open-ended interpretations. They were not expected to interpret the text as fact or to answer factual questions related to the text.

The White rural children from Roadville also developed literacy at home, where they were taught to interpret texts as a set of facts, and creativity in interpretation was considered lying. Reading was closely associated with proverbs and other moral lessons. In the Heath (1983) study, learning in the two communities differed, but neither community prepared children for school literacy:

> Roadville and Trackton residents have a variety of literate traditions, and, in each community, these are interwoven in different ways with oral uses of language, ways of negotiating meaning, deciding on action, and achieving status .... In Roadville, the absoluteness of ways of talking about what is written fits church ways of talking about what is written. Behind the written work is an authority, and the text is a message that can be taken apart only insofar as its analysis does not extend too far beyond the text and commonly agreed upon experiences .... In Trackton, the written word is for negotiation and manipulation—both serious and playful. Changing and changeable, words are the tools performers [community members] use to create images of themselves and the world they see. For Roadville, the written word limits alternatives of expression; in Trackton, it opens alternatives. Neither community's way with the written word prepares it for the school's ways. (pp. 234–235)

Heath's research shows how language and literacy in the home and community are part of the group's culture. Different communities, such as those of Trackton and Roadville, incorporate different beliefs about the uses for literacy. Numerous literacy development studies in African American communities discuss strategies for providing meaningful literacy experiences for Black children in school settings.

Dissonance between home and school literacy experiences can be addressed by teacher mediation. Van Ness (1981) described how a Koyukon-Athabaskan teacher used a discourse style and actions that allowed Koyukon-Athabaskan students to self-determine many of their actions and also did not publicly call on students who were uncertain or demonstrated divergent behavior. Bernhardt (1982) studied reading lessons in first- through third-grade classrooms and also described that Alaskan-Athabaskan teachers allowed Athabaskan students to help control the discourse in the ways of community participation structures. Battle (1993) in a study of kindergartners' storybook reading described how a teacher used a more interactive discourse style with Mexican American children to gain higher levels of participation. These studies demonstrate how teachers, especially those with native-language backgrounds that match the culture and linguistic background of their students, can adapt their discourse styles in reading lessons to make them more compatible with home discourse structures of the students.

The use of *code-switching*, that is, switching back and forth from the student's native language to English, usually with sentences or phrases (Pérez & Torres-Guzmán, 2002), has also been studied in school literacy lessons. Numerous studies document the use of code-switching within Spanish/English bilingual communities (Battle, 1993; de Silva, chap. 9, this volume; Huerta-Macías & Quintero, 1992; Zentella, 1981). Yoon (1992) described how code-switching is used in a Korean community. Two interesting code-switching phenomena were found: a change of the part of speech in the process of making small nonequivalence constituent switches, and an introduction of Korean operating verbs, which were inflected to indicate the degree of respect due to the conversational partner. Guthrie and Guthrie (1987) in a study of Cantonese bilingual students have described how the teacher, also a Cantonese speaker, used code-switching especially for word meanings and to check for understanding. The uses and ways of code-switching were similar to reports of code-switching in the local Chinese American community.

Other studies suggest similar approaches that reformulate literacy practices in the school so that the content, language goals, social context, and conversational context of classroom literacy practices reflect a wider range of the community literacy practices found in diverse communities (Irvine & Elsasser, 1988; Ivaniĉ & Moss, 1991; McLaughlin, 1989). Structuring school literacy in community-centered approaches capitalizes on the social-communicative nature of literacy.

For example, Moll et al. (1990) examined and documented the origin, use, and distribution of knowledge and skills, "funds of knowledge," in Hispanic households. He also examined the existing methods of instruction in schools. Moll's research team worked with teachers in an after-school study group using the data to develop methods of literacy instruction that build on the resources of the community. For example, teachers found out that some children were learning language and literacy skills related to the building trades from their fathers and were able to build on these developing skills and to invite community members to share their knowledge in classroom literacy activities. The teacher study group, in turn, provided a social context for informing, assisting, and supporting teachers in developing innovations (Moll et al., 1990).

Delgado-Gaitan (1990) also found that children's homework was the most common printed text and literacy practice among the working-class, Mexican-immigrant families she studied. Similarly, Goldenberg and Gallimore (1991) found that school had a major impact on the literacy interactions of Latino kindergartners at home where almost half of observed literacy activities involved using school materials. Several studies of Latino families (Delgado-Gaitan, 1990; Goldenberg, Reese, & Gallimore, 1992; Mulhern, 1994) have found that in households with children in kindergarten and first grade, the children were the initiators of much of the home literacy activities, with children reading and writing alone, with their mothers, and with siblings. Mulhern (1994) described how Yesenia, a child in her study, invented her own homework to do with her mother and sisters, using writings tasks to "establish or affirm relationships with them" (p. 275).

The family literacy movement of the 1980s studied literacy practices in various diverse communities, and many designed programs incorporating some aspects of the home literacy practices. Ada (1988) and Huerta-Macías (1995) studied the incorporation of culturally familiar and relevant content in family literacy programs serving Mexican Americans. In these programs, stories (e.g., folktales, fables) from the home culture or language and themes (e.g., herbal medicines) related to the home culture, as well as "code-switching" interactive style of the home, were incorporated. Auerbach (1995) described how a literacy program for Haitians involved learners in selecting curriculum goals and themes in an attempt to ensure the relevance and appropriateness of content. It was established that the themes that parents identified in this family literacy program went beyond literacy practices that supported their children in school; they focused on many social and political issues developing literacy for their own purposes. Gadsden (1995) likewise reported that African American parents in a literacy program in Philadelphia explored literacy activities, purposes, questions, and issues that arose in their families and within their cultural and urban context.

Auerbach (1995) raised concerns about the proliferation of family literacy programs and the "dangers of a deficit perspective on family literacy" (p. 643) that aims to change parents' inabilities and beliefs about literacy and propose school-like literacy interactions (e.g., storybook reading, journal writing) with their children. Although most of the programs officially claim to oppose deficit perspectives and to embrace family strengths, she has argued that, in fact, this very "anti-deficit rhetoric" has become so pervasive that it masks fundamental underlying differences in values, goals, ideological orientations, and pedagogical approaches.

There is enormous diversity in community and home literacy practices among and within cultural and linguistic groups. Auerbach (1989) reviewed the available research and found that rather than being literacy impoverished, the home environments of poor, undereducated, and language-minority children often are rich with literacy practices and literacy tools and materials. More important, numerous studies (Auerbach, 1995; Heath, 1983; Moll, 1992; Purcell-Gates, 1995) extensively documented that culturally and linguistically diverse families not only value literacy, but see it as the single most powerful hope for their children.

School Biliteracy Studies

A few studies in bilingual and English as a second language (ESL) classrooms for children of limited English proficiency have begun to examine children's literacy development within these classrooms. These studies provide some individual student or teacher cases of biliteracy that can be examined to identify literacy practices that might be successfully implemented in other classrooms. For instance, the observations of a successful teacher in fostering literacy in two languages for a small group of Puerto Rican children (McCollum, 1991), or the process of literacy awareness and development in only-English classes for a group of Cambodian children (Hornberger, 1990) illustrates cases where children are developing literacy in varied classrooms.

Focus on Reading. Verhoeven (1990) studied immigrant Turkish bilingual children in the Netherlands. The Turkish children's reading in Dutch was compared with the reading of Dutch native-speaking children. Although the bilingual Turkish children were less efficient reading Dutch texts than were the Dutch monolingual children, nonetheless, they used comparable strategies for word recognition and reading comprehension. The bilingual Turkish children with higher oral proficiency in Dutch also performed better on the reading tasks. A finding that points to the sociocultural nature of literacy was that Verhoeven found that the Turkish students' performance on Dutch literacy tasks appeared to be related to their sociocultural orientation or ability to identify with the Dutch language and culture. In a subsequent study, Verhoeven (1994) found that when Turkish children were compared to each other rather than to Dutch children, the Turkish children's metalinguistic competence was more predictive of their ability to transfer skills from Turkish to Dutch reading than were their Dutch oral language skills.

Phonological awareness of bilinguals and the transfer of this ability to English has been an area of much current interest. Durgunoğlu, Nagy, and Hancin-Bhatt (1993) examined the phonological awareness of Spanish-speaking first graders. After assessing Spanish phonological awareness, the children were taught several tasks in English to study the transfer of knowledge across task and language. Tasks that used onsets and rimes with English-like pseudo words were taught to Spanish-speaking children and later tested with an English word recognition test that included onsets and rimes of real words. Durgunoğlu et al. found that Spanish phonological awareness and Spanish word knowledge predicted the children's performance on the English-like pseudo-word and English real-word tasks. The Spanish-speaking children transferred the phonological awareness acquired in Spanish performing on the English tasks without formal instruction in English phonological awareness. Durgunoğlu et al. concluded that the metalinguistic process was similar and underlying in the two languages, thus facilitating the transfer.

Other studies with diverse languages have concluded that young bilingual children transferred metalinguistic awareness, for French–English (Bruck & Genesee, 1995), Mandarin–English (Bialystok, 1997), and Hebrew–English (Geva & Wade-Woolley, 1998).

Studies on the role of background knowledge and reading in bilingual contexts have found that second-language students require careful prereading preparation to activate and expand background knowledge for comprehension. Children also need to be made aware of the rhetorical organization of texts, and need to read extensively to become productive readers. Langer, Bartolome, Vásquez, and Lucas (1990) examined the ways that Mexican American students construct meaning when reading Spanish and English narrative and informational school materials. They found that the student's use of good *meaning-making strategies*, ability to relate the text to prior experience or learning, made the major difference in how well they comprehended in both Spanish and English; language competence in Spanish helped pupils understand and respond to questions in both languages; the students' familiarity with genre affected their ability to construct meaning in both languages; and the kinds of questions the students were asked during and postreading affected their ability to communicate their understanding of the texts (Langer et al., 1990). In another study the use of metacognitive strategies, such as self-questioning, resulted in significant gains in English comprehension for third-grade Spanish-dominant students (see Muñíz-Swicegood, 1994).

Miramontes (1990) found that students in her study developed elaborate coping strategies for biliteracy and schooling in general. She looked at the oral reading and the patterns of successful performance of bilingual children described by their teachers as "mixed (language) dominance." Using miscue reading analysis, Miramontes identified a significant number of the students who had good oral reading and comprehension strategies previously undetected or underrated by their teachers.

Children acquiring reading in a second language who may have difficulty with word recognition processes may be assisted with learning specific strategies. Verhoeven (1990) summarized that reading research suggests that successful bilingual readers use three main strategies with words: (a) phonemic mapping, that is, sounding out the word, (b) looking for orthographic patterns, and (c) sight or visual recognition of words already represented in memory (Verhoeven, 1990, p. 92).

Research conducted cross-culturally and cross-linguistically can provide insights for consideration in bilingual literacy programs. For example, Pritchard (1990) examined how *cultural schemata*, experience with and knowledge of the topics/ideas and referents, influence 11th-grade U.S. and Palau students' reading-processing strategies as they read culturally familiar and unfamiliar passages in their own language. The study found differences related to cultural familiarity in the rate and sequence of connections that readers made between individual propositions in the text; students recalled more idea units and produced more elaborations with fewer distortions for the culturally familiar passages. Pritchard concluded that cultural schemata appear to influence readers, processing strategies, and the level of comprehension they achieved.

In university studies with ESL students, Carrell (1987) found three types of schemata used to organize, understand, and interpret written text: *linguistic schemata*, based on prior language development; *content schemata*, based on prior knowledge of the content area or concepts of the text; and *text schemata*, based on knowledge of the rhetorical structure of the narrative or expository selection. The features of a particular text and the use of schemata imply readers are likely to have developed connections through their previous personal and literacy experiences. The connections have important implications for schema theory and effective instruction, especially for culturally and linguistically diverse students. For efficient comprehension, readers must be able to relate text material to their own knowledge (Au et al., 1986; Carrell, 1987). Studies of both children and adult readers have shown that comprehension improves when the reading material contains culturally familiar content (Reyes, 1987; Rigg, 1986). Texts with familiar content allow readers to make accurate predictions as they read, freeing them to read faster and with less dependence on visual cues. Such texts tend to activate entire networks of relevant concepts developed from the reader's own experience. Thus, bilingual readers when confronted with reading English texts containing familiar cultural material may comprehend the text content within the larger sociocultural context of their own related experiences rather than as isolated facts. They are more likely to connect implicit as well as explicit information to their prior experience and knowledge.

Comprehension can be improved by building background knowledge or helping readers activate relevant background experience before they read (Hudson, 1982; Johnson, 1982). Comprehension also improves when the text's narrative structure is consistent and thus predictable, rather than inconsistent, shifting unexpectedly from one style to another (Rigg, 1986). Other suggestions include reading literature from the student's own culture and reading texts from the new culture using metalinguistic and metacognitive strategies to become familiar with its style and content (Edelsky, Draper, & Smith, 1983). Raphael and Brock (1993) described a case study of a Vietnamese student's success with gaining meaning when participating in a group social context in a literature-based reading program.

Most bilingual students need specific instruction in comprehension of content materials. Comprehension studies suggest that the use of metalinguistic and metacognitive strategies helps students integrate personal information to text and information within the text. For bilingual students whose personal information may not contain the referents needed to make sense of content area texts, it becomes necessary to have specific instruction on comprehension of these materials. Other suggestions include providing instruction in previewing, skimming, adjusting reading rate, recognizing the author's purpose, making inferences, and separating fact from opinion (Jensen, 1986). Specific instruction in these reading strategies can assist bilingual students in comprehending content area material in both languages and in bridging the gap between first-language literacy and second-language.

Focus on Writing.   Research on writing and how it is used and taught has proliferated (Barton, 1991; Edelsky, 1986; Vernon & Ferreiro, 1999), extending interest in studying writing processes (Atwell, 1987; Harste et al., 1984), fostering variety in genres, and recognizing the rhetorical traditions that prevail across languages (Connor & Kaplan, 1987; Kroll, 1990; Peyton, Staton, & Richardson, 1990; Teberosky, 1991). The transfer of first-language writing and reading abilities into English has been shown to differ—with writing being more difficult—and to vary somewhat depending on first-language groups (Carson, Carrell, & Silberstein, 1990; Davis, Carlisle, & Beeman, 1999).

In a case study of writing with Spanish-dominant students (Moll & Díaz, 1987), the researchers worked with teachers from several schools in biweekly sessions focused on extending the students writing and changing teachers' skill instructional practices. Using Vygotsky's (1978) hypothesis, that a very different assessment of children's abilities was attainable by contrasting what they can do when working alone to what they can do when working in collaboration with others, they created writing tasks that included collaboration with other students and community. The content of the writing tasks was also modified to capitalize on the available cultural and community resources. Teachers asked students to write (individually, in pairs, and in collaboration with the teacher) about issues of significance to them using community information collected through homework assignments, such as questionnaires and interviews. Moll and Díaz (1993) concluded that "Whether students were fluent or not in English, they participated in comparable, demanding intellectual activities; the goal of writing for communication remained invariant, ways of achieving the goal varied depending on the characteristics of the students and the resources" (p. 76).

Hadaway (1990) described how a context for purposeful writing was created for bilingual students in Austin, Texas. A letter exchange program between public school students and university teacher education students was established; students were matched so that bilingual students corresponded in Spanish and the topics were of the correspondents' choosing. This study illustrates an educational context that is responsive to what Edelsky (1989) called interspeech community written language variations, for example, differences in the syntactic and semantic choices (e.g., flowery, elaborate closures in Spanish and brief, clipped closures in English) between the Spanish and English letter-writing styles. The letter-writing activity also illustrated to university students (all prospective teachers) and public school students a more purposeful and authentic use of school literacy.

Other studies of writing suggest that immersion in writing activities that emphasize process rather than product increases students' control over writing conventions like grammar and spelling and helps them develop a sense of audience, voice, and fluency (Atwell, 1987; Calkins, 1986; Davis et al., 1999; Edelsky, 1986; Gutiérrez, 1992; Hansen, 1987). The use of process approaches to writing with some culturally diverse students has been challenged (Delpit, 1991;

Reyes, 1987) for their focus on voice and fluency at the cost of teaching the more socially acceptable discourses. However, Smitherman (1994) reported that for the narrative–imaginative essays of the 1989 NAEP, African American students who used Black English Vernacular discourse patterns performed better when compared to their African American peers who did not use this discourse style. Smitherman recommended that teachers focus on ideas:

> .Once you have pushed your students to rewrite, revise; rewrite, revise; rewrite, revise; and once they have produced the most powerful essay possible, then and only then should you have them turn their attention to BEV [Black English Vernacular] grammar and matters of punctuation, spelling, and mechanics. (p. 95)

In combination, these studies of learner behaviors and teacher interaction have important implications for organizing classrooms as communities to maximize the development of literacy among bilingual students as a base for all learning. Linguistically diverse students need opportunities for interaction with both teachers and English-speaking peers because the type of literacy used with each of these two groups is different. Teachers focus primarily on content and the language requisite to learning and classroom management. On the other hand, peers focus on the socially appropriate ways of using language and literacy for communication.

SUMMARY

Within a sociocultural theoretical frame, viewing literacy as multiple literacies acknowledges the native and home literacy practices that learners bring to the school literacy tasks. It allows for investigating and validating students' multiple literacies and cultural resources affirming cultural identify in order to inform school literacy practices and build a community of learners. The interpretations of texts and applications of literacy made by members of linguistically diverse groups may reflect their community cultural context but may not meet with the expectations and interpretations of the schools' mainstream group definition of literacy.

The learner brings to the literacy task all the experiences with the world to construct meaning. The teacher, through social mediation, can assist culturally and linguistically diverse student literacy development. Aside from the schema and cultural differences between languages, it is important for teachers to understand that there are significant differences in text structures and discourse across languages. Linguistically and culturally diverse students will expect text and discourse to be patterned according to the conventions and constraints of their native language and their community discourse patterns.

As teachers, we need to understand that our particular language and literacy socialization contributes to how we create classroom literacy contexts and to how we set standards or expectations for school literacy. The more we learn about the diverse linguistic experiences of our students, the better prepared we will be to create appropriate literacy environments.

■ ACTIVITIES

1. Visit a classroom or school playground and observe the language and cultural diversity of the students. How do children relate to each other? Are there any natural ethnic or cultural groupings occurring? Do the linguistically different children use different languages when addressing perceived members of their linguistic group or perceived English speakers?

2. Survey five or six persons about their definitions of literacy. If they do not define literacy within a "social change" context, ask them if they think "literacy is linked to power structures in society." Bring the data collected from the survey to class, share in small groups, and categorize the definitions. Summarize from your findings what the general public understands as the definition of literacy. What implications does the general public's understanding of literacy have for school literacy programs?

3. Select a section of the newspaper to read for which you have little background knowledge, for example, business, sports, or technology. Read an article through once and write the key points or topics that you understood. Reread the article and underline or circle the key words or phrases for which you do not have prior knowledge or experience. Analyze the role these words or phrases play in the comprehension of the whole text. Discuss with your classmates what this experience would be like if you were reading in a second language.

SUGGESTED READINGS

Auerbach, E. (1995). Deconstructing the discourse of strengths in family literacy. *Journal of Reading Behavior, 27*, 643–661.
Hornberger, N. H. (1994). Continua of biliteracy. In B. M. Ferdman, R. M. Weber, & A. G. Ramírez (Eds.), *Literacy across languages and cultures* (pp. 103–139). Albany: State University of New York Press.

Jiménez, R. T. (2000). Literacy and the identity development of Latina/o students. *American Educational Research Journal, 37*(4), 971–1000.

Moll, L., Vélez-Ibáñez, C., & Greenberg, J. (1990). *Community knowledge and classroom practice: Combining resources for literacy instruction.* Arlington, VA: Development Associates, Inc.

Wong Fillmore, L. (1991). Second-language learning in children: A model of language learning in social context. In E. Bialystok (Ed.), *Language processing in bilingual children* (pp. 49–69). Cambridge, England: Cambridge University Press.

REFERENCES

Ada, A. F. (1988). The Pajaro Valley experience: Working with Spanish-speaking parents to develop children's reading and writing skills in the home through use of children's literature. In T. Skutnabb-Kangas & J. Cummins (Eds.), *Minority education: From shame to struggle* (pp. 223–238). Clevedon, England: Multilingual Matters.

Alton-Lee, A., Nuthall, G., & Patrick, J. (1993). Reframing classroom research: A lesson from the private world of children. *Harvard Educational Review, 63*, 50–84.

Anderson, A., & Stokes, S. (1984). Social and institutional influences of the development and practice of literacy. In H. Goelman, A. Oberg, & F. Smith (Eds.), *Awakening to literacy* (pp. 24–37). Portsmouth, NH: Heinemann.

Anderson, A. B., Teale, W. B., & Estrada, E. (1980). Low-income children's preschool literacy experience: Some naturalistic observations. *Quarterly Newsletter of the Laboratory of Comparative Human Cognition, 2*, 59–65.

Atwell, N. (1987). *In the middle: Writing, reading, and learning with adolescents.* Portsmouth, NH: Boynton/Cook.

Au, K. H. (1993). *Literacy instruction in multicultural settings.* Fort Worth, TX: Harcourt Brace.

Au, K. H., Crowell, D., Jordan, C., Sloat, C., Speidel, F., Klein, T., & Tharp, R. G. (1986). Development and implementation of the KEEP reading program. In J. Orasanu (Ed.), *Reading comprehension: From research to practice* (pp. 235–252). Hillsdale, NJ: Lawrence Erlbaum Associates.

Au, K. H., & Mason, J. (1981). Social organizational factors in learning to read: The balance of rights hypothesis. *Reading Research Quarterly, 17*, 115–152.

Auerbach, E. (1989). Toward a socio-contextual approach to family literacy. *Harvard Educational Review, 59*, 165–181.

Auerbach, E. (1995). Deconstructing the discourse of strengths in family literacy. *Journal of Reading Behavior, 27*, 643–661.

Ballenger, C. (1999). *Teaching other people's children: Literacy and learning in a bilingual classroom.* New York: Teachers College Press.

Barton, D. (1991). The social nature of writing. In D. Barton & R. Ivanic (Eds.), *Writing in the community* (pp. 1–13). Newbury Park, CA: Sage.

Barton, D., & Hamilton, M. (1998). *Local literacies: Reading and writing in one community.* London: Routledge.

Battle, J. (1993). Mexican-American bilingual kindergartners' collaborations in meaning making. In D. J. Leu & C. K. Kinzer (Eds.), *Examining central issues in literacy research, theory, and practice. Forty-second yearbook of the National Reading Conference* (pp. 163–170). Chicago: National Reading Conference.

Bernhardt, C. (1982). Tuning-in: Athabaskan teachers and Athabaskan students. In R. Barnhardt (Ed.), *Cross-cultural issues in Alaskan education* (Vol. 2, pp. 144–164). Fairbanks: Centers for Cross-Cultural Studies, University of Alaska.

Bialystok, E. (1986). Factors in the growth of linguistic awareness. *Child Development, 57,* 498–510.

Bialystok, E. (1997). Effects of bilingualism and biliteracy on children's emerging concepts of print. *Developmental Psychology, 33*(3), 429–440.

Bloome, D. (1989). Beyond access: An ethnographic study of reading and writing in a seventh grade classroom. In D. Bloome (Ed.), *Classrooms and literacy* (pp. 58–77). Norwood, NJ: Ablex.

Bloome, D., & Green, J. (1992). Educational contexts of literacy. *Annual Review of Applied Linguistics, 12,* 71–85.

Bruck, M., & Genesee, F. (1995). Phonological awareness in young second language learners. *Child Language, 22,* 307–234.

Bruner, J. S. (1983). *Child's talk: Learning to use language.* New York: Norton.

Bruner, J. (1996). *The culture of education.* Cambridge, MA: Harvard University Press.

Calkins, L. M. (1986). *The art of teaching writing.* Portsmouth, NH: Heinemann.

Carrell, P. L. (1987). Content and formal schemata in ESL reading. *TESOL Quarterly, 21,* 461–481.

Carson, J. E., Carrell, P. L., & Silberstein, S. (1990). Reading–writing relationships in first and second language. *TESOL Quarterly, 24,* 245–266.

Cazden, C. B. (1988). *Classroom discourse: The language of teaching and learning.* Portsmouth, NH: Heinemann.

Clay, M. M. (1979). *Reading: The patterning of complex behavior.* Portsmouth, NH: Heinemann.

Connor, U., & Kaplan, R. B. (Eds.). (1987). *Writing across languages: Analysis of L2 text.* Reading, MA: Addison-Wesley.

Cook-Gumperz, J. (1986a). Literacy and schooling: An unchanging equation? In J. Cook-Gumperz (Ed.), *The social construction of literacy* (pp. 16–44). Cambridge, England: Cambridge University Press.

Cook-Gumperz, J. (Ed.). (1986b). *The social construction of literacy.* Cambridge, England: Cambridge University Press.

Cummins, J. (1989). *Empowering minority students.* Sacramento: California Association for Bilingual Education.

Davis, L. H., Carlisle, J. F., & Beeman, M. M. (1999). Hispanic children's writing in English and Spanish when English is the language of instruction. In L. T. Shanahan & F. B. Rodriguez-Brown (Eds.), *National Reading Conference Yearbook, 48* (pp. 238–248). Rochester, NY: National Reading Conference.

Delgado-Gaitan, C. (1990). *Literacy for empowerment: The role of parents in children's education.* London: Falmer Press.

Delgado-Gaitan, C., & Trueba, H. (1991). *Crossing cultural borders.* Bristol, PA: Falmer Press.

Delpit, L. D. (1991). The silenced dialogue: Power and pedagogy in education other people's children. In M. Minami & B. P. Kennedy (Eds.), *Language issues in literacy and bilingual/multicultural education* (pp. 483–502). Cambridge, MA: Harvard Educational Review.

Delpit, L. D. (1993). The politics of teaching literate discourse. In T. Perry & J. W. Fraser (Eds.), *Freedom's plow* (pp. 285–295). New York: Routledge.

Delpit, L., & Dowdy, J. K. (2002). *The skin that we speak: Thoughts on language and culture in the classroom.* New York: New Press.

50

Díaz, R. M. (1983). Thought and two languages: The impact of bilingualism on cognitive development. In E. W. Gordon (Ed.), *Review of research in education* (Vol. X, pp. 23–54). Washington, DC: American Education Research Association.

Díaz, R. M., & Klingler, C. (1991). Towards an explanatory model of the interaction between bilingualism and cognitive development. In E. Bialystok (Ed.), *Language processing in bilingual children* (pp. 167–192). Cambridge, England: Cambridge University Press.

Durgunoğlu, A. Y., Nagy, W. E., & Hancin-Bhatt, B. J. (1993). Cross-language transfer of phonological awareness. *Journal of Educational Psychology, 85,* 453–465.

Dyson, A. (1984). Learning to write/Learning to do school. *Research in the Teaching of English, 6,* 233–264.

Dyson, A. H. (1993). *Social worlds of children learning to write in an urban primary school.* New York: Teachers College Press.

Edelsky, C. (1986). *Writing in a bilingual program: Había una vez.* Norwood, NJ: Ablex.

Edelsky, C. (1989). Putting language variation to work for you. In P. Rigg & V. G. Allen (Eds.), *When they don't all speak English: Integrating the ESL student into the regular classroom* (pp. 96–107). Urbana, IL: National Council of Teachers of English.

Edelsky, C., Draper, K., & Smith, K. (1983). Hookin' 'em in at the start of school in a "whole language" classroom. *Anthropology and Education Quarterly, 14,* 257–281.

Erickson, F. (1977). Some approaches to inquiry in school-community ethnography. *Anthropology and Education Quarterly, 8,* 515–544.

Erickson, F. (1984). School literacy, reasoning and civility: An anthropologist's perspective. *Review of Educational Research, 54,* 525–544.

Erickson, F. (1993). Transformation and school success: The politics and culture of educational achievement. In E. Jacob & C. Jordan (Eds.), *Minority education: Anthropological perspectives* (pp. 27–51). Norwood, NJ: Ablex.

Fagan, W. T. (1995). Social relationships of literacy. *Reading Teacher, 49,* 260–262.

Ferdman, B. M. (1991). Literacy and cultural identity. In M. Minami & B. P. Kennedy (Eds.), *Language issues in literacy and bilingual/multicultural education* (pp. 347–390). Cambridge, MA: Harvard Educational Review.

Ferreiro, E., & Teberosky, A. (1982). *Los sistemas de escritura en el desarrollo del niño.* México, DF: Siglo Veintiuno Editores. (English trans., *Literacy before schooling.* Exeter, NH: Heinemann, 1982.)

Flores, B., Cousin, P. T., & Díaz, E. (1991). Transforming deficit myths about learning, language and culture. *Language Arts, 68,* 369–379.

Freire, P. (1970). *Pedagogy of the oppressed.* New York: Seabury Press.

Freire, P., & Macedo, D. (1987). *Reading the world and the word.* S. Hadley, MA: Bergin and Garvey.

Gadsden, V. (1995). Representations of literacy: Parents' images in two cultural communities. In L. Morrow (Ed.), *Family literacy connections in schools and communities* (pp. 287–303). Newark, NJ: International Reading Association.

Gee, J. (1990). *Social linguistics and literacies: Ideology in discourse.* London: Falmer Press.

Gee, J. (1992). Socio-cultural approaches to literacy (literacies). *Annual Review of Applied Linguistics, 12,* 31–48.

Gee, J. P. (2000). Discourse and sociocultural studies in reading. In M. L. Kamil, P. B. Mosenthal, P. D. Pearson, & R. Barr (Eds.), *Handbook of reading research* (Vol. III, pp. 195–207). Mahwah, NJ: Lawrence Erlbaum Associates.

Gersten, R., & Woodward, J. (1995). A longitudinal study of transitional and immersion bilingual education programs in one district. *Elementary School Journal, 95*, 223–239.

Geva, E., & Wade-Wooley, L. (1998). Component processes in becoming English–Hebrew biliterate. In A. Y. Durgunoğlu & L. T. Verhoeven (Eds.), *Literacy development in a multilingual context: Cross-cultural perspectives* (pp. 85–110). Mahwah, NJ: Lawrence Erlbaum Associates.

Gibson, M. A. (1993). The school performance of immigrant minorities: A comparative view. In E. Jacob & C. Jordan (Eds.), *Minority education: Anthropological perspectives* (pp. 113–128). Norwood, NJ: Ablex.

Goldenberg, C., & Gallimore, R. (1991). Local knowledge, research knowledge, and educational change: A case study of early Spanish reading improvement. *Educational Researcher, 20*, 2–14.

Goldenberg, C., Reese, L., & Gallimore, R. (1992). Effects of literacy materials from school on Latino children's home experiences and early reading achievement. *American Journal of Education, 100*, 497–536.

Goodman, K. S. (1992). Why whole language is today's agenda in education. *Language Arts, 69*, 188–199.

Goodman, Y. M. (1990). *How children construct literacy*. Newark, DE: International Reading Association.

Green, J., & Dixon, C. (1996). Language of literacy dialogues: Facing the future or reproducing the past. *Journal of Literacy Research, 28*, 290–301.

Greenfield, P. M. (1991). Book review. In M. Minami & B. P. Kennedy, *Language issues in literacy and bilingual/multicultural education* (pp. 333–344). Cambridge, MA: Harvard Educational Review.

Guthrie, L. F., & Guthrie, G. P. (1987). Teacher language use in a Chinese bilingual classroom. In S. R. Goldman & H. T. Trueba (Eds.), *Becoming literate in English as a second language* (pp. 205–234). Norwood, NJ: Ablex.

Gutiérrez, K. D. (1992). A comparison of instructional contexts in writing process classrooms with Latino children. *Education and Urban Society, 24*, 244–262.

Hadaway, N. L. (1990). Reading and writing for real purposes in the English as a second language classroom. *Reading Education in Texas, 6*, 67–73.

Hakuta, K., Ferdman, B. M., & Díaz, R. M. (1987). Bilingualism and cognitive development: Three perspectives. In S. Rosenberg (Ed.), *Advances in applied psycholinguistics: Reading, writing and language learning* (Vol. II, pp. 284–319). New York: Cambridge University Press.

Hansen, J. (1987). *When writers read*. Portsmouth, NH: Heinemann.

Harste, J., Woodward, V., & Burke, C. (1984). *Language stories and literacy lessons*. Portsmouth, NH: Heinemann.

Hartle-Schutte, D. (1993). Literacy development in Navajo homes: Does it lead to success in school? *Language Arts, 70*, 642–654.

Heath, S. (1983). *Ways with words*. New York: Cambridge University Press.

Heath, S. (1986). Sociocultural contexts of language development. In *Beyond language: Social and cultural factors in schooling language minority children* (pp. 143–186). Los Angeles: Evaluation, Dissemination and Assessment Center, California State University.

Hornberger, N. (1990). Creating successful learning contexts for bilingual literacy. *Teachers College Record, 92*, 212–229.

Hornberger, N. H. (1994). Continua of biliteracy. In B. M. Ferdman, R. M. Weber, & A. G. Ramírez (Eds.), *Literacy across languages and cultures* (pp. 103–139). Albany: State University of New York Press.

Hornberger, N. H. (2003). Revisiting the continua of biliteracy: International and critical perspectives. *Language and Education: An International Journal.*

Hudson, T. (1982). The effects of induced schemata on the "short circuit" in L2 reading: Nondecoding factors in L2 reading performance. *Language Learning, 32*, 1–31.

Hudson, T. (1991). A content comprehension approach to reading English for science and technology. *TESOL Quarterly, 25*(1), 77–104.

Huerta-Macías, A. (1995). Literacy from within: The Project FIEL curriculum. In G. Weinstein-Shr & E. Quintero (Eds.), *Immigrant learners and their families: Literacy to connect generations* (pp. 91–99). McHenry, IL: Center for Applied Linguistics & Delta Systems.

Huerta-Macías, A., & Quintero, E. (1992). Code switching, bilingualism, and biliteracy: A case study. *Bilingual Research Journal, 16*, 69–90.

Igoa, C. (1995). *The inner world of the immigrant child.* New York: St. Martin's Press.

Irvine, P., & Elsasser, N. (1988). The ecology of literacy: Negotiating writing standards in a Caribbean setting. In B. A. Raoth & D. L. Rubin (Eds.), *The social construction of written communication* (pp. 304–320). Norwood, NJ: Ablex.

Ivaniĉ, R., & Moss, W. (1991). Bringing community writing practices into education. In D. Barton & R. Ivaniĉ (Eds.), *Writing in the community* (pp. 193–223). Newbury Park, CA: Sage.

Jensen, L. (1986). Advanced reading skills in a comprehensive course. In F. Dubin, D. E. Eskey, & W. Grabe (Eds.), *Teaching second language reading for academic purposes* (pp. 103–124). Reading, MA: Addison-Wesley.

Jiménez, R. T. (2000). Literacy and the identity development of Latina/o students. *American Educational Research Journal, 37*(4), 971–1000.

Johnson, P. (1982). Effects on reading comprehension of building background knowledge. *TESOL Quarterly, 16*, 503–516.

Kantor, R., Miller, S. M., & Fernie, D. E. (1992). Diverse paths to literacy in a preschool classroom: A sociocultural perspective. *Reading Research Quarterly, 27*, 185–201.

Kroll, B. (Ed.). (1990). *Second language writing: Research insights for the classroom.* New York: Cambridge University Press.

Ladson-Billings, G. (1994). *The dreamkeepers: Successful teachers of African American children.* San Francisco: Jossey-Bass.

Lakoff, G. (1987). *Women, fire, and dangerous things: What categories reveal about the mind.* Chicago: University of Chicago Press.

Lanauze, M., & Snow, C. (1989). The relation between first- and second-language writing skills: Evidence from Puerto Rican elementary school children in bilingual programs. *Linguistics and Education, 1*, 323–339.

Langer, J. (1984). Examining background knowledge and text comprehension. *Reading Research Quarterly, 68*, 629–481.

Langer, J. (1991). Literacy and schooling: A sociocognitive perspective. In E. H. Hiebert (Ed.), *Literacy for a diverse society: Perspectives, practices, and policies* (pp. 9–27). New York: Teachers College Press.

Langer, J. A., Bartoleme, L., Vásquez, O., & Lucas, T. (1990). Meaning construction in school literacy tasks: A study of bilingual students. *American Educational Research Journal, 27*, 427–471.

López, M. E. (1999). *When discourses collide: An ethnography of migrant children at home and in school.* New York: Peter Lang.

Mayher, J. (1993). How the system is used to make meaning. In L. M. Cleary & M. D. Linn (Eds.), *Linguistics for teachers* (pp. 564–577). New York: McGraw-Hill.

McCollum, P. (1991). Cross-cultural perspectives on classroom discourse and literacy. In E. H. Hiebert (Ed.), *Literacy for a diverse society: Perspectives, practices, and policies* (pp. 108–121). New York: Teachers College Press.

McGee, L. M., & Purcell-Gates, V. (1997). Conversations: So what's going on in research in emergent literacy? *Reading Research Quarterly, 32*, 310–318.

McIntyre, E. (1992). Young children's reading behaviors in various classroom contexts. *Journal of Reading Behavior, 23*, 339–371.

McLaughlin, D. (1989). The sociolinguistics of Navajo literacy. *Anthropology and Education Quarterly, 20*, 275–290.

Merino, B. J., Trueba, H. T., & Samaniego, F. A. (1993). Towards a framework for the study of the maintenance of the home language in language minority students. In B. J. Merino, H. T. Trueba, & F. A. Samaniego (Eds.), *Language and culture in learning* (pp. 5–25). Washington, DC: Falmer Press.

Miramontes, O. B. (1990). A comparative study of English oral reading skills in differently schooled groups of Hispanic students. *Journal of Reading Behavior, 22*, 373–394.

Moll, L. (1992). Literacy research in community and classrooms: A sociocultural approach. In R. Beach, J. L. Green, M. L. Kamil, & T. Shanahan (Eds.), *Multidisciplinary perspectives on literacy research* (pp. 211–244). Urbana, IL: National Council on Teachers of English.

Moll, L., & Díaz, S. (1987). Teaching writing as communication: The use of ethnographic findings in classroom practice. In D. Bloome (Ed.), *Literacy and schooling* (pp. 193–222). Norwood, NJ: Ablex.

Moll, L., & Díaz, S. (1993). Change as the goal of educational research. In E. Jacob & C. Jordan (Eds.), *Minority education: Anthropological perspectives* (pp. 67–79). Norwood, NJ: Ablex.

Moll, L. C., & González, N. (1994). Lessons from research with language-minority children. *Journal of Reading Behaviour, 26*, 439–456.

Moll, L., Vélez-Ibáñez, C., & Greenberg, J. (1990). *Community knowledge and classroom practice: Combining resources for literacy instruction*. Arlington, VA: Development Associates.

Mulhern, M. M. (1994). *Webs of meaning: The literate lives of three Mexican-American kindergartners*. Unpublished doctoral dissertation, University of Illinois at Chicago.

Mulhern, M. M. (1997). Doing his own thing: A Mexican-American kindergartner becomes literate at home and school. *Language Arts, 74*, 468–476.

Muñiz-Swicegood, M. (1994). The effects of metacognitive reading strategy training on the reading performance and student reading analysis strategies of third grade bilingual students. *Bilingual Research Journal, 18*, 83–98.

National Center for Education Statistics. (1995). *National Assessment of Educational Progress (NAEP), 1995 Report*. Washington, DC: U.S. Department of Education.

National Center for Education Statistics. (1999). *National Assessment of Educational Progress (NAEP), 1999 Long-term trend reading summary*. Washington, DC: U.S. Department of Education.

Ogbu, J. (1983). Minority status and schooling in plural societies. *Comparative Education Review, 27*, 168–190.

Olson, D. (1986). Intelligence and literacy: The relationship between intelligence and the technologies of representation and communication. In R. Sternberg & R. Wagner (Eds.), *Practical intelligence* (pp. 338–361). New York: Cambridge University Press.

Pérez, B. (1994). Spanish literacy development: A descriptive study of four bilingual whole-language classrooms. *Journal of Reading Behavior, 26*, 74–94.

Pérez, B. (2004). *Becoming biliterate: A study of two-way bilingual immersion education*. Mahwah, NJ: Lawrence Erlbaum Associates.

Pérez, B., & Torres-Guzmán, M. E. (2002). *Learning in two worlds: An integrated Spanish/English biliteracy approach* (3rd ed.). Boston: Allyn & Bacon.

Peyton, J. K., Staton, J., & Richardson, G. (1990). The influence of writing task on ESL students' written production. *Research in the Teaching of English, 24*, 142–171.

Pinker, S. (1994). *The language instinct: How the mind creates language*. New York: Morrow.

Prince, D. D., & Lawrence, L. A. (1993). *School readiness and language minority students: Implications of the first national education goal*. Washington, DC: National Clearinghouse for Bilingual Education.

Pritchard, R. (1990). The effects of cultural schemata on reading processing strategies. *Reading Research Quarterly, 25*, 273–295.

Purcell-Gates, V. (1993). Issues for family literacy research: Voices from the trenches. *Language Arts, 70*, 670–677.

Purcell-Gates, V. (1995). *Other people's words: The cycle of low literacy*. Cambridge, MA: Harvard University Press.

Ramírez, J. D., Yuen, S. D., Ramey, D. R., & Pasta, D. (1991). *Final report: Longitudinal study of structured English immersion strategy, early-exit and late-exit bilingual education programs for language-minority children, Vol. 1*. (No. 300-87-0156). Washington, DC: U.S. Department of Education.

Raphael, G. E., & Brock, C. H. (1993). Mei: Learning the literacy culture in an urban elementary school. In D. J. Leu & C. K. Kinzer (Eds.), *Examining central issues in literacy, research theory, and practice* (pp. 179–188). Forty-Second Yearbook of the National Reading Conference. Chicago: National Reading Conference.

Reyes, M. de la L. (1987). Comprehension of content area passages: A study of Spanish/English readers in third and fourth grade. In S. R. Goldman & H. T. Trueba (Eds.), *Becoming literate in English as a second language* (pp. 107–126). Norwood, NJ: Ablex.

Rigg, P. (1986). Reading in ESL: Learning from kids. In P. Rigg & D. S. Enright (Eds.), *Children and ESL: Integrating perspectives* (pp. 55–92). Alexandria, VA: Teachers of English to Speakers of Other Languages.

Rosaldo, R. (1989). *Culture and truth: The remaking of social analysis*. Boston: Beacon Press.

Sánchez, R. (1993). Language variation in the Spanish of the Southwest. In B. J. Merino, H. T. Trueba, & F. A. Samaniego (Eds.), *Language and culture in learning* (pp. 75–93). Washington, DC: Falmer Press.

Scinto, L. F. M. (1986). *Written language and psychological development*. New York: Academic Press.

Scribner, S., & Cole, M. (1981). *The psychology of literacy*. Cambridge, MA: Harvard University Press.

Shore, B. (1996). *Culture in mind: Cognition, culture, and the problem of meaning*. New York: Oxford University Press.

Smitherman, G. (1994). "The blacker the berry the sweeter the juice": African American student writers. In A. H. Dyson & C. Genishi, *The need for story: Cultural diversity in classroom and community* (pp. 80–101). Urbana, IL: National Council of Teachers of English.

Snow, C. E., Burns, M. S., & Griffin, P. (Eds.). (1998). *Preventing reading difficulties in young children*. Washington, DC: National Academy Press.

Solsken, J. W. (1993). *Literacy, gender and work in families and in school.* Norwood, NJ: Ablex.

Strauss, C., & Quinn, N. (1998). *A cognitive theory of cultural meaning.* Cambridge: Cambridge University Press.

Street, B. (1995). Foreword. In G. Weinstein-Shr & E. Quintero (Eds.), *Immigrant learners and their families: Literacy to connect generations* (pp. i–vi). McHenry, IL: Center for Applied Linguistics & Delta Systems.

Street, B. V. (1984). *Literacy in theory and practice.* New York: Cambridge University Press.

Sulzby, E., & Teale, W. (1991). Emergent literacy. In R. Barr, M. L. Kamil, P. Mosenthal, & P. D. Pearson (Eds.), *Handbook in reading research* (Vol. II, pp. 727–757). New York: Longman.

Taylor, D., & Dorsey-Gaines, C. (1988). *Growing up literate: Learning from inner-city families.* Portsmouth, NH: Heinemann.

Teale, W. H. (1987). Emergent literacy: Reading and writing development in early childhood. In J. E. Readence & R. S. Baldwin (Eds.), *Research in literacy: Merging perspectives* (pp. 45–74). Rochester, NY: National Reading Conference.

Teberosky, A. (1990). Nuevas investigaciones sobre la adquisición de la lengua escrita. *Lectura y Vida, 11,* 23–27.

Teberosky, A. (1991). Re-escribiendo noticias: Una aproximación a los textos de niños y adultos. *Anuario de Psicología, 47,* 65–88.

Tharp, R. (1994). Research knowledge and policy issues in cultural diversity and education. In B. McLeod (Ed.), *Language and learning: Educating linguistically diverse students* (pp. 129–167). Albany, NY: State University of New York Press.

Torres-Guzmán, M. E. (1992). Stories of hope in the midst of despair: Culturally responsive education for Latino students in an alternative high school in New York City. In M. Saravia-Shore & S. F. Arvizu (Eds.), *Cross-cultural literacy: Ethnographies of communication in multiethnic classrooms* (pp. 477–490). New York: Garland.

Traugott, E. C. (1987). Literacy and language change: The special case of speech act verbs. In J. Langer (Ed.), *Language, literacy, and culture: Issues of society and schooling* (pp. 111–127). Norwood, NJ: Ablex.

Trueba, H. T. (1993). Foreword. In C. J. Faltis (Ed.), *Joinfostering: Adapting teaching strategies for the multilingual classroom* (pp. xi–xv). New York: Macmillan.

Tucker, G. R. (1986). Implications of Canadian research for promoting a language-competent American society. In J. A. Fishman (Ed.), *The Ferfusonian impact* (Vol. 2, pp. 361–369). Berlin: Mouton.

Ungerer, F., & Schmid, H. J. (1996). *An introduction to cognitive linguistics.* London: Longman.

Valdés, G. (1996). *Con respeto: Bridging the distances between culturally diverse families and schools.* New York: Teachers College Press.

Valenzuela, A. (1999). *Subtractive schooling: U.S.-Mexican youth and the politics of caring.* Albany, NY: State University of New York Press.

Van Ness, H. (1981). Social control and social organization in an Alaskan Athabaskan classroom. A microethnography of "getting ready" for reading. In H. T. Trueba, G. P. Guthrie, & K. H. Au (Eds.), *Culture and the bilingual classroom: Studies in classroom ethnography* (pp. 120–138). Rowley, MA: Newbury.

Verhoeven, L. T. (1990). Acquisition of reading in a second language. *Reading Research Quarterly, 25*(2), 90–114.

Verhoeven, L. T. (1994). Transfer in bilingual development: The linguistic interdependence hypothesis revisited. *Language Learning, 44,* 381–415.

Vernon, S. A., & Ferreiro, E. (1999). Writing development: A neglected variable in the consideration of phonological awareness. *Harvard Educational Review, 69*(4), 395–415.

Vygotsky, L. S. (1978). *Mind and society*. Cambridge, MA: Harvard University Press.

Weinstein-Shr, G. (1990). Literacy and social process: A community in transition. In B. Street (Ed.), *Cross-cultural approaches to literacy* (pp. 272–293). Cambridge, England: Cambridge University Press.

Wells, G. (1986). *The meaning makers*. Portsmouth, NH: Heinemann.

Wertsch, J. V. (1998). *Mind as action*. Oxford: Oxford University Press.

Wong Fillmore, L. (1976). *The second time around: Cognitive and social strategies in second language acquisition*. Unpublished doctoral dissertation, Stanford University, Stanford, CA.

Wong Fillmore, L. (1979). Individual differences in second language acquisition. In D. J. Fillmore, D. Kempler, & W. S. Wange (Eds.), *Individual differences in language ability and language behavior* (pp. 203–228). San Diego, CA: Academic Press.

Wong Fillmore, L. (1991). Second-language learning in children: a model of language learning in social context. In E. Bialystok (Ed.), *Language processing in bilingual children* (pp. 49–69). Cambridge, England: Cambridge University Press.

Yoon, K. K. (1992). New perspective on intrasentential code-switching: A study of Korean-English switching. *Applied Psycholinguistics, 13*, 433–449.

Zentella, A. C. (1981). *"Hablamos los dos. We speak both": Growing up bilingual in El Barrio*. Unpublished doctoral dissertation, University of Pennsylvania.

3

Writing Across Writing Systems

Bertha Pérez

When children come to school they have already developed the genesis of writing in their first language and culture. This early learning is the foundation of future learning and what schools do can help or hinder the transition into school literacy. If we design instruction so children continue their literacy development as a natural progression from what they have already learned to do well, school literacy instruction might be more effective. How can the teacher view the child's competencies in writing in his or her first language, and what implications does this have for writing in a second language?

This chapter reviews selected research on emergent writing, describes a variety of writing systems, discusses learning to write in a second writing system, and examines the implications for the classroom.

EMERGENT WRITING

Emergent literacy research has described how children come into literacy through a gradual and integrated development. Literacy develops when children have encounters with print, presumably written in a language which the child speaks, and have social interactions around print with adult or older readers and writers. Much of the research on emergent literacy (Dyson, 1984; Ferreiro & Teberosky, 1982; Graves, 1983; Harste, Woodward, & Burke, 1984; Hernández-Chávez & Curtis, 1984; Teale & Sulzby, 1986; Tolchinsky Landsman & Levin, 1985; Vernon & Ferreiro, 1999) has found that many preschoolers have a surprisingly remarkable knowledge of print and have developed some print conventions on their own. Researchers have worked with children from a variety of racial, ethnic, and cultural backgrounds, and from a range of socioeconomic levels. Children from these studies provide evidence that, given literate environments where a variety of print and texts as well as literate users are available, children construct ideas about reading and writing that they have not been taught.

Emergent literacy in a variety of different languages has been studied, for example, in Spanish (Ferreiro & Teberosky, 1982; Teberosky, 1990), English (Harste et al., 1984), Hebrew (Tolchinsky Landsman, 1990), and Chinese (Chi, 1993). Interestingly enough, many similarities in the process of development were found across languages and writing systems. Young children developed a variety of hypotheses and strategies that are developmentally ordered for obtaining meaning from the print in their homes and communities, and for their first written productions. Many children naturally develop reading and writing as a continuum of their language acquisition process as influenced by their own interests and curiosity. The natural process of written language acquisition is described by Tolchinsky Landsman (1990) and Ferreiro (1990) as a Piagetian assimilation schema process. Piaget's (1959) theories describe children's developmental tasks in a schema framework where new learning must be assimilated and accommodated. In the acquisition of writing, children use their developing knowledge and experience to generate hypotheses that assist them in constructing or giving meaning to written productions. The facts that children construct their own representations and explanations about writing, that similarities occur in different linguistic environments, and that the processes children exhibit appear to be developmentally ordered, have led some researchers to characterize the acquisition of writing as a "psychogenetic process, in a Piagetian sense" (Ferreiro, 1990).

The literature on emergent literacy stresses the important role of print or text and of the presence of opportunities for the children to observe adults and older siblings reading and writing. In the development of literacy, the object of knowledge is the writing system. The writing system is a cultural artifact. The process of becoming literate occurs in a context of social interactions (Scribner, 1984; Vygotsky, 1978; Wertsch, 1998) and through the interpretation of cultural representations of literacy. Luria (1980) expanded on Vygotsky's "psychogenesis of cultural forms of behavior" (Vygotsky, 1978, p. 424) and directly studied writing as a developmental activity.

What happens when a child has learned or is learning to create meaning from print in a particular writing system and is then confronted with a different writing system? Which are the developmental data or evidence of prior competence with regard to print in any language that must be taken into consideration by the teacher? What are the literacy instruction objectives? In order to decide what is appropriate for any given child, but in particular for a child whose prior learning and experience is in a language other than English, how do we select and organize the great quantity of tasks, materials, and theories about literacy that constitute the framework for reading and writing instruction in schools? In other words, how do we integrate (a) what we know about the development of literacy, (b) what we observe children doing with their own writing system, and (c) what we present in classrooms as first- or second-language literacy instruction?

The Process of Writing Development

Is what we consider writing different from what children consider writing? Any definition of writing would probably include graphic displays that are understood as a code for a spoken or potentially spoken message, and writing as a social practice (Moll, Sáez, & Dworin, 2001). Learning a writing system is similar to learning a language in that the fundamental objective is communication; it is different in that writing requires interaction with print or text. Dyson (1984, 1993) studied children's writing development as it relates to purpose and is situated within the social contexts and power relationships that exist with children's experiences. She defined these contexts as multiple worlds, the symbolic world, the peer social world, the official teacher's world, and the wider world (Dyson, 1993). Dyson concluded that children develop written language in different ways related to their individual social styles and their need to create meaning using symbols. She speculates that children, in particular culturally diverse children, may encounter tensions as they negotiate different meanings for literacy within school contexts and between the home and the school worlds.

In the emergent literacy literature of the last 15 years, we have example after example of how children learn to write their native language and how they come to define writing. Children also explore the arbitrariness of the symbols that are written down to stand for the word or idea that they can speak. Children do not learn the writing system as a collection of unrelated symbols; they first attempt to establish a relation between the symbols and the language units they represent (Tolchinsky Landsman, 1990). In the initial stages of the writing development, children seem to progress through similar steps across the different writing systems.

Distinguishing Writing From Drawing

Early in their awareness of print or text, children begin to distinguish between graphic representations that they consider writing and those they consider drawing. Very young children (before the age of 4) may produce writing and drawings that are graphically indistinguishable. However, from looking closely at scribbles, Harste et al. (1984) concluded that "Children as young as three, regardless of race or socio-economic status, differentiated writing from drawing .... Generally the children's art was characterized as being global, centralized and connected .... Their writing, on the other hand, was typically linear, spaced, and located off center" (pp. 127–128). Children differentiate between the use of lines in drawing to outline or to give an image of the contours of an object and the organization of lines in graphic representations that resemble the writing system for their cultural group. They distinguish that the lines used to write may have nothing to do with the form of the object, and the organization of the writing may have nothing to do with the organization of the parts of the object. For example, very young children when asked to write "house" may in fact attempt to draw lines that resemble a *house*; as children develop an awareness of writing they may scribble lines that do not in any way resemble a house and will read their written production as *house* (Ferreiro, 1990, p. 15).

Ferreiro and Teberosky (1982) found that young children could learn to make several distinctions between written productions and other graphic symbols. They distinguished:

- Drawing from writing.
- Pictures from print.
- Letter from numerals.
- Letters from punctuation.
- Letters from words.
- Print from cursive writing.

Children quickly come to recognize the arbitrariness of writing and the need to arrange their graphic productions in linearly distinctive units separated by regular spaces similar to the writing systems of their native languages (Tolchinsky Landsman, 1990). They also view written marks as substitute objects, for the physical objects or ideas.

Ferreiro and Teberosky (1982), Tolchinsky Landsman (1990), Clay (1991), and other researchers have begun to discover the principles that children use in constructing what Ferreiro called "children's theories" about writing and literacy. Among these principles are:

- *The principle of minimum quantity*: How many letters or symbols must exist for print to say something? Children in the Ferreiro study learning Spanish expected at least three letters and no more than six or seven for a word to be readable. Children also hypothesize about the relationship of a word to the referent object—for example, a big house needed more letters than a little house, a cow needed more letters than a fly, and that words that related things such as hens and chickens could be written in the same way with only a variation in the size of the letters.
- *Internal quality variations*: Not only is the number of letters important but also the variety is important. Can the same letter repeated be readable? Children's theories about the readability of repeated letters seem to vary based on language system.
- *Objective differences in writing*: How can they create graphic differentiations for different meanings? The need for a wide variety of graphics or letters to make different constructions for distinct words creates a problem especially when children only know a limited number of letters or symbols, for example, those of their names or family names.
- *The phonetization or syllabic hypothesis*: Depending on the language, how do children begin to attempt a correspondence between the spoken language and the written symbols? Children begin to look for similar letters or symbols to write for similar pieces of sounds, and many children hypothesize that they must write a minimum of one letter or symbol for each syllable. This may occur more with children learning more syllable-timed languages, such as Spanish (Ferreiro, 1990).
- *The alphabetic hypothesis* (for children learning alphabetic languages): Children attempt to use letters to represent individual sounds. In their attempt to construct a theory, children often eliminate the irregularities in the orthography of the given language.

Table 3.1 outlines the principles that children use in constructing the syllabic and alphabetic hypothesis.

The emergence of writing seems to follow a process of increasing differentiation, from general (distinction between drawing and writing and linearity) to more specific features (letters/characters for particular vocalizations). This movement toward the particular graphic features of the writing system constitutes the figurative side of the

TABLE 3.1
Spanish-Speaking Children's Literacy Development

First Level	
Distinguishing between drawing, writing, and numbers	(drawing of house) casa 4

Second Level	
String of letters stand for objects/names	casa
Quantitative principle of: Minimum quantity Maximum quantity	vum fatisa
Qualitative principle of: Internal variations Letters must be different and use vowels	eeee ≠ word ssss ≠ word sede

Third Level	
Syllabic—minimum of one letter for each syllable	oa for sopa aaia for calabaza seoa for cebolla
Syllabic—alphabetic beginning of correspondence	spa for sopaa lasa for calabaza miosa for mariposa
Alphabetic	kasa for casa sopa for sopa calabasa for calabaza ceboya for ceboilla

child's writing system development. The developing knowledge of these graphic features is the raw material children use to work out their own constraints. These constraints seem to be general across writing systems.

WRITING SYSTEMS

Writing is a way of recording language by means of graphic symbols. Some languages have been written for a very long time (e.g., Chinese, Greek), many have existed in written form for somewhat shorter lengths of time (most European languages), and still others are just today developing writing systems, such as Hmong (Olsen & Mullen, 1990) and some Native American languages (Leap, 1993).

Although the development of speech seems to have come about as a result of evolutionary changes in the biology of the brain, writing seems to have developed as a result of cultural changes. Therefore, it would appear that the only essential prerequisite for a child to be able to read and write is belonging to a literate culture group.

According to Pinker (1994), in all known writing systems, the symbols designate only three kinds of linguistic structure: the *morpheme*, the *syllable*, and the *phoneme*. The morpheme is the smallest meaningful unit in a language. For example, words like *kind* that cannot be divided without changing meanings are morphemes, and other morphemes serve grammatical functions—for example, the prefix *un-* in *unkind*, the suffix *-ly* in *kindly*, or verb tenses as *-s* in *talks*. The syllable is a unit in speech often longer than one sound and shorter than a word, and the phoneme is the smallest unit of sound that can distinguish two words; for example, the words cat and mat differ only in their initial sound /c/ and /m/, or the words mat and met only differ in their vowel sound /a/ and /e/. The number of phonemes varies from one language to another. English is often considered to have 44 phonemes: 24 consonants and 20 vowels (Richards, Platt, & Weber, 1985). Most writing systems can be classified into three main types according to the units of language that they represent: *logographic, syllabary*, and *alphabetic* (Rayner & Pollatsek, 1989). Let us consider each in turn.

The Logographic Writing System

In the logographic writing system, most symbols represent words or morphemes rather than having a grapheme–phoneme correspondence. However, more current scholarship is describing the writing system as morphosyllabic (see Chang, chap. 7, this volume). Chinese is the most widely used logographic writing system today. An estimated half-million children in the United States live in communities and homes where the Chinese logographic writing system is used.

This morphemic writing system appears to have served the Chinese well, despite the fact that readers are at a loss when they face new or rare words. The majority of Chinese characters are constructed based on the radical plus remainder system, where the remainder is usually a predictable phonetic component. Speakers of many dialects can share texts, although they may pronounce the words differently. Relatively few changes have occurred over time; thus, very old documents are readable by today's speakers of the many different Chinese dialects (Pinker, 1994). The characters or symbols of Chinese writing may represent quite different-sounding words in the various dialects of Chinese, but they represent specific form and meaning. The character is the building block for multi-morphemic words, and characters can be combined to form multi-part or compound words and derivatives (Hoosain, 1991; Ju & Jackson, 1995). Figure 3.1 gives examples of the Chinese characters building-block organization. Note that the characters of Chinese writing may also represent the same meaning in two languages, Chinese and Japanese, for example.

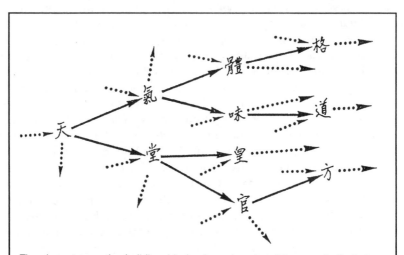

The character as the building block of words. A solid arrow indicated an actual combination of characters forming a word, listed below with their English translations. A dotted arrow indicates that an indeterminate number of other combinations is possible, involving characters preceding or following the character in question. The characters, independently, can usually function as linguistic words, as follows:

'sky'	天	'weather'	天氣
'gas'	氣	'heaven'	天堂
'hall'	堂	'gas'	氣體
'body'	體	'smell'	氣味
'taste'	味	'grand'	堂皇
'king'	皇	'waiter'	堂官
'official'	官	'physique'	體格
'matrix'	格	'taste'	味道
'road'	道	'official'	官方
'square'	方		

FIG. 3.1. Examples of Chinese characters. From Hoosain (1991), *Psycholinguistic Implications for Linguistic Relativity: A Case Study of Chinese*, p. 17. Hillsdale, NJ: Lawrence Erlbaum Associates, Publishers. Reproduced with permission.

The Syllabary Writing System

In the syllabic or syllabary writing system the symbols represent syllables rather than phonemes. Cherokee, a Native American language, is
an example of a language with a syllabic writing system. Chief Sequoya
is credited with the development of the Cherokee writing system in
the early 1820s.

Japanese is a combination of the logographic and syllabic system.
The stems of Japanese words are written with Chinese characters,
which are called *Kanji* and encode morphemes; other elements of the
language are represented by means of a syllabary. Actually, Japanese
uses two sets of written syllabic symbols, the *Katakana* and *Hiragana*
(Taylor, 1981). Taylor explained that "each letter of Katakana is a fragment of a simple Chinese character, hence the name Kata (fragment)
+ Kana (borrowed name). Each letter of Hiragana (cursive or smooth
borrowed name) is fashioned from a cursive form of a simple character" (Taylor, 1981, p. 21). Figure 3.2 illustrates Katakama, Kanji, and
Hiragana symbols.

The Alphabetic Writing System

In the alphabetic writing system, the symbols represent phonemes of
the language. The correspondence of phonemes to graphemes (the
written symbols or letters) varies with greater or less correspondence
from language to language. Historically, alphabetic writing systems
were the last to be invented. It is generally assumed that alphabetic
writing evolved from Egyptian hieroglyphics, through Phoenician
writing that represented the consonants only, to Greek writing that
represented both consonants and vowels. English, Spanish, Italian,
Vietnamese, and many other languages use the Roman or Latin alphabetic writing system. Other alphabetic writing systems include the Semitic (modern Hebrew and Arabic), the Cyrillic (Russian and other
eastern European languages), and the Greek (Pinker, 1994).

English is an alphabetic language that poses some complicating
challenges for second-language learners. As with all alphabetic systems, the written symbols or letters are referentially meaningless, that
is there is no relation between the written symbols of a word and the
object that the word represents. For example, there is no relationship
between the word "car" and the size or qualities of the object—car.
The phonological value assigned to the written symbol is also abstract, generally governed by the surrounding letters or rules with
many exceptions, for example, the sound represented by the phoneme /a/ in "cat" and in "car." English orthography relies on represent-

Sound	Katakana	Kanji	Hiragana	Add (")	Sound: voiced	Add (˚)	Semi-voiced	
ha	ハ	八波	は	ば	ba	ぱ	pa	take both (") & (˚)
hi	ヒ	比	ひ	び	bi	ぴ	pi	
f, hu	フ	不	ふ	ぶ	bu	ぷ	pu	
he	ヘ	阝部	へ	べ	be	ぺ	pe	
ho	ホ	保	ほ	ぼ	bo	ぽ	po	
ka	カ	加	か	が	ga			take only (")
ki	キ	幾	き	ぎ	gi			
ku	ク	久	く	ぐ	gu			
ke	ケ	介計	け	げ	ge			
ko	コ	己	こ	ご	go			
na	ナ	奈	な					take neither (") nor (˚)
ni	ニ	仁	に					
nu	ヌ	奴	ぬ					
ne	ネ	祢	ね					
no	ノ	乃	の					

FIG. 3.2. Katakama, Kanji, and Hiragana symbols. From Taylor (1981) Writing Systems and Reading. In G. E. Mackinnon & T. G. Waller (Eds.), *Reading Research: Advances in Theory and Practice* (Vol. 2), p. 21. New York: Academic Press. Reproduced with permission.

ing spoken language through an alphabetic system that does not closely relate to the surface sounds of words. According to Smith (1997), "orthographies may be defined as either *shallow* or *deep*, depending on the ease of predicting the pronunciation of a word from its spelling" (Smith, 1997, p. 161). Some languages with shallow orthographies, such as Spanish, Italian, and Serbo-Croatian, spell words as they sound—with high degree of sound–symbol correspondence. English is said to have a deep orthography. English word spelling can reflect morphological relations rather than maintaining a consistent sound, for example, the sounds of the letter c in police, political, and politician. English also conserves historical spellings or spellings that connote the etymology of words, for example, the ph in philosophy and sophisticated to denote the Greek origins.

Is There an Ideal Writing System?

Ideally, a writing system should have a one–one relation between its written symbols and the spoken language units they represent. That is, an alphabetic system should have one letter or grapheme for each phoneme or sound of the language, and no more. And each letter should always represent the same phoneme. Similarly, in syllabic writing or logographic writing there should be one symbol for each distinct syllable or word, no more and no less. In actual fact, except for some theoretical writing systems (e.g., Esperanto), we do not find that ideal situation in any of the writing systems in use. A symbol may represent various phonemes, the same phoneme may be represented by various symbols; sometimes there are more symbols than phonemes, at other times there are more phonemes than symbols, and so on. The more regular the fit, the easier it is to predict and to learn the writing system once we know the language. English is particularly irregular and thus harder to predict.

When we first develop the writing system of our native language, we develop, confirm, modify, and discard hypotheses about the encoding of our language until we develop a set of habits that involve an almost automatic association between the symbols and the language units they represent and the skill for rapid writing of the symbols. As the associations are learned, and when they are learned early and naturally, the great effort involved in learning them is minimized. Hebrew- and Arabic-speaking children soon master writing with speed and dexterity from right to left on the page, Japanese or Chinese children learn to write the Chinese characters with seeming ease, and English-speaking children begin to work out the irregularities between their spoken and written systems and learn the writing system of their language and culture.

LANGUAGE DISCOURSE DIFFERENCES

Written text has a style that is different from oral language. Although, oral language is an integral part of the home culture and everyday social life, literacy opens up broader worlds to readers that may not be available in a purely oral culture. Written language employs vocabulary that is more varied and is described as "literary" or "written." As one reads, the vocabulary encountered in print may become part of one's oral language. Thus, the more a person reads, the higher is the probability that literary vocabulary will be infused in their speech.

Written language is also much more dense—that is, it contains more words per unit than comparable spoken units of language. The order of the words or *text structures* will also be ordered in ways that are distinct from spoken or oral language. For example, seldom will one find the following ordering of clauses and phrases in oral speech:

> She had been 13 when the house they left behind two years ago signaled the end of the old and the beginning of the new.

The inversions and orderings illustrated in this sentence, taken from a children's book, are more typically found in written text.

Beyond the mastery of the mechanics of the writing system, children also learn the text structures and discourse styles used for writing in their native language and their cultural community. The discourse and text structures can vary significantly across languages. For example, English discourse and text structures for narratives and expository writing, especially in the literature and materials for children, are represented in a linear structure. It is hierarchically represented as the stories progress from introduction of characters, plot, event(s), and resolution of problem in a linear fashion. For the Asian American (see Chang, chap. 7, this volume) and for Native Americans (see McCarty & Watahomigie, chap. 4, this volume), texts are constructed in more circular fashion using a different story grammar. Spanish and other Romance languages, along with Russian and other Slovak languages, have a linear structure but may use a story grammar that allows for much digression and commentary along the way to constructing the text (see Fig. 3.3).

LEARNING A SECOND SYSTEM OF WRITING

Research shows that we transfer our writing knowledge and skills to a second language (Hudelson, 1986; Peyton & Seyoum, 1989). However, it is less clear just how this transfer is affected when learning a second-language writing system. Obviously, if both languages use the same symbols—say, the letters or graphemes of the Roman alphabet—the problems of learning to write and to identify the symbols are less difficult. The problems consist of associating familiar symbols to a different sound system. Such is the case of Spanish and English.

If the two languages use different symbols, but some of the symbols show some resemblance across languages, part of the trouble will be in learning new symbols and part in getting accustomed to new asso-

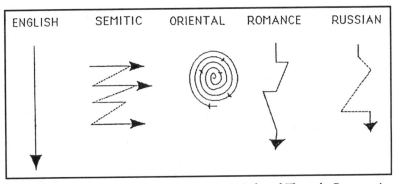

FIG. 3.3. Discourse structure illustration. "Cultural Thought Patterns in Intercultural Education," by R. Kaplan, 1970, *Language Learning, 16,* 1–20. Reprinted with permission.

ciations for symbols that are similar to those of the native language, for example, the cyrillic alphabet of Russian.

For alphabetic systems that do not resemble each other, for example, Thai or Korean, and English, the learner has to learn new symbols not previously associated with their first language. However, the learner already knows that the symbols represent phonemes and will begin a process of developing hypotheses about the correspondence of the symbols with the phonemes of the second language.

In the case of Chinese (logographic) and English (alphabetic) languages, the differences are so fundamental that hardly any transfer at all may be expected to occur. Chinese characters can represent words or morphemes and can be written vertically down and in columns from right to left. Chinese writers learning an alphabetic system do bring a knowledge of the fundamental principle that the symbols on the piece of paper have meaning and stand for something in a language. Bialystok (2001) reported that on a task that asked children to match printed words to spoken words with incongruity between the size of the word and the size of the referent object, the younger Chinese-English bilingual children found the task very difficult. However, older Chinese-English bilinguals did better and Bialystok concluded that "they sorted out the correspondences used in the two writing systems .... The experience of working through representational rules in two different systems clarified the rules for both, making them more explicit and more accessible" (p. 163).

A writer of a Semitic language learning to write English faces a distinct set of tasks. Semitic writing (e.g., Hebrew and Arabic) is alphabetic but the forms are completely different from the Roman alphabet. Semitic languages usually omit the short vowels and represent only the consonants and some long vowels. Most Semitic systems are written and read from right to left. In learning English, children must discover the new directionality and learn to encode the vowels as well as the consonants.

Ferdman (1991) summarized the task of becoming literate in a second language system as "being skilled in the use of methods of representation such as the alphabet, writing implements, books, and so on, the literate person must be familiar with a particular configuration of meanings in context, to comprehend appropriately the content of what is encoded and decoded" (p. 353).

IMPLICATIONS FOR THE CLASSROOM

Transfer of Literacy Process Skills

Beyond discrete linguistic skills, there are numerous process skills that transfer from literacy in a first language to a second language. This transfer of literacy process skills can assist students in learning literacy in a second language. Literate students will understand that a written language is a code, and there are particular rules for decoding (reading) and encoding (writing) and making meaning. They will understand that the written language differs from the spoken language, but that there are conventions to help the reader make the written text sound as much like oral speech as possible when read aloud (e.g., periods, commas, quotation marks, boldface). Literate students will have strategies for confronting a written text, and they may look for physical cues that help them analyze the nature or genre of the document (letter, poem, grocery list, story, and so on).

Literate students will know how to read for meaning in a paragraph, how to organize and classify details, how to form images of what is read. Problem solving for deciding on strategies to use with unknown words, such as using context clues (looking just before or just after a new work to find its meaning restated) or consulting a dictionary or peer. Having developed literacy in one language helps the student understand the concepts and purposes of reading and writing in a second language.

It is not enough to make broad comments on differences between writing systems and the transfer of literacy process skills to understand the learning tasks faced by persons trying to learn two systems either simultaneously or within a short developmental period. The teacher will have to keenly observe the students' attempts at interpreting print in the classroom, inquire about prior literacy experiences in the native language, and explore the community environment where children may have first encountered print and the need for literacy in order to assess what possible emergent literacy children have in their first language and bring to the classroom.

If teachers do not have the basic understanding of writing development to make sense of the behaviors that children are exhibiting, literacy behaviors of children go unobserved and unsupported. Teachers need to observe and gather information that will assist them to see otherwise unnoticed signs of literacy development in students. When teachers can see the strategies that children are using to interact and make sense of print and when those strategies can be viewed within the context of a natural, ordered, developmental process, teachers can support, reinforce, and provide a context for the continued development of these processes. The things that a teacher "attends to" reveal to children what the teacher values about their learning and about them. When teachers talk with children about their first-language knowledge, the teacher places value on the first language. Teachers must know the power they have over children and the effect that teacher attention can have on developing literacy and learning. When teachers understand this, they begin to think differently and respond differently to children's use of their first language and writing knowledge in learning English literacy. Teachers can begin to discover the creative, ingenious, and inventive ways that linguistically diverse children construct meaning in their first and second language.

When teachers become overly concerned with requirements for written text to deal with teacher-chosen topics and to be within narrowly define standards for writing (Alton-Lee, Nuthall, & Patrick, 1993), children will be restricted in the ways they can express themselves through written symbols (Dyson, 1984; Edelsky, 1986; Ferreiro & Teberosky, 1982).

The Complexities of Theory Construction

Understanding the development process that children go through, as well as knowing about the writing systems that culturally diverse students are exploring, provides teachers with new ways of looking at how children are developing literacy. Literacy and, in particular, writing are culturally situated in that the tools of writing (the symbols, text, discourse organization, etc.) are culturally determined and valued by the different culture groups (home culture, ethnic culture, classroom culture) to which the learner belongs (Sluys, 2003). Literacy is socially mediated by the more capable members of the learner's groups (parents, siblings, teachers, classroom peers). How these more capable members mediate the use of literacy will determine the uses that the learner will attempt, develop, and adapt. For example, Moll, Vélez-Ibáñez, and Greenberg (1990) described how adults mediate certain uses of writing in his funds of knowledge in the households they studied. On the other hand, Purcell-Gates (1995) described how the lack of mediation or the lack of use of literacy by parents within a household can lead to children not seeing any value or need for writing.

Literacy is also constructed. That is, the culture group may have multiple levels of literacies and literacy uses; the more capable members of the group use literacy with children, but the bottom line is that for children to learn to write they must "construct" and test their theories themselves. Without this process of experimentation and construction children will not develop writing.

SUMMARY

Many children from linguistically diverse communities have developed the genesis of writing in their native language before they come to school. This early learning is the foundation and nexus for second-language literacy development. The development of writing, as all of literacy uses and functions, is constructed by the learner within the various sociocultural contexts in the child's world.

The task of learning to write is made easier or harder depending on the writing system. The more sound–symbol correspondence the spoken language has with the written language, the easier it is to predict the writing system once we know the language. English does not have a high predictable correspondence; in fact, there are numerous exceptions to most rules and thus English is hard to predict, especially for second-language learners.

■ ACTIVITIES

1. Working in small groups, collect a sample of five or six texts written in a variety of languages and writing systems (e.g., food packaging, newspapers, children's books). Eliminate any English translation but try to conserve as much of the pragmatic context of the print. Each group presents their samples to another group asking the second group to attempt to answer the following questions: (a) What is the purpose of the material? (e.g., to inform, entertain, direct)? (b) What type of writing, or system of writing, does it represent? (c) What language does it represent and how did you deduce the language? (d) Hypothesize how you can deduce when the symbol is a

letter, a graphic, a number, and so on; hypothesize how you can deduce words, phrases, sentences, and paragraphs. (e) Hypothesize what the text "says" or "means."

2. Interview or have a discussion over a piece of text with a preschool or kindergarten second-language learner using the qualitative and quantitative principles described in the chapter. Can you decipher the "theories" the child has formed about reading and writing?

3. Walk or ride around a culturally and linguistically diverse community and notice the use of print, advertisements, and availability of newspapers in languages other than English. What does the availability of print materials in languages other than English connote about the community members?

SUGGESTED READINGS

Clay, M. (1993). *An observation survey: Of early literacy achievement.* Portsmouth, NH: Heinemann. (Also, Escamilla, K., Andrade, A. M., Basurto, A., & Ruiz, O., 1995. *Instrumento de observación de los logros de la lecto-escritura inicial: Spanish reconstruction of an observation survey.* Portsmouth, NH: Heinemann.)

Dyson, A. H. (1993). *Social worlds of children learning to write in an urban primary school.* New York: Teachers College Press.

Sluys, K. V. (2003). Writing and identity construction: A young author's life in transition. *Language Arts, 80*(3), 176–184.

Taylor, I. (1981). Writing systems and reading. In G. E. MacKinnon & T. G. Waller (Eds.), *Reading research: Advances in theory and practice* (Vol. 2, pp. 15–27). New York: Academic Press.

Vernon, S. A., & Ferreiro, E. (1999). Writing development: A neglected variable in the consideration of phonological awareness. *Harvard Educational Review, 69*(4), 395–415.

REFERENCES

Alton-Lee, A., Nuthall, G., & Patrick, J. (1993). Reframing classroom research: A lesson from the private world of children. *Harvard Educational Review, 63*, 50–84.

Bialystok, E. (2001). *Bilingualism in development.* Cambridge, England: Cambridge University Press.

Chi, M. (1993, February). *Writing development of ESL students.* Paper presented at National Association for Bilingual Education Annual Conference, Anaheim, CA.

Clay, M. M. (1991). *Becoming literate: The construction of inner control.* Portsmouth, NH: Heinemann.

Dyson, A. (1984). Learning to write/Learning to do school. *Research in the Teaching of English, 6*, 233–264.

Dyson, A. H. (1993). *Social worlds of children learning to write in an urban primary school.* New York: Teachers College Press.

Edelsky, C. (1986). *Writing in a bilingual program: Había una vez*. Norwood, NJ: Ablex.

Ferdman, B. M. (1991). Literacy and cultural identity. In M. Minami & B. P. Kennedy, *Language issues in literacy and bilingual/multicultural education* (pp. 347–390). Cambridge, MA: Harvard Educational Review.

Ferreiro, E. (1990). Literacy development: Psychogenesis. In Y. M. Goodman (Ed.), *How children construct literacy* (pp. 12–25). Newark, DE: International Reading Association.

Ferreiro, E., & Teberosky, A. (1982). *Los sistemas de escritura en el desarrollo del niño*. México, DF: Siglo Veintiuno Editores. (English trans., *Literacy before schooling*. Exeter, NH: Heinemann, 1982.)

Graves, D. H. (1983). *Writing: Teachers and children at work*. Exeter, NH: Heinemann.

Harste, J., Woodward, V., & Burke, C. (1984). *Language stories and literacy lessons*. Portsmouth, NH: Heinemann.

Hernández-Chávez, E., & Curtis, J. (1984). The graphic sense hypothesis or "You can't read firecrackers." In C. Rivera (Ed.), *Placement procedures in bilingual education: Education and policy issues* (pp. 121–151). Clevedon, England: Multilingual Matters.

Hoosain, R. (1991). *Psycholinguistic implications for linguistic relativity: A case study of Chinese*. Hillsdale, NJ: Lawrence Erlbaum Associates.

Hudelson, S. (1986). ESL children's writing: What we've learned, what we're learning. In P. Rigg & D. S. Enright (Eds.), *Children and ESL: Integrating perspectives* (pp. 23–54). Washington, DC: TESOL.

Ju, D., & Jackson, N. E. (1995). Graphic and phonological processing in Chinese character identification. *JRB: A Journal of Literacy, 27*, 299–315.

Kaplan, R. (1970). Cultural thought patterns in inter-cultural education. *Language Learning, 16*, 1–20.

Leap, W. L. (1993). American Indian English and its implications for bilingual education. In L. M. Cleary & M. D. Linn (Eds.), *Linguistics for teachers* (pp. 207–219). New York: McGraw-Hill.

Luria, A. (1980). *Higher cortical functions in man*. New York: Basic Books.

Moll, L. C., Sáez, R., & Dworin, J. (2001). Exploring biliteracy: Two student case examples of writing as a social practice. *Elementary School Journal, 101*, 435–449.

Moll, L., Vélez-Ibáñez, C., & Greenberg, J. (1990). *Community knowledge and classroom practice: Combining resources for literacy instruction*. Arlington, VA: Development Associates, Inc.

Olsen, L., & Mullen, N. A. (1990). *Embracing diversity: Teachers' voices from California's classrooms*. San Francisco: California Tomorrow.

Peyton, J., & Seyoum, M. (1989). The effect of teachers strategies on students' interactive writing: The case of dialogue journals. *Research in the Teaching of English, 23*, 310–334.

Piaget, J. (1959). *The language and thought of the child*. London: Routledge & Kegan Paul.

Pinker, S. (1994). *The language instinct: How the mind creates language*. New York: Morrow.

Purcell-Gates, V. (1995). *Other people's words: The cycle of low literacy*. Cambridge, MA: Harvard University Press.

Rayner, K., & Pollatsek., A. (1989). *The psychology of reading*. Englewood Cliffs, NJ: Prentice Hall.

Richards, J., Platt, J., & Weber, H. (1985). *Longman dictionary of applied linguistics*. Essex, England: Longman Group UK.

Scribner, S. (1984). Literacy in three metaphors. *American Journal of Education*, *93*, 6–21.

Sluys, K. V. (2003). Writing and identity construction: A young author's life in transition. *Language Arts*, 80, 3, 176–184.

Smith, M. C. (1997). How do bilinguals access lexical information? In A. M. B. de Groot & J. F. Kroll (Eds.), *Tutorials in bilingualism: Psycholinguistic perspectives* (pp. 145–168). Mahwah, NJ: Lawrence Erlbaum Associates.

Taylor, I. (1981). Writing systems and reading. In G. E. Mackinnon & T. G. Waller (Eds.), *Reading research: Advances in theory and practice* (Vol. 2, pp. 15–27). New York: Academic Press.

Teale, W. H., & Sulzby, E. (1986). Introduction: Emergent literacy as a perspective for examining how young children become writers and readers. In W. H. Teale & E. Sulzby (Eds.), *Emergent literacy* (pp. vii–xxv). Norwood, NJ: Ablex.

Teberosky, A. (1990). Nuevas investigaciones sobre la adquisición de la lengua escrita [New investigations of the acquisition of written language]. *Lectura y Vida*, *11*, 23–27.

Tolchinsky Landsman, L. (1990). Literacy development and pedagogical implications: Evidence from the Hebrew system of writing. In Y. M. Goodman (Ed.), *How children construct literacy* (pp. 26–44). Newark, DE: International Reading Association.

Tolchinsky Landsman, L., & Levin, I. (1985). Writing in preschoolers: An age related analysis. *Journal of Applied Psycholinguistics*, *6*, 319–339.

Vernon, S. A., & Ferreiro, E. (1999). Writing development: A neglected variable in the consideration of phonological awareness. *Harvard Educational Review*, *69*(4), 395–415.

Vygotsky, L. S. (1978). *Mind and society*. Cambridge, MA: Harvard University Press.

Wertsch, J. V. (1998). *Mind as action*. Oxford: Oxford University Press.

II

LANGUAGE AND LITERACY ACQUISITION IN DIVERSE COMMUNITIES

4

Language and Literacy in American Indian and Alaska Native Communities

Teresa L. McCarty
Lucille J. Watahomigie

Two million American Indians and Alaska Natives reside in the United States, representing 175 languages and more than 550 federally recognized tribes (see Fig. 4.1). Nearly one quarter of the Indigenous population are school-age children who attend a variety of schools: federal schools operated by the Bureau of Indian Affairs (BIA), tribal or community-controlled schools funded through grants and contracts with the federal government, public schools, private schools, and mission or parochial schools. Although many of these schools are located on reservation lands and have a majority American Indian/Alaska Native enrollment, 56% or more than 250,000 Indigenous students attend public schools with less than 25% Indian/Alaska Native enrollment (National Center for Education Statistics, 2000).

This situation suggests some of the linguistic, cultural, and educational diversity glossed by the title of this chapter. We explore that diversity here, at the same time pointing out common historical and contemporary experiences that enable us to consider American Indi-

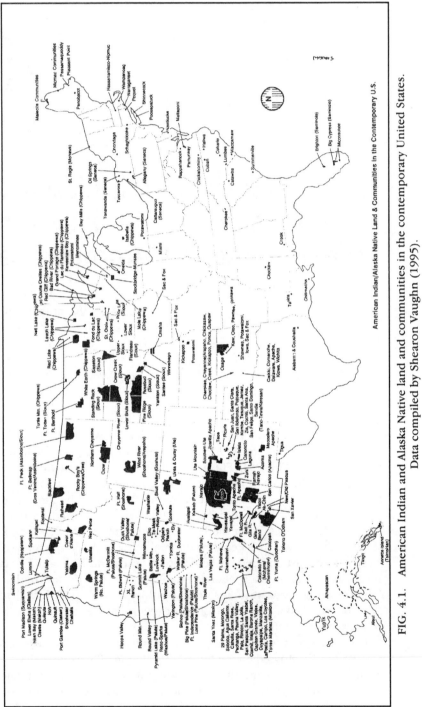

FIG. 4.1. American Indian and Alaska Native land and communities in the contemporary United States. Data compiled by Shearon Vaughn (1995).

ans and Alaska Natives as a group.[1] Our discussion represents the combined perspectives of local and outside educator-researchers. Lucille Watahomigie is Hualapai and the founder of the nationally recognized Hualapai bilingual/bicultural program at Peach Springs School in northwestern Arizona. Teresa McCarty is non-Indian, a social-cultural anthropologist and a university-based teacher and researcher. For more than two decades we have collaborated on a variety of local, regional, and national projects in American Indian/Alaska Native education. In this chapter, we look both forward and backward to examine the sociocultural context for language and literacy development in American Indian and Alaska Native communities today. We begin with a discussion of historical antecedents.

THE SOCIOHISTORICAL CONTEXT OF AMERICAN INDIAN/ALASKA NATIVE EDUCATION

> 'I don't know what to put in a journal,' the teacher wrote. 'I've never been good at writing. I have a writing handicap.'

The American Indian teacher who wrote these lines submitted them as her first entry in a dialogue journal for our university course on literacy and biliteracy in American Indian classrooms. Her words speak volumes on the disenfranchising legacy of formal schooling for Indigenous people in the United States, and on the continuing impacts of that legacy. A graduate of English-only federal Indian boarding schools, this teacher had been convinced from her schooling that the linguistic and cultural resources she brought to the classroom were irrelevant, even a "handicap" to her English literacy. The teacher had been effectively blocked by her school experiences from entering what Smith (1988) called the language and literacy "club." And teachers who do not view themselves as full and unqualified "members of the club" have difficulty admitting children to it.

This teacher's experience is all too common. To understand this situation and its implications for language and literacy development among Indigenous students today, we must look critically at the history of schooling for American Indians and Alaska Natives in the United States. It is a history unlike that of any other ethnolinguistic group, because schooling for American Indians and Alaska Natives

---

[1]Following the Indian Nations at Risk Task Force Report (U.S. Department of Education, 1991) and protocol established by the *Journal of American Indian Education*, we use the terms *American Indian* and *Alaska Native* to refer to Indigenous groups in the United States. To clarify specific cases, we also use the term *Native Hawaiian* to refer to Indigenous groups in Hawaii. The term *Indigenous* includes all peoples who are descendants of the first inhabitants of what is now the United States.

was until very recently primarily a federal responsibility. The sources of that responsibility are educational provisions in treaties beginning in 1794, and federal legislation. The U.S. Constitution recognizes a special government-to-government relationship between tribes and the U.S. Congress, which includes broad federal authority and trust responsibilities on the part of the U.S. government (U.S. Department of Education, 1991, p. xi). In 1819 Congress approved the Civilization Fund Act, acknowledging and formalizing the federal responsibility for the schooling of American Indians. The title of that legislation is a disturbing but accurate portrayal of government officials' view of their role at the time; education was synonymous with forced assimilation or "civilization." The statement of one Commissioner of Indian Affairs sums up the historic thrust of federal Indian education policy: The goal in Indian education, he stated, was to remove "the stumbling blocks of hereditary customs and manners," and of these, *"language is one of the most important"* (quoted in Medicine, 1982, p. 399; emphasis added).

Such repressive policies lasted well into the 20th century. The primary means for their enforcement was the removal and placement of children in distant federal boarding schools, many located at military forts that had been the sites of intense Anglo–Indian conflict only a few years before. Stories abound of young children being kidnapped from their homes at an early age and brought by Indian agents in horse and wagon to the boarding schools (see, e.g., Sekaquaptewa, 1969). There, students' hair was cut and they were issued cast-off army clothing, subjected to harsh and humiliating militaristic discipline that included weekly parades before the school superintendent, and forbidden to speak their native language. Drills and manual labor accompanied a curriculum in English, arithmetic, and, for boys, preparation for the trades; girls studied homemaking. Often students did not see their parents for months or years. Children who fled these conditions, if caught, faced being shackled by school officials intent on preventing further escapes. Galena Sells Dick, who taught and directed the Navajo bilingual program at Rough Rock Community School in Arizona, described her boarding-school experience this way:

> [We] were punished and abused for speaking [our] native language …. If we were caught speaking Navajo, the dormitory matrons gave us chores like scrubbing and waxing the floors, or they slapped our hands with rulers. Some students had their mouths "washed" with yellow bar soap. Thankfully I never experienced this last punishment. (Dick & McCarty, 1996, p. 73)

Only in the last several decades have these policies and practices been replaced by ones intended to encourage Indigenous control over education and the meaningful incorporation of Indigenous languages and cultural knowledge into school curricula. Most of these changes began in the 1960s, in the context of the Civil Rights Movement and a rising tide of political and cultural activism (see, e.g., Lomawaima & McCarty, 2002; McCarty, 1997). Along with other Civil Rights reforms and the 1968 Bilingual Education Act, the Indian Education Act of 1972 and the 1975 Indian Educational Assistance and Self-Determination Act provided for curriculum development and teacher preparation in Indigenous languages, and enabled tribes and Indigenous communities to operate their own schools. Additional legislation allowed for the construction and improvement of public schools on Indian reservations. Later in this chapter we discuss the promising educational developments growing out of these reforms.

The policies and practices of the past left a profoundly negative imprint, however, as the teacher's comments at the beginning of this section suggest. Today, American Indian/Alaska Native students are significantly overrepresented in low-ability, skill-and-drill tracks and experience the highest school dropout rates in the nation—over 40% (U.S. Department of Education, 1991). The Indian Nations at Risk Task Force attributes these outcomes to linguistically and culturally irrelevant curricula, low educator expectations, loss of tribal elders' wisdom, and a "lack of opportunity for parents and communities to develop a real sense of participation" (U.S. Department of Education, 1991, pp. 7–8). Moreover, although complete linguistic assimilation never was achieved, the English-only practices carried out in boarding schools did exact a price. Convinced by a brutally punishing school experience that, as one bilingual teacher told us, "our language is second best," many parents vowed that their children would learn English, even at the expense of the heritage language and culture.

Contemporary language and literacy issues in American Indian/ Alaska Native communities must be understood in light of this sociohistorical context. To be sure, tremendous differences exist between tribal communities in terms of their histories and contacts with Euro-Americans. What all groups share is a unique status as the first North Americans and hence a special political relationship with the U.S. Congress. That relationship entails both legal and moral obligations on the part of the federal government. It also has entailed an unparalleled history of experience for Indigenous students in Anglo-American schools. One consequence of that experience was enormous sociocultural dislocation, including the loss of many Indigenous languages and internalized ambivalence by adults and children about the value of those languages. The teacher's comment quoted at the beginning of this section suggests the depth of these feelings. At the same time, many Indigenous languages have survived and remain a vital part of contemporary community life.

The present situation, then, is complexly colored with the struggles of the past and the resultant individual situations of tribes and Indigenous communities today. We do not and cannot speak for them all. What follows is a discussion of the parameters of diversity among Indigenous groups, some shared concerns relating to languages and literacies, and suggestions for the specific ways in which Indian and non-Indian educators can capitalize on the resources Indigenous students bring to school to develop multiple literacies, and an affirming sense of self and community.

LANGUAGE AND CULTURE DIVERSITY AMONG INDIGENOUS COMMUNITIES TODAY

Language Diversity

A bilingual teacher explains her reaction to the myth that all American Indians share a common language and culture: "People often say to me, 'You're American Indian,' and they expect all American Indians to understand the same language. I have to explain that there are nearly 200 American Indian languages, and that most are as different as Russian and Japanese. We've all experienced those kinds of situations."

No one knows precisely how many languages once were spoken by the people native to what is now the United States and Canada, although one prominent scholar estimates over 300 (Krauss, 1998). We do know that in the past and today, Indigenous peoples can be characterized as much by their linguistic and cultural diversity as by what they share in common. Most scholars agree that of the original 300+ Indigenous North American languages, between 150 and 210 are still spoken in the United States today (Goddard, 1996; Krauss, 1998; McCarty & Zepeda, 1995; Zepeda & Hill, 1992). Twenty-six of these languages are spoken in Arizona and New Mexico alone (Martin & McCarty, 1997). Within major language groups, people often speak distinct dialects, some so different they merit being treated as separate languages. Table 4.1 gives some idea of this remarkable linguistic variety.

But linguistic labels mask the immense differentiation that exists with regard to *proficiency* in Indigenous languages. For languages with large numbers of speakers—Navajo in the Southwest, for example—there are still speakers of all ages, with about half the school-age population identified as speakers of Navajo (Holm & Holm, 1995). But even among Navajos, who claim over 150,000 speakers, a marked shift toward English is under way, as past education policies coupled

TABLE 4. 1
American Indian and Alaska Native Languages in the United States

Category	Language Family	Locations and Examples of Speakers
Eskaleut	Eskimo-Aleut	Alaska (*Yupik, Aleut, Inupiaq*)
Na-Déné	Athabaskan	Western Sub-Arctic (*Athabaskan*); Northwest Plateau (*Carrier-Chilcotin*); Plains (*Kiowa-Apache*); Southwest (*Navajo, Western Apache*); California/North Pacific Coast (*Hupa, Tlingit*)
Algonquian	Algonquian-Ritwan	Great Lakes/Northeast (*Chippewa, Ojibwe, Abenaki, Menominee*); Southeast (*Powhatan*); Central States (*Shawnee, Omaha, Kickapoo*); Northern Plains (*Cheyenne, Arapaho, Blackfeet, Cree*)
Mosan	Chimakuan	Northwest Pacific Coast (*Quileute*)
	Salishan	Northwest Plateau and Coast (*Quinault, Coeur d'Alene, Shuswap, Columbia, Flathead*)
Aztec-Tanoan	Uto-Aztecan	Plains (*Comanche*); Southwest (*Hopi, O'odham, Southern Paiute, Yaqui/Yoeme*); Great Basin/Nevada/California (*Shoshone, Bannock, Paiute, Chemehuevi*)
	Tanoan	Arizona/New Mexico (*Tewa, Tiwa, Jemez*)
	Kiowan	Plains (*Kiowa*)
Penutian	California Penutian	Northern California (*Maidu, Wintu, Patwin, Miwok*)
	Chinook-Tsimshian	Northwest Pacific Coast/Washington/Oregon (*Chinook*)
	Klamath-Sahaptian	Northwest Plateau/Washington/California (*Nez Perce, Sahaptin, Yakima, Klamath, Modoc, Warm Springs*)
Hokan	Hokan	Northern California (*Karuk, Washo*)
	Yuman	Arizona/Southern California (*Cocopa, Havasupai, Hualapai, Kumeyaay, Ipai, Maricopa, Mohave, Tipai, Quechan*) Central California (*Chumash*)
	Salinian-Seri	Northern California (*Shasta*)
	Shastan	Central and Northern California
	Pomoan	(*Northern, Northeastern, Eastern, Central, Southeastern, Southern, and Kashaya Pomo*)

(continued on next page)

TABLE 4.1 (continued)

Category	Language Family	Locations and Examples of Speakers
Siouan-Yuchi	Siouan	Eastern Plains (*Mandan, Hidatsa, Winnebago, Ponca, Osage*); Western Plains (*Teton, Yankton, Assiniboine, Crow*); Central Plains (*Dakotan*)
	Yuchi (Euchee)	South Carolina/Gulf Coast/Oklahoma (*Euchee*)
Iroquoian	Iroquois	Great Lakes/Northeast (*Seneca, Oneida, Onandaga, Mohawk*); Southeast/Atlantic Coast/Oklahoma (*Cherokee*)
Caddoan	Caddoan	Eastern Plains (*Arikara, Pawnee, Wichita*)
Gulf	Muskogean	Southeast/Oklahoma (*Choctaw, Chicasaw, Creek, Seminole*)
	Natchez	Gulf Coast (*Natchez*)

Note. The classification of Indigenous North American languages differs throughout the literature. This is partly due to differing views of what constitutes a discrete language versus a dialect of the same language. This classification is a synthesis of several accounts, including Goddard (1996), Hinton (1998), and Mignon and Boxberger (1997). It does not include all American Indian/Alaska Native languages, but is intended to illustrate the range of variation. In addition, some locational information includes both Indigenous homelands and current locations of speakers resulting from the forced relocation of tribes (e.g., Cherokee, Kickapoo, and Euchee).

with exposure to English mass media, technology, and the larger society all take their toll. Among many other groups, only a handful of elderly speakers remain; in some cases, the heritage language has been lost entirely or is spoken by adults but no longer transmitted as a child language.

As the threat of language loss has grown, many tribes have implemented language policies asserting the primacy of the native language for all business conducted on tribal lands. Some tribes, such as the Tohono O'odham of southern Arizona, have developed education standards to assist schools in implementing tribal language policies. In California, where 50 Indigenous languages are spoken—none as a mother tongue by children—some younger tribal members work as language apprentices to elderly speakers in order to learn and revitalize the heritage language (Hinton, 1998). Among the Navajo and Hualapai of Arizona and the Crow of Montana—groups in which there are still child speakers—heritage language immersion and bilingual programs serve the dual purposes of maintaining the native language and facilitating children's acquisition of English (see, e.g., Crawford, 1995; McCarty, 1995, 2003). Yet in other communities, such as some Pueblos in Arizona and New Mexico, there is strong resistance to teaching the native language in school, as language is believed to be the province of the family and community rather than outside institutions.

Compounding these differences in the status of *spoken* languages is the great differentiation of *written* forms of Indigenous languages, and of native-language literacies. Some Indigenous languages have relatively long written histories. Yup'ik, Navajo, and Cherokee, for example, all have been written for well over a century. Other languages, such as Hualapai and O'odham, have developed practical writing systems in the past 30 years, largely as an outgrowth of bilingual education programs. For virtually all Indigenous groups, spoken language has historically taken precedence over written language as a critical marker of ethnic identity. "Although it is true," Tohono O'odham linguist Ofelia Zepeda writes, "that certain ideas were 'written' before contact with Europeans—as in petroglyphs, rock writing, calendar sticks, and so on—it is clear that the interpreters or the literate people of these writings were but a select few" (Zepeda, 1992, pp. x–xi).

Nonetheless, through their school boards and tribal councils, many communities today actively promote literacy in the heritage language. The great need is for authentic native-language texts. Development of a writing system is the first step in meeting this need. Most Indigenous languages now have practical orthographies—locally developed writing systems through which native-language literacy can be taught and learned. Orthographies for different languages vary widely, with some using adaptations of the Roman alphabet and others using their own symbols, including syllabaries.

But just as differences of opinion exist about whether the native language should be taught in school, there is no universal agreement with regard to writing the heritage language. Many tribal members believe that oral tradition is the truest form of the heritage language, and oppose attempts to write it down (see, e.g., Pecos & Blum-Martinez, 2001). The issue becomes even more complex when questions of standardization arise: Whose dialect should be written down? Whose variety should be accepted as the "standard"?

Such questions reflect honest differences of opinion that must be acknowledged and respected. Each speech community has its own language norms and values. And, although native-language literacy is valued by some and not by others, virtually all Indigenous communities desire literacy for children in English—but not at the cost of the heritage language.

In light of this situation, the framework for language and literacy development presented here advocates what Zepeda (1992, 1995) called the *literacy continuum* (see also Hornberger, 1989; McCarty & Dick, 2003). Within this continuum, Indigenous children are encouraged to connect orality with literacy as each child "reaches deep into a past, a past he or she shares with a community—a past thousands of years old" (Zepeda, 1995, p. 11). What the literacy continuum helps us understand is that all students come to the classroom with a storehouse of cultural and linguistic knowledge; in the case of American Indian and Alaska Native students, that knowledge typically includes storytelling traditions, the flow and structure of oral narratives, and the importance of oral traditions within the community (Zepeda, 1995). To the extent that classroom environments allow students to draw on this reservoir of oral tradition, children can apply that knowledge to acquire literacy in the native language, English, or both. Later in this chapter we provide specific suggestions for how this might be done.

In concluding our discussion of linguistic diversity, it is important to point out that different as they are among themselves, the structures of American Indian and Alaska Native languages in no way resemble those of English or other Indo-European languages. Anything that can be said in English can, of course, be said in any Indigenous language. Indigenous languages, however, are typologically distinct. Aside from their different phonemic structures, American Indian and Alaska Native languages, in general, handle verbs and nouns much differently than does English. For example, the distinctions between singular, past, perfect, or progressive tense verbs in English (verbs marked with -s, -ed, -en, and -ing endings) are not at all natural to a speaker of Crow, which has one ending for singular verbs with singular subjects and another for plural verbs (Kates & Matthews, 1980). A teacher of Crow students, therefore, could expect them to omit the -s ending on present tense/other person-singular verbs, in an intuitive effort to "regularize" the English forms (McCarty & Schaffer, 1992, p. 125).

Cultural Diversity

It is a given that language and culture are inextricably linked. Just as it is a myth to assume that all American Indians speak a common language, it is equally fallacious to assume the presence of a single, monolithic "Native American culture." Reflecting their distinctive social-ecological environments, individual tribal groups evolved rich and varied cultural traditions that historically ranged from matrilineal to patrilineal kinship systems; horticulture to fishing, hunting, and gathering; shamanism to priesthoods; and dispersed, pastoral lifestyles to concentrated village and town life. Anglo-European colonialism and the usurpation of Indigenous lands did much to destroy and distort these lifeways. Like some Indigenous languages, many cultural traditions were lost as well. Yet in most Indigenous communities today, there remains a strong cultural core that melds traditional ways of living and values with cultural forms introduced from outside the community. These new cultural forms, along with elements of traditional cultural systems, are in many places directly incorporated into children's socialization and have taken on new meaning as representative of ethnic identities.

The Hualapai of northern Arizona provide one example of the dynamics of cultural change and its meaning for children today. Hualapai is within the family of Yuman languages (see Table 4.1), spoken by peoples Indigenous to the region extending from the southern Pacific to the mountains and deserts of Arizona. *Hwal bay* or Hualapai means People of the Tall Pines, and refers to descendants of 12 of the 13 bands who traditionally occupied the arid plateau that stretches over a sixth of the state of Arizona (Watahomigie & McCarty, 1996). Until the late 1800s, the Hualapai lived by gathering wild plants, hunting game, and planting gardens of corn, beans, squash, and melon. Because extended families lived in close proximity, interaction between the generations was easy and natural, and children were enculturated by peers, parents, and grandparents. Storytelling, origin accounts, family and tribal history, and lessons about the land and the Hualapai way all were part of this enculturation, and the province of parents and elders.

This sociocultural foundation was ruptured in the late 1800s by genocidal U.S. military campaigns, the imprisonment of 12 Hualapai bands at a military fort on the Colorado River, and, after their subsequent escape, by their involvement in wage labor. Most of the Hualapai population of 1,700 now lives in the town of Peach Springs, on the million-acre Hualapai reservation south of the Grand Canyon (see Fig. 4.1). Straddling the Santa Fe Railroad and U.S. Highway 66, Peach Springs includes a K–12 public school—the only educational facility within 40 miles of the reservation—a post office, general store, two gas stations, and the tribal government and U.S. Public Health Service offices. Homes built under federal Housing and Urban Development (HUD) projects line both sides of the Santa Fe Railroad tracks.

Wage labor, cattle raising, and settlement in the town have replaced traditional forms of economic and social organization. HUD housing has had a nucleating effect on extended families; this and the mobility associated with wage work have undermined traditional forms of cultural interaction. Television, video, and radio all compete with traditional forms of communicative interaction, simultaneously opening compelling new use contexts for English.

Yet a core of the traditional Hualapai lifeway remains integral to contemporary community life. Within a close network of kin, extended families continue to trace relationships back many generations. Food-sharing and ceremonial gatherings unite the community, and traditional forms of oratory, arts, and crafts are still known and a great source of pride. Community-organized storytelling and dance activities provide new forms for old customs, and for transmitting tribal history and the Hualapai language (Watahomigie & McCarty, 1997).

Beginning in the mid-1970s, bilingual educators at Peach Springs School worked to capitalize on these cultural and linguistic resources, providing bilingual instruction and a curriculum emphasizing contemporary and traditional Hualapai life. At the same time, the bilingual/bicultural program made a concerted effort to reach out to community elders, involving them in the creation of curriculum and as linguistic and cultural experts in the classroom. Although Peach Springs School reflects the changing community environment, the bilingual/bicultural program seeks to provide children with a valued identity *as Hualapais*, and the academic skills necessary to grow and learn.

In many ways, the situation at Peach Springs is typical of rural reservation communities. Visitors to the larger Navajo or Pine Ridge Sioux reservations, for example, will observe physical features (housing, schools, and government facilities), similar to those at Peach Springs. Visitors also are likely to observe a similar blending of traditional and contemporary cultural forms. Yet beneath these surficial similarities, each community and tribal group is unique. Moreover, there are immense cultural differences between rural/reservation and urban Indian communities, and equally great differences between Indigenous communities in the "lower 48" and those in Alaska and Hawaii. Thus, the patterns and norms of each community must be understood in their own sociocultural context. Reading resources at the end of this chapter are intended to facilitate such an understanding.

Diversity in Communication and Interaction Patterns

Many writers have attempted to identify common cognitive or interactional styles among American Indian/Alaska Native learners. Indigenous students frequently are described as nonverbal learners, a characterization associated with holistic or nonanalytical thinking and an emphasis on affective versus cognitive variables in learning (Jimenez, 1983; Kaulbach, 1984; Marashio, 1982; McShane & Plas, 1984; Rhodes, 1988; Tharp, 1989). Often, such characterizations are applied to large, undifferentiated populations such as "Algonquians and Athabaskans," "urban Indians," "northern Indians," and even "traditional Indian cultures" (see, e.g., Diessner & Walker, 1989, p. 87; More, 1989, pp. 17–19; Ross, 1989; Walker, Dodd, & Bigelow, 1989, pp. 64–65; Wauters, Bruce, Black, & Hocker, 1989, pp. 54–55).

Generalizations such as these do little more than stereotype. One obvious danger in such stereotypes is that they can be used to justify remedial, nonacademic, and nonchallenging curricula for Indigenous students. In their extreme form, such generalizations raise far more alarming concerns. For example, Ross (1989, p. 72) asserts that "Traditional Native American mode of thinking is uniquely different from modern man." He then goes on to characterize "Native American thinking" as a right-brain process that is "holistic versus analytic" and "feminine versus masculine," and that involves "imagination versus reading," "dance versus writing," "inability to think in work versus neatness," and being a "poor speaker versus planning" (Ross, 1989, pp. 74–75).

Beyond their racist and sexist content, such claims are, of course, patently false. Yet even as we reject these claims, we recognize that children from diverse ethnolinguistic backgrounds do bring to the classroom unique learning dispositions developed in the context of their socialization within families and communities. These dispositions may stand in opposition to school-based interactional, organizational, and communicative structures—a situation that, as Swisher and Deyhle (1993, p. 90) note, "can have a significant effect on whether students learn or fail." Hence, understanding these differences *as they reflect distinct sociocultural environments* can suggest curricular and pedagogical innovations that enable educators to strategically use Indigenous students' knowledge and experiences in support of their literacy development (Au, 1993).

For example, working in Warm Springs, OR, the ethnographer Susan Philips investigated the structures for verbal participation and learning in the Indian community and in the classroom (Philips, 1983/1993). Although Philips observed an emphasis on silent observation and supervised participation in community-based learning activities, she likened interaction in the classroom to a "switchboard" in which the teacher called on individual students and forced them to perform on demand in front of the class. Teachers in Philips's study interpreted students' reluctance to respond under these conditions as evidence of their shyness or boredom. At the same time, however, Philips observed students willingly cooperating in small groups where they directed the activities themselves. The differences in readiness to participate in interaction, Philips concludes, "are attributable to the way in which interaction is organized and controlled." The practical implication of these findings "is that in Indian classrooms the participant structures preferred by the Indian students can be used successfully ... for the transmission of curriculum content" (Philips, 1983/1993, p. 133).

A case study from the Navajo community of Rough Rock, Arizona, further illustrates Philips's point and the need to evaluate cultural differences within individual social settings. At Rough Rock, a team of ethnographers and bilingual curriculum developers found that the same students identified as nonverbal and nonanalytic, when presented with familiar cultural–linguistic curricular content became highly verbal, ventured opinions and spoke up in class, and easily made inductive generalizations, a form of analytical thinking (McCarty, Wallace, Lynch, & Benally, 1991). These outcomes were attributed to a bilingual, inquiry-based curriculum that not only drew its overt content from the local community, but that in its pedagogical approach reinforced patterns of learning in natural situations outside the classroom. Specifically, those patterns assume a constructive, interactive learning process in which children use inductive processes to build increasingly sophisticated understandings of the world. Traditionally, young girls, for instance, mastered the art and economics of rug weaving not through lecture or didactic instruction, but by observing an experienced weaver and in the context of the life tasks of which weaving is part, making inferences and generalizations about the process (Begay, 1983). These teaching–learning interactions closely parallel the assumptions underlying classroom inquiry: Knowledge is built incrementally through the recursive expansion of children's prior understandings, in meaningful dialogue and socially significant interactions.

The Rough Rock data highlight the conditions under which inquiry, analytical thinking, and "speaking up" can be effective instructional components in American Indian classrooms (McCarty et al., 1991). "This work reminds us," Au (1993) notes, "that, while becoming informed about cultural differences, we should be careful to avoid stereotypes that suggest that certain groups of students cannot benefit from literacy learning activities that require their active, constructive involvement" (p. 119).

In combination with qualitative case studies by Philips for Warm Springs, Au (1980) for Native Hawaiians, and others (e.g., Heath, 1982), the Rough Rock data also point out that undifferentiated characterizations of learning styles can obscure the complex social-behavioral processes underlying students' out-of-school learning experiences, which influence their receptivity to particular pedagogical approaches. Hence, even as we recognize that Indigenous students share much in common in terms of the learning dispositions they bring to school, we also must recognize that these dispositions emerge in and are nurtured by the particular features of a given sociocultural environment. It is these particulars that determine the patterns of communication and interaction distinctive to each tribe and local community.

LINKING HOME, COMMUNITY, AND SCHOOL

How can educators respond to both the diversity and the unity in Indigenous students' experiences in ways that effectively link home, community, and school? The remainder of this chapter provides data from real schools and communities that address this question, and that simultaneously show how teachers can engage the literacy continuum.

Teachers can enhance their ability to build on Indigenous students' cultural, linguistic, and personal resources by first learning more about those resources. One obvious way to do this is to work in partnership with parents, grandparents, and community elders. This can involve home visits as well as parental visits to the classroom. An even more effective way to acquire this knowledge is for teachers, students, and parents to explore their community together, in a manner not unlike the way children naturally acquire knowledge of their language and community.

Lipka and Ilutsik (1995; see also Lipka, Mohatt, & the Ciulistet Group, 1998) provide a useful model for doing this. In their work in southwest Alaska, these educators noted the "widespread belief that Yup'ik only 'gets in the way' of English and Western knowledge" (p. 201). To reverse this situation, "Not only do we want the elders to share their knowledge with us, but we want to show the larger community—particularly the next generation—that the elders' knowledge 'counts,' that their language holds wisdom, and that their stories teach values, science and literacy" (p. 201).

To achieve these goals, Ilutsik—a Yup'ik bilingual teacher—and Lipka—an ethnographer and teacher educator—developed a school change group, the *Ciulistet* (literally, Teacher Leaders). The Ciulistet is composed of teachers, teacher aides, and elders who work collaboratively on the co-creation of curriculum. Over several years the group was remarkably successful in formalizing an Indigenous knowledge base in mathematics and science that also teaches Yup'ik language and culture. For example, the Ciulistet researched the math and science concepts embedded in everyday fish-camp experiences. "Fish camps were chosen," Lipka (1994) states, "because Yup'ik people still engage in catching and processing fish for the year, and their work groups are still organized in traditional ways" (p. 17). By videotaping fish-camp activities and analyzing the videotapes, the Ciulistet was able to articulate an Indigenous knowledge base that not only included mathematics and science, but that also revealed the complex social relationships intrinsic to Yup'ik subsistence. Yup'ik elders also have provided curricular content on hunting, trapping, weather forecasting, the geometry of parka making, and storyknifing, a traditional storytelling form in the snow or mud using a knife and specific symbols to represent various characters (Ilutsik, 1994; Lipka, 1994; Lipka et al., 1998; Lipka & McCarty, 1994).

In this collaborative learning–teaching process, "Two-way learning occurred, and both Western and Yup'ik systems were valued" (Lipka, 1994, p. 18). For Yup'ik students, knowledge from their own heritage provided concrete connections to abstract mathematical and scientific concepts. Students saw, for instance, "that mathematical systems have evolved from the concrete to the abstract, are based on familiar patterns and ways of ordering, and relate to concrete and cultural symbols" (Lipka, 1994, p. 25). Language and literacy development became natural and integral components of this learning.

Equally significant, Yup'ik community members have had a direct voice in their children's education—a process that, as Ilutsik (1994) describes, involved a painful yet necessary transformation:

> Many of our own people and many other educators were painfully aware that we were different, and that difference—based on culture and language—had been internalized in a negative sense. In that respect, we had to get over our feeling of inferiority, especially if we were truly going to be the "leaders" in education as the term Ciulistet implies. (p. 10)

This transformation occurred "by valuing Yup'ik language and knowledge and by providing an opportunity for elders and the school community to visualize the possible ways in which everyday tasks and knowledge can be a basis for learning in school" (Lipka, 1994, p. 26).

In facilitating changes such as those initiated through the Ciulistet, it is important to respect and validate the norms for interaction within the community. Discriminatory structures, as Cummins (1989) points out, "are manifested in the *interactions* that minority students and communities experience with *individual* educators" (p. 51). In this regard, educator Vivian Ayoungman (1995) cautions that "the *form* of educators' presentation may be as important as the message itself" (p. 184). Speaking of her work with Siksika (Blackfeet) community members, Ayoungman (1995) writes:

> Prior to one parent meeting I chaired as vice principal, a parent whispered, "I hope she doesn't use big words." Overhearing this, I conducted the session in Siksika. It turned out to be quite a productive meeting; use of the native language literally invited parental participation, and many who rarely spoke in public actively participated.

Ayoungman goes on to urge that parents and grandparents not be "used as 'tokens'":

> From our experience, elders appreciate having specific information on what is expected of them so they can contribute productively. One suggestion ... is that [teachers] identify the specific information they seek, and request this of elders invited to the school. Arrangements should also be made to assist elders' travel and ensure their comfort. Elders have said they sometimes feel out of place at school because there is no one to greet or direct them to where they are supposed to go. (pp. 184–185)

Educators, then, must be aware of and responsive to a wide range of local cultural features, including formally articulated knowledge such as that tapped by the Ciulistet in Alaska, as well as more subtle expectations and rules for communicative interaction, such as those Ayoungman highlights for the Blackfeet community. For teachers unfamiliar with the community, formal study can aid such understandings. Ethnographic accounts such as those on Warm Springs (Philips, 1983/1993), Rough Rock (McCarty, 2002; McCarty et al., 1991), and other works cited at the end of this chapter, are good places to begin. Yet even for teachers who are from the community, and especially for those who are not, it is necessary from time to time to become students themselves, and to explore the community together with parents, elders, and children.

The bilingual/bicultural program at Peach Springs provides an additional illustration of how this might be done. At Peach Springs, learning extends well beyond the classroom walls. Students and teachers work together on community videography projects, interviewing elders on local oral history, photographing the varied geological formations of the nearby Grand Canyon, and investigating other aspects of the natural and social environment. Students learn the art of basket weaving from elders, conduct field studies of the petroglyphs and pictographs of their ancestors, and undertake the comparative study of Hualapai ethnobotany and Western plant science. Throughout these projects, language development is integrated with challenging content area study, enabling students to learn through multiple literatures—including the oral literature of their community—multiple technologies, and, most important, their own prior knowledge and experience.

Studies such as these can be adapted and carried out in any community. Like the work of the Ciulistet, such community studies bridge the continuum of literacy, providing a seamless transition from oral tradition to the formal development of language, literacy, and biliteracy in school. Further, community studies offer a wealth of opportunities to bring parents and elders directly into the language and literacy learning process. All of this enriches the shared experiences of teachers, students, and community members, increases the pool of knowledge for future learning, and builds the general climate of support for education.

Certainly efforts such as these are not minimal; they require considerable time and commitment on the part of teachers and community members alike. But the stakes are high, and the benefits to Indigenous students amply reward the extra effort such collaborative work entails. We are reminded here of the words of one grandmother and long-time resident of Rough Rock: "If a child learns only the non-Indian way of life," she remarked, "you have lost your child." Working side by side with the community, educators have an obligation to help ensure that such a loss does not occur.

LEARNING THE SCHOOL LANGUAGE AND THE SCHOOL WAYS: THE LITERACY CONTINUUM IN PRACTICE

The pedagogies presented in this chapter presuppose a set of educator assumptions that both reflect and help construct an image of the child—and eventually, the adult—and her or his language and learning potential. Consider again the teacher's reference to a "writing handicap" quoted earlier. This statement exposes the teacher's negative image of her own literacy, demonstrating how potently self-fulfilling, even among professional educators, deficit-view assumptions can be. Transform those assumptions into ones that view bilingualism and multiculturalism as assets, and an entirely different image emerges.

In the case of this teacher, we encouraged her to write in her native language if she chose, without worrying about form, and from her own experience. Over the duration of the course, she filled a large notebook with her reflections on the teaching and learning of language and literacy in American Indian classrooms. She also began to write bilingual poetry. The teacher's final journal entry best reveals the power of her revisioned literacy: "I feel I really *am* a literary person," she wrote.

There are clear implications in this account for elementary and secondary educators, especially those working with American Indian and Alaska Native students. In classrooms, curriculum and pedagogy are the mirrors in which students see themselves reflected, and through which they construct images of themselves as thinkers, learners, and users of language. Educators have the ability to strategically manipulate those mirrors in ways that ensure that the image students see and develop is one of self-affirmation, efficacy, and trust (McCarty, 1993b).

To illustrate these possibilities, we present several classroom vignettes. The vignettes are extracted from our videotapes and ethnographic observations in schools in the Western United States (see, e.g., McCarty, 1993a, 1997; McCarty & Schaffer, 1992; Watahomigie, 1988). Although the classrooms vary in their social and demographic characteristics, they share these essential features: All are environments rich in oral and written language, and places where students have the opportunity to learn about themselves and the wider world through the heritage language and English. In short, these are classrooms that in many small and large ways effectively engage the literacy continuum, enabling students to draw on the language and culture resources of their communities to exploit their literacy learning potential.

We begin with a first-grade classroom on the Tohono O'odham reservation in southern Arizona:

> The room is abuzz with activity. All students in the class are O'odham, but there is great variety in their O'odham and English language proficiencies. Several children sit at a table listening to audiotapes of favorite stories in O'odham. Elsewhere in the room, students work in pairs to create stories in English from wordless picture books. Within each pair, one student is stronger in O'odham, while the other is more proficient in English. If a writer has a question about spelling, the partner can help; invented spellings are encouraged. In another part of the room, three students read from an English big book, helped by their tutor, a third grader. The teacher, a fluent speaker of O'odham and English, walks among the groups, stopping to ask or respond to a question, or to listen as students read their completed stories. The walls in and outside the classroom offer colorful displays, in O'odham and English, of students' artistic and written work. Later in the morning, the teacher gathers students together for a traditional O'odham round dance and song. The children participate joyfully in this, concluding the activity by greeting each visitor-observer in O'odham.

Several hundred miles to the northeast, in a high school language arts class in a town bordering the Navajo reservation:

> In this classroom of Navajo students, the non-Indian teacher and her students sit around a long seminar table, reading and discussing the poems they have written. Over the past two weeks, the class has read works of fiction, nonfiction, and poetry dealing with a theme they selected: love. At other tables around the room, a few students work with a partner on their poems, sharing drafts and clarifying meanings. The poems are written in English, but much of the discussion about them is in Navajo. The teacher, whose first language in English but who has studied Navajo, encourages students to use their native language. When students are satisfied with their final versions, they will publish them in a class anthology. Later, stu-

dents will select other themes to research and write about: fear, fantasy, success, and a study of the local community. The most exciting aspect of this work, the teacher confides, is the autonomy she and students feel in "determining what and how they're going to learn."

In a second-grade class in the interior of the Navajo reservation:

Students work in small clusters around the room. Most students speak Navajo as their first language. The classroom exudes purposeful activity. Several students work together on a mural, using butcher paper stretched across a row of desks. The teacher, a native of the local community, explains that students are illustrating "what happens in our community that reflects the government in any way." Their government unit grew out of students' questions about the recent presidential election; they are studying local, tribal and national government. On one wall is a chart with a brainstorming web showing students' questions and their existing knowledge of Navajo tribal government. Another display shows a brainstorming web of [then-President] Bill Clinton. As the mural group continues its work, several other students work at a research center, reading books on Arizona landmarks. Their findings will be incorporated into writing projects on Navajo tribal government. The teacher explains that students also have interviewed local officials to learn more about the history of government in their community. All classroom activities are intended to answer real questions posed by students themselves. As they engage in their various projects, students share their ideas, writings, and laughter in Navajo. The teacher monitors the progress of each group, asking and answering questions as they arise. Later, the class comes together to see and hear an illustrated story on local government created by the mural group. The morning concludes with a quiet time for journal writing in Navajo.

Finally, from an urban middle school language arts class in the San Francisco Bay area:

This is a multicultural learning environment. There are five American Indian students in the class, representing five tribal groups. All have grown up in the city. Only three speak the heritage language, but all say they return to their home reservations at least once a year. In addition to these students, the class is composed of Anglo, Latino, and African-American students, as well as several students who have recently immigrated from Vietnam. The African-American teacher leads the class in a discussion of Scott O'Dell's *Island of the Blue Dolphins*. Based on historical events involving the Chumash of the central California coast, the book's plot captivates students; they easily relate to the main character, Karana, who survives against all odds after being left on a deserted island. On this particular day, the class is joined by a respected local Indian educator, who provides cultural information on the Chumash and asks students to critically consider the impact of missionization on California Indians. He also shares stories about such customs as the naming rituals referenced in the book, using examples from his native Lakota Sioux oral tradition. Later, the students will work in small groups to research questions arising from this discussion and their reading. As the bell rings, the teacher tells us that over the next few weeks, he plans to introduce other multicultural literature to encourage cross-cultural inquiry.

How do these classrooms exemplify the literacy continuum? First, they capitalize on the power of *story* to connect literacy learning to children's lives. As children hear a favorite book on audiotape, listen to the factual and fictional stories of their peers, create poetry together, and participate in the unfolding of oral texts, they experience, in those moments, the joining of oral and written narrative forms. Through a rich variety of learning enterprises—mural making, story making from wordless books, song, literature discussion, and their own research and writing—students are encouraged to apply their prior knowledge of oral narratives to the creation of written texts. Orality and literacy, Indigenous and Western narrative forms, are united in ways that allow students to use what they know to develop new language abilities and to inquire about the world.

Second, in joining spoken and written narrative forms, these teachers draw narrative *content* from the culture of the community and the students. The teachers of Navajo students do this by grounding language and literacy learning in larger investigations based on student-generated themes. The O'odham teacher does this by blending Native stories, song, and dance in a multifaceted language experience. Although his classroom is organized more conventionally, the urban middle school teacher also maximizes the cultural resources available in his multicultural community. His choice of literature, the involvement of local cultural experts, and the self-selection students exercise in their follow-up projects all access the distinctive resources of students and their communities.

Within the literacy continuum, both the native language and English have value and a place. The classrooms profiled here show how domains for native language use can be established and activated. By their presence and their own bilingualism, the O'odham and Navajo teachers model the value of the native language. But language lessons in these classrooms go even deeper. In the Tohono O'odham classroom, the teacher pairs English- and O'odham-proficient students. Their varying backgrounds and abilities in O'odham and English, and their teacher's bilingualism, become the foundation for strengthening each child's language abilities and resources for new learning. In the classrooms with English monolingual teachers, the teachers nonetheless validate the heritage languages of their students. One teacher does this through formal study of the local language and by encouraging student interaction in Navajo. The urban middle school teacher takes advantage of the linguistic knowledge of local experts. Although these latter two classrooms do not provide a genuinely bilingual learning environment, both teachers bring the languages of their students into the life of the classroom in natural and academically challenging ways.

In all four classrooms, students become aware of the psychological power of words. "This power is different from that which is held by a select few," Zepeda (1992, p. x) writes; "This is the power ordinary people can have with words." And this is the essence of the literacy continuum: There is no single, uniform literacy; no one, straight-line path to literacy; nor is the literacy club open only to a privileged few. Instead, there are multiple literacies, many paths, and a variety of ways for children to acquire and use their literacy potentials. Noteworthy about the teachers and classrooms described here are the specific ways they make use of Indigenous students' unique backgrounds to expand their literacy learning potentials. In the process, the image each child sees reflected, and is helped to construct, is one of unqualified and lifelong membership in the language and literacy club.

READING AND WRITING IN THE HERITAGE LANGUAGE AND ENGLISH

In discussions of literacy in two languages, we may take for granted the presence of print in those languages. In the case of Indigenous languages, such a situation cannot be assumed; the lack of native-language print materials is a formidable obstacle to native-language literacy. Simply put, there are not enough good texts in Indigenous languages, and publishers see few market incentives to produce more (McCarty, 1993b, 2002).

The situation is far from hopeless, however, as tribes, schools, and Indigenous communities have produced a number of excellent native-language materials. In most cases, this has required literally beginning "from scratch." At Peach Springs, the Hualapai Bilingual/ Bicultural Program began its work by first creating a practical orthography for the language. In the words of the former bilingual program coordinator, staff members had to "become their own linguists" (Watahomigie & McCarty, 1994, p. 33). They then generated a list of community and student characteristics and ways of teaching, as a foundation for developing a child-centered curriculum (see Fig. 4.2). Over time, and through sustained staff and parent involvement in on-site workshops and university-based institutes, the Hualapai bilingual

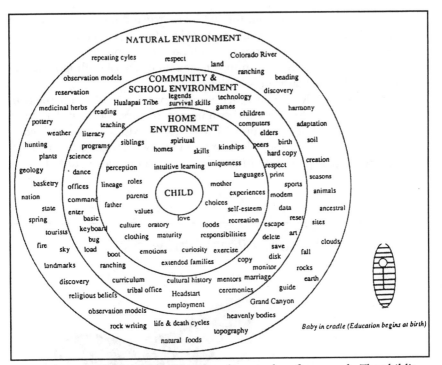

FIG. 4.2.   Hualapai bilingual/bicultural curriculum framework: The child's interactive learning environment. From Watahomigie (1988).

staff developed a host of curriculum materials—attractively illustrated children's literature, expository texts, a grammar, dictionary, and a series of teacher guides with cultural–environmental units—used in the Peach Springs School.

At Rough Rock, the bilingual/bicultural program has undertaken similar efforts, producing written and audio materials on Navajo history and life. Like the Hualapai materials, these are based on the stories and knowledge of the local community. Rough Rock bilingual teachers and teacher assistants also have become the authors of children's storybooks in Navajo. From their own life accounts and those passed down from elders, teachers have developed a small but growing collection of authentic Navajo literature. Desk-top publishing, the talents of local artists, and a small printing budget have turned those texts into high-quality, beautifully illustrated works (McCarty, 1993b).

Figure 4.3 provides an example of these teacher-developed texts. In Jessie Caboni's *Łį́į́tsooí ayázhi nináyiijááh* [*Yellowhorse bringing lambs home*] (Caboni et al., 1995), children learn of the gentle, smart horse whose owner saddled him with gunnysacks, filled the pockets with newborn lambs from the field, and trusted the horse to return safely home with his newborn charges. Materials such as these not only open new possibilities for biliteracy development, they also allow students and the community to see their school's bilingual teachers as published authors—in Navajo.

Both Rough Rock and Peach Springs provide models for the *process* by which educators and community members can initiate local Indigenous literacy programs. These schools also provide *pedagogical* models for literacy development in two languages. At Peach Springs, the approach to biliteracy development has included:

Łį́į́ltsooí Ayázhí Nináyiijááh

Jessie Caboni Hane' Áyiilaa
Gilberto Jumbo Na'azhch'ąą'
Afton Sells Naaltsoos Ałkéé' Niinínil

Doo dah na'ałgo'da jiniigo t'áá éí t'éiyá hwoł naaldloosh łeh. T'áá akwííjį dibé bikéé' chojooł'įígo nahayéii łeh. Łį́į́ bidą́ą́ dóó tł'oh ayóo yee yaa áhályą́ą́ nít'éé'. Łahda bilasáana yaanéí'áah łeh. Éí binahji' t'áá bí hooghaniji' nizhónígo nináhályeedgo yíhooł'aa'. Dibé taah nánił déé'da, nidáá' déé'da, bizh'dichi'go t'áá bí hooghaniji' nizhónígo anáhályeed silį́į́.

FIG. 4.3. Excerpts from a staff-developed Navajo storybook, *Łį́į́ltsooí ayázhi nináyiijááh* [*Yellowhorse bringing lambs home*]. From Caboni et al. (1995).

1. Assessment of children's language strengths using a test of oral English and a locally developed home language survey and Hualapai oral language assessment.

2. Use of a natural, communication-based approach throughout the curriculum.

3. Use of the native language and English for distinct learning purposes, with concepts developed in one language reinforced and expanded in the other language.

4. Process-oriented reading and writing in two languages, including literature study and thematic units, independent reading, storytelling and story sharing, computer publishing, writing workshops, journal writing, dictation, and chart writing (Watahomigie, 1988).

Similar features are evident in Rough Rock's pre-K–12 bilingual/bicultural program, which has emphasized cooperative classroom structures, process-oriented language and literacy development, and a criterion-referenced system for monitoring and assessing student progress (Dick, Estell, & McCarty, 1994; McCarty, 2002, pp. 148–159; McCarty & Dick, 2003). Rough Rock elementary teachers organize their classrooms around learning centers at which students engage in Navajo and English literature studies, listening activities, art, computer publishing, and research projects related to thematic units. A thematic unit in one third-grade class, for instance, focused on the four sacred mountains identified in Navajo oral tradition. Study of these landmarks facilitated natural connections between literature, oral history, geography, and geology.

The text in Fig. 4.4 exemplifies what children can do under these instructional conditions. In *Dził t'áá díílíígo siniligíí' baahashne'* [*The story of the four sacred mountains*], Laverne Teller, then a third grader, shares what she has learned from her exploration of these landmarks and their importance to her community. Full of rich description, her text demonstrates a sophisticated understanding of Navajo history, geography, directionality, and color symbolism.

At places such as Rough Rock and Peach Springs, teachers and students have created new contexts for Indigenous literacies. This, in turn, has catalyzed community consciousness about the heritage language and its significance as a pedagogical tool. As parents and grandparents have seen their children learning and growing through bilingual/bicultural/biliteracy programs such as these, community attitudes toward literacy forged in the boarding schools have begun to change. "I thought only the Anglos wrote books," one Rough Rock elder told us. Parents and grandparents now have tangible demonstrations of texts produced by local educators in their own language. By

FIG. 4.4.   Samples of a student-produced text, *Dził t'áá dį́įlíigo siniligii'
baahashne'* [*The story of the four sacred mountains*], by Laverne Teller,
Grade 3.

bringing the texts of their everyday lives directly into the process of
schooling, American Indian and Alaska Native parents, teachers, and
students validate the multiple literacies that constitute the complex
dynamics of their communities.

SUMMARY

Developments such as those reported here for Peach Springs, Rough
Rock, the Ciulistet, and the work under way in many other Indigenous
communities are the antithesis of what schooling historically has been
for American Indian and Alaska Native students. Clearly, reversing
past patterns requires far more than changing pedagogy alone, and

many of the necessary bureaucratic and institutional changes are outside the control of individual educators. Educators are, nevertheless, critical participants within the educational system who have the power to re-envision and reform that system.

In this chapter we have described some of the forces for positive change emanating from the work of Indigenous and non-Indigenous educators in diverse school–community settings. Much remains to be done in challenging deficit views, labels that limit, and historical relationships of domination and exclusion. Yet we are confident that current efforts in bilingual, bicultural, and biliteracy education for Indigenous students will open new doors for them and for future generations of American Indians and Alaska Natives. This statement by bilingual educator Galena Sells Dick, a graduate of the boarding schools, suggests that such a process is already well under way: "When we went to school, all we learned about was Western culture. We were never told the stories that Rough Rock children are now told, and write themselves. We're telling those stories now. In the process, we are reversing the type of schooling we experienced. We see both sides of it and we're helping children make connections to their own language and lives" (1998, p. 25).

■ ACTIVITIES

1. Invite a local American Indian/Alaska Native cultural-educational resource person to class to discuss Indigenous language education and literacy. What issues are unique to your region of the country or community? What issues are shared with other Indigenous communities in the United States? What are the characteristics and resources of Indigenous students where you live or teach? What recommendations does the resource person have for implementing pedagogies that are antiracist and linguistically and culturally responsive?
2. In pairs or small groups, research educational, language, and literacy issues of particular Indigenous communities. (See the bibliography and suggested readings at the end of this chapter for resources.) Ideally, this research should be done in consultation with one or more Indigenous educators and include a site visit to a local American Indian/Alaska Native education program, classroom, and/or school. Allow time for all groups to present and discuss their findings. What are the implications of this research for educators of American Indian/Alaska Native youth?
3. Initiate a literature study using the published narratives of Indigenous people, such as Helen Sekaquaptewa's (1969) *Me and Mine*, Francis

La Flesche's (1963) *The Middle Five*, Polingaysi Qoyawayma's (1964) *No Turning Back*, and Esther Burnett Horne's *Essie's Story* (Horne & McBeth, 1998). (See suggested readings at the end of this chapter.) What themes emerge from these texts? What do accounts such as these suggest for understanding and applying the concept of a literacy continuum? What do these accounts suggest in terms of language and literacy issues in contemporary Indigenous communities?

4. Make an inventory of children's and adolescents' literature by, for, and about American Indians and Alaska Natives. To the extent possible, consult publishers such as the Rough Rock Community School in Arizona (RRTP, Box PTT, Chinle, AZ 86503), the Hualapai Bilingual Program in Peach Springs, AZ (PO Box 360, Peach Springs, AZ 86434-0360), or other local, regional, or tribal outlets. Meet in small groups to critically review the literature surveyed. (*Note:* Slapin, Seale, & Gonzáles's [1989] book, *How to Tell the Difference: A Checklist for Evaluating Native American Children's Books*, Slapin & Seale's [1988] *Books Without Bias*, and McCarty's [1995] article "What's Wrong with *Ten Little Rabbits?*" will be helpful in undertaking such a review; see suggested readings.) What themes emerge from the literature you review? What inaccuracies, stereotypes, or other problems do you observe? Which texts are most appropriate and useful? How might educators use such texts to bridge the literacy continuum and to develop in the classroom a positive and proactive image of the child?

SUGGESTED READINGS

Bergstrom, A., Cleary, L. M., & Peacock, T. D. (2003). *The seventh generation: Native students speak about finding the good path*. Charleston, WV: ERIC Clearinghouse on Rural Education and Small Schools.

Cajete, G. (1994). *Look to the mountain: An ecology of indigenous education*. Durango, CO: Kivaki Press.

Goodman, Y., & Wilde, S. (Eds.). (1992). *Literacy events in a community of young writers*. New York: Teachers College Press.

Kawagley, A. O. (1995). *A Yupiaq worldview: A pathway to ecology and spirit*. Prospect Heights, IL: Waveland Press.

Klug, B. J., & Whitfield, P. T. (2003). *Widening the circle: Culturally relevant pedagogy for American Indian children*. New York: RoutledgeFalmer.

La Flesche, F. (1963). *The middle five: Indian schoolboys of the Omaha Tribe*. Lincoln: University of Nebraska Press.

Lipka, J., with Mohatt, G. V., & the Ciulistet Group. (1998). *Transforming the culture of schools: Yup'ik Eskimo examples*. Mahwah, NJ: Lawrence Erlbaum Associates.

Lomawaima, K. T. (1994). *They called it Prairie Light: The story of Chilocco Indian school*. Lincoln: University of Nebraska Press.

Lomawaima, K. T. (2004). Educating Native Americans. In J. A. Banks & C. A. M. Banks, *Handbook of research on multicultural education* (2nd ed., pp. 441–461. San Francisco: Jossey-Bass.

McCarty, T. L. (1995). What's wrong with *Ten Little Rabbits? New Advocate, 8*, 97–98.
McCarty, T. L. (2002). *A place to be Navajo—Rough Rock and the struggle for self-determination in Indigenous schooling.* Mahwah, NJ: Lawrence Erlbaum Associates.
McCarty, T. L., & Zepeda, O. (1995). Indigenous language education and literacy [Special issue]. *Bilingual Research Journal, 19.*
McLaughlin, D. (1992). *When literacy empowers: Navajo language in print.* Albuquerque: University of New Mexico Press.
Philips, S. (1983/1993). *The invisible culture: Communication in classroom and community on the Warm Springs Indian Reservation.* Prospect Heights, IL: Waveland Press.
Qoyawayma, P. (1964). *No turning back: A true account of a Hopi Indian girl's struggle to bridge the gap between the world of her people and the world of the white man.* Albuquerque: University of New Mexico Press.
Sekaquaptewa, H. (1969). *Me and mine: The life story of Helen Sekaquaptewa* (as told to Louise Udall). Tucson: University of Arizona Press.
Slapin, B., & Seale, D. (Eds.). (1988). *Books without bias: Through Indian eyes.* Berkeley, CA: Oyate.
Slapin, B., Seale, S., & Gonzáles, R. (1989). *How to tell the difference: A checklist for evaluating Native American children's books.* Berkeley, CA: Oyate.
Swisher, K. G., & Tippeconnic, J. W., III (Eds.). (1999). *Next steps: Research and practice to advance Indian education.* Charleston, WV: ERIC Clearinghouse on Rural Education and Small Schools.
U.S. Department of Education. (1991). *Indian nations at risk: An educational strategy for action. Final report of the Indian Nations at Risk Task Force.* Washington, DC: Author.
Wallis, V. (2002). *Raising ourselves: A Gwich'in coming of age story from the Yukon River.* Kenmore, WA: Epicenter Press Alaska Book Adventures.

REFERENCES

Au, K. H. (1980). Teaching reading to Hawaiian children: Finding a culturally appropriate solution. In H. Trueba, G. P. Guthrie, & K. Hu-pei Au (Eds.), *Culture and the bilingual classroom* (pp. 137–152). Rowley, MA: Newbury House.
Au, K. H. (1993). *Literacy instruction in multicultural settings.* Fort Worth, TX: Harcourt Brace.
Ayoungman, V. (1995). Native language renewal: Dispelling the myths, planning for the future. *Bilingual Research Journal, 19*, 183–187.
Begay, S. (1983). *Kinaaldá: A Navajo puberty ceremony* (rev. ed.). Rough Rock, AZ: Navajo Curriculum Center.
Caboni, J., with Jumbo, G., & Sells, A. (1995). *Łį́į́ltsooí ayázhi nináyiijááh* [Yellowhorse bringing lambs home]. Chinle, AZ: Rough Rock School.
Crawford, J. (1995). *Bilingual education: History, politics, theory and practice* (rev. ed.). Los Angeles, CA: Bilingual Educational Services, Inc.
Cummins, J. (1989). *Empowering minority students.* Sacramento: California Association for Bilingual Education.
Dick, G. S. (1998). I maintained a strong belief in my language and culture: A Navajo language autobiography. *International Journal of the Sociology of Language, 132*, 23–25.
Dick, G. S., Estell, D. W., & McCarty, T. L. (1994). Saad naakih bee'enootííłjí na'alkaa: Restructuring the teaching of language and literacy in a Navajo community school. *Journal of American Indian Education, 33*, 31–46.

Dick, G. S., & McCarty, T. L. (1996). Reclaiming Navajo: Language renewal in an American Indian community school. In N. H. Hornberger (Ed.), *Indigenous literacies in the Americas: Language planning from the bottom up* (pp. 69–94). Berlin and New York: Mouton de Gruyter.

Diessner, R., & Walker, J. L. (1989, August). A cognitive pattern of the Yakima Indian students. *Journal of American Indian Education* [Special issue], pp. 84–88.

Goddard, I. (1996). Introduction. In I. Goddard (Vol. Ed.) & W. C. Sturtevant (Gen. Ed.), *Handbook of North American Indians: Vol. 17. Languages* (pp. 1–16). Washington, DC: Smithsonian Institution.

Heath, S. B. (1982). Questioning at home and at school: A comparative study. In G. Spindler (Ed.), *Doing the ethnography of schooling* (pp. 103–131). New York: Holt, Rinehart and Winston.

Hinton, L. (1998). Language loss and revitalization in California: Overview. *International Journal of the Sociology of Language, 132,* 83–93.

Holm, A., & Holm, W. (1995). Navajo language education: Retrospect and prospects. *Bilingual Research Journal, 19,* 141–167.

Hornberger, N. H. (1989). Continua of biliteracy. *Review of Educational Research, 59,* 271–296.

Horne, E. B., & McBeth, S. (1998). *Essie's story: The life and legacy of a Shoshone teacher.* Lincoln: University of Nebraska Press.

Ilutsik, E. (1994). The founding of Ciulistet: One teacher's journey. *Journal of American Indian Education, 33,* 6–13.

Jimenez, R. (1983). Understanding the culture and learning styles of Hispanic students. *Momentum, 10,* 15–17.

Kates, E. C., & Matthews, H. (1980). *Crow language learning guide.* Crow Agency, MT: Bilingual Materials Development Center.

Kaulbach, B. (1984). Styles of learning among Native children: A review of the research. *Canadian Journal of Native Education, 11,* 27–37.

Krauss, M. (1998). The condition of Native North American languages: The need for realistic assessment and action. *International Journal of the Sociology of Language, 132,* 9–12.

La Flesche, F. (1963). *The middle five: Indian schoolboys of the Omaha Tribe.* Lincoln: University of Nebraska Press.

Lipka, J. (1994). Culturally negotiated schooling: Toward a Yup'ik mathematics. *Journal of American Indian Education, 33,* 14–30.

Lipka, J., & Ilutsik, E. (1995). Negotiated change: Yup'ik perspectives on indigenous schooling. *Bilingual Research Journal, 19,* 195–207.

Lipka, J., & McCarty, T. L. (1994). Changing the culture of schooling: Navajo and Yup'ik cases. *Anthropology & Education Quarterly, 25,* 266–284.

Lipka, J., with Mohatt, G. V., & the Ciulistet Group. (1998). *Transforming the culture of schools: Yup'ik Eskimo examples.* Mahwah, NJ: Lawrence Erlbaum Associates.

Lomawaima, K. T., & McCarty, T. L. (2002). When tribal sovereignty challenges democracy: American Indian education and the democratic ideal. *American Educational Research Journal, 39,* 279–305.

Marashio, P. (1982). "Enlighten my mind ..." Examining the learning process through Native Americans' ways. *Journal of American Indian Education, 21,* 2–9.

Martin, J., & McCarty, T. L. (1997). The Southwest culture area. In M. Mignon & D. L. Boxberger (Eds.), *Native North Americans: An ethnohistorical approach* (2nd ed., pp. 253–307). Dubuque, IA: Kendall/Hunt.

McCarty, T. L. (1993a). Creating conditions for positive change: Case studies in American Indian education. In L. Malave (Ed.), *NABE Annual Conference Journal* (pp. 89–97). Washington, DC: National Association for Bilingual Education.

McCarty, T. L. (1993b). Language, literacy, and the image of the child in American Indian classrooms. *Language Arts, 70,* 182–192.

McCarty, T. L. (1995). What's wrong with *Ten Little Rabbits? New Advocate, 8,* 97–98.

McCarty, T. L. (1997). American Indian, Alaska Native, and Native Hawaiian bilingual education. In J. Cummins (Vol. Ed.) & D. Corson (Series Ed.), *Encyclopedia of language and education, Vol. 5: Bilingual education* (pp. 45–56). Dordrecht, Netherlands: Kluwer.

McCarty, T. L. (2002). *A place to be Navajo—Rough Rock and the struggle for self-determination in Indigenous schooling.* Mahwah, NJ: Lawrence Erlbaum Associates.

McCarty, T. L. (2003). Revitalising Indigenous languages in homogenising times. *Comparative Education, 39,* 147–163.

McCarty, T. L., & Dick, G. S. (2003). Telling The People's stories: Literacy practices and processes in a Navajo community school. In A. I. Willis, G. E. Garcia, R. B. Barrera, & V. J. Harris (Eds.), *Multicultural issues in literacy research and practice* (pp. 101–122). Mahwah, NJ: Lawrence Erlbaum Associates.

McCarty, T. L., & Schaffer, R. (1992). Language and literacy development. In J. Reyhner (Ed.), *Teaching American Indian students* (pp. 115–131). Norman: University of Oklahoma Press.

McCarty, T. L., Wallace, S., Lynch, R. H., & Benally, A. (1991). Classroom inquiry and Navajo learning styles: A call for reassessment. *Anthropology & Education Quarterly, 22,* 42–59.

McCarty, T. L., & Zepeda, O. (1995). Introduction: Indigenous language education and literacy. *Bilingual Research Journal, 19,* 1–4.

McShane, D. A., & Plas, J. M. (1984). The cognitive functioning of American Indian children: Moving from the WISC to the WISC-R. *School Psychology Review, 13,* 61–73.

Medicine, B. (1982). Bilingual education and public policy: The cases of the American Indian. In R. V. Padilla (Ed.), *Ethnoperspectives in bilingual education research: Bilingual education and public policy in the United States* (pp. 395–407). Ypsilanti: Eastern Michigan University.

Mignon, M., & Boxberger, D. L. (Eds.). (1997). *Native North Americans: An ethnohistorical approach* (2nd ed.). Dubuque, IA: Kendall/Hunt.

More, A. J. (1989, August). Native Indian learning styles: A review for researchers and teachers. *Journal of American Indian Education* [Special issue], pp. 15–28.

National Center for Education Statistics. (2000). *Characteristics of American Indian and Alaska Native education.* Washington, DC: U.S. Department of Education, Office of Educational Research and Improvement.

Pecos, R., & Blum-Martinez, R. (2001). The key to cultural survival: Language planning and revitalization in the Pueblo de Cochiti. In L. Hinton & K. Hale (Eds.), *The green book of language revitalization in practice* (pp. 75–82). San Diego: Academic Press.

Philips, S. U. (1993). *The invisible culture: Communication in classroom and community on the Warm Springs Indian Reservation.* New York: Longman, and Prospect Heights, IL: Waveland Press. (Original work published 1983)

Qoyawayma, P. (1964). *No turning back: A true account of a Hopi Indian girl's struggle to bridge the gap between the world of her people and the world of the white man.* Albuquerque: University of New Mexico Press.

Rhodes, R. W. (1988). Native American learning styles: Implications for teaching and testing. In Arizona Department of Education (Ed.), *Proceedings of the Eighth Annual Native American Language Issues Institute* (pp. 11–21). Choctaw, OK: Native American Language Issues Institute.

Ross, A. C. (1989, August). Brain hemispheric functions and the Native American. *Journal of American Indian Education* [Special issue], pp. 72–76.

Sekaquaptewa, H. (1969). *Me and mine: The life story of Helen Sekaquaptewa* (as told to L. Udall). Tucson: University of Arizona Press.

Slapin, B., & Seale, D. (Eds.). (1988). *Books without bias: Through Indian eyes*. Berkeley, CA: Oyate.

Slapin, B., Seale, S., & Gonzáles, R. (1989). *How to tell the difference: A checklist for evaluating Native American children's books*. Berkeley, CA: Oyate.

Smith, F. (1988). *Joining the literacy club: Further essays into education*. Portsmouth, NH: Heinemann.

Swisher, K., & Deyhle, D. (1993). Adapting instruction to culture. In J. Reyhner (Ed.), *Teaching American Indian students* (pp. 81–95). Norman: University of Oklahoma Press.

Tharp, R. (1989). Culturally compatible education: A formula for designing effective classrooms. In H. T. Trueba, G. Spindler, & L. Spindler (Eds.), *What do anthropologists have to say about dropouts?* (pp. 51–66). New York: Falmer Press.

U.S. Department of Education. (1991). *Indian nations at risk: An educational strategy for action. Final report of the Indian Nations at Risk Task Force*. Washington, DC: Author.

Walker, B. J., Dodd, J., & Bigelow, R. (1989, August). Learning preferences of capable American Indians of two tribes. *Journal of American Indian Education* [Special issue], pp. 63–71.

Watahomigie, L. J. (1988). *Hualapai Bilingual Academic Excellence Program: Blending tradition and technology. Model replication training manual*. Peach Springs, AZ: Peach Springs School District No. 8.

Watahomigie, L. J., & McCarty, T. L. (1994). Bilingual/bicultural education at Peach Springs: A Hualapai way of schooling. *Peabody Journal of Education, 69*, 26–42.

Watahomigie, L. J., & McCarty, T. L. (1996). Literacy for what? Hualapai literacy and language maintenance. In N. H. Hornberger (Ed.), *Indigenous literacies in the Americas: Language planning from the bottom up* (pp. 95–113). Berlin and New York: Mouton de Gruyter.

Wauters, J. K., Bruce, J. M., Black, D. R., & Hocker, P. N. (1989, August). Learning styles: A study of Alaska Native and non-Native students. *Journal of American Indian Education* [Special issue], pp. 53–62.

Zepeda, O. (1992). Foreword. In Y. Goodman & S. Wilde (Eds.), *Literacy events in a community of young writers* (pp. ix–xi). New York: Teachers College Press.

Zepeda, O. (1995). The continuum of literacy in American Indian communities. *Bilingual Research Journal, 19*, 5–15.

Zepeda, O., & Hill, J. (1992). The condition of Native American languages in the United States. In R. H. Robins & E. M. Ehlenbeck (Eds.), *Endangered languages* (pp. 135–155). New York: Berg.

5

Language, Culture, and Literacy in Puerto Rican Communities

María E. Torres-Guzmán

Organizing quality literacy instruction requires knowing the sociocultural context of the learner (Freire, 1972; Freire & Macedo, 1987; Street, 1992). The scarcity of literature on the Puerto Rican learner and the complexity of their sociocultural circumstances make knowing about them and organizing quality literacy programs a bit problematic. This is true for Puerto Ricans or any other Spanish-speaking group because the labeling of all Spanish speakers as "Hispanic" in the last few decades and the lack of disaggregated data along the lines of ethnicity (Nieto, 1995a) tend to make more difficult the differentiated comparisons between Latino groups (Vélez-Ibañez & Greenberg, 1992) and analysis of in-group variability. With better statistical data, our ability to explain the differences and complexities of relations between education, occupation, income, and schooling performance and completion would infinitely improve. Yet even if better data were available, Hidalgo (1992) cautioned that, "the statistical profile of Puerto Ricans in the United States does not reveal the rich Puerto Rican cultural traditions, nor how those values undergo modification in the U.S." (p. 28).

The historical educational failure of Puerto Ricans in the United States is well documented (Fitzpatrick, 1987; Latino Commission on Educational Reform, 1992; New York Board of Education, 1958; Rodríguez, 1989; and others). Explanations for such failure run a gamut from the cultural deficit, cultural difference, and sociocultural perspectives to the within-school structural, involuntary immigrant, and resistance models (Jacob & Jordon, 1987). Some of these theories have more explanatory power than others. Some are adhered to because of their ability to portray what it means to be a Puerto Rican from an insider's perspective. The reality, however, is that schools still operate in very traditional ways based on negative, historically discriminatory stereotypes, and many school personnel are still ignorant of who their students are and where they come from. Furthermore, even when they are predisposed to learn, school personnel often want simple, unidimensional explanations and solutions.

Simple solutions are difficult to come by, particularly because language, culture, literacy, and identity are intertwined in complex ways. As Walsh (1991) stated, "There is no simple connection nor static relation for Puerto Ricans between language, culture, and existence. Instead, there is an elaborate multiplicity of meanings and representations that inscribe how Puerto Ricans come to know ... what it is to be Puerto Rican" (p. 131). Erickson (1990) elaborated this notion of complexity and dynamism when developing the concept of heteroglossia[1] within a community:

> What is it, after all, to be Puerto Rican today in Williamsburg? Is it to speak Spanish? Perhaps, but not necessarily all the time, and some persons may be Puerto Rican yet not speak Spanish. Is it to know how to slice mangos skillfully along their long axis, so as to pare away as much as possible of the delicate pulp from between the fruit's skin and its irregularly shaped woody core? ... Where in the heteroglossia of Williamsburg, Brooklyn in 1988 was there a fixed set of cultural traits by which one was defined as Puerto Rican? Nowhere was there a fixed set; that is not the way culture and social identity work in the modern world .... Ethnic culture and identity is much more rich and dynamic than a trait list, and so can education be that affirms culture and identity. (pp. 40–41)

In the United States, a multiethnic society with coexistent, variant conceptions of literacy, Puerto Rican individuals are engaged in the creation of cultural identities while becoming literate (Ferdman, 1991). The defining of self—as an individual, as part of a group, and in

---

[1]Heteroglossia, in this context, refers to the multiple meanings of culture and social identity that operate within a single community, be it an inherited traditional culture or ways of speaking, thinking, judging, and acting that have been invented or recombined intergenerally.

relation to the cultural image embedded in the literacy program—occurs in the context of the power relationships established with the U.S. society and from its colonial relationship with Puerto Rico.

Given the scarcity of information and the complexity of the relationship, I present a profile of literacy among Puerto Rican children. The profile is embedded in a perspective that views literacy as socially constructed and through which cultural values, standards, behaviors, and practices are communicated intergenerationally and renegotiated in social interactions among adults, between adults and children, and among children at play, at home, in school, and in church and other community settings (Pérez & Torres-Guzmán, 1996). Of particular importance is the group's core values in relation to language. The chapter ends by exploring programs in which literacy has been organized ideologically (Street, 1992) with the dynamism and the complexity of the conditions of Puerto Ricans in the United States in mind. The discussion of these examples serves to highlight the viability of some recommendations made in the educational policy literature on effective ways of educating Puerto Rican and Latino children.

THE SOCIOCULTURAL CONDITIONS
OF PUERTO RICANS IN THE UNITED STATES

There is great diversity among Puerto Ricans. They are a mixture of Indian, European, and African peoples; some are lighter and others darker. There are almost as many Puerto Rican living on the mainland as on the Island of Puerto Rico. Among those on the mainland, Santiestevan and Santiestevan (1984) proposed three distinct categories: recent arrivals, migrants moving back and forth according to work or family demands, and United States-born second, third, and fourth generation. Unlike other Latino groups, Puerto Ricans are U.S. citizens by birth, whether living on the Island or on the mainland. The ease of movement back and forth and the economic dependency of the Island on the mainland has created a constant circular migration, what C. E. Rodríguez (1989) called *el va y ven* [the coming and going]. Some of the movement is due to the availability of seasonal work, that is, migrant work. Others come and go in response to the close familial relationships they maintain. And others spend longer periods of time in the United States for one reason or another and, according to Cafferty and Rivera-Martinez (cited in Nieto, 1995a), at least one in three Puerto Ricans has lived in the United States at one point or another for periods of less than 10 years. The constant coming and going to and from the island has sociohistorical and political roots in its colonial relationship with the United States and has had an impact on the educational and economic conditions of the Puerto Ricans in the United States (Hidalgo, 1992; Nieto, 1995a). Hidalgo proposed that the educational conditions must be viewed in the context of migration, levels of acculturation, and the colonial heritage. Nieto proposed a context of three recurrent themes: the legacy of colonialism; the roles of racism, ethnocentrism, and linguicism; and the quest for self-determination.

A Statistical Profile

In 2000, there were 1,137,336 Puerto Rican school age children (less than 18 years old) on the mainland, 44% of them living in homes headed by married couples. In these homes, 88% of the adults were employed, the majority in non-professional job categories. The household income was less than $25,000 in 61% of the cases. Over one-third (37%) of the Puerto Rican children are living in poverty. The conditions under which Puerto Rican children live are likely to be better understood when they are contrasted with the conditions of the general U.S. population: The employment rate for the general population is 69%; a significantly larger portion of families are headed by couples (68%); a greater percentage of adults have finished high school (80.9%); and fewer children live in poverty (34.6%) (U.S. Bureau of the Census, 2000).

The majority (67.4%) of the Puerto Rican population, according to the 1990 Census data, is still concentrated in inner cities on the East Coast. In the last few decades, however, Puerto Ricans have tended to disperse outside these concentrated pockets, and the areas where Puerto Ricans once predominated are becoming increasingly heterogeneous (Latino Commission on Educational Reform, 1992). In New York City, for example, the change has been dramatic. In 1968 and in 1977, the percentage of Puerto Ricans in the Latino population was 89 and 81, respectively. The current estimate is that half of all Latinos living in New York are Puerto Rican (DeCamp, 1991).

In 1991, 45% of Puerto Rican adults in New York City had finished high school. There was an approximate 10 percentage point difference between high school completion among Puerto Ricans and other Hispanic groups. Although both lagged behind the White population, the gap was wider for the Puerto Rican. This was also true for college completion. Among Puerto Ricans, only 6.6% of adults were college graduates, whereas among other Latino groups the number was 13% (Rosenberg, 1992). Literacy is important in the adaptation of the newcomer to a world of greater complexity and higher technology

(García, 1994). Even when using what Street (1992) called autonomous measures of literacy, it has been difficult to assess the literacy rates among Latinos in the United States in Spanish. The English literacy rates (prose, document, and quantitative, as determined by the 1985 Young Adult Literacy Survey conducted by National Assessment of Educational Progress) among Puerto Rican adults lag behind other Hispanics as well as African Americans (National Assessment of Educational Progress, 1986).

Puerto Rican Culture

Culture is both inherited and negotiated daily; it is dynamic and difficult to capture in a list of traits. It is critical to know both that which is characteristic of the group and how individuals approach who they are and what it means to be Puerto Rican.

The traditional values, beliefs, and ways of being and evaluating that children receive from their parents are important to understand, because children are not empty vessels when they enter the classroom. They carry with them the experiences they have lived, the cultural heritage of their families, the core values of the ethnic group, and the resources in their community. Knowing about these cultural ways can influence communication in classrooms.

Some of these cultural ways can be found in behaviors. Nieto (1995b), for example, told of a teacher who for 2 years ignored a nonverbal wrinkling of the nose that many Puerto Ricans use to signify "what?" This occurred because the teacher had no notion that it meant anything until she went to a staff development workshop that mentioned it (p. 115). Byers and Byers (cited in Ogbu, 1991) used differences in the meaning of "eye contact" between teachers and Puerto Rican/Latino children to explain misinterpretation of each other's behavior. Puerto Ricans learn to look down to show respect when they are being reprimanded. White teachers, on the other hand, expect a child look at them directly when being chastised. What is polite for the Puerto Rican is misinterpreted as rude and an admission of guilt by the teacher. Teachers do not know about the cultures of their students and have vague notions of what this might mean with respect to teaching strategies and schools are reticent in accommodating to cultural diversity.

Some of the less tangible concepts recurrent in the literature on Puerto Rican culture that are often misinterpreted by outsiders, among others, are *educado* [educated] (Hidalgo, 1992; Nieto, 1995b; Salgado, 1985), *respeto* [respect] (Hidalgo, 1992; Nieto, 1995b; Torres-Guzmán,

1992; Torruellas, Benmayor, Goris, & Juarbe, 1991; Valdivieso & Nicolau, 1992; Walsh, 1991), *dignidad* [2] [dignity] (Torruellas et al., 1991), *capacidad* [3] [capability] (Nieto, 1995b), and *humilde* [4] [humble] (Nieto, 1995b). These words have deep meaning for many Puerto Rican students; they are values that have been constructed in the social reality of their families and of the community in which they live. Nieto (1995b) documented how wanting to be somebody does not necessarily mean getting good grades, but to be *educado* in the Latino sense of being respectful, polite, and obedient. [5] She alerted the reader to how this behavior can be misinterpreted to mean "quiet and reserved, a departure from what are considered to be important characteristics of intellectually curious children in other cultures" (p. 128). There is evidence of this type of misinterpretation in Salgado's (1985) story of a Puerto Rican girl whose teacher thought that her behavior was peculiar. The mother, meanwhile, perceived her daughter to behave as a "good child" (p. 47).

These examples of values and behaviors suggest that a different world view may give young learners a distinctive sense of what demonstrating competence means. They are concepts that provide a sense of ethnic group definition to the child and from which he or she looks at the outside world; they "are important not just for their functional value, but also as symbols" (Ferdman, 1991, p. 190). The transmitted way of making sense of the world is consistently present but constantly contested by the lived circumstances of the population wherever they may be, on the island, in the *va y ven*, or within the United States. Values that are transmitted intergenerationally and held as ethnic-group features can be adopted more or less strongly by an individual. A particular feature may pose internal contradictions for a Puerto Rican youngster who is in search of identity, particularly when it is a

---

[2]"'Dignidad' and 'respeto' ... [mean] ... allowing a measure of self-worth to all" (Torruellas et al., 1991, p. 194). Torruellas et al. gave the example of how when a parent is speaking about class identity, she says *Nosotros los pobres* [we, the poor]. She is not only showing she is not ashamed, she is trying to teach her children that there is *dignidad* [dignity] in the person and the collective lot in life and that this ought to be *respetado* [respected].

[3]"*Capacidad* ... [is] ... a combination of maturity, a sense of responsibility and capability" (Nieto, 1995b, p. 161). The concept is also used to encourage an individual with a sense of being potentially able, as used in the expression *eres capaz* [you are capable of]. Nieto gives the example of Marisol as taking on a larger share of the family responsibility as a demonstration of *capacidad*.

[4]*Humilde* means "humble, and soft-spoken but also very strong" (Nieto, 1995b, p. 161); it is humble in the positive sense, suggesting an unassuming character. Nieto presents Marisol as an individual with dogged determination to do well in life and stay in school, and as a soft-spoken, unassuming (that is, not aggressive) person who upholds strong family values and interacts with respect.

[5]See Walsh (1991) for an extensive discussion on the difference between "educated" and *educado*.

cultural characteristic that is not valued by the peers that matter to him or her. The cultural values can become the salvation for some and the source of difficulty for others.

Beyond the individual's feelings about the cultural features of an ethnic group, there are institutional responses to them. In speaking about Puerto Rican students, Frau-Ramos and Nieto (1991) pointed out that success or failure is not so much due to who the students are or what they bring with them as to "the way in which students' race and ethnicity are valued or devalued in society" (p. 7). "Because literacy education tends to be left primarily to the school, children become literate in the cultural image represented by their school" (p. 189). In other words, the cultural image may not be the ethnic cultural image, but one that comes from the dominant society. What happens in literacy education programs depends on the extent to which the school gives messages of acceptance and cultural heterogeneity and the extent to which the individual student uses his or her Puerto Rican background as a cultural referent to interpret the meaning of the processes and symbols involved in these programs.

Understanding the dynamism of culture and how it influences what happens in literacy education can lead to an understanding of the need to develop institutional interventions that take into account the existential issues of being Puerto Rican in the United States and challenging existing stereotypes and misunderstandings about Puerto Ricans. There is literature that begins to challenge the commonly held assumptions about Puerto Ricans. Diaz Soto's work (1988a, 1988b, 1990, 1993), for example, begins to challenge the stereotype that poverty and single-parenting leads to failure. She documented home environments of children who are successful in school and those who are not. The children come from a variety of home contexts—homeless, poor, and single-parent homes as well as two-parent, working-class homes. Her study suggests that the traditional variables quoted in the literature—poverty, single-parent status, and so forth—are not the most important variables to examine. Instead, she found that the child's degree of language proficiency, the parents' educational aspirations for their children, and the levels of parental controlling strategies were more significant factors. Rubio (1995), who documented parental involvement in a dual-language school in Philadelphia, also found that parental aspirations, language attitudes, and language proficiency were important factors to consider when looking at schooling among Puerto Rican children. Hidalgo (1994) documented more closely the adaptation strategies associated with school achievement used by Puerto Rican families in the United States. In an ethnographic study of families, she documented the supportive roles extended families play in single-parent homes. She featured a single mother of a successful child and suggests that where the traditional two-parent family does not exist, the extended family plays a substitute role for both the mother and the child.

Torruellas et al. (1991) suggested that parents communicate the importance of school literacy to their children within a framework of strong support and a highly collective family experience (also found by Auerbach, 1989; Hidalgo, 1994). They told the story of how Ester Huertas, a woman from El Barrio,[6] got involved with her children's schooling. In Ester's words:

> I would dictate the letters [to them] even though I didn't know if they were writing them down correctly .... I always sat down with them until they finished their homework. I'd talk to them about how important it was to study, knowing that I never had the chance. (p. 194)

Torruellas et al. (1991) also recounted how Ester jumped into bed with pencil and paper after washing dishes and how her sons sat around her while she worked and helped her out with their limited knowledge of Spanish. "When she [got] frustrated for not being able to express something correctly, they [told] her to write it anyway and to ask for help in class the next day. Her children [were] returning the support she [had] given them, and [wanted] her to continue in school" (p. 195).

Although there is evidence that Puerto Rican families do not participate in school events in traditional ways and that literacy events in the home do not look like those of their middle-class White counterparts, there is considerable evidence that they provide support in invisible[7] ways that are strong determinants for academic success. Torruellas et al. (1991) documented how the struggles of the mother to improve herself are examples for the children also to work for a better lot in life. Rubio (1994) documented the parents' efforts to fight the "drogos" [drug pushers] in the community as a way of supporting school efforts and giving young children a clear message about the importance of schooling. Torres-Guzmán (1995) documented how the informal interactions of the teacher and parents in the community are

---

[6]El Barrio is the name of a New York City Puerto Rican community located in East Harlem.

[7]Invisible in the sense that Philip (1983) used the adjective to describe what are unconscious practices and symbols held dear by a group as an identifier of membership. For example, learning by practicing and individualism are values held by the dominant society; some nonmainstream groups may coincide with the mainstream values, but others would prefer learning by observing and would consider learning as a collective task. Although some individuals may be able to verbalize their preferences (mainstream or not), many do not consider their preferences as subjects worthy of discussion; they just are what they are. For others, particularly those whose preferences clash with the given way of doing things, making visible and discussing personal preferences in public ways is vital to establishing equity.

ways in which the teacher seeks to guide and ward off parental involvement in the schooling of young adolescents. Nieto (1995b) documented how parents instill in children the desire to "be someone." In other words, if involvement is reframed to less ethnocentric ways, one may come to view homes as resources (Moll, 1995; Volk, 1994). A change in perspectives would suggest that schools ought not to look at the homes of children of poverty and culturally different groups solely as places "to be improved," but as social entities possessing intellectual, affective, and survival strategies that may be relevant to establishing more effective learning environments in school.

The Language Context and Identity

As stated previously, the language in which literacy practices are enacted and measured is important among Puerto Ricans. Spanish is the language of the Island, although there is a history of bilingualism[8] due to its colonial relationship to the United States. Instruction in English as a second language is made available on the island from elementary grades onward. Although many on the island are not against knowing more than one language, the politics of bilingualism is presently associated with the struggle around political status. The first legislative act of the pro-statehood government in 1993 was to repeal a "Spanish as an official language" law and to establish a new language law that recognized Spanish and English as "indistinguishable" within the context of official business in Puerto Rico. In the United States, the issues of bilingualism take on a different meaning; bilingualism is intrinsically connected to and at the "heart of Puerto Rican identity" (Hidalgo, 1992, p. 11). It means the ability to interact in the native language, Spanish, while acquiring a new way of interacting through English. As a result, some attention must be given to the issues of educational language policy and sociolinguistic patterns found in the community within the United States.

C. E. Rodríguez (1989) reported that within the United States although "an astonishing 91 percent still speak Spanish at home, ... an almost equal percentage speak English too." In other words, Spanish continues to be a language in use in many Puerto Rican households within the United States. The Language Policy Task Force (1984) and L. Torres (1989) documented a pattern of use of Spanish and English in the life cycle of Puerto Ricans in El Barrio. They proposed that the first generation speaks primarily Spanish, with English playing a sec-

---

[8]From 1898, when Puerto Rico came under U.S. colonial rule, until 1946, the language of instruction was English. Since 1946, English has been taught as a second language.

ondary role, if any (usually English plays a passive role). The second generation shifts to English upon entering elementary school and as its members begin to interact with English-speaking children. When this second generation reaches a young adult age and begins to assume more adult responsibilities, its members return to Spanish as the language of preference. Urciuoli (1990) proposed that people build their sense of language around relationships as much as they build relationships around language. The second generation returns to Spanish as its members build relationships around adult responsibilities (Language Policy Task Force, 1984). They associate with the adult Spanish-speaking network (L. Torres, 1989) and their child-rearing interactions tend to be in Spanish most of the time (Urciuoli, 1990; Zentella, 1978).

Urciuoli (1990) also proposed that relationships with the non-Spanish-speaking world are dictated by the linguistic ease with which they can be formed. He found that relationships are established with greater linguistic ease between Puerto Ricans and African Americans in contrast to the linguistic risk Puerto Ricans experience in their relationships with middle-class Whites. Despite the risk factor, Zentella (cited in Walsh, 1991) found that Puerto Ricans use 35% to 40% more English than other Spanish-speaking groups.

The phenomenon of code-switching, the mixing of the two languages, has been studied by a few. L. Torres (1989) found that the patterns of language switching among the first generation could best be described as primarily borrowing, the use of single words in English within the grammatical construction of the Spanish language. The second generation, however, used more complex strategies such as borrowing entire phrases. Its members produced expressions that are word-for-word translations not grammatically wrong in Spanish, but that would not be produced in a Spanish dialect. Poplack (1981) and Zentella (1978) suggested that this more complex code-switching does not arise from insufficient control of the language. Instead they viewed these patterns of speech more positively, because the ability to switch between two languages requires highly developed skills in both languages. They proposed that the type of code-switching correlates with the degree of proficiency in the two languages (i.e., children who are more proficient in the two languages tend to use code-switching in more complex ways). Alvarez (1988) found that code-switching contributed to the stability of bilingualism in the Puerto Rican community. In other words, bilingualism is a manifestation and expression of self-determination within the context of the United States.

Another pattern among Puerto Ricans is strong support for the development of proficiency in both languages. Fernández, Henn-Reinke, and Petrovich (1989), in a study of Hispanic education in five large cities, found that Puerto Rican students were the most likely to report that their parents encouraged them to use both languages. M. E. Torres (1989), Rubio (1995), and others have found that parents value their children's opportunities to be bilingual. Díaz Soto (1993) found that parents of higher achieving students believed that the maintenance of Spanish was extremely important and they also envisioned a gradual exposure and transition to English.

Bilingual competency appears to be important for the Puerto Rican student population as well. Fernández et al. (1989) found that 92.6% of the Puerto Rican students reported using Spanish. A large segment of this population (81.5%) reported that they spoke Spanish pretty well or very well. A higher percentage (93.4%) stated they spoke English pretty well or very well. A little more than half (55.3%) of the Puerto Rican students reported that they tended to speak mostly or solely in English with schoolmates, but when asked what language they used to speak with their best friend, the response category with the highest percentage (42.7%) was "both Spanish and English."

The use of Spanish does have particular significance at home and at school. The majority (74.6%) of the Puerto Rican ninth-grade students interviewed by Fernández et al. (1989) reported speaking Spanish at home exclusively or most of the time, and only 19.3% reported speaking both languages. Urciuoli (1990) also found that parents expected their children to speak to them in Spanish as a sign of respect. Marisol, a student interviewed by Nieto (1995b), spoke about the importance of speaking Spanish in relation to her identity as a Puerto Rican:

> I'm proud of it [being Puerto Rican]. I guess I speak Spanish whenever I can .... To me its important, you know, because I have to stand up for Puerto Ricans, to say like for the Whites probably it's more important for them too, just like the Blacks ....
>
> I used to have a lot of problems with one of my teachers 'cause she didn't want us to talk Spanish in class and I thought that was like an insult to us, you know? Just telling us not to talk Spanish, 'cause they were Puerto Ricans and, you know, we're free to talk whatever we want .... I could never stay quiet and talk only English, 'cause sometimes, you know, words slip in Spanish. You know, I think they should understand that. (p. 127)

Flores, Attinasi, and Pedraza (1981) and Zentella (1978) also found that children have clear language preferences, and that their choices are dynamic and convey different meanings in different contexts. Shultz (cited in Zentella, 1981) found that Puerto Rican children determined what language to speak based on their perceptions of the level of dominance of the addressee, the situation they were in, and the topic. Shultz also found that for successful participation in the classroom, children must not only have the right answer, they must also know when and how to offer it. In addition to these rules, in the bilingual classroom, the child must also learn when Spanish, English, or both languages are appropriate for all or parts of various classroom events. Zentella (1981) found that teachers' and students' attitudes and behaviors in relation to mixing the languages were different according to subject matter. If the subject of the class was one of the languages, English or Spanish, there was less tolerance of code-switching. In other subjects, where the correct answer is what is sought, response in either language was acceptable.

These findings lend validity to the claim that highly complex skills are required to live bilingual lives and that the "language–culture nexus" (Marsiglia & Halase, 1992) is the terrain where young Puerto Ricans forge their ethnic identities.

It is also "a visible site of contradiction for bilinguals" (Walsh, 1991, p. 132). Despite the persistent data pointing to a relationship between speaking Spanish and Puerto Rican identity, Flores et al. (1981) found that among El Barrio residents, speaking Spanish did not necessarily ensure high self-esteem, nor did speaking English ensure assimilation. Schmidt (1987), the daughter of a Puerto Rican immigrant mother and an American father, described how her family colluded with what she calls "forced non-bilingualism," because they did not want her to suffer the consequences of being bilingual. The results were feelings of low self-esteem and frustration as a result of the linguistic repression she faced. This did not deter her from identifying as part Puerto Rican, nor from being interested in learning other languages. Zentella (1990) studied the language attitudes of mainland Puerto Rican adolescents upon returning to the island; some of them had lost Spanish significantly and others spoke a New York Puerto Rican dialect. The majority (81%) of those she interviewed were comfortable with the notion of Puerto Rican identity without a language requirement—that is, they did not have to speak the Spanish spoken in Puerto Rico to be Puerto Rican. She found that these youngsters were faced with the contradiction of thinking of themselves as Puerto Rican while struggling with the hostility and ridicule inflicted on them by islanders who adhered to the view that the Puerto Rican language was threatened by the impoverished language they spoke. Despite their difficulties with some of the islanders' attitudes and behaviors, these mainland youngsters understood that they fared better than the islanders in gaining employment in the early 1980s because of their knowledge of English. With respect to learning English as a sign of assimilation, A. P. Rodríguez (1988) found that Puerto Rican students were attitudinally more open toward the acquisition of English when they viewed the second language as necessary for personal gain or the achievement of success rather than for total integration into mainstream society.

As Erickson (1990) and Ferdman (1991) pointed out, identity in not static and the relationship between language, culture, schooling, and literacy is complex. Because of the importance of the relationship between language and identity, the results of the Fernández et al. (1989) study on the level of literacy among ninth graders are significant. They found that on a 4-point scale of *very well* to *not at all*, only 55.8% of the Puerto Rican students reported reading Spanish *very well* or *pretty well*, and that an almost equal number felt they wrote it considerably well. More of them reported being able to write *pretty well* in English (88.3%), and an almost equal number also felt they wrote *pretty well*. In other words, more than half of the high school Puerto Rican youngsters self-report being able to access and produce texts in Spanish. Yet their literate behaviors in Spanish are limited. When asked what type of materials they read regularly in either of the languages, more than two-thirds mentioned that they read newspapers, magazines, comic books, and books in English three to four times a week. Less than one-fifth reported reading such materials in Spanish. More than one-fourth (26%) said they did not like to read in Spanish and 31.1% said they did not read very well. The relationship between spoken and written language suggests that the Puerto Rican students' adherence to the significance of speaking Spanish is about cultural identity, that is, that the maintenance of Spanish functions as a core value (Smolicz, 1981) in the group's cultural identity. As Ferdman (1991) pointed out, for "many Puerto Ricans in the United States, the Spanish language is not just a means of communication; it also represents their identification as Latinos and their difference from the majority culture. Even if Spanish reading and writing ability is absent, the desire to conserve some degree of Spanish speaking ability may reflect a desire to maintain distinctiveness from the surrounding society" (p. 190). This may in addition suggest why only a small portion of language minorities participate in programs that foster native language literacy. There is evidence that most school literacy programs are interventions of assimilation to English; "68 percent of fourth grade, 65 percent of eighth grade and 82 percent of 11th grade language minority students receive neither bilingual nor English-as-a second language" (Baratz, cited in Valdivieso & Nicolau, 1992). Furthermore, the responses of these high school students also suggest the scarcity of environmental print and publications within the United States in languages other than English.

THE CULTURE OF SCHOOLS AND CLASSROOMS

In this section, I focus on four examples of instruction that approach "literacy as a cognitive skill ... embedd[ed] as cultural practice"

(Hornberger, 1990, p. 2). They illustrate how literacy is "intrinsically linked to cultural and power structures in society" (Street, 1992, p. 5). As Roth (1984) proposed, "schools, acting as agents for the culture, control the extent to which personal knowledge may enter into the public knowledge of school curriculum," and in all four cases, students are able to define their participation, to create a cultural context in which the skills of decoding and encoding are practiced, and to renegotiate the culturally and socially significant information coded in the text. These programs also represent "stories, memories, narratives and readings of the world" (Giroux, 1987, p. 177) that belong to the students. The stories show how students become active in their learning, using their cultural experiences as resources for learning and then going beyond these to negotiate their identities within the context of the United States. These are stories of empowerment (Cummins, 1986) for Puerto Rican students; they represent the experiences many of us would like to see increase within school walls, because only when these examples become the norm will there be an increase in school completion and school achievement. In addition, I make connections with educational policy recommendations that come from studies documenting the resistance of Puerto Rican students to schooling, which is manifested in high dropout rates and the low performance on standardized achievement tests (De Acosta, 1993; Fernández & Vélez, 1989; Frau-Ramos & Nieto, 1991; Grannis & Torres-Guzmán, 1990; Hakuta, 1987; Latino Commission on Educational Reform, 1992; Valdivieso & Nicolau, 1992). These four programs illustrate how as educational settings and institutions begin to accommodate the cultural and linguistic needs of their students, we may begin to witness the *capacidad* of Puerto Rican children.

The Bronx Middle School Project[9]

Upon taking a course on reading and language arts, Marceline, a graduate student, invited her professor, Carmen Mercado, to apply some of the literacy theories in her culturally diverse sixth-grade classroom. The majority of the students were Latino and they came from low-income homes.

Inspired by Pearson and Dole's (1987) article on direct instruction and Brice-Heath's work with collaborative partnerships, they set out to challenge the low-level curriculum characteristic of inner-city schools. Both researcher and teacher believed in the *capacidad* of

---

[9]The narratives of the Bronx Middle School and Esperanza High are abbreviations of project descriptions found in Torres-Guzmán, Mercado, Quintero, and Rivera Viera (1994).

their students, and their objectives were to "put ethnography into the hands of those who would use it to improve their knowledge of what was happening to them in their learning and their skills in oral and written language" (Brice-Heath, 1985, p. 18) and to improve the school-related literacy skills of the students.

They took advantage of Marceline's flexible schedule (Valdivieso & Nicolau, 1992)—two double periods. This allowed them to do interdisciplinary curriculum planning (Frau-Ramos & Nieto, 1991; Latino Commission on Educational Reform, 1992; Valdivieso & Nicolau, 1992), integrating language arts and social studies by combining whole language methodology (Slavert, 1991) and the study of communities. The organization of the curriculum permitted a variety of activities with different types of groupings (Valdivieso & Nicolau, 1992): whole group, small groups, individual work, and presentations by guest speakers. They altered the roles and relationships in the classroom. The students were to assume greater responsibility for the learning and teaching process and they were expecte. to know when they need help from more capable others (Vygotsky, 1978), be it from peers, family, adults in the classroom, or other authorities. The adults became collaborators with each other and the students and saw their role as "helping students (1) remain focused, (2) explore and take advantage of the many opportunities that present themselves to create sources of data, and (3) reflect on what they [had] done and what they [were] learning from their research activities" (p. 108).

The students went beyond the adults' expectations; they renegotiated the cultural text. They chose topics of deep personal interest, such as drugs, teen pregnancy, AIDS, the homeless, and childhood illnesses, and focused their research questions directly on understanding what the topics meant in their lives. They legitimized their personal knowledge and interest by making it public. They learned how to write for different purposes, how to generate information in a variety of ways, how to organize and analyze the data collected, and how to prepare an oral presentation.

They engaged in "literate thinking" (Wells, 1986), where the emphasis is on practicing literacy. They produced a variety of texts: minutes of group meetings (which they called scribe notes), documents of research plans, transcriptions of interviews, proposals for conference presentations, abstracts, and speeches. They learned about the power of writing as a tool for learning and its relationship to reading, talking, and thinking. Not only did their portfolios show improvement in the quality of their work over time, their standardized reading scores, as measured by the Degrees of Reading Power (DRP) test, revealed dramatic gains. A 4-point gain is considered significant, whereas some students went up as much as 16 points.

There were other significant gains as well. Students' self-confidence, identity, and self-worth improved when they presented as conferences and realized that their audience valued what they had to say and saw them as authorities. The experience brought some of them closer to their families and relatives, and it helped them see other adults in the community as resources. Furthermore, the experience helped students show the care and compassion they felt for others (Valdivieso & Nicolau, 1992). One student gave up his lunch hour to help other students do their research; some began to voice their concern for the less fortunate in their neighborhood, and the class wrote to city authorities about the unfairness of some of their policies.

Most important, they saw that cooperation (Frau-Ramos & Nieto, 1991; Latino Commission on Educational Reform, 1992; Valdivieso & Nicolau, 1992) permitted them to engage in work that they felt was "hard" and beyond their individual *capacidad*; it was how they created the collective text. They attributed being able to do this to the fact that the adults also created spaces for them to "discover on their own," to experience "real life, and to see the world from the perspective of 'a teenager'" (Torres-Guzmán, Mercado, Quintero, & Rivera Viera, 1994, p. 109). Literacy was embedded in the cultural practice of becoming ethnographers and being Puerto Ricans who knew and loved their community.

The Esperanza High School Project

The Esperanza High School Project began more formally as a university–community collaborative that was to document the development of a bilingual/bicultural, empowerment-oriented alternative high school and to provide staff development for its teachers. The school was in one of the poorest Puerto Rican communities in Brooklyn and was housed in a community-based organization. Eventually, the documentation and staff development centered on how *empowerment* was manifested in a variety of domains—instruction, curriculum, and organization.

One of the examples of how empowerment was defined centered on enabling students as learners of English, a new language for many. The teacher had organized instruction by altering the relationship between the learner and the text. She had adapted a lesson taken from the regular 10th-grade English text by using culturally relevant instructional methods (Frau-Ramos & Nieto, 1991; Latino Commission on Educational Reform, 1992; Valdivieso & Nicolau, 1992).

With a change in the suggested order of instruction provided by the text, the kinds of social relationships and cultural knowledge involved in the literacy event changed (Sola & Bennett, 1985). Instead of reading the selection, followed by the identification of the vocabulary and follow-up activities, the teacher did the reverse. She began by introducing the vocabulary, relating the words to the students' lived experiences (that is, by acknowledging the personal experience in public ways), and then proceeded to read the text.

Understanding that they had some prior knowledge of the concepts discussed, she positioned the students in a lateral relation to the text. The unit was about civil rights and the vocabulary related to concepts such as racism, discrimination, segregation, emancipation, ghetto, and freedom. The teacher elicited an affective and cognitive response to the topic by using examples provided by the students. By validating the voices of students through the retelling of their experiences in the form of examples, the teacher was acknowledging they had something to say about the topic. Traditionally the text is viewed as the authority; here the student was also an authority. The interaction of the student with the text could be critically transformed. The reading of the text could be seen as the process of renegotiating truths established by the collective discussion between the teacher and the students and contrasted with, or complemented by, what was presented in the text.

Close examination of the classroom practices of this teacher demonstrated how she repeatedly used the students' language, lived experiences, and culture as pedagogical tools to legitimize new social relationships of power (Torres-Guzmán, 1992). Students became active participants (Valdivieso & Nicolau, 1992) in molding their own learning and in negotiating and contesting the meaning of the text. The content became accessible and the learning process became meaningful and purposeful. Furthermore, the learning environment created in this alternative school provided spaces for the students to explore their own relationships as individuals to the broader societal context—that is, it fostered students' quest for self-determination.

The Dual Language Middle School Project[10]

The Dual Language Middle School Project is a university–school collaborative that during its second year focused on teacher reflective thinking about classroom practices (Frau-Ramos & Nieto, 1991; Latino Commission on Educational Reform, 1992; Valdivieso & Nicolau, 1992) in the teachers' English and Spanish literature

---

[10]This narrative is based on my work with the Dual Language Middle School.

groups. The teachers were videotaped during 2 weeks in December and 2 weeks in February. They individually viewed the tapes and selected a problem they were grappling with and a 5-minute video clip that demonstrated it. The teacher group viewed the tape as a way to stimulate collective reflection. In the teacher group, members began to think about the relationship between cultural background knowledge, lived experiences, and the text; interaction with text in oral versus literate forms; the linguistic diversity of the students and the organization of interaction with text; the reading abilities of individual students; and more.

The following shows the difference between teachers thinking individually and in a group about expectations they have for their students. More important, it serves to illustrate that even when teachers believe in children, the structures that are set up for teachers to communicate and help each other are very important in ensuring that instruction reflects those beliefs (Latino Commission on Educational Reform, 1992; Valdivieso & Nicolau, 1992).

Upon viewing a tape of her teaching, one of the teachers decided that she would share with the other teachers a segment that showed a problem of practice in the Spanish literature class. She was teaching Quiroga's short story "Anaconda." The text, she felt, was difficult and challenging. The difficulty of teaching this type of text was exacerbated by the linguistic diversity and the variety of cultural experiences the students had had. The range of levels of comprehension was wide.

When the teacher group viewed the tape, the discussion centered around many themes: (a) the opportunities the teacher gave each of the students to respond to her questions, (b) the sequence of teaching this text versus other texts used during the year, (c) the balancing of more difficult and less familiar and more familiar and easier texts, and (d) the instructional techniques used by the teacher to bring in lived experiences, cultural knowledge, and common experiences as a way of teaching the main concepts and key vocabulary for comprehension. There were multiple interpretations about what happened in the incident in the tape and how that moment played itself out during the year.

The collective conclusions were critical. One of the conclusions centered around the use of culturally relevant teaching strategies and the other around collective expectations. After watching the segment of the videotape, some of the teachers felt they had learned about the power of cultural relevance. The teacher had used childhood experiences to connect the students with the reading; she had also created a rainstorm activity that contributed to the students making meaning of the story's central concept, *albergar* (meaning "shelter"). The teachers concluded that by using prior experiences, making cultural knowledge visible, and creating common experiences, the teacher had physically and emotionally brought all the students into the discussion of what *albergar* meant. The second conclusion centered on their expectation of the *capacidad* of their students. The teacher who was showing the videotape had individually concluded that the Quiroga text was too difficult. She had decided that in a linguistically and culturally heterogeneous setting, she would start with less difficult and more relevant texts. The group of teachers helped her see something different. The transformation in thinking occurred when the teachers assured her of the value of her work. They talked about how they could see the progress of those students during subsequent semesters. They felt that the students were not the only ones to benefit; the teachers did too. They were able to engage in and enjoy higher order thinking with these students during the subsequent literature class as a result. The struggle of teaching a "difficult" text early in the year had created better literature readers in both languages and created room from a variety of "cultural texts" in the long run because it went beyond what students knew. The teachers also felt that the initial readings would set the pace and the standards for the year. They were not unrealistic about this conclusion, because they also agreed on the need for a balance of texts of different degrees of difficulty and on the role of student interest. Expectations, they discovered, were established not just individually, but collectively; they also demonstrated that higher expectations are established when there is a long-range vision of curriculum. They realized that focusing on specific moments of teaching through the videotapes helped them in very concrete ways to understand the cultural practice of literacy in their school setting.

Abriendo Caminos

Abriendo Caminos is a GED (General Equivalency Diploma) program housed in a community-based organization in Philadelphia. Hornberger and Hardman (1991) documented how Puerto Rican cultural practices transform the instruction of a traditional curriculum so that students feel comfortable bringing into class their cultural ways, and they also showed how the explicit teaching of culture and history reinforced, expanded on, and helped students renegotiate their identity as Puerto Ricans within the U.S. context. Like Esperanza High, the students in this program had dropped out of school. Abriendo Caminos created an environment that affirmed their identity, conveyed a message of belonging, and supported their *capacidad* to struggle against all odds.

Hornberger and Hardman (1991) described a very traditional GED curriculum text in English and Spanish. The Spanish translation of the material was in a Spanish variety other than that known to them, and the errors of article usage were easily identified by the students. Despite the traditional curriculum, the literacy events were embedded in cultural practices around relationships. For example, when a student brought in her concern about poverty in Latin America, she received a solidarity response from her classmates and the instructor. The students also demonstrated their sense of belonging through participation in the election of a representative to the ASPIRA Club Federation Board. They applied the literacy skills they were learning in organizing the campaign for their candidate, which included a rap theme song in both Spanish and English. They acknowledged the community as a resource when they interviewed Puerto Rican professionals as a way of exploring career paths. And they redefined an individualized classroom task to conform to their preferred collaborative approach.

In addition, Hornberger and Hardman (1991) showed how the "program explicitly [taught] cultural awareness to its students" (p. 18) by helping the students explore their values and goals and introducing them to community cultural and social resources. Jose, a counselor for program students, felt "that one reason these students [did] well in the Abriendo Caminos program despite having dropped out of school ... [was that in the program it was] ... ok to be Puerto Rican, while at school it [was] as if everything they are [was] working against them from the first day they show[ed] up" (p. 20). Hornberger and Hardman found that the topics and issues of identity were as important for classes taught in English as for those taught in Spanish and concluded, as the Language Policy Task Force (1984) among others did, that "for this case, anyway, language is apparently separable from ethnic identity" (p. 21). In other words, it was its symbolic cultural value that was maintained by the group. They also found that tensions within the group were not around language; they centered on the differences associated with the experiences, values, and behaviors of the mainland as opposed to those from the island, that is, the tensions of the circular migration.

SUMMARY

School literacy is organized to establish relationships among people and cultural traditions; these traditions are not always inclusive of Puerto Ricans and the result for this population is low literacy rates, high dropout rates, and low achievement scores on standardized tests. But there are alternatives. These alternatives require that school personnel and policymakers believe in the *capacidad* of the Puerto Rican students and in establishing high expectations. They also require establishing bilingualism, biliteracy, cultural relevance, and multiculturalism as goals of instruction. Furthermore, they require creating alternative school structures and providing staff development to enable the teaching and support staff to implement the alternatives effectively. The foregoing examples bring to life some 'of the possibilities. Although the task is not an easy one, they do suggest some directions to take for ensuring the success of Puerto Rican children.

■ ACTIVITIES

1. Select five families to visit. Ask the parents what they mean when they say a child *es capaz* [is capable]. Analyze the differences in meaning. How similar or different are their meanings in comparison with what was presented in the chapter?

2. Select a few students who are language minority and, minimally, understand the two languages. Ask the students to describe to you at least three instances of things their parents say when they are angry. If the student doesn't provide a clear indication of the language spoken by the parents, ask the student directly. What language does your parent speak in when they are scolding you? And so forth. What you want to find out are ways parents use language to indicate respect and seriousness to children.

3. Develop a parent survey. Figure out how to best ask these questions for the parents in your community, birthplace, migration patterns, and immigration stories. For example: Where were they born? If born in the United States, how many generations have been in the United States in their family? What are some stories about their family's trip to the United States that they remember hearing as a child? If the parents were born elsewhere, how long have they been in the United States? What did they like most of their country of origin? What do they like most about the United States? Ask them to tell you one important story of their trip to, arrival in, or years in the United States? Remember that language and presentation are important.

4. Go to the Internet and visit http//:www.latinolink.com. Also search out other sites using key words from the chapter. *Hint:* Another name for Puerto Rican is Boricua. Or do a library search on Puerto Ricans. You may want to focus on migration patterns, political sta-

tus and colonialism, language use, children's literature, art, or another topic. Write a journal entry about what you found and how it differs from the sense you got from this chapter.

SUGGESTED READINGS

Díaz Soto, L. (1988). The home environment of higher and lower achieving Puerto Rican children. *Hispanic Journal of Behavioral Sciences, 10,* 161–167.

Hidalgo, N. M. (1992). *"i saw puerto rico once": A review of the literature on Puerto Rican families and school achievement in the United States.* Boston: Center on Families, Communities, Schools and Children's Learning.

Rodríguez, C. E. (1989). *Puerto Ricans: Born in the U.S.A.* Boston: Unwin Hyman.

Torres-Guzmán, M. E. (1992). Stories of hope in the midst of despair: Culturally responsive education for Latino students in an alternative high school in New York City. In M. Saravia Shore & S. Alvizu (Eds.), *Cross cultural literacy: Ethnographies of communication in multiethnic classrooms* (pp. 477–490). New York: Garland.

Zentella, A. C. (1990). Returned migration, language and identity: Puerto Rican bilinguals in dos worlds/two mundos. *International Journal of the Sociology of Language, 84,* 81–100.

REFERENCES

Alvarez, C. (1988). *The social significance of code-switching in narrative performance.* Unpublished doctoral dissertation, University of Pennsylvania, Philadelphia.

Auerbach, E. R. (1989). Toward a social-contextual approach to family literacy. *Harvard Educational Review, 59,* 165–181.

Brice-Heath, S. (1985). Literacy or literate skills? Consideration for ESL/EFL learners. In P. Larson, E. L. Judd, & S. Hesserschmidt (Eds.), *On TESOL 114: A brave new world for TESOL* (pp. 15–25). Washington, DC: TESOL.

Cummins, J. (1986). Empowering minority students: A framework for intervention. *Harvard Educational Review, 56,* 18–36.

De Acosta, M. (1993). *The Cleveland Hispanic community and education: A struggle for voice.* Cleveland, OH: Cleveland State University.

DeCamp, S. (1991). *The linguistic minorities in New York City.* New York: Community Services Society.

Díaz Soto, L. (1988a, March). *The home environment and Puerto Rican children's achievement: A researcher's diary.* Paper presented at the National Association for Bilingual Education Conference, Houston, TX.

Díaz Soto, L. (1988b). The home environment of higher and lower achieving Puerto Rican children. *Hispanic Journal of Behavioral Sciences. 10,* 161–167.

Díaz Soto, L. (1990). *Families as learning environments: Reflections on critical factors affecting differential achievement.* University Park, PA: Pennsylvania State University.

Díaz Soto, L. (1993). Native language for school success. *Bilingual Research Journal, 17,* 83–97.

Erickson, F. (1990). Culture, politics and educational practice. *Educational Foundations, 4*, 21–46.

Ferdman, B. M. (1991). Literacy and cultural identity. *Harvard Educational Review, 60*, 181–204.

Fernández, R., Henn-Reinke, K., & Petrovich, J. (1989). *Five cities high school dropout study: Characteristics of Hispanic high school students*. Washington DC: ASPIRA Association.

Fernández, R. R., & Vélez, W. (1989). *WHO STAYS? WHO LEAVES? Findings from the ASPIRA five cities high school dropout study*. Washington DC: ASPIRA Association.

Fitzpatrick, J. P. (1987). *Puerto Rican Americans: The meaning of migration to the mainland*. Englewood Cliffs, NJ: Prentice Hall.

Flores, J., Attinasi, J., & Pedraza, P. (1981). La carreta made a u-turn: Puerto Rican language and culture in the United States. *Daedalus, 110*, 193–217.

Frau-Ramos, M., & Nieto, S. (1991). *"I was an outsider": Dropping out among Puerto Rican youths in Holyoke, Massachusetts*. Boston: University of Massachusetts, Mauricio Gastón Institute for Latino Community Development and Public Policy.

Freire, P. (1972). *Pedagogy of the oppressed* (M. B. Ramos, Trans.). New York: Herder and Herder.

Freire, P., & Macedo, D. (1987). *Literacy: Reading the word and the world*. New York: Bergman & Harvey.

García, K. (1994). Culture, ethnicity, and language for Puerto Rican women. *Equity & Excellence in Education, 27*, 34–36.

Giroux, H. A. (1987). Critical literacy and student experience: Donald Graves' approach to literacy. *Language Arts, 64*, 175–181.

Grannis, J., & Torres-Guzmán, M. E. (1990). Hispanic students in the New York City Dropout Prevention Program. In J. C. Grannis (Ed.), *Evaluation of the New York City Dropout Prevention Initiative 1985–86 through 1987–88: Final longitudinal report, Volume one*. New York: Teachers College, Columbia University.

Hakuta, K. (1987). Degree of bilingualism and cognitive ability: Mainland Puerto Rican children. *Child Development, 58*, 72–88.

Hidalgo, N. M. (1992). *"i saw puerto rico once": A review of the literature on Puerto Rican families and school achievement in the United States*. Boston: Center on Families, Communities, Schools and Children's Learning.

Hidalgo, N. M. (1994). Profile of a Puerto Rican family's support for school achievement. *Equity and Choice, 10*, 14–22.

Hornberger, N. H. (1990). Creating successful learning contexts for biliteracy. *Penn Working Papers in Educational Linguistics, 6*, 1–21.

Hornberger, N. H., & Hardman, J. (1991). Literacy as cultural practice and cognitive skill: Biliteracy in a Cambodian adult ESL class and Puerto Rican GED program. In D. Spener (Ed.), *Biliteracy: Theory and practice* (pp. 147–169). Philadelphia: National Clearinghouse on Literacy Education.

Jacob, E., & Jordon, C. (1987). Theme issue: Explaining the school performance of minority students. *Anthropology & Education Quarterly, 18*, 259–367.

Language Policy Task Force. (1984). *Speech and ways of speaking in a bilingual Puerto Rican community*. New York: Center for Puerto Rican Studies, Hunter College.

Latino Commission on Educational Reform. (1992). *Toward a vision for the education of Latino students: Community voices, Student voices* (Vols. I & II). New York: New York City Board of Education.

Marsiglia, F. F., & Halase, O. (1992, April). *Ethnic identity and school achievement as perceived by a group of selected mainland Puerto Rican students*. Paper presented at the annual meeting of American Educational Research Association, San Francisco, CA.

Moll, L. (1995). Bilingual classroom studies and community analysis: Some recent trends. In C. Baker & O. Garcia (Eds.), *Policy and practice in bilingual education: Extending the foundations* (pp. 273–280). Philadelphia: Multilingual Matters.

National Assessment of Educational Progress. (1986). *Literacy: Profiles of America's young adults*. Princeton, NJ: Education Testing Service.

New York Board of Education. (1958). *Puerto Rican study: The education and adjustment of Puerto Ricans in New York City*. New York: New York City Board of Education.

Nieto, S. (1995a). A history of the education of Puerto Rican students in U.S. mainland schools: "Losers," "outsiders," or "leaders"? In J. A. Banks & C. A. McGee Banks (Eds.), *Handbook of research on multicultural education* (pp. 388–411). New York: Macmillan.

Nieto, S. (1995b). *Affirming diversity* (2nd ed.). White Plains, NY: Longman.

Ogbu, J. U. (1991). Cultural diversity and school experience. In C. E. Walsh (Ed.), *Literacy as praxis: Culture, language, and pedagogy* (pp. 25–50). Norwood, NJ: Ablex.

Pearson, P. D., & Dole, J. A. (1987). Explicit comprehension instruction: A review of research and a new conceptualization. *The Elementary School Journal, 88*, 151–185.

Pérez, B., & Torres-Guzmán, M. E. (1996). *Learning in two worlds* (2nd ed.). White Plains, NY: Longman.

Philip, S. U. (1983). *The invisible culture: Communication in classroom and community on the Warm Springs Indian Reservation*. White Plains, NY: Longman.

Poplack, S. (1981). Syntactic structure and social function of codeswitching. In R. P. Duran (Ed.), *Latino language and communicative behavior* (pp. 169–184). Norwood, NJ: Ablex.

Rodríguez, A. P. (1988, March). *Why do we want to learn English? Ask us!* Paper presented at the Annual Meeting of the National Association for Bilingual Education. Houston, TX.

Rodríguez, C. E. (1989). *Puerto Ricans: Born in the U.S.A.* Boston: Unwin Hyman.

Rosenberg, T. J. (1992). *Poverty in New York City, 1991: A research bulletin*. New York: Community Service Society of New York.

Roth, R. (1984). Schooling, literacy acquisition and cultural transmission. *Journal of Education, 166*, 291–308.

Rubio, O. (1994). *Una buena educación: A study of parental values, beliefs, and aspirations in a dual language school*. Unpublished doctoral dissertation, University of Pennsylvania.

Rubio, O. (1995). "Yo soy voluntaria." Volunteering in a dual-language school. *Urban Education, 29*, 396–409.

Salgado, R. (1985). The Puerto Rican family. In *Puerto Ricans in the mid '80s: An American challenge*. Alexandria, VA: National Puerto Rican Coalition.

Santiestevan, H., & Santiestevan, S. (Eds.). (1984). *The Hispanic almanac*. Washington, DC: Hispanic Policy Development Project.

Slavert, R. (1991). Integrating computerized speech and whole language in the early elementary school. In C. E. Walsh (Ed.), *Literacy as praxis: Culture, language, and pedagogy* (pp. 115–129). Norwood, NJ: Ablex.

Schmidt, J. A. (1987). Pitfalls of "forced non-bilingualism." *San Jose Studies, 13*, 15–23.

Smolicz, J. (1981). Core values and cultural identity. *Ethnic and Racial Studies, 4*, 75–90.

Sola, M., & Bennett, A. T. (1985). The struggle for voice: Narrative, literacy and consciousness in an East Harlem school. *Journal of Education, 167*, 88–110.

Street, B. (Ed.). (1992). *Cross-cultural approaches to literacy*. Cambridge, England: Cambridge University Press.

Torres, L. (1989). Code-mixing and borrowing in a New York Puerto Rican community: A cross-generational study. *World Englishes, 8*, 419–432.

Torres, M. E. (1989). Attitudes of bilingual education parents toward language learning and curriculum and instruction. *NABE Journal, 12*, 171–185.

Torres-Guzmán, M. E. (1992). Stories of hope in the midst of despair: Culturally responsive education for Latino students in an alternative high school in New York City. In M. Saravia Shore & S. Alvizu (Eds.), *Cross cultural literacy: Ethnographies of communication in multiethnic classrooms* (pp. 477–490). New York: Garland.

Torres-Guzmán, M. E. (1995). Recasting frames: Latino parent involvement (Reprint). In C. Baker & O. Garcia (Eds.), *Policy and practice in bilingual education: Extending the foundations* (pp. 259–272). Philadelphia: Multilingual Matters.

Torres-Guzmán, M. E., Mercado, C. I., Quintero, A. H., & Rivera Viera, D. (1994). Teaching and learning in Puerto Rican/Latino collaboratives: implications for teacher education. In E. R. Hollins, J. E. King, & W. G. Hayman (Eds.), *Teaching diverse populations: Formulating a knowledge base* (pp. 106–127). Albany: State University of New York Press.

Torruellas, R. M., Benmayor, R., Goris, A., & Juarbe, A. (1991). Affirming cultural citizenship in the Puerto Rican community: Critical literacy and the El Barrio Popular Education Program. In C. E. Walsh (Ed.), *Literacy as praxis: Culture, language, and pedagogy* (pp. 183–219). Norwood, NJ: Ablex.

Urciuoli, B. (1990). The political topography of Spanish and English. The view from a New York Puerto Rican neighborhood. *American Ethnologist, 18*, 295–310.

U.S. Bureau of the Census. (1994). Current population reports. *Population characteristics: The Hispanic population in the United States*. Washington, DC: U.S. Department of Commerce.

Valdivieso, R., & Nicolau, S. (1992). *Look me in the eye: A Hispanic cultural perspective on school reform*. Palo Alto, CA: American Institutes for Research in the Behavioral Sciences.

Vélez Ibañez, C. G., & Greenberg, J. B. (1992). Schooling processes among U.S. Mexicans, Puerto Ricans, and Cubans: A comparative, distributive, and case study approach. In T. Weaver (Ed.), *Hispanics in the United States* (pp. 270–280). Houston, TX: Arte Publico Press.

Volk, D. (1994). A case study of parent involvement in the homes of three Puerto Rican kindergartners. *Journal of Educational Issues of Language Minority Students, 14*, 89–113.

Vygotsky, L. S. (1978). *Mind in society: The development of higher psychological processes*. Cambridge, MA: Harvard University Press.

Walsh, C. E. (1991). *Pedagogy and the struggle for voice: Issues of language, power, and schooling for Puerto Ricans*. New York: Bergin & Garvey.

Wells, G. (1986). *The meaning makers*. Portsmouth, NH: Heinemann.

Zentella, A. C. (1978). *Code-switching and interactions among Puerto Rican children* (Sociolinguistic Working Paper No. 50). Austin, TX: Southwest Educational Development Laboratory.

Zentella, A. C. (1981). *Ta'bien, You could answer me en cualquier idioma*: Puerto Rican codeswitching in bilingual classrooms. In R. P. Duran (Ed.), *Latino language and communicative behavior* (pp. 109–131). Norwood, NJ: Ablex.

Zentella, A. C. (1990). Returned migration, language and identity: Puerto Rican bilinguals in dos worlds/two mundos. *International Journal of the Sociology of Language, 84*, 81–100.

6

Language and Literacy in Vietnamese American Communities

To thi Dien

In an address to the California Education Summit in San Francisco, in February 1994, Professor Kenji Ima stated that Southeast Asian students have the lowest reading scores, below African American and Latino groups. His finding is the result of a decade of comparative research on students' achievement in San Diego city schools. Ima expressed his surprise and dismay about the language-learning failure of Southeast Asian students: Why, in the midst of all claims about Asian academic miracles, did we miss that? His finding leads to an unavoidable inference: Southeast Asian students' needs have not been served, our educational system is guilty of neglect toward them, they are truly suffering educational harm.

The 1992 University of California at Los Angeles demographic report revealed that the Asian population as a whole had become more diverse and bipolar: many well-to-do and many poor; many succeeding, reinforcing the model minority image; many just shattering it, with scores standing at the bottom, the lowest among at-risk youth. The "model minority myth" (Aoki, 1993) and aggregated data on Asian academic achievement failed to recognize the wide spectrum of variations between students from different Asian ethnicities and have

137

masked the needs of the new immigrants from Southeast Asian shores. According to Yau and Jiménez (2003), "prevailing stereotypes of Asian American academic success may be responsible for the institutional neglect and lack of concern for the special needs of struggling Asian American students" (p. 196).

In an effort to redress the situation, this chapter attempts to increase the body of knowledge of pre- and in-service teachers, to enable them to better understand and more adequately respond to the needs of all their students, and to take a step toward the ideal of equity for all.

This chapter focuses on language and literacy learning within the Vietnamese American context. It proposes to examine three aspects of literacy. The first section delves into elements of the Vietnamese language and its main phonetic, grammar, and lexical differences with English. The second section examines native literacy in its cultural context, that is, how Vietnamese cultural upbringing and its norms, habits, and values influence Vietnamese students' learning style and literacy learning in speaking, reading, and writing. The final section attempts to capture the impact and consequences of learning the school language and the school ways as perceived by a selected group of Vietnamese parents and students.

These three sections are preceded by a review of the sociohistorical context of Vietnamese migration to the United States, and an overview of the different ethnic and language groups from Southeast Asia.

By increasing the awareness and understanding of teachers about the sociocultural context of literacy within Vietnamese communities, it is hoped that the literacy of the classroom will be made more congruent with the literacy of the Vietnamese home and cultural traditions. This will allow Vietnamese students to enrich their academic tasks at schools with the knowledge and experience they bring from their cultures and to succeed in school without the risk of cultural dislocation.

THE VIETNAMESE MIGRATION TO THE UNITED STATES: HISTORICAL, DEMOGRAPHIC, SOCIAL, ECONOMIC, EMOTIONAL, AND EDUCATIONAL DATA

History

Vietnam intersects with the United States at many dire times of their respective histories. From 1964 to 1975, there were the pain and shame of the Vietnam war, where the United States sacrificed 58,000 of its children and Vietnam lost countless millions of its military and civil populations. In the last days of April 1975, the nationalist government of South Vietnam collapsed into the hands of the North Vietnam communist regime. Within a few weeks, Vietnamese refugees erupted in the United States. The encounter was a shock for both sides. The average American had few opportunities to interact with the Vietnamese. Before the 1975 exodus, only a handful of Vietnamese, mostly exchange students, numbering 603 in 1964, according to R. Takaki (1989), could be found scattered in universities throughout the 50 states. Overnight, 135,000 Vietnamese poured onto American shores. The nation was unprepared. Military organizations such as the Marine Corps in Camp Pendleton and the Red Cross were called on to deal with the newcomers as with unexpected disasters. This was the first big wave.

The second big wave of Vietnamese refugees to come to the United States swelled in 1978, peaked in 1980, then gradually dwindled down from 1981 to 1983. Subsequently, some Vietnamese refugees arrived but they never reached the proportion of the first two waves. The Refugee Report of December 1988 mentioned 547,205 as the total number of Vietnamese refugees in the United States, a little over half a million souls in 13 years, important but hardy massive compared to the millions of Cuban arrivals from 1960 to 1974. Caplan, Whitmore, and Choy (1989) stated that "they appear as an insignificant segment of our population soon to be absorbed in the melting pot" (p. 4).

The impact of the Vietnamese influx reached alarming dimensions, however, from the point of view of California schools. Nearly two thirds of the Vietnamese refugees chose to settle in this state. To the early refugees who came directly to California, four more groups added to the California Vietnamese population: (a) U.S.-born children of Vietnamese parents, not included in the refugee count because they are American citizens, (b) internal secondary migration from the other 49 states, (c) newcomers from Southeast Asian refugee camps via refugee processing centers, through the United Nations High Commission for Refugees, and (d) later immigrants who came directly from Vietnam without a lengthy stay in Southeast Asian camps, such as the Amerasian, the political prisoners, and their families. The latter came through the Humanitary Operation, which is a component of the Orderly Departure Program, or ODP, under the auspices of the Department of State. As of January 1996, the ODP is still functioning.

Nearly two decades after the fall of the South Vietnam Nationalist regime to the Communist powers of the North, President Clinton lifted the economic embargo against Vietnam, in February 1994, and, on July 11, 1995, announced the normalization of diplomatic relationships between Vietnam and the United States of America. Incidentally, Pierre Huard, a French scholar, stated in his *Connaissance du Vietnam* (Huard & Durand, 1954) that the first diplomatic mission of the United States to Asia headed toward Vietnam, and not Japan or China. U.S. President Jackson sent Edmond Robert, twice, in 1832 and 1836, to the court of Vietnamese Emperor Minh Mang, who did not receive him.

Demographic Data

Demographic data show that the most salient trait of the Vietnamese refugee population is its youth. Data-BiCal is a publication of the California State Department of Education, Bilingual Education Office. A spring 1994 count of limited-English and fluent-English proficient Vietnamese students in California public schools ranked the Vietnamese second after the Hispanics for the number of limited-English students. California schools have been experiencing the most impact of new arrivals from Vietnam.

Social Aspect of the Vietnamese Migration to the United States

What Is a Refugee?   The 1957 Convention related to the Status of Refugees defined refugees as anyone who "owing to well-founded fear of being persecuted for reasons of race, religion, nationality, membership of a particular social group or political opinion, is outside of the country of his nationality and is unable, or owing to such fear, is unwilling to avail him-herself to the protection of that country." A refugee is different from an immigrant, as fear is different from hope and danger from opportunity. Immigrants usually have a choice. They chose their host country, had time to prepare for the move, and were often seeking economic betterment. Refugees, for the most part, have been unprepared for their trips, escaping political forces while running for their lives. A refugee is a person who essentially flees from a perceived danger, whereas an immigrant is attracted by another country's promises. Kunz, as cited by Ann Shapiro (1988), proposed several kinetic models for refugee flight, such as the "push-pressure-plunge" versus the "pull" for immigrants. Kunz emphasized that resistance to uprooting oneself and the absence of positive original motion to settle elsewhere characterize all refugee decisions and distinguish the refugee from the migrant. One can say that an immigrant is attracted by the situation in another country because the grass is greener there, whereas for the refugees, the grass is burning under their feet and they have no choice but to jump out. Mark Liff (1980) quoted Carl Sternberg, executive director of the International Rescue Committee, who said, "People do not run unless a situation is unbearable" (p. 16).

Economic Aspect

The absence of preparation places the refugees in an economically disadvantaged situation when compared with the immigrants. Refugees generally come with less capital than the immigrant, because they have not had the opportunity to plan their move. The Refugee Policy Group (1985) cited Barry Chiswick's study (1980), which analyzed the economic progress of immigrants and found that immigrants who migrate for political reasons take longer to close the gap in earnings between them and nonimmigrants of similar background than do those who migrate for economic reason. Political immigrants here can be equated with refugees. Refugees are in a way involuntary immigrants. Tran Minh Tung (Tung, Rahe, Looney, Ward, & Liu, 1979), a Vietnamese psychiatrist, stated: "Their expatriation was unexpected, their trip unplanned and their departure precipitous: hence the absence of any preparation, material or psychological, which could have somewhat cushioned the impact of the transplantation ... unlike the migrants who responded to the prospects of better life and tried to make it good on their own terms, in the land of their choice" (p. 5). Ngin (1990) echoed this by saying that "unlike a contemporary immigrant whose decision to migrate to a new country is usually well thought out, a refugee does not make plans to migrate" (p. 49).

When they do plan their clandestine journey, as in the case of the majority of the boat people, their concerns are more focused on the escape side than the resettling side. Many have invested their fortune in the preparation for their escape and arrived in the United States empty-handed. Caplan et al. (1989) noted that the poverty rates of Indochinese refugees who have been in the United States 4 months or less reached 80%. Census Bureau data indicated that the poverty rate for the total U.S. population at the same time was 15%. Seventy-five percent of all the refugees sampled in Caplan, Whitmore, and Choy's 1981–1986 research received some sort of public assistance. The researchers concluded that virtually all the Indochinese refugee population "began their American lives on welfare" (Caplan et al., 1989, p. 56).

In San Diego County, Ima cited a panel study that found that just over one-sixth of "first wave" (pre 1978) Indochinese refugees were welfare dependent, whereas fully two thirds of the "second-wave" (post-1978) Indochinese families were dependent on public assistance. An explanation for the second-wave dependency on public assistance might be that these people were more likely to come from rural settings, less likely to be literate, less likely to know English, and less likely to bring occupational skills transferable to the U.S. job market. The second wave arrived in the United States during more difficult economic times, all of which has exacerbated the difficulties of their social and psychological adjustment. Ima and Rumbaut (1988) stated that "their children attending San Diego schools are, by and large, children of poverty" (p. 25).

The Emotional Aspect of the Vietnamese Migration to the United States

Ima and Rumbaut (1989), investigators of the Southeast Asian Refugee Youth Study (SARYS), noted that "the trauma of the Indochina war and of their migration as refugees to the U.S. ... take a psychological toll on the parents of the Southeast Asian students" (p. 25). For the Vietnamese boat people, the trauma and the disruptive uprooting of the exodus are compounded by the memory of war and the harrowing experience of a clandestine sea voyage. Describing the education conditions in refugee camps in Hong Kong, Mark Liff, an educational writer for the *New York Daily News*, stated that he saw youngsters drawing pictures of boats repetitively. He reported the remark of one camp worker: "For many of them, the boat is an obsession—even a nightmare ... whenever we tried to get one student to draw something other than a boat, or to give up his drawing, he would break down and cry" (Liff, 1980, p. 16). It seemed that these children mentally cling to these drawings as a symbol of security amid the frightening uncertainty of their transient existence. Liff (1980) quoted another worker saying, "most children ... refuse to talk about their flight from Vietnam" (p. 16).

Van Luu, a Vietnamese refugee herself, stated that "the interval between deciding to leave their homes and arriving in a safe camp can be long and very harrowing." One of the main hindrances to safe passage has been piracy. U.S. officials interviewing the victims often write the initials "RPM" in their case histories. RPM stands for "rape, pillage, and murder" (Van Luu, 1989, p. 63). Another witness of the emotional ordeal of the Vietnamese refugees is Nguyen Thanh Liem, who, with Henkin (Nguyen & Henkin, 1981), stated that prior to their exodus, in Vietnam, the Vietnamese "witnessed destruction every day" (p. 47). Feelings of anxiety, fear, desperation, helplessness, skepticism, and pessimism are commonplace among people who are born and raised in wartime. Liem added that "many refugees spent an initial period in camps where feelings of uncertainty, anxiety and statelessness are intensified" (Nguyen & Henkin, 1981, p. 49). Because of their refugee situation, the longing for home is much alive, strong, and real. Tung et al. (1979) said that for many Vietnamese refugees, a form of nostalgia continuously impacts the tone of their lives and feelings.

Those from rural backgrounds with little prior education or transferrable occupational skills experienced more difficulties in their resettlement than the more educated, urban folks. Yet separations and losses are inevitable for all displaced people. The 1988 Indochinese Health and Adaptation Research Project (IHARP) study, reported by Ima and Rumbaut, found rates of clinically significant psychological distress among Indochinese adults that were more than four times greater than those among American adults. For a great number of refugees, the experience of mental distress is expressed under the guise of physical symptoms (Tung et al., 1979). The newcomers who find adjustment most difficult are those who are without their families (Ngin, 1990). For newcomers, going to school can be a traumatic experience where fear of the unknown is coupled with separation anxieties. A quiet and nonthreatening environment is essential to postwar children.

The Educational Level of Refugees From Vietnam

The Vietnamese refugees who arrived in 1975 were for the most part well-educated professionals. The subsequent waves had lover levels of education and lacked English-language fluency. Caplan et al. (1989) found that 80% of surveyed students reported that no household member knew any English on arrival in this country, and most had parents with little education. Caplan et al. used a scale from 0 to 10 to assess survival English proficiency: 0 means *none*, 3 means *read street signs*, 4 means *shop for food*. Eighty-five percent of the study sample fall in the 0 to 3 categories; the remaining 15% cluster around 4. Caplan et al. documented that 86% of the Vietnamese adults sampled did not go to college and 36% had only elementary education. The SARYS Vietnamese Parents sample were more educated than the Caplan et al. group, with an average of over 9 years of education. Their English-language proficiency at the time of the SARYS survey was not documented.

DIFFERENT ETHNIC AND LANGUAGE GROUPS FROM SOUTHEAST ASIA

The term *Southeast Asian* refers to more than five ethnic groups, clearly distinct from one another in their countries of origin (Fig. 6.1 shows the Southeast Asian region), histories, beliefs, values and tradi-

tions, and oral and written languages. They are the Cambodian or
Khmer, the Lao, the Vietnamese, the ethnic Chinese from Cambodia,
Laos, and Vietnam, and the numerous ethnic minority groups of the
highland of Laos such as the Hmong, the U-Mien, the Kammu, and the
Lahu (Lewis et al., 1992).

Because the focus of this chapter is on the Vietnamese language
and literacy, only a brief overview of the four other languages is presented here. Southeast Asians "speak different languages which are
not mutually intelligible" (Huynh, 1988, p. 5). The national language
of Cambodia is Cambodian or Khmer. It is a nontonal language, as opposed to Chinese, Lao, Hmong, and Vietnamese, which are tonal,
meaning that the pitch levels, called tones, change the meaning of
words. Cambodian or Khmer written language is based on Sanskrit,
an old language from India. It has 33 consonants and 36 vowels. It is
an alphabetical system, written from left to right and from top to bot-

FIG. 6.1.   Southeast Asia.

tom. Besides the common secular genres, the Cambodians have a special genre reserved exclusively for sacred texts.

The national language of Laos is Lao, but many hilltribe people speak their own dialects. Lao is a tonal language. Like Cambodian, it is based on Sanskrit but is different from Cambodian. It has an alphabetical system with 32 consonants, 28 vowels, and 4 tonal markers.

The Chinese from Vietnam, Laos, and Cambodia speak different tonal languages, such as Cantonese, Tiu Chiv, Hainan, and Mandarin. They, however, use only the Chinese written system as Chinese in other parts of the world. The Chinese written system is logographic; it is a concept-based system as opposed to the phonemic-based ones of the Cambodian/Khmer, Lao, Vietnamese, H'mong, and most of the Western languages such as French and English. The 18th-century German philosopher Leibnitz admired the symbolic nature of the Chinese written system and concluded that its logographs have the potential of becoming a universal language, similar to mathematical and scientific notations.

Figure 6.2 illustrates some of the written languages of Southeast Asia. All five languages of Southeast Asia are noninflective—that is, none change the form of a word for grammatical reason. The singular, plural, masculine, feminine, past, future, and present tenses are indicated by the context or separate words.

ELEMENTS OF THE VIETNAMESE LANGUAGE

According to Nguyen (1966, 1980), Vietnamese is not genetically linked to Chinese. Some claim that it belongs to a family called the Austro-Asiatic family, others to the Mon-Khmer language group. Nguyen quoted Henri Maspero, a French researcher, who stated that modern Vietnamese "seems to have resulted from a mixture of many elements" (p. 9). Vietnamese is tonal and monosyllabic. It has 11 vowels, 18 single consonants, 8 double consonants, and 5 diacritical or tone markers. The relatively large number of vowels comes from the fact that there are three variations of a (a, ă, â), three of o (o, ô, ơ), two of e (e, ê), and two of u (u, ư). The consonants are the same as in English except that d has two variations (d, đ) and that f, j, w, and z do not exist in the Vietnamese alphabet.

The five diacritical marks create six tones, going from low to high, with the middle tone being devoid of any mark. Diacritical marks are functional—that is, they change the meaning of words in a drastic way: Similar words do not have similar meanings, and cannot be grouped under similar categories. For example, the term *ma* has six meanings: ma (ghost), má (mom or cheek), mà (however, that, which), mã

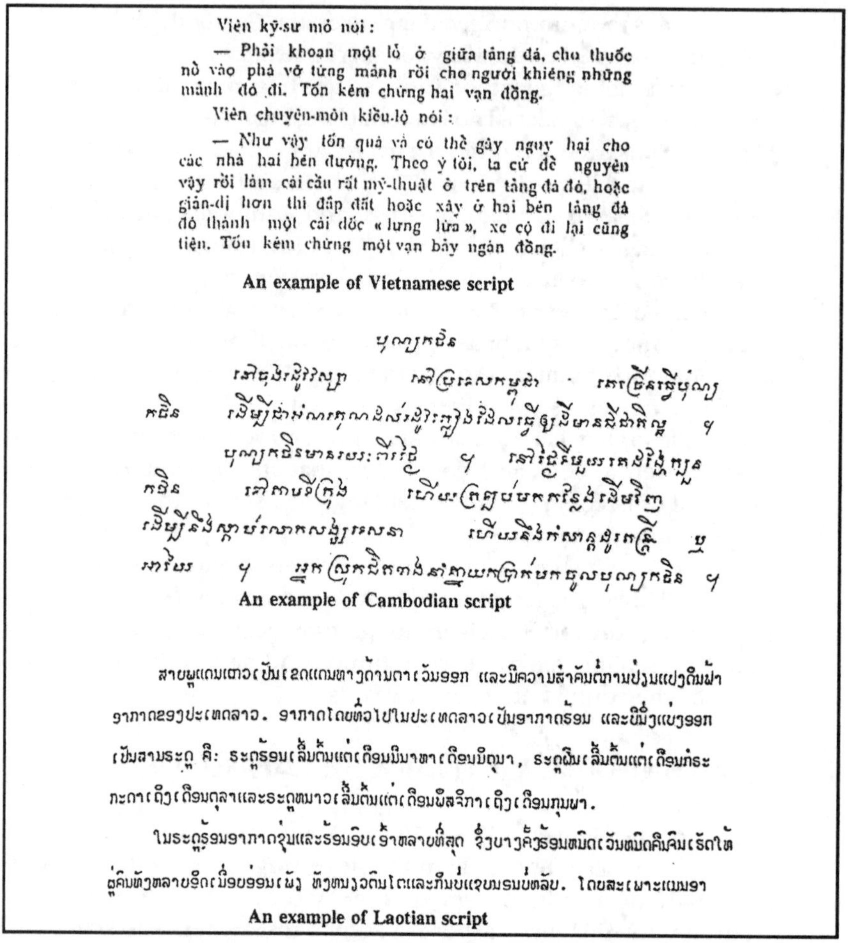

Viên kỹ-sư mỏ nói :

— Phải khoan một lỗ ở giữa tảng đá, cho thuốc
nổ vào phá vỡ từng mảnh rồi cho người khiêng những
mảnh đó đi. Tốn kém chừng hai vạn đồng.

Viên chuyên-môn kiều-lộ nói :

— Như vậy tốn quá và có thể gây nguy hại cho
các nhà hai bên đường. Theo ý tôi, ta cứ đề nguyên
vậy rồi làm cái cầu rất mỹ-thuật ở trên tảng đá đó, hoặc
giản-dị hơn thì đắp đất hoặc xây ở hai bên tảng đá
đó thành một cái dốc « lưng lừa », xe cộ đi lại cũng
tiện. Tốn kém chừng một vạn bảy ngàn đồng.

An example of Vietnamese script

An example of Cambodian script

An example of Laotian script

FIG. 6.2.   Selected written languages of Southeast Asia.

(horse), mạ (grave), ma (young rice sprouts). There is no logical connection between these words that are only one mark different from one
another. These marks combined with vowel variations make the exact
pronunciation of Vietnamese names almost an impossibility to the
nonliterate in Vietnamese. In contrast, for Vietnamese speakers, written Vietnamese is relatively easy to learn because it is entirely phonetic:
There are consistent sound-to-symbol correspondences.

Prior to the French domination, in the late part of the 19th century,
Vietnamese used the Chinese written system in government transactions and in education. Thus, literate Vietnamese, Chinese, Japanese,
or Koreans were able to "carry on a conversation with their writing
brushes" (Nguyen, 1980, p. 14) without having to pronounce the Chi-

nese written symbols in the same way. In the 17th century, Catholic missionaries, from Spain, Portugal, Italy, and France, worked out a Roman script to translate prayer books and catechisms. A Vietnamese–Portuguese–Latin dictionary was written around 1649 by a French Jesuit missionary named Alexander de Rhodes and published in Rome in 1651 (Nguyen, 1980). When South Vietnam became a French colony, in 1867, this Roman script was adopted by Vietnamese scholars and, subsequently in the early 1900s, became the national language of Vietnam. The Romanization makes Vietnamese a romance language, a legitimate but largely ignored sister of French, Spanish, Italian, and Portuguese, all using the Roman alphabet. This fact also gives the literate Vietnamese student a familiarity with the English alphabetic written system and a head start over the Cambodian, Lao, or Chinese students in some literacy tasks. However, word pronunciation, syllable and sentence stresses, grammatical construction, and essay composition present areas of difficulties, traps into which Vietnamese students often fall in their attempts to master the English language.

Pronunciation (Phonemic) Differences Between Vietnamese and English

The Vietnamese students will be quick in catching English vowel sounds, except for the difference between short and long vowels, which should be stressed. In contrast, they will find English consonants and especially consonant clusters real tongue twisters. The most noticeable strategy used by Vietnamese beginners is to simplify the English word by dropping one or two consonants or replacing them with a familiar one. For example, "milk" becomes "mik," "clusters" becomes "cludter," "the" becomes "de" or "ze." The plural form of nouns, ending with "s," gets neglected: "two tables" becomes "two table." Vietnamese speakers of English will also have the tendency to soften the plosive "p" in initial position, because "p" does not occupy this position in the Vietnamese language, except in combination with "h" as in "phở." "r," "t," and "d" require special attention because these consonants are pronounced differently in Vietnamese and in English. A contrastive analysis of Vietnamese and English sounds is illustrated in Table 6.1.

Stresses on syllables within a word and on words within a sentence constitute another area of difficulty for Vietnamese learners of English. Stresses modify the phonemic value of orthographically similar syllables. This is puzzling to readers of entirely phonetic languages such as Vietnamese where there is only one way to pronounce a com-

TABLE 6.1

Contrastive Analysis of Vietnamese and English Sounds

Vowel sounds

1. Vietnamese students have great difficulty in recognizing and producing the following four English vowel sounds, which do not exist in Vietnamese.

/ɪ/ bit	/æ/ bad
/ʋ/ book	/a/ cot

Because these sounds do not exist in their native language, the Vietnamese tend to pronounce bit as beat, look as luke, bad as bed, and cot as caught. The recognition and production of these sounds can be taught by contrasting them in minimal pairs.

/i/	and	/ɪ/	/ɛ/	and	/æ/
seat		sit	bed		bad
deep		dip	leg		lag
/u/	and	/ʋ/	/ə/	and	/a/
fool		full	sawed		sod
luke		look	caught		cot

2. Vietnamese have no /r/-controlled vowels; therefore, Vietnamese students may have trouble saying such words as arm, heard, and airport.

Consonant sounds

1. Five English consonant sounds do not exist in Vietnamese:

/c/ chair	/j/ judge	/ø/ thin	/ð/ those	/z/ zip

The teacher may wish to reinforce the recognition and production of the sounds by contrasting /c/ with /j/, /ø/ with /ð/, and /z/ with /s/. Students should learn these sounds in all three positions, initial, middle, and final. Focus on one sound at t time by following three steps:

    a. Model the sound (and illustrate the place and manner of articulation if necessary).
    b. Ask students to recognize or identify the sound.
    c. Ask students to produce the sound.

2. The following 15 consonant sounds do not occur in the final position in Vietnamese, causing difficulties for Vietnamese students when they occur in the final position.

/b/ rob	/f/ laugh	/š/ push
/d/ bed	/v/ love	/z/ rouge
/g/ bag	/ø/ bath	/l/ school
/č/ search	/ð/ breathe	/r/ sir
/j/ large	/s/ bus	/z/ freeze

Consonant sounds (*con't.*)

3. Final consonants are not released in Vietnamese. Thus, Vietnamese students tend to drop English final consonant sounds. Some possible problems are:
   a. The plural endings and third-person singular endings.
   b. The -ed of past-tense verb endings.
   c. Difficulty understanding when English is spoken with juncture.
   d. Substitution of final consonant sounds:

/b/ and /p/	/d/ and /t/	/f/ and /v/
cub cup	mad mat	leaf leave
/s/ and /z/	/ð/ and /ø/	/č/ and /j/
loose lose	wreathe wreath	search surge
/s/ and /š/	/k/ and /g/	
class and clash	back bag	

4. The Vietnamese language has no consonant clusters. Such words as problem, street, and desks may be difficult.

---

bination of letters. Consider the phonetic values of *a* in hum*a*n and in hum*a*nity. They are not the same. Vietnamese students need to learn word stresses and stresses in sentences in order to be able to read and speak intelligibly.

In the domain of phonemic differences, it is also relevant to mention the difficulty Vietnamese students will have with polysyllabic words. English words appear immeasurably long to us. We shorten them whenever we can. California is just "Cali," and Sacramento, "Sacto," to us. New York, Texas, Florida, and Hawaii are left alone, as well as Oregon and San Diego. The rule of thumb seems to indicate that the Vietnamese tolerate up to three syllables per word. Beyond that, they pull out their scalpel of word surgeon and invariably shorten them.

Grammatical Structures–Syntactic Differences

It is impossible to list all the syntactic differences between Vietnamese and English within the format of this chapter. Only a few are highlighted here. The English plural and singular nouns are both a pronunciation and a grammatical difficulty for Vietnamese. English verb tenses are another hardship. However, the English-language structure that appears most complex to Vietnamese learners is the word order in negative and interrogative sentences. Questions and negations are relatively simple to build in Vietnamese. We change an affirmative sentence into an interrogative one by adding "*no?*" to its end, and into a negative sentence by placing "*no*" before the action verb. For example, from *"Anh đi học"* (you go to school), we get *"Anh đi học không?"* (you go to school, no?) and a simple negative one: *"Anh không đi học"* (you no go to school). All of these Vietnamese sentences begin with the subject. In English, the introduction of the auxiliary represents a major difficulty, not only with *"Do you go to school?"* but also with *"You do not go to school, do you?"* These structures need special reinforcement to be comfortably used to Vietnamese learners.

Vietnamese uses adjectives without auxiliary. *The sky is blue* becomes *the sky blue*. Because adjectives follow nouns in Vietnamese syntax, beginning learners who have yet to master English grammar will fall back on the structures of their maternal tongues. Thus, with literal translation, *the black dog which runs after the red ball* can be described as *the dog black runs after the ball red*.

Lexical Structures–Semantic Differences

Three lexical differences are selected here: the prepositions, the personal pronouns, and the articles or classifiers. They unravel an interesting and perhaps unique worldview, categorization of things under heaven, and perception of social order.

Prepositions. English space prepositions are stating objective locations regardless of the position of the speakers. For example, in English, one would say: the plane is *"in"* the sky, the child is playing *"in"* the kitchen, cars run *"in"* the street. In Vietnamese, the position of the respondent is to be taken into consideration: the plane is above (him or her), the child is inside, cars are outside. Thus, the one single preposition *"in"* can be translated three ways. For prepositions indicating direction, both the point of origin and the destination of the speaker or subject are to be considered. "I go to the library" can be expressed three ways in Vietnamese: (a) tôi đi thu' viện (I go the library); (b) tôi đi ra thu' viện (I go *out to* the library); or (c) tôi đi vô thu' viện (I go *into* the library). In the first case (a), I state my intention, no direction is needed, no preposition is used. In the case of (b), the choice of preposition depends on the point of origin, I go *out* (of my house to) the library. In the last instance (c), I am close to my destination as I enter the library, I go *into* the library.

Vietnamese prepositions are more relational than objective. According to Patricia Nguyen My Huong as mentioned by Nguyen Dinh Hoa in his *Language in Vietnamese Society* (Nguyen, 1980), English prepositions represent a set of lexical difficulties for ESL (English as a second language) students because they are sometimes ambiguous. Consider the English expression, "I work *out of* my house." For Vietnamese learners of English, that may mean "I work *outside of* my house," which is not the case. Teachers of Vietnamese need to be very explicit in their explanation of such an expression in order to avoid misunderstanding. They may want to paraphrase it with "I work inside of my house, I use my house as the place of work, I work from my house, and receive clients in my house."

In English, some commonly used verbs such as "to do, to get, to look, to give" change their meanings when prepositions are added to them. The complexity of these semantic variations is difficult for learners of English as a second language. They usually have a hard time seeing the difference between "look over" and "overlook," "give out," "give up," "give in," "done with," "done in," "get over with," and so on. Ample explanation, a large variety of examples, and dramatic illustrations are absolute necessities if the goal of English mastery is to be reached by speakers of other languages than English. Above all, teachers of Vietnamese students need to realize that there is no one-to-one correspondence between words in Vietnamese and in English. Vietnamese words do not fit clear-cut grammatical categories of most Indo-European languages.

Personal Pronouns. The differences between the use of pronouns in English and their use in Vietnamese deserve special consideration. Pronouns reflect an implicit sense of social order, which for the Vietnamese is stratified and hierarchical. There are no equivalent terms in Vietnamese for the commonly used pronouns "I" and "you." The words "I" and "you" can be easily rendered in French by "*je, tu, vous,*" in Spanish by "*yo, tu, usted,*" in Chinese by "*hwa, ni, ni men.*" This is not the case in Vietnamese. There is no immediate, out-of-context, single translation of the dyad "I–you" in Vietnamese. In this language, choices are multiple. The answer to an ordinary "How are you" greeting can be translated in 12 to 20 ways, depending on the social position and status of the speaker in regard to the one being addressed. Nguyen Dinh Hoa described the Vietnamese system of personal pronouns as "unique," but it seems that there exists a similar system in the Korean language as well.

Nguyen stated in *Language in Vietnamese Society* (1980) that:

> Terms of relationship are used in address and reference in lieu of personal pronouns. When a man and his son carry on a conversation, the set of the pronouns *I–you* as "father–child" or "child–father" is used depending on which one is talking. (p. 12)

The English words "I" and "you" are used in conjunction with a verb that, most of the time, indicates an action done by one to the other. "I" becomes "you" when the direction of the action changes, that is, when "I" ceases to be the subject and becomes the object in the transaction defined by the verb. In a conversation between A and B, in English, for example, they take turns being or using "I" or "you," depending on who initiates the conversation. If I say "I am speaking to you," that puts me in the driver's seat and you are supposed to listen. But you can say the same sentence and you, in turn, become the person designated by the pronoun "I" and I become the "you." Switching roles entails switching words. A significant part of the English verbal message is the verb around which pronouns are rotating. In Vietnamese, this gyrational movement is unnecessary. The same word is used by a person to designate him- or herself whether he or she is the addressor or addressee—that is, in grammar terminology, the subject or the object. The Vietnamese personal pronouns are not dependent on an action but on an interpersonal relationship between the parties. Such rapport remains the same throughout the transaction regardless who initiates it. In a parent–child conversation, the child maintains his or her rank whether he or she speaks or is spoken to. So the conversation between a parent and a child may go like this:

> Child: Is parent going to play with child?

> Parent: Yes, parent will play with child, after dinner.

The preceding dialogue can also happen in English but within some contexts such as a family circle. The words "I" and "you" cannot be literally translated in Vietnamese without a context. Each context, each relationship has its own set of I–you. Once the right association is found, it remains identical throughout the communication as long as the parties continue to be the same and maintain the same interpersonal ties.

One of the difficulties for the English-speaking, non-native student of Vietnamese is to know how to select the proper pronoun to match the status and the degree of familiarity between speakers. A knowledgeable person who likes to play with words may subtly move from one to another set of pronouns to signal feelings and thoughts. For example, switching from a term of endearment to an impersonal pronoun is the equivalent of a change of heart and a dismissal, or call a casual acquaintance by a familiar term and you are labeled ill-mannered and "fresh." Young Vietnamese are aware of this sophisticated game that only a few can master. Teachers have reported their puzzlement about the behavior of some Vietnamese pupils. These children, after rapid-fire discussions with their friends in their native language on the playground, declare—when called to translate for the school administration—that they don't know how to speak Vietnamese. Are they lying? Why are they denying the obvious? The reason lies in the complexity of the Vietnamese language. These students do not know the right terminology, the proper relational words to address older, unrelated people. They somehow are aware that their playground vocabulary is acceptable only between peers. They follow the unspoken rule of propriety without knowing how to relate this to their teachers. Their answer is not a lie, but an incomplete truth: They don't know how to speak Vietnamese within that context with its own set of corresponding relevant vocabulary.

From this use of pronouns, one can draw some inferences about the mode of communicative behavior of the Vietnamese. Prior to any utterance, the unspoken rule of language propriety asks for a recognition of the nature of a relationship. The context and the relative status of the addressor to the addressee need to be gauged. Ranking, evaluating, appraising, judging take place in the selection of pronouns. Knowing one's place is reflected in such choices. Educating a child is to show the child his or her role in a larger system of kinship where human beings are immersed. Education is an introduction to the social system. This socialization purpose of education is undoubtedly not unique to the Vietnamese, but its intimate linkage with the use of pronouns is remarkable. Part of the family education of young Vietnamese children includes the teaching of the "right" appellation, the rightful naming, the sine qua none condition for socially acceptable conversations. Nguyen (1980) arrived at a similar conclusion when he noted that in the Vietnamese

> status minded society, the position—official or social—of each individual is clearly defined, not so much in terms of rights and obligations (as in a Western bureaucracy for instance), but mainly in terms of inter-personal behavior. (p. 34)

One can logically conclude that, for speakers of Vietnamese, prior to engaging in verbal expressions the situation and relationship is assessed. Communication takes place in the recognition of context and relations. The "I–you" dyad is not unilinear from "I" to "you," but global and holistic, "I" equal, inferior, superior to "you," and close, distant, or indifferent to one another, in an atmosphere of respect, contempt, or otherwise. Rank, status, social, personal history, and present feelings are condensed in this pronoun choice. The individual does not interact as an individual but as a son in a parent–child relationship, as an apprentice in a master–apprentice relationship, or as a worker in an employer–employee relationship. Furthermore, the playing of the role of son, apprentice, student, or worker persists 24 hours a day. The personal pronouns in this case can be called the interpersonal pronouns.

What does their constant use do to users? What are the influences of these interpersonal pronouns on thought patterns and concepts? How does it influence literacy? Hayakawa, in *Language in Thought and Action* (1952), stated that "A great deal of our education involves learning concepts .... It is through concepts that we are able to make sense of experience" (p. 292). Concepts are lenses through which humans perceive the world. Concepts and words influence our worldview and they also possess the power to shape our psyche. To quote Hayakawa,

> Words have power to mould ... thinking, to canalize ... feeling, to direct ... willing and acting. Conduct and character are largely determined by the nature of the words we currently use to discuss ourselves and the world around us. (p. 2)

If we subscribe to the thought that language determines a vision of the world then the Vietnamese world—as expressed by the absence of "I–you" general personal pronouns—is a web of interpersonal relations. I would venture to advance that the perceived quietness of the majority of the Vietnamese students in class, especially at the beginning of a school year, is not totally attributable to their lack of mastery of the English language but, in part, to the engrained attitude of gauging the concerned parties and situating the nature of the relationship in a context. I have observed with Vietnamese speakers that a confusion of roles or the absence of definite roles entails a slowness in utterances.

In addition, the Vietnamese carry this hierarchical world shaped by language in their literacy tasks. There is a hierarchy of reading materials: Instructional textbooks have more status than informative or pleasure reading materials. Vietnamese parents encourage their children to work hard in mastering teachers' selected textbooks but discourage the use of trade books, which are often considered frivolous and a waste of time. Yet familiarity with storybooks, frequency of reading for pleasure, and length of reading time are known to correlate with proficiency in spelling and writing. It is therefore reasonable to advance that their native-language patterns may partly account for the Vietnamese lower scores in verbal tests as documented by Caplan et al. (1989) and Ima and Rumbaut (1988).

Articles and Classifiers.   If personal-pronoun patterns in the Vietnamese language negatively influence the Vietnamese students' scores on verbal tests, the Vietnamese classifiers, on the contrary, seem to give them a head start in mathematics. In acquiring their language, native Vietnamese speakers are taught to recognize nature, shape, and number; in other words, they are given descriptive geometry early on when they learn how to speak. They learn groups and sub-groups, and their possible combinations, through classifiers, which, like articles in English, stand before nouns. Classifiers add to the meaning of nouns by indicating to which groups the nouns belong. They are data organizers. For English-speaking students, nothing in the English language gives clues to the sameness of a pear, an apple, and an orange, or a violin, a cello, and a guitar. Classifiers in the Vietnamese language give clues to the characteristics of what is being mentioned. The fruit terms have the *fruit* classifier and musical instrument terms are preceded by the *musical instrument* classifier. Psychological measurements of the capacity for abstraction in English tests lose their exactness when translated into Vietnamese because answers are given away in the Vietnamese language. It seems as if the Vietnamese classifiers help Vietnamese students succeed in mathematics. Ima and Rumbaut (1988), in a study on Southeast Asian refugee youth (SARYS) in San Diego city schools, stated that "almost half of all Vietnamese students (49%) are in the top of 10% nationally in math skills, and four out of five Vietnamese students … are in the top 40% (or above average) in the U.S. in math skills" (p. 36). Caplan et al. (1989) conducted a similar study in five metropolitan locations throughout the United States. Despite differences in sampling and location, the results are remarkably compatible between the SARYS research and that of Caplan et al. The superior scores of the Vietnamese in mathematics may be due in part to the mental gymnastic that is necessary for mastering the categorizations inherent in the Vietnamese language.

THE CULTURAL CONTEXT OF LANGUAGE LEARNING

Language is defined by function and context. People use literacy to achieve their goals in a variety of contexts. Culture dictates the what in learning, the how and the do's and don't's in expressing oneself. Students in learning and literacy situations bring with them cultural dispositions and patterns of behavior that enable or paralyze them, depending on the degree of compatibility with the new milieu. This section addresses the influence of Vietnamese cultural contexts on learning. The issue is a complex one. Generalizations are unavoidable, but with them there lies the danger of stereotyping: The Vietnamese in America are more or less influenced by the Vietnamese sociohistorical and cultural contexts, but the degree of intensity of such influence on various individuals is difficult to assess and to measure. It cannot be stressed enough that the goal of describing a culture here is to further the understanding of that culture. It should not be understood as, nor used for, labeling and stereotyping. For the sake of simplicity, I focus on aspects of learning and literacy, such as speaking, reading, and writing in the native tongue, in which salient traits of Vietnamese thinking and learning can be observed. Practical recommendations for teachers of Vietnamese students follow as the results of such observations.

Learning: Vietnamese Style

Howard Gardner described an experience that he had in 1987 at the lobby of the Jinling hotel in Nanjing, China, that gave him a "telling lesson" in the difference between Chinese and American ideas of education. His observation hit home for me because, in this particular instance, the Vietnamese and the Chinese behave the same way. This is how the story began. The key to Gardner's room was

> attached to a large plastic block with the room number embossed on it. When leaving the hotel, a guest was encouraged to turn in the key, either by handing it to an attendant or by dropping it through a slot into a receptacle. Because the key slot was narrow and rectangular, the key had to be aligned carefully to fit snugly into the slot. (p. 54)

Gardner (1989) had with him a son who was 1½. This toddler loved to bang the key into the slot. Sometimes he succeeded in pushing it through, but most of the time, he did not. This did not bother his father, because the child was exploring and had a good time. It seemed, however, that the hotel attendants did not feel the same way. Each time the toddler approached the slot, they rushed out to help him by guiding his hands. Gardner observed that teaching by holding hands was indeed widespread in China. Without overstating his position, Gardner suggested that education for young Chinese focused on skill learning and conformity to an ideal, whereas educators of young Americans would stress the sense of independence and creativity in their students.

I was intrigued by Gardner's statement and decided to conduct a small experiment of my own. I proceeded to describe Gardner's situation and his son's activities to my Chinese and Vietnamese students, then asked them what would they have done in such instance. They invariably expressed their approval of the attendants' intervention, and would also guide the child's hands. When I reflected on Vietnamese education, I would venture to say, without stereotyping, that the Vietnamese, too, value conformity to "ideals," be they truth or beauty, harmony, or correctness. Vietnamese students seem to unconsciously strive toward these ideals. Their attitude is shown in their frequent criticism of themselves, in their relentless effort to duplicate the perfect movement, to reach the perfect grade. Their activities appear to be less dictated by a desire to express themselves and more by a thrust toward perceived ideals. They learn by admiration. Role models are essential for them. Teachers of Vietnamese children will do well in showing them samples of what could be considered the perfect A+ papers. To avoid possible plagiarism, keep these samples varied, from different sources, with different styles, different illustrations, and organizational plans.

Speaking: Oral Language Communication

The first moments of literacy usually happen in the context of a family. Vietnamese are no exception to this human condition, but the configuration and the dynamics of the Vietnamese family shape the nature, the functions, and the roles of communication within it. It has been said that the family, as a natural support kinship system, is the "cornerstone of Asian psyche and society" (Tung, Rahe, Looney, Ward, & Liu, 1989, p. 61). Tung et al. defined a family as a multigenerational, sizable, extended network grouping, with a set of precisely defined loyalties and responsibilities, which bind its members with obligations of mutual support and dependency. Nguyen and Henkin (1981) contended that the individual had no place in Vietnamese society. Family ties and kinship network defined his or her identity. The Vietnamese individual thinks and behaves not as an independent person responsible for and to him or herself, but as a son or daughter dependent on and responsible to his or her parents, or as a brother or sister dependent on and responsible to other brothers, sisters, and relatives. The family is the first social support system of the individual. In Vietnam, it often was the only one. From the 18th century to 1975, Vietnam had been at war. It had no health and property insurance, a shaky money system, and embryonic social welfare services. The Vietnamese only had the family as a relatively permanent and dependable source of financial, social, and emotional support. It represented the most important factor in the socialization for the Vietnamese child.

The functional aspect of literacy aims at identifying the uses and approaches of literacy of a social group; in other words, social relations influence literacy. Most Vietnamese children grow up immersed in the extended family. Communication within a close, extended family is similar to that of a villagelike community system: It relies on extensive shared background, intimate knowledge of various members' personal idiosyncracies, and the expectation of a lifelong, sustained relationship. From early childhood, the Vietnamese child is intimately involved in several families and included into the stream of communicative life around them. The environment of Vietnamese boys and girls during their first years of life is indeed a very human one, with constant and ample amount of input from a variety of kinship people.

However, within such a circle, children are not considered suitable for regular conversation with adults. They are exposed to adult talk as silent observers, not as participants. They learn by observation, imitation, and practice. Adults teach through modeling and exhortation. Explanation of the reason behind adults' acts or words is not usually expressed. Given this cultural and social environment, the most suitable mode of learning is visual and experiential, rather than verbal. Vietnamese families and communities favor a high-context mode of communication between its members. The term *high context* was coined by E. T. Hall in the *Silent Language* (1964). It refers to a mode of communication wherein the greater part of the meaning is drawn from a context, that is, from a situation or a particular environment, and a smaller part from the verbal message.

Vietnamese adults do not try to be consistent with the young. Reward and punishment vary up and down according to the occasions, moods, and feelings of authority figures. In order to survive, children learn to be flexible around people, to predict their reactions, and to mold their communication to the necessity of the moment. They focus on interpersonal relationships and are keen to interpret the meaning of people's behaviors. Flexibility and adaptability are the keys to their survival. Like Trackton children described by Heath in *Ways With Words* (1983), the Vietnamese children "manage their social interaction, shifting tactics in accordance with their estimation of the audience moods" (p. 82).

The Vietnamese children, like Trackton children, are surrounded by a tightly bound community that offers wide exposure to many different individuals and numerous opportunities for practicing interpretation of motives, intentions, and predispositions of individuals. The goals and meanings of communications are embedded with high cues and are nonverbal. Vietnamese toddlers from both genders are often teased and challenged verbally and nonverbally by adults and older children. Adults may say hurtful things to engage younger children in some sort of response. They may tease through make-believe, lies, or overt showing of aggression, and they playfully push younger ones to the limit of their emotional endurance and verbal wits.

The young Vietnamese are expected to react to overt provocations and keep their "cool" within a rigid hierarchical structure of authority, expressed through proper appellations, which specify the rank of each family member in the authority structure. To know one's place is to know which I–you dyad to use, the difference in status between oneself and others, the social distance, and the amount of respect that one is expected to show through one's discourse.

How does one make requests or ask questions within such context? One does not. A Vietnamese student, who is brought up in, and influenced by, the Vietnamese cultural environment, will not likely ask questions and make requests. The preferred Vietnamese pattern for information seeking seems first to be quiet and attentive listening to the teacher's talk, and observation of the teacher's behavior, followed by an intense and noisy peer-group activity to process the given information, discuss its implication, and eliminate unsuitable individual interpretations, followed by a group resolution of the issue. A classroom atmosphere in which teachers offer personalized, affectionate, and motivating relationships and allow for peer-group discussion is helpful and encourages Vietnamese children to participate creatively and with reduced anxiety.

The U.S. or American culture is a low-context culture. Communication is often based on clear and explicit expression, whereas understanding in high-context communities, such as the Vietnamese, requires knowledge of implicit, widely known, understated assumptions. Students who have internalized the Vietnamese high-context cultural trait will be less eager to speak and more ready to observe and listen. Their initial quietness may be mistaken for dullness, shyness, ignorance, passivity, or laziness. But if these students are placed in a classroom where there is trust and understanding, they may reveal themselves as unstoppable conversationalists, after their initial reserve. The students who are used to high-context communication will be more comfortable with small-group exchanges than whole-class sharing. They also will do well in a one-to-one communication, and their teachers' individualized attention will carry a great deal of weight.

This author has experienced the influence of a power relation on speech. In an oral language placement test, Vietnamese students in her class were stiff and inarticulate, as if they were dull and linguistically deprived. When the author began small talk with them, the pressure of formalism was lifted, and the students became animated and were able to express themselves elaborately and with a great amount of wit. Wong Fillmore (1995) related similar experiences described by teachers of project KEEP (Kamehameha Early Education Project) in Hawaii. KEEP project teachers studied the modes of communication of their students at home and at school. They found different patterns of discourse, beliefs and expectations, social power, activities, and participant structures. They tailored their teaching patterns accordingly. They used question, feedback, and modeling extensively. They allowed for a high degree of peer collaboration. They developed independent peer-learning centers in which children work cooperatively. Group discussion began with shared experience, instructional conversations, small-group conversations in which students and teachers jointly engaged in discourse. This contextual change created a break-through for Hawaii students' academic success. Teachers were acting as creators of contexts and facilitators rather than sole source trans-mitters of knowledge. This author believes KEEP findings and changes in teaching pattern will benefit the Vietnamese students as well. The context modification will break the mold of conformist obe-dience expected of Vietnamese students by their culture and liberate their creativity in the quest for a literacy that is authentic to their per-sonal nature.

Writing: Expressing Oneself Through the Written Word

It is difficult for Vietnamese people in general and Vietnamese stu-dents in particular to express their thoughts in writing. Explanation of this trait is twofold: the high regard for the written word, and the fear of misinterpretations. The Vietnamese culture values literacy. A learned person enjoys high social status. One expects pearls of wis-dom from such a learned person, written down, in black on white for posterity, worthy of preservation and transmission from generation to generation like a sacred text. The trivial nitty-gritty of everyday life, the ordinary, is not considered suitable matter for written literacy.

Schooling in Vietnamese culture is believed to be the transmis-sion of philosophical, beautiful, or useful thoughts, as in literature and technical knowledge where the informal and the familiar are ex-cluded. Writing in the Vietnamese culture is a serious business that cannot, should not, be taken lightly. The Vietnamese culture im-poses formal patterns and structures on communications appropri-ate to various circumstances. Vietnamese students prefer to internalize a few well-understood principles, and to express them-selves concisely in writing rather than acquiring a broad coverage of shallowly understood materials and becoming prolific writers. When fulfilling a school assignment for writing, they tend to be brief and pompous; they rely on generalities or commonly understood folk wisdom. Without necessarily copying one another, their papers may actually look similar.

Teachers of Vietnamese students would do well if they taught struc-tures and formulas first, before attempting to ask the students to ex-press their thoughts and the content of what they would want to convey. It is less anxiety provoking if before a writing assignment Viet-namese students first know the pragmatics of the English culture, that is, what is proper, what is considered polite or rude, refined or vulgar, in English. In other words, Vietnamese students feel more secure if they know the parameters of what is considered acceptable and proper behaviors in the American culture. As John Ree (1980) stated, "the first job of teaching English ... entails teaching elements of English as a second culture" (p. 3). The author added, "One may be able to get by, as many have, with broken English without offending too many speakers of the dominant language but he/she may not get very far with 'broken culture,' or breaking social rules, without creating ill will toward the speakers of the dominant group" (p. 3).

It is also commonly observed that Asian students do not volunteer an answer or write down their thoughts unless they are sure about the social and academic correctness of their answers. American children are often asked to try and try again if at first they fail. Vietnamese children will feel discouraged and humiliated if they fail. They also cherish accuracy more than speed. Wong Fillmore (1995) found that the Asian students she and her team studied had difficulties in dealing with written and other assignments, until the students had "achieved a level of comfort with their new surrounding" and had reached "an intermediary level of proficiency in the language they were learning" (p. 40). Writing activities that are self-selected and self-directed can be puzzling to Vietnamese students, who depend on adults for guidance and directions. Competitive and individual learning may not agree with Vietnamese learners. Autocratic models of teaching seem to suit their learning styles better.

The reluctance to confide one's thoughts on paper can be explained by another cultural trait: the fear of misinterpretations by outsiders. This trait can be observed in other Asian groups such as the Chinese in Vietnam, who still carry business transactions with no paper trail. Words between trusted individuals are for them as binding as signatures. Vietnamese often hesitate to confide anything on paper, least of all their true feelings. They do not know who will be the recipient of their written message, and how their message would be understood or used, once taken out of context. This reluctance to write was reinforced by "confessions" that nationalist Vietnamese southerners went through under the domination of the Communists from North Vietnam. In these confessions, officials from the former South Vietnam government and officers of the defeated nationalist army were coerced to write their autobiographies, describing their activities and political involvement, year by year. They were required to go through this exercise many times. Discrepancies between various copies were the object of intense police interrogation. As a result, they learn that the less you put down on paper, the less you would be grilled.

My advice to teachers of Vietnamese reluctant writers is to select topics within the realm of communalities rather than issues that are too close to their hearts. Say no to topics such as "write about your exodus from your country" or "describe a member of your family." Select instead noninvolved topics such as "describe a town that you know," "a ball game you have attended," "the marketplace," "you and your friends' activities during leisure times," "the summary of a book just read in class," and so forth. Other topics may be welcomed once the students feel at home with the teacher and are willing to open up to the trusting climate of the classroom, which has fostered intimacy and made them feel safe enough to uncover their feelings and discover their identity. Writing one's thoughts and feelings may stir up issues of changing identities for immigrant children. Tobin and Friedman, as quoted by Shapiro (1988), who studied the adjustment and formation of refugee identity, stated that the greatest threat to identity in refugees and immigrants is not the feeling of belonging in three cultures—the native, the host, and the refugee cultures—but the feeling of belonging to none. Learning to behave appropriately and to succeed academically is critical to one's self-identification.

Regarding cultural identity, Kelly (1981) noted that many Vietnamese who came to the United States were motivated by a desire to maintain their own cultural, religious, social, and economic patterns as they had known them. They showed little diligence in adopting new ways. Tran Minh Tung explained this attitude as the dilemma between identity and integration. Vietnamese expatriates are often torn between a desire to hold onto the past, onto their old image of self and the world, and the necessity to conform to the norms of the host society. Some may have decided that they belong to the new country and they had better live up to their new identity, and these are more open to cooperation and involvement. Some others simply go along with the world around them but use a dual standard to accommodate the demands of their own and the American communities.

Tran Minh Tung et al. (1989) observed a pervasive attitude of passivity among Vietnamese refugees in general. None of them is really comfortable and satisfied with what they are doing. Nguyen and Henkin (1981) noted that success for many Vietnamese involves meeting prescribed obligations. For students, the way to fulfill their part of the social obligations is by studying hard and achieving academically. Yet there is a problem here. What will happen when Vietnamese children claim independence from the authority of the kinship system and pursue their own self-fulfillment? The Vietnamese culture offers little support to its members in their acculturation to this "land of the free," and in the development of a high degree of self-reliance in their quest of personal happiness. The gap between the American way of life and the Vietnamese traditions creates a double bind for Vietnamese students and a double cultural marginality.

Fortunately, the Vietnamese family structure is not embedded in concrete. It is a dynamic phenomenon subject to the influence of social transactions. Yet there is cause for concern. Although statistics on divorce and single-parenthood within the Vietnamese community are lacking, there is anecdotal evidence of family breakdown. The loss of support and monitoring that follow family crises affects the academic and social development of a growing number of Vietnamese children who are joining the ranks of at-risk students, in need of services that the family and the culture are unable to deliver. There is hope, though. Caplan et al. (1989) noticed that the Vietnamese children they studied felt "intrinsic gratification with learning, the out of school relevance of learning to the long term well-being of their family, pride in sharing teamwork, conviction that things will work in their favor" (p. 158).

Reading: Literacy Activities in the Vietnamese Community

Because literacy is highly regarded, large Vietnamese communities in the United States offer a fairly wide range of print materials to their members. Chung (1988) found 1,090 different titles published in America in the Vietnamese language since 1975. This number can be broken down to 150 titles on teaching and learning English, 200 nonfiction publications on religion, psychology, and self-improvement, and 740 remaining titles are novels and translations on a wide range of subjects. These titles appeal to adults, literate in Vietnamese, more than young readers who are learning their mother tongue. To help the latter in Vietnamese-language development, the Vietnamese communities conduct after-school and weekend classes, staffed by volunteers. The curriculum of these programs includes Vietnamese reading and writing, civics, folklore, and poetry, as well as the history and geography of Vietnam (Chung, 1988).

Due to the dearth of leisure reading materials for children, and because the Vietnamese culture favors the aural–oral mode of language transmission over reading, one does not see daily bedside reading to children as often as among literate American families. Vietnamese parents do not always encourage their children, especially adolescents, to read fiction. They want to maintain some control over the ideological influence of novels, which, for many parents, are considered pervasive with unbridled expressions of passion, vivid and wild imagination, against traditions. As I mentioned briefly in the section on personal pronouns, reading materials are classified into the serious and the frivolous. Serious reading is encouraged and the frivolous discarded as a waste of time. Teachers of Vietnamese students need to emphasize the importance of reading for information seeking and the development of creativity. This effort is crucial in reversing the dismaying trend of Vietnamese students receiving very low verbal scores, mentioned by Kenji Ima in his communication to the California Education Summit of 1994.

Vietnamese parents, however, express their pride in children who know how to read English. They value this technical knowledge and often rely on such skills to find their way in this new land. Children are often counted on to be mediators in the family's communications with social institutions. Their proficiency in English gives them added status and responsibilities.

My advice to teachers of Vietnamese students is to make reading assignments relevant to their social contexts, and tailored to their ages and family needs. Knowing how to read job applications, welfare communiqués, hospital information sheets, advertisements, directions to utilities and social agencies, manuals for operation of appliances, and consumer information is useful. These technical skills need to be developed in the classroom. Teachers of Vietnamese children, and of any children in transition, have to become pragmatists and focus on the usefulness of language. This does not mean that fiction and poetry are to be excluded. When teaching fiction, teachers can bridge the gap between the language of fiction and the language used in everyday discourse through plays, skits, and simulations. Vietnamese students will then have opportunities to practice oral and written language under the teacher's guidance, incorporate useful expressions for communication in the real world, and truly develop the language skills they need to operate in their lives, for themselves and for their families.

PERCEPTION OF EDUCATION BY VIETNAMESE PARENTS AND STUDENTS

In 1992, I conducted a study of parents' and students' perceptions of school services at Yerba Buena High school in San Jose, California, which had and still has a large concentration of Vietnamese students. Part of the research involved interviews that were taped, transcribed, and analyzed. This study indicated that education has a unique, special place in the value scales of the Vietnamese parents who were interviewed. They expressed hope and expectations of high academic achievement for their children. They want their children to take full advantage of the educational opportunities that they themselves had missed in their youth. In order to preserve confidentiality, students identify themselves by a number that they selected. The father of a student, who called himself number 165, used the term *"hu,"* which means damaged, spoiled, rotten, wasted, out of service, to qualify a dropout from school. The father said that he can bear poverty, he can be content in poverty, as long as his children get an education. His children's education is his only hope in life. He thinks of himself as an uneducated man, a man "who lacks the words." He felt that this deficiency left him with no future. He said:

> In our country [Vietnam], poor people do not have the opportunity to go to school. I had to earn my living at an early age. Now in America, without the words, I can't do anything, anything worthwhile. I work just to survive, day by day. My hope lies with my children. I don't want to become desperate. I will do all I can to keep them in school.

"All I can" is translated into emotional pressure and environmental control. The father appealed to his son's sense of family responsibility. He said:

> My son is the eldest in the family. He has to set the right path for his younger siblings. If he goes "*hu*" [rotten] then all his younger ones will follow and will be "*hu*."

The father, who is working part-time, wanted to see his son study, under his eyes, at home. Playing is a waste of time, a futile exercise. He said:

> I don't want my son to play outside. I don't want him to go to the outside world too young, too soon, he may pick wrong habits. If he plays, I want him to play with his classmates from time to time but absolutely with no one else. Besides, he doesn't want to play.

This father gave positive strokes for all educational efforts. He was proud to convey to the interviewer his son's eagerness for school matters. Under the father's eyes, even the most venerated traditional celebrations should not interfere with schooling. He said, "My son went to school even on the day of the Vietnamese Lunar New Year. What can he do at home? Just hanging around, wasting his time." For this man, time away from school was time wasted.

This obsession with education is translated into an obsession for high grades with the father of a 16-year-old girl, number 18. They came to California after a long stay in a small Kentucky town, where the names of the honor-roll students were published in the local newspaper. He proudly announced that he was very well known in his town because all of his children who went to school had their names published in the local newspaper every month as honor-roll students. Education as the future for their children was the motivation behind number 2's and number 10's parents' immigration to the United States, a move that took 7 years of preparation and all their fortune. Student number 10's mother happily stated: "Upon hearing about the American law about repatriation of Amerasians, I adopted my Amerasian daughter. Now all six of my children are here and going to school and my adopted one is getting married. The American education is the best in the world."

Her only dream, the education of her children, came through. Her husband echoed the same thought. He said, "In my generation, very few people can go abroad to get an education. Now our only hope is the future of our children." The mother expressed her willingness to endure all hardships if her children studied and had a bright future. That would be a great satisfaction for her. From her perspective, her children are most fortunate. She kept them motivated by reminding them about her own life. She said, "Before [as a child] I had a painful and limited life. I was not as lucky as you. Now, you should be happy going to school and working toward your future."

Parents' Concern for "Too Much" Freedom

Vietnamese parents are concerned about too much freedom for the young. They deplored what they perceived as lax discipline in American schools. They want to see order and adult control at school and in the streets. After moving to California from Kentucky, student number 18 did not maintain straight As. Her grades wandered into Bs from time to time. To the average parent, this drop would be acceptable. This student's father reacted by increasing control and used emotional pressure to motivate her, telling her to set the right path for her younger siblings to follow. The father deplored the laxness of discipline in California public schools. He expressed the thought that teachers should schedule firmly. He said:

> About activities of the Vietnamese Club, for example, at rehearsal, even though it is a cultural event, there should be an exact time, teachers should say exactly when, say, a play rehearsal begins and when it ends. And it should be on school grounds, it cannot be at somebody's house ... I want my daughter to join the club to develop her skills but I want some control. [Without the strict scheduling, the students] may just play around and not rehearse.

For this parent, teachers were indulging students. When his daughter's grades were falling, from A to B, he questioned her. The reason she gave was that she was talking in class. To his mind, her teacher did not exercise enough control. For the teacher, the matter was in the hands of the students. It was up to them to correct their own behaviors. Student number 18's father disagreed and said:

> I went to see her teacher and requested that he change her place. His reply
> was that he wanted students to self-correct. It seems unreasonable to let
> students self-correct for the whole year. It is fine to leave things in their
> hands for a while. After a week, for example, it is imperative that change be
> made. If students do not self-correct, then we should force them to, by re-
> arranging sitting places.

His sense of control bordered paranoia. He could not understand that
strong bonding between people can be developed without the emi-
nence of danger, as it was for him during the Vietnam war with his com-
rades at arms. When his daughter announced that she liked her
classmates as much as family members, he imagined the worst. He said:

> After we moved here for a year, one day my daughter came home very ex-
> cited. She announced that her classmates treated one another like family
> members. To you is that good news or bad news? Do you know what I
> thought? I was thinking about the strong influence of the group ... like the
> army. It was frightening. I was thinking very hard on this. Were Vietnamese
> students in big fight with Mexican students or something? How come that
> they treat one another like that [bonded and close as if they were family
> members]? Without any fighting and treating one another like family, I had
> a serious suspicion that she had contact with gang members.

In a prior interview with his daughter, she revealed the fact that she
was overjoyed with seeing ethnic minorities like herself at school, after spending her first 10 years in the United States with only White students in a small Kentucky town. Another mother was also concerned
about the control of her son, number 20, an 11th grader, who wanted
to become a business person or a computer expert. She said:

> What is most unbearable in America is my great fear about my son becom-
> ing involved with the wrong friends and smoke this and that with nobody
> watching him in the streets. Parents cannot have a tranquil heart in this
> country. We are sad and afraid that he gets into a "no-good" situation.

But she had a gleam of hope. She said, "I am glad that there is order in
school, thanks to you teachers and staff, you help my son succeed.
And then there is the police outside of school."

In the parents' minds, the children's futures were inseparable from
getting good grades and going to college. Parents' expectations and
demands for academic success from their children, their vision of
bright futures through education, their own regrets for missed educational opportunities, and their insistence on the control of the young
by school staff were recurrent themes in the interviews with Vietnamese parents. Recreation, freedom, leisure, communication, and intimacy were not mentioned as priorities on parents' agendas. Yet they

were on the children's. The yearning for parents' understanding, and the yearning for trust, communication, and freedom succinctly expressed in the survey were articulated again and again, with eagerness, passion, and despair in the students' interviews.

Students' Valuing Education

Some interviewed Vietnamese students echoed the parents' wishes for good schooling and focused their whole working time on this single objective. Most of the students paid great attention to their grades. They felt a great deal of mental anguish even at a slight, commonly acceptable drop, such as from A to B. Ima and Rumbaut (1988) noted that for most Vietnamese youth, life is centered around getting an education. Personal preferences tend to be subordinated to this perceived collective priority (Ima & Rumbaut, 1988). Student number 26 described her life in the first 5 months to the United States as school, homework, sleep. She said:

> I go to school ... go home when school is finished, concentrate on homework, put my effort into finishing homework, and, if I have some free time in the evening, I lie down to watch cartoons for a while and fall asleep.

Student number 165 liked school, thought school was fun, social studies interesting, mathematics difficult, Vietnamese language class useful. He said that Vietnamese do not have problems because they: "work and play, ... school."

Student number 26 explained at great length how she missed an A in mathematics by 2 points. It was such a serious matter for her, she felt quite depressed about it and almost cried. Student number 27 reported that she was very sad when she received a less than excellent grade at school. A newcomer of 9 months to the United States, she intended to spend all of her free summer time studying English. She said:

> My friends asked me to join them to go to work this summer. At first, I wanted to work, to earn some money, to have money to spend on a few little things, but now, on second thought, ... like my mother said ..., I am new here, I better put all my effort in studying. While others go to work, I want to hone my English skills.

This single-mindedness for academic success was not always rewarded. A junior, student number 8, received a D in mathematics, felt dumb and desperate, and withdrew from his friends. He blamed himself, said that he hated himself. He said:

I found schooling easier before, but it became more and more difficult. Now I don't know why but, I forget everything I learn. It is weird! ... I don't want to play, I don't want to talk to my friends. I just want to sit here with my books open and force myself to learn.

He did not live with his parents but with an older brother and his new bride. His sister-in-law was interviewed. She said she urged him to seek help. She advised him to take his falling grades as a temporary state, to stop being so concerned about them, and go out to have fun, but to no avail. Student number 8 stubbornly stayed home and sulked. His only distraction and consolation were to listen to music.

What is the motivation behind their single-mindedness for schooling? Academic success was considered as a moral obligation by some Vietnamese students interviewed. For them, failure at school stood as a moral failure, the incapacity to fulfill one's duty and carrying out one's responsibility toward the family. For students 165, 27, and 18, the eldest of many siblings, it was their sense of responsibility toward the younger ones, a responsibility reinforced by parents' constant remarks. These students are reminded that they are the leaders; they set the path, the example as role models for others to follow. These ideals had been internalized. These Vietnamese students seemed to have made a personal commitment to fulfill their moral obligation. Student number 18, who had good grades but ran away from home two times, said in a said voice, "I am the role model [to younger siblings] ... I've done a lot of bad things so ... how can I be good to them?" The sense of moral obligation was sometimes expressed as a sense of reciprocity, of returning a favor for a favor. Another student, number 27, was alone with her mother in Vietnam, while her father had escaped to the United States. About her falling school grades, she said, "I was very sad. My mother worked very hard to raise me, to take care of everything for me, alone without [the help of] my father." She felt that she had to do her part, which was to apply herself diligently and succeed in school. This moral obligation was felt even if the parents were not present. At the time of the interview, student number 8's mother was in Vietnam and his father was "somewhere" in the United States. Yet he resented his school failure and blamed himself bitterly.

Among the motivating factors for academic success expressed by students were traces of competitive behavior, the "keeping up with the Joneses" syndrome, and the fear of being put down because one could not keep up with the demands. Student number 27 mentioned that her aunts and uncles "belittled me, because I cannot succeed even though it was easy."

Not all interviewees shared this kind of focus on school matters. Student number 13 dropped out of school and was suspended for truancy a whole semester. When asked about the reason for his action, he said:

> I used to hang around with uh … friends, you know. They asked me to cut school …. Everyday, every time I met them uh … they asked me, 'cause I have a car …. So I'm gonna try and see to, uh … to blame … you know, ever'thing on them. If a friend asks you to cut and you feel like cutting too, and 'cause … you cut with them.

Student number 13's saving grace was his mother, the person to whom he is most indebted. She registered him back to school and he decided to stay, although teachers really did not care. Student number 13 said that teachers

> just give you some assignment, go ahead and do it …. You don't turn it in the day it's due …. They don't even remind you to do it or whatever …. They don't show anything like they care about you.

Students' Dreams of White-Collar Careers

No matter what their attitudes were toward school, most Vietnamese interviewees expressed their intent to pursue higher education and dreamed about white-collar careers. Asked whether he will go to college, student number 13, who dropped out of school for a whole semester, said, "I am undecided yet. I think I am. I think, but I'm not sure. I think I have to … I have to go to college." After 9 months in the United States, student number 27 wants to be "good in English so I can go to college, in the future." A sophomore, student number 18, said, "There are a few careers I would like to have. I am planning to either major in fashion designing or maybe a lawyer, or business or accounting. There's a lot of things I'd like to be."

One year after his arrival in the United States, student number 17, in his sophomore year, wanted his counselor to point him to "the route to go to college, step by step." Student number 10 wanted to be a computer designer, student number 20 a business or computer major, student number 21 a teacher like her father. In that sense, they were fulfilling the dreams of their parents who had not enjoyed schooling opportunities in their youth. As student number 27 stated, she wanted to please her mother who was also her friend and confidant.

The findings of my study are similar to the findings of other research. Caplan et al. (1989) remarked that the Vietnamese reflect an adaptive style that is active, pragmatic, and instrumental, based on a work ethic of personal effort. Vietnamese ethics as reflected in popular literature emphasize the value of hard work combined with patience. Caplan et al. stated that both older and younger generations share these values: A correlation of .83 was found between the samples of parents and high school students on the measure of importance attributed to the value items. This indicated an extremely high level of consensus between generations. SARYS reached similar conclusions. By using a set of items that measured the parents' level of agreement or disagreement with a range of cultural values and choices, Ima and Rumbaut (1988) created an index of cultural values. A list of 26 values was presented. The respondents were to indicate which values they considered most important. Ninety-eight percent or more of the respondents rated the following items at the highest levels on the scale measuring perceived importance:

- Education and achievement.
- A cohesive family.

Ima and Rumbaut found that the parents who strongly held traditional values and who bonded with their ethnic group were more likely than others to have children with high academic achievement. The statistical analyses pointed to the traditional values of family and community cohesiveness of parents as strong predictors of children's academic success. SARYS also found that the more convinced the parents were that as Southeast Asians they would never have equal status with the mainstream Americans in the United States, the higher were the grade point averages (GPAs) attained by their children. The authors attributed this to the motivational role of ethnic pride and identity. They had observed resilience, self-justification, and determined effort in both parents and children. They concluded, like Caplan et al., that the educational achievement of Southeast Asian students is undergirded by strong familial identity and sustained community support.

This has been observed by many other researchers. Nguyen and Henkin (1981) stated that individual success is highly valued in American and Vietnamese society but with a difference: Americans view success as their own, whereas the Vietnamese thinks about success for his or her family or primary group. When one congratulates a successful Vietnamese candidate, recognition is due to the parents and the entire family. Family ties are important even in the case of physical separation of members from one another. In split families, the sense of responsibility, the expectation of support, and the communality of norms persist. Mortland (1987) noted that "family is not just one of the organizing principles of Southeast Asian life but in many ways it *is* the principle" (p. 307). The refugees' family, as an institution, is the greatest strength and the biggest asset of the refugee population.

However, it seemed that, for some others, the family bonds had been deteriorating. The main factors appeared to be a clash in perspectives between some of the Vietnamese parents and their respective students. The parents' philosophy was expressed in both ethical and pragmatic terms. They emphasized duties and responsibilities, and the "sizing-up of educational opportunities" that they had missed in their childhood. Not all children's feelings, attitudes, opinions, and behaviors were consistent with their parents' exhortations, philosophy, and demands. Many Vietnamese students had expectations of their own. Although parents were concerned about schooling and their children's future, some Vietnamese students questioned the present, the cultural conflicts at school, the communication with family members and peers, their growing needs for intimacy, and their sense of self-worth.

The school climate as perceived by some interviewed Vietnamese students was marred by the isolation of students within their ethnic groups and interethnic conflicts. Besides problems of communication with the family, some of the Vietnamese students interviewed at Yerba Buena expressed their frustration with racial discrimination among students and from some of the teachers and administrators. Student number 17 said that other students, mostly Mexicans, threw dirty towels at him in the bathroom, looked at him and said things that he did not understand, and played soccer "at his head" (i.e., without consideration). Student number 2 was very annoyed when she was teased by Mexican American classmates in her ESL period. She said, "They teased me, looked at me, said something in Spanish to their friends and laughed at me."

Student number 18 hoped that racism would stop. She said, "I mean, it's like, 'cause Mexicans always make ... say things about Vietnamese and then ... Vietnamese get mad and always have to say something back to Mexicans and then we end up fighting."

Student number 4 speaks English fluently, having been in the United States for 12 years. Yet she did not mix well with other ethnic groups. She said, "I prefer Vietnamese friends. I don't get along with American people .... Oh, I don't know. I don't get along with American or Mexican people ... I hang around with Vietnamese."

SUMMARY

From the preceding pages, you may have noticed that Vietnamese children as a group are motivated to learn, and are pushed by their parents into achieving in school. They aspire to white-collar positions and they are aware of the high level of literacy that such positions usually require. The Vietnamese students interviewed expressed their willingness to forego immediate gratification and to concentrate their efforts in schooling. It seems as if their personal identities are linked with school achievement; to fail in school equates with becoming spoiled and rotten, that is, to deteriorate as a moral person to one who cannot fulfill obligations. Although researchers, such as Ima and Caplan, have documented Vietnamese students' success at the national and local levels, not all Vietnamese students are succeeding, and many do so only with tremendous effort because of the incongruence between school expectations and the students' initial cultural preliteracy patterns. When we examine the modalities of oral language acquisition of the preliterate Vietnamese children and the shift from oral to written language as observed in selected Vietnamese households, we see that the ways of home are not always compatible with the ways of schools.

I would suggest the following to teachers who want to help Vietnamese students:

1. First, an attitude of openness is recommended to teachers of culturally diverse students. Recognize the many ways of learning and motivation of your students, which are built in their culture, reinforced by parents' exhortations, literature, and mass media. Human beings are born with infinite potential. Cultures are actualizations of some of that potential. To know more aspects of culture is to know more about humankind. Teachers would then live up to what an ancient Greek author had wished: "I am a human being, and nothing which is human is foreign to me." Although we appear dissimilar, we all belong to the same species and can enrich one another.

2. Second, make the contact with a new culture a personal and enjoyable experience for yourself and your students. Your openness to your students is a professional obligation. Make it a personal obligation. You are not learning a new culture only because you have got to teach these kids, but because you want to be a learner and they bring aspects of humanity that will enrich your mind and your heart. You can return the favor so that the learning and teaching act is an act of mutual enrichment. The classroom then will become a true community of learners.

3. The Vietnamese students aspire to personal attention from their teachers, as ambassadors of the American culture and respected authority figures. An encouraging remark from you goes a long way in their lives. It is capable of reinforcing and restoring their sense of self-confidence and self-worth, often shaky in situations that involve culture and language switching. Their sense of indebtedness to your attentive kindness may also last a lifetime,

because once they consider you a member of their family, they do not let you go. The author of these lines still receives letters and visits from students whom she taught some 30 years ago.

4. Allow time for yourself to observe; practice some kid-watching. Not all students embed all aspects of his or her culture. Intergroup variations offer a wide range of possibilities. No single chapter can get at all cases. There is no substitute for your own contacts and judgment in situ and at a given time. Take time to arrive at your own conclusions. There is no fast microwave-like device or cooking advice for teachers of culturally diverse students. You are on your own. Hopefully, this chapter has given you some guidelines, some sort of lamppost, or check points, on your cultural journey.

5. Be a lifelong learner. Because you are at the explosion time of the information age, one of its concurrent explosions is the cultural multiplicity found in the student population of the United States. Don't let things happen to you. Embrace your time and flow along.

■ ACTIVITIES

1. Invite a local Vietnamese American cultural educational resource person, such as a member of the Vietnamese PTA, to speak to your class about concerns for Vietnamese children. Ask about existing educational resources for primary-language education and literacy rates. What are the needs unique to your region of the country or community? What issues are shared with other Vietnamese communities in the United States? What are the characteristics of the Vietnamese families and students where you live or teach? What recommendations does the resource person have for implementing pedagogies that are linguistically and culturally responsive to the Vietnamese children's needs and parents' expectation?
2. Visit a local after-school Vietnamese-language program. Observe and describe teacher–students, students–teacher, and students–students interactions in this context. Notice the variations in the quality of communications such as teachers' and students' attitudes, the tones of their voices, pitch, rate, and amplitude. Notice the frequency of such occurrences. What conclusions can you temporarily formulate with regard to teachers' and students' roles, expectations, preferred modes of communication, and learning style?
3. Visit a local Vietnamese bookstore. Estimate the inventories, that is, number of titles in efferent and esthetic materials. What kind

dominates the display of books? Compare your inventory with that of popular American bookstores, such as B. Dalton and Barnes & Noble. What conclusions can you possibly draw? What characteristics of the Vietnamese literary community can you infer from this comparison? What are the implications of your conclusions for the education of Vietnamese youths?

4. Interview a few Vietnamese students at various ages, say, 5, 7, and 16, who have been in the United States for 3 or more years. Identify their perceptions of the different ways of using language at home and at school. What are the language and literacy uses of the oral and the written language they have acquired in their native tongue? Are these uses different than in English?

5. In pairs or in small groups of three to five, initiate a literature study using translated works of popular Vietnamese folktales. What themes emerge from these stories? What kind of light do these themes shed on the attitude of the Vietnamese learners toward literacy, the role of the parents and teachers in shaping literacy tasks, and their expectations of the young? What conclusions can you temporarily draw from this study about Vietnamese learning styles and their attitude toward literacy? What implications can you draw for the education of Vietnamese students in the classroom setting?

SUGGESTED READINGS

Chung, C. H. (1988). The language situation of Vietnamese in America. In S. L. Wong (Ed.), *Language diversity: Problems or resources* (pp. 276–292). Rowley, MA: Newbury House.

Huynh, D. T. (1988). *The Indochinese and their cultures*. San Diego: San Diego State University, Multifunctional Resource Center.

Olsen, L. (1988). *Crossing the schoolhouse borders: Immigrant students and the California public schools*. San Francisco: California Tomorrow.

Van Luu, L. (1989). *The hardships of escape for Vietnamese women*. In E. H. Kim, L. V. Villanueva, & Asian Women United of California (Eds.), *Making more waves* (pp. 60–69). Boston: Beacon Press.

Yau, J., & Jiménez, R. (2003). Fostering the literacy strengths of struggling Asian American readers. *Language Arts, 80*(3), 196–205.

REFERENCES

Aoki, E. M. (1993). Turning the page: Asian Pacific American children's literature. In V. Harris (Ed.), *Teaching multicultural literature* (pp. 109–135). Norwood, MA: Christopher-Gordon.

Caplan, N., Whitmore, J. K., & Choy, M. H. (1989). *The boat people and achievement in America: A study of economic and educational success*. Ann Arbor: University of Michigan Press.

Chung, C. H. (1988). The language situation of Vietnamese in America. In S. L. Wong (Ed.), *Language diversity: Problems or resources* (pp. 276–292). Rowley, MA: Newbury House.

Gardner, H. (1989, December). Learning Chinese style. *Psychology Today, 23*(12), 54–57.

Hall, E. T. (1964). *The silent language*. Garden City, NY: Anchor Press.

Hayakawa, S. I. (1952). *Language in thought and action*. London: Allen & Unwin.

Heath, S. B. (1983). *Ways with words: Language, life, and work in communities and classrooms*. Cambridge, England: Cambridge University Press.

Huard, P., & Durand, M. (1954). *Connaissance du Vietnam*. Paris: Ecole Française d'Extrême Orient, Imprimerie Nationale.

Huynh, D. T. (1988). *The Indochinese and their cultures*. San Diego: San Diego State University, Multifunctional Resource Center.

Ima, K. (1994, March). *Vietnamese student achievement*. Speech delivered to California Education Summit, San Francisco.

Ima, K., & Rumbaut, R. G. (1988). *The adaptation of Southeast Asian refugee youth: A comparative study*. Washington, DC: Final Report to the Office of Refugee Resettlement.

Kelly, G. P. (1981). Contemporary American policies and practices in the education of immigrant children. In J. Bhatnager (Ed.), *Educating immigrants* (pp. 113–130). New York: St. Martin's Press.

Lewis, J., Kam, R., Vang, L., Elliott, M., Yang, T., & Crystal, E. (1992). *Minority cultures of Laos: Kammu, Lua', Lahu, Hmong, and Mien*. Folsom, CA: Southeast Asia Community Resource Center.

Liff, M. (1980). Indochinese refugees—The newest American. *American Education, 10*, 6–16.

Mortland, C. A. (1987). Secondary migration among Southeast Asian refugees in the United States. *Urban Anthropology, 16*(3–4), 46–53.

Ngin, C. S. (1990). The acculturation pattern of Orange County's Southeast Asian refugees. *Journal of Orange County Studies, 3/4*, 46–53.

Nguyen, D. H. (1966). *Vietnamese English dictionary*. Rutland, VT: Charles Tuttle.

Nguyen, D. H. (1980). *Language in Vietnamese society*. Carbondale, IL: Asia Books.

Nguyen, T. L., & Henkin, A. B. (1981). *Between two cultures: The Vietnamese in America*. Saratoga, CA: Century XXI Publishing.

Ree, J. J. (1980). English for Asians as a second language: problems and strategies. In J. Koo & R. Saint Clair (Eds.), *Bilingual education for Asian American: Problems and strategies, Series in socio-linguistics, #1*. Hiroshima: Bunka Hyoron.

Refugee Policy Group. (1985). *How are refugees doing? Adaptation and integration of recent refugees to the U.S.* Washington, DC: Author.

Shapiro, A. (1988). Adjustment and identity formation of Lao refugee adolescents. *Smith College Studies in Social Work, 58*(3), 99–112.

Takaki, R. (1989). *Strangers from different shores: A history of Asian Americans*. New York: Penguin Books.

Tung, T. M., Rahe, R. H., Looney, J. G., Ward, H. W., & Liu, W. T. (1979, October). *The Indochinese refugee mental health problem: An overview*. Paper presented at the First Conference on Indochinese Refugees, George Mason University, Fairfax, VA.

Tung, T. M., Rahe, R. H., Looney, J. G., Ward, H. W., & Liu, W. T. (1989, June). *Southeast Asian refugee mental health: Fourteen years later*. Paper presented at the

National Conference on Indochinese Communities: Health, Needs and Responses, Melbourne, Australia.

Van Luu. L. (1989). *The hardships of escape for Vietnamese women*. In E. H. Kim & L. V. Villanueva (Eds.), *Making more waves* (pp. 60–69). Boston: Beacon Press.

Wong Fillmore, L. (1995). Second language learning in children. A model of language learning in social context. In E. Bialystok (Ed.), *Language processing by bilingual children* (pp. 49–69). Cambridge, England: Cambridge University Press.

Yau, J., & Jiménez, R. (2003). Fostering the literacy strengths of struggling Asian American readers. *Language Arts, 80*(3), 196–205.

7

Language and Literacy in Chinese American Communities

Ji-Mei Chang

Along with the increasing number of newly arrived immigrants, major school districts across the country have been experiencing an increase in the number of diverse languages spoken in their schools. For example, according to the U.S. Bureau of the Census (1994), the following school systems reported having more than 100 languages spoken in their schools: New York City, Chicago, Los Angeles, and Fairfax County, Virginia. The Chinese language (1.2 million speakers) ranked sixth among the top 10 languages spoken in these four school systems, after English (198.6 million), Spanish (17.3 million), French (1.7 million), German (1.5 million), and Italian (1.3 million). Proportionately in the most populous states, New York and California, Chinese-speaking students represent the largest group within the Asian American student population. In the 1990–1991 school year, Chinese-speaking limited English proficient (LEP) students were the second largest LEP group in New York and California (Chang, 1993). However, diversity in language exists within Chinese-speaking LEP and second-language learners commensurate with the language diversity among the general Chinese American populations.

179

The major purpose of this chapter, then, is to provide relevant information regarding the Chinese language and the sociocultural context of selected Chinese American communities. The importance of these issues lie within the inner-city Chinese American and recent Chinese immigrant populations. Within the Chinese American population there is diversity in culture, Chinese language, and dialects. Furthermore, Chinese immigrants tend to maintain a close relationship with their homeland, subscribing to Chinese culture and values, and speaking Chinese dialect(s) in their private lives. The author intends to achieve two specific objectives: to enhance teachers' awareness and understanding of the complexity of the Chinese language and its orthographic effects on individuals becoming literate in the Chinese language; and to help teachers generate opportunities for inner-city Chinese American LEP students' social, language, and literacy development.

This chapter is divided into three parts. Part one describes the diversity and commonalities within Chinese American communities on issues related to Chinese oral and written languages. Part two presents specific orthographic effects on becoming literate in the Chinese language to help teachers understand specific reading, writing, and mathematical problem-solving behaviors for some Chinese American LEP learners who had prior school experiences in Chinese language. In part three, the author presents a sociocultural perspective of the home–school–community learning environment of a selected group of inner-city Chinese American LEP students. This information is described with the intent of heightening teachers' awareness of these students' unique needs, as well as suggesting ways to generate opportunities to learn among the learners who may not fit the image of Asian model minority students in our schools.

DIVERSITY AND COMMONALITY WITHIN THE CHINESE AMERICAN COMMUNITY

Chinese Americans represent a heterogeneous group of Chinese immigrants from China, Taiwan, Hong Kong, Southeast Asia, and other countries. Wong (1988) provided a detailed account of the Chinese immigration history and language situation of various Chinese American communities. Briefly stated, because of political, economic, and social influences, there have been many fluctuations in the size and composition of the Chinese American community over the past 130 years. Regardless of how large or small a percentage of Chinese speakers there were within a school system, they were likely to reflect the linguistic heterogeneity found in the various Chinese American communities.

Wong (1988) also observed that linguistic diversity within the Chinese American community varied according to the time when the different groups of Chinese immigrants arrived in the United States. However, only a relatively small number of Chinese dialects have played dominant roles within Chinese American communities and schools (Guthrie, 1985; Wong, 1988). In public schools, until the late 1980s and early 1990s, only the Cantonese-speaking students had the option of enrolling in Chinese bilingual classrooms in major metropolitan school districts across the country. As the number of Chinese immigrants from Taiwan and mainland China increased, Mandarin bilingual classrooms became increasingly available when parents began demanding them. Currently, however, a majority of Chinese and Chinese American parents choose to place their children in English-only instructional programs in most school districts.

This section presents a brief account of various aspects of two distinctively different systems of Chinese spoken and written languages to help the reader understand the complexity of the Chinese language, and how it may impact Chinese-speaking students' literacy development.

Chinese Spoken Language

Among the Chinese people, approximately 94% speak Han, a branch of the Sino-Tibetan language group (Cheng, 1987; Li & Thompson, 1981; Wong, 1988). The speakers of Sino-Tibetan languages reside in East and Southeast Asia. Chinese speakers of the Han language dominate the East Asian mainland. Han consists of seven different dialects (see Table 7.1). As indicated by Wang (1973), "It is the dialects along the southern coast, however, that have been carried to many parts of the world by Chinese emigrants" (p. 52), for example, Cantonese.

Li and Thompson (1981) point out that Mandarin and Cantonese, both Han languages, differ in many ways; however, because they are spoken in the same country, they are not referred to as different languages, but as dialects. Becoming fluent in either Mandarin or Cantonese spoken language does not necessarily mean that one can transfer or generalize naturally between these two dialects. Some dialects are closely related and some are mutually unintelligible. Furthermore, within the major dialects there is also diversity among the subdialects.

DeFrancis (1984, 1989) indicated that the main types of Chinese spoken language are Mandarin (about 750 million speakers), Wu or Shanghainese (about 85 million speakers), and Cantonese (about 50 million speakers). Mandarin is the standard Chinese language in three regions: People's Republic of China; Taiwan, Republic of China; and

TABLE 7.1
Linguistic Diversity Within the Chinese Language

Major Dialects of the Han Language Group	Percentage[a] of Speakers in Total Chinese Population in China
1. Mandarin[b]	70
2. Wu	7.5
3. Xiang	3.5
4. Gan	2
5. Hakka	2.5
6. Min Nan (e.g., Taiwanese)	2.5
7. Min Pei (e.g., Fuzhou)	1.2
8. Yue (e.g., Cantonese)	4.5

[a]Percentage obtained from Grimes (1992) as estimated in 1984.
[b]Mandarin is the national language for the Republic of China in Taiwan and the People's Republic of China.

Singapore. Mandarin is officially called *Putonghua* (Common Speech) in People's Republic of China, *Guoyu* (National Language) in Taiwan, Republic of China, and *Hwayu* (Chinese Language) in Singapore. The Chinese writing system that is based on Mandarin is also the written standard (DeFrancis, 1989).

Han is a tonal language, which means that each speech sound has a range of tones signifying different meanings. Each Han dialect varies in its tonal system and pronunciations. Taking Mandarin as an example, in each of its base syllables four tones are used to convey a variety of meanings. Other dialects have even more tones; for example, Cantonese has seven tones. The four tones in Mandarin are described by Wang (1973) as "rising, falling, level and dipping .... In addition to the tone every syllable must also have a nucleus to carry the tone, usually a vowel. The tone and the nucleus are the two obligatory components of the Chinese syllable" (p. 56).

Chinese spoken language and written language are two separate and different systems; hence, for all Chinese-dialect speakers, becoming literate in the Chinese language demands a mastery of a separate morphosyllabic writing system (DeFrancis, 1989), as well as their spoken language. It is very common for literate Chinese people to use the index finger of one hand to write in the palm of their other hand, while attempting to communicate with another literate person who does not speak the same dialect. In short, Chinese characters often denote the same meaning, but are pronounced differently in each dialect. Because spoken language and written language are two separate different systems, Chinese speakers of other than Mandarin dialect will not always find consistency in matching their spoken and written languages, that is, a one-on-one match between spoken syllable and Chinese print. It is common for local newspapers that are published for Cantonese speakers to often add additional characters in order to correspond with Cantonese spoken language.

Chinese Written Language

According to DeFrancis (1989), "The Chinese writing system must be classified as a syllabic system of writing. More specifically, it belongs to the subcategory that I have labeled meaning-plus-sound syllabic systems or morphosyllabic systems" (p. 115). He used the term *morphosyllabic* to serve two purposes. The first is to replace the terms *logographic, wordsyllabic,* and *morphemic* in order to reflect the nature of the majority of Chinese characters, the basis of the Chinese writing system, which represents both a single syllable and a single morpheme. The second purpose is to heighten the awareness of the public that over 80% to 90% of Chinese characters represent sound elements. Hence, the Chinese writing system is not just pictographic or ideographic as commonly believed by some Western writers. DeFrancis stated, "In actual fact, there never has been, and never can be, a full system of writing based on the pictographic or ideographic principle" (p. 114).

In comparison with the English language, DeFrancis (1989) suggested that although English graphemes represent phonemes, Chinese graphemes represent syllables, or syllabic phonemes as termed by Boodberg (1937). DeFrancis further stated that "There are in current Chinese some 1,277 syllabic phonemes counting tones, about 400 not counting tones ... there are 40 phonemes in English and 400 toneless and 1,300 tonal syllabic phonemes in Chinese" (p. 116).

As mentioned earlier, changing the tone of one syllable will alter its meaning significantly. For example, in the case of Mandarin, there are four different characters that represent four tones of a base syllable. Characters are the basis of Chinese writing system, called "zi" (字). In the case of the base syllable of /ch'ih/ there are four tones: The first tone indicates "eat" and is represented by a character of (吃); the second tone, "late," is (遲); the third tone, "tooth," is (齒); and, the fourth tone, "wing," is (翅). Adding to this complexity, within each tone of /ch'ih/ there are also anywhere from 11 to 23 characters representing that particular tone as illustrated in a dictionary. For example, the second tone of /ch'ih/ also conveys the following meanings of "hold" (持), "pond" (池), "spoon" (匙), and so on, up to 22 possible meanings. These examples reflect the diversity and challenge encountered by beginning readers as they attempt to master Chinese homophones, as well. It is even more challenging for many young Chinese Americans who are learning Chinese as a second language through a community-based Chinese school 2 hours a week. For example, in the spoken language, "碼頭" /ma-tou/ (pier) can be confused by "馬頭" /ma-tou/ (horse head), or " 議員 " /yi-yuan/ (councilman) for "一元" /yi-yuan/ (one dollar).

Over thousands of years, as Chinese written language evolved, it also yielded a large number of Chinese homophones, that is, words that sound the same but have different meanings, like read and red in English. In both oral and written form, these homophones can only be distinguished by specific contexts (Sheridan, 1983). The difficulty in identifying Chinese homophones was one of the major reasons against the Romanization of the Chinese language (Hoosain, 1986).

Chinese Character Formation.   In DeFrancis's (1989) analysis, there are both continuity and change in the evolution of the Chinese writing system represented by characters. He stated:

> Chinese characters were created by speakers of many different varieties of Chinese and often reflect the peculiarities of their speech. There have been historical changes in word order; and, the characters have been shuffled around to adapt to these changes. Characters have died out as the words that they represented have become obsolete. New characters and new combinations of characters have been created to express new words that have entered into the vocabulary. In common with all writing systems with a long history, the pronunciation of the symbols has changed greatly over time. (p. 95)

Chinese characters are formed on the basis of six general principles or Liu-Shu (六書) (see Table 7.2). Chinese writings were found engraved in tortoise shells and ox bones dated back to 1200 BC. The evolution of Chinese characters stemmed from the shell and bone scripts to modern standard characters over thousands of years (DeFrancis, 1989; Wang, 1973). Due to the dialectical differences, the sounds and shapes of these characters have undergone certain changes, but the principles of character formation and internal structure remained fairly stable. For example, of the 2,000 to 3,000 characters that have been found on ancient tortoise shells and ox bones, about half can still be read today (Wang, 1973).

Each character is constructed through specific strokes, and Wang (1973) indicated that "There are approximately 20 distinct strokes in the language, so that strokes are the closest counterparts to the 26 letters of the Latin alphabet" (p. 53). Early in their schooling, Chinese

TABLE 7.2
Description of Chinese Character Formations

Six Categories	Brief Descriptions and Examples
1. Pictographs 象形 (Hsiang Hsing)	Characters formed on the basis of pictures, marks made by creatures, or objects. For example, Fish:
2. Ideographs 指事 (Chih Shih)	Characters formed by various kinds of substitution to convey an idea or event in a metaphorical way. For example, Fight: It is formed by drawing two people fighting using weapons.
3. Compound ideographs 會意 (Hui I)	Characters formed by combining two or more pictographs and/or ideographs to convey abstract ideas or events. For example: Double/Pair: It is formed by having two birds held in one hand.
4. Phonetic compound 形聲 (Hsing Sheng)	Characters formed by two parts: a radical dictates the meaning or category; a phonetic the pronunciation. For example, Dog: It is formed by a radical of " 犭 " indicating the shape of a dog, and a phonetic " 句 " the bark of a dog.
5. Loan characters	Characters formed by assigning a new meaning or idea to an existing character that share the same pronunciation to address the shortage of Chinese characters. For example,

(continued on next page)

TABLE 7.2 *(continued)*

Six Categories	Brief Descriptions and Examples
假借 (Chia Chieh)	" 北 " (north) was loaned from " 背 " (back) which borrowed from the idea that the back of the house is usually facing north. Ideally, Chinese houses will locate in north while facing the south.
6. Analogous characters 轉注 (Chuan Chu)	Characters formed at different time and different geographic locations to convey similar ideas or meaning. They often share an identical radical but different phonetic. For example, " 父 " (Father/Dad) and " 爸 " (papa) are analogous characters. In " 爸 " the phonetic " 巴 " /ba/ denote the speech sound. Each one defines the other.

Note. The drawing and examples are adopted from Chen (1977).

students learn to write Chinese characters following a specific order or sequence, often through a laborious process to achieve mastery in handwriting and calligraphy. The Chinese character " 永 " /yung/ (eternal) symbolizes eight basic strokes used in many Chinese characters and is commonly used in school or home practices for calligraphy writing. Chinese calligraphy is a highly valued and "cultivated art form that has long been prized in Chinese culture, much as painting is valued in the Western world" (Wang, 1973, p. 53). Table 7.2 provides a brief description of how Chinese characters evolved.

The first three groups of characters, pictographs, ideographs, and compound ideographs, are the earliest Chinese primitive scripts. They represent interesting features of early attempts to represent concrete objects or the idea of Chinese written symbols. However, in their original forms, they consisted of a relatively small percentage of all characters because there were limitations in creating sufficient numbers of symbols for concrete objects and abstract ideas.

The fourth category of characters, phonetic compounds, represents about 80% to 90% of all Chinese characters. This is the reason DeFrancis (1989) used the term *morphosyllabic* to describe Chinese writing system as stated earlier. The radicals, or " 部首 " *bu-shou*, which signifies meaning, are also characters formed as pictographs. Modern Chinese dictionaries are arranged by radicals, along with the numbers of the strokes, for users to look up Chinese characters or words. There are approximately 189 to 214 radicals in use today (Wang, 1973).

Characters formed within the category of phonetic compound provide potential semantic as well as phonetic clues to readers. For example, the characters associated with tree or log will likely share a bu-shou, " 木 " /mu/ (log) and characters associated with water will have another bu-shou of " 氵 " /swuei/ (water). The large percentage of phonetic compounds within the Chinese written system also reflects the reliance on the tonal sound feature of the Chinese language.

Due to shifting or changing in pronunciation of Chinese spoken languages over thousands of years, the sound clues used in phonetic compounds may or may not be a reliable source for modern readers to use for deciphering unknown characters or words. However, readers continue to access the sound clues in characters when necessary (Chang, Hung, & Tzeng, 1992; Tzeng, 1983; Tzeng, Hung, & Wang, 1977). For example, among Chinese people, the most common reading strategies to decipher unknown characters are to utilize the possible sound clues as follows:

- If two graphic components of a character are side by side, the strategy is to read the one on either side.
- If the character is formed by layers, the strategy is to try the sound clue presented in the center.

The last two categories of characters shown in Table 7.2 represent variations in character formation needed to address the functional use of existing characters or radicals to cope with expansion of Chinese written language.

Chinese Characters Versus Chinese Words. Chinese characters more closely resemble a morpheme in English, not an English "word." In the Chinese language, words are called " 詞 " /tz'u/ whereas the characters are called " 字 " /zi/. Although there are some one-character words, most modern Chinese spoken words are formed by two- or three-character words. For example, the word for "park" in Chinese is a two-character-word (公園) formed by the characters for "public" (公) and "garden" (園). The word for "library" in Chinese is a three-character word (圖書館) formed by the characters for "picture" (圖), "book" (書), and "building" (館).

Furthermore, each of the characters within any multiple-character words can also be combined with other character(s) to form new compound words, such as "book-store" (書店), or "picture-draw-book" (圖畫書) (picture storybook). Such a morphological feature of Chinese "word" formation can both enhance and challenge beginning readers. A detailed description of such challenges is presented in the section on reading: acquisition and vocabulary development.

Chinese Writing and Phonetic Systems. The Chinese writing system currently in use is represented by two closely linked versions: the traditional and simplified writing systems. The effort to simplify Chinese characters can be traced back in the early 1930s (Yang, 1996). Since the mid-1950s, the People's Republic of China (PRC) has systematically simplified a large number of characters in an attempt to make Chinese written language easier to read and write. Currently, schools in Taiwan, Republic of China (ROC), Hong Kong, and most of the overseas Chinese-language schools in North America continue to use the traditional writing system. The PRC and Singapore have adopted the simplified writing system. Chinese-language programs in major universities in North American tend to introduce both writing systems to their students; and, it is expected that all students who have completed 2 years of study in any reputable Chinese program in this country will be able to read both the traditional and simplified writing systems (Sun, 1996).

Because the Chinese spoken and written languages are two separate systems, two phonetic systems have been developed and adopted to assist beginning readers to access Chinese print. For example, the *Pinyin system* (spell sound), using the Roman alphabet, was developed and used in the PRC. The *Zhuyin system* (denote sound), formed by non-Roman phonetic symbols, was developed and used in Taiwan, ROC. The Zhuyin system was aimed at promoting the pronunciation of the national language, Mandarin, in Taiwan, ROC. Textbooks or children's readers published in Taiwan for the primary grades are often printed either solely in Zhuyin symbols or with each text item accompanied by Zhuyin symbols for pronouncing each of the characters. It is common for preschoolers in Taiwan, ROC, to have their early reading experiences in the Zhuyin system.

In sum, the major points presented in this section are:

- Chinese speakers represent heterogeneous groups of people from different regions with different social and cultural histories.
- Although Chinese-language dialects vary greatly between as well as among major dialect groups, they do have a common written language. When literate Chinese are unable to communicate orally, they often rely on written forms to convey meaning when communicating among different Chinese dialect groups.
- Over 80% to 90% of Chinese characters are formed on the basis of combining both semantic and phonetic clues, such as those formed

by the principle of *phonetic compounds*. Hence, the Chinese writing system can be better described as a morphosyllabic rather than as a logographic or morphemic writing system.

- Chinese words are formed differently from English words. Chinese characters are more closely related to English morphemes. Chinese spoken words often consist of more than one character.
- Currently there are two phonetic and two writing systems used among Chinese in different parts of the world.

SELECTED ORTHOGRAPHIC EFFECT OF CHINESE LANGUAGE ON ACADEMIC DEVELOPMENT

This section highlights the features of the Chinese language that differ from English, and those features of the Chinese writing system that were observed to have an influence on literacy and numeracy development among individuals becoming literate in Chinese language. A generic term, *Chinese language*, is used in the discussions in this section to indicate that all Chinese native speakers, regardless of specific dialects, are likely subjected to similar Chinese orthographic effect as highlighted in each of the following areas. Implications and recommendations for classroom instruction in the academic areas of mathematics, writing, and reading are also presented.

Mathematics: The Influence of Chinese Language on Place-Value Understanding

The discussion of Chinese orthographic effect on students' mathematical performance is drawn from research conducted by Miura and her associates (Miura, 1987; Miura, Kim, Chang, & Okamoto, 1988; Miura & Okamoto, 1995). These scholars have claimed that numbers are inseparable from language and that individuals becoming literate in Asian languages that have roots in ancient Chinese, such as Chinese, Japanese, and Korean, share a common numerical language structure. In essence, the numerical names in these three languages are congruent with the traditional base 10 numeration system. According to Miura and Okamoto (1995, cited in National Council of Teachers of Mathematics (NCTM), 1989):

> In this system, the value of a given digit in a multidigit numeral depends on the face value of the digit (0 through 9) and on its position in the numeral; the value of each position increases by powers of 10 from right to left. In learning the counting sequence, children must memorize a base sequence of counting words. Higher numbers of the sequence are generated accord-

ing to a set of rules (Gelman & Gallistel, 1978), and in the Base 10 system, higher members of the sequence are generated by multiples of 10. Understanding place value, the meaning assigned to individual digits in a multi-digit numeral, is a crucial step in children's construction of number concepts. (p. 17)

This group of researchers argued that spoken numerals (e.g., eleven, twenty, thirty) in an alphabetic language such as English are not congruent with the base 10 system; that is, the elements of tens and ones contained in these numerals are not apparent in the spoken word. Consequently, an alphabetic language system may not provide sufficient scaffolding for some children as they advance from single digits to multidigit concepts in learning place value. In comparison, children from Asian language groups whose numerals are congruent with the base 10 system benefit more readily from the relationship between spoken numerals and the concepts. For example, the numeral 11 is spoken as ten-one, 20 as two-tens, and 31 as three-tens-one, and so on. The advantage is that the spoken numerals correspond with the written form; hence, these Chinese/Asian American children are able to tap into their memory of number names from one to ten and to generate the remaining numbers using the base 10 system (Miller, Smith, Zhu, & Zhang, 1995; Miura & Okamoto, 1995).

Miura and Okamoto (1995) conducted studies and have hypothesized that the "variations in the number naming systems were expected to influence children's cognitive representation of number ... and children whose cognitive representation of number reflected the Base 10 system would have a better understanding of place-value concepts" (p. 18). Their research compared various language groups, and their findings support the claim that the number counting system may contribute to differences in mathematics performance between students from Asian language groups and other language groups.

The implications for teaching suggested by Miura and Okamoto (1995) are that whenever possible, it is important for Chinese/Asian American students to learn number concepts in their primary language, or that these concepts be reinforced in their primary language. This may seem contrary to common belief and school practices that say that because Chinese/Asian American students tend to perform well in mathematics, they can be mainstreamed early into an English-only environment. Such an arbitrary decision may not be an optimal learning environment for some Chinese-speaking/ESL (English as a second language) learners who fail to perform well in mathematics as expected. These students could be affected by a lack of understanding of the abstract and academic concepts presented orally in English. They could also fail to grasp the basic concept of place value. In short, mathematics is a language-based subject area; hence, it is critical to provide these Chinese-speaking students math instruction in their primary language.

Based on a research study conducted among inner-city Chinese American LEP students and their LEP parents (Chang, Lai, & Shimizu, 1995), parents reported feeling most comfortable when supervising mathematics homework; however, this did not extend to word problems written in English. A word of caution: It is likely that some of these parents will have idiosyncratic approaches to computing and solving mathematics problems. For some students, the way mathematical computations and problem-solving steps have been introduced at home may be different from their teacher's approach, thus creating confusion for the child. For example, parents may not teach long division or fractions in the same steps presented in a classroom. Prior to formal assessment of these children in math, it would be useful to consider these possible sources that contribute to students' learning blocks.

Writing: Thought Processes and Grammar

Chinese and English languages differ not only in sounds and word formations, they also differ in syntax, such as combining words to form sentences and discourse style. Li and Thompson (1976) claimed that Chinese is a topic-prominent language, and that English is a subject-prominent language with respect to how both languages structure their sentences. Tsao (1980) argued that in a Chinese written discourse unit, the topic is more important than the subject. In other words, "the grammatical meaning of subject and predicate in Chinese is topic and comment, rather than actor and action" (Chao, 1968, p. 69). This insight may help teachers understand how some Chinese students use language in their rhetoric, particularly in essays.

Robert B. Kaplan (1966) first suggested that there are specific cultural thought patterns revealed through his extensive work in *contrastive rhetoric*, a form of comparative analysis of students' presentation of written materials for achieving specific purposes (cf. Connor & Kaplan, 1987). Though his work was subsequently challenged, the findings of modern contrastive rhetoric studies, centering around the social construction of knowledge within discourse communities, may sensitize teachers to enhance ESL writers' ability to meet the expectation of the English-speaking readers in selected contexts (Leki, 1991).

In contrast to subject-predicate sentence structure observed in English writing, the topic-comment structure of the Chinese written discourse unit consists of a topic chain, which can have more than one clause linked by a topic, and the subject of each clause bears some semantic relations to the topic. Such a writing practice may likely foster or reflect recursive or interactive thought processes. This is evident in analyzing written discourse produced in English language by Chinese-speaking ESL and LEP students in the beginning stages.

If our Chinese-speaking students are made aware of cultural and textual differences in rhetoric tradition between English and Chinese, it may help them establish positive self-concept (Leki, 1991) when experiencing difficulty in timed essay examination. In fact, many Chinese-speaking teacher education students face challenges in passing the written portion of the California Basic Educational Skills Test (CBEST), but they have little or no difficulty passing the mathematics of the CBEST.

Furthermore, the use of English verb tenses and inflections of word endings are all new entities for Chinese speakers. Chinese spoken language is essentially noninflective, and verbs have no morphological inflection. Chinese characters remain intact in any written form or context regardless of syntactical changes. Tzeng (1983) stated, "Grammatical marking elements, such as tense, number, gender, and so on, are introduced by adding other morpheme characters rather than modifying the form of a particular character" (p. 79). In addition, tense and mood are not marked in Chinese written language as they are in English (Tsao, 1980). However, Chinese has rich aspect markers that indicate events completed or an action being carried out, and more (Comrie, 1976). Chinese-speaking individuals can be expected to produced oral or written statements with inconsistent use of verb tense and word endings signifying plural nouns or third-person singular verbs, and so on.

It is also common for many ESL or LEP students to use English articles, such as "a," "an," and "the," randomly in both speech and written work because articles are not used in Chinese spoken and written language. In addition, the use of gender-specific pronouns is not required in Chinese spoken language, so it is also common even for educated adults to mix he and she in conversations, although they can usually monitor the correct use in written language. Modern Chinese written language uses a radical " 女 " signifying female to distinguish gender difference in personal pronouns. In addition, the use of sentences and the use of punctuation marks are essentially Western concepts that are imposed on the Chinese written language.

The orthographic differences observed between the Chinese and English languages suggest that English writing mechanics need to be introduced to these learners in meaningful contexts through interactive teaching and frequent modeling. During the transitional phases before they master English sentence structures, these students may be more likely to produce run-on sentences, influenced by Chinese written discourse style. The use of the semicolon may be one strategy to help some overcome run-on sentences initially before they become proficient in English language. A writer with a recursive thought process may not be able to easily break the flow of ideas into the concise and linear fashion of subject-predicate sentence structures required in English. Thus, may use the semicolon to overcome the transferring of their Chinese sentence or rhetoric structures during the initial phases of English writing. These students will need modeling and support through both process- and textual-oriented instruction to build their English written expression to an acceptable manner (Leki, 1991). Using webbing or concept-mapping skills (e.g., Buckley & Boyle, 1981; Heimlich & Pittelman, 1986) may be another way to help them transform recursive thoughts into a more linear outline format to construct their written work. In addition, the use of rubrics, or a set of criteria, in holistic scoring (e.g., Herman, Aschbacher, & Winters, 1992) for written work may also help these individuals pinpoint areas of need in their effort to gain mastery in different types of written genre.

Reading: Acquisition and Vocabulary Development

Monolingual Chinese children observed in Taiwan, ROC, learn about 3,000 new characters from official textbooks during their elementary school years. These characters will, in turn, generate more "multi-character words" as the children gradually become fluent readers. It has been shown that by the end of the sixth grade, about 7,000 words have been introduced in elementary school textbooks in Taiwan, ROC (Stevenson et al., 1982). Elementary graduates are capable of reading daily newspapers with little or no difficulty, provided they have age-appropriate spoken vocabulary, general information, and information on current events. Similar to English readers, Chinese readers who have opportunities to develop general information, receptive and expressive vocabularies, and sufficient motivation are more likely to become literate in the Chinese language, as observed in different reading research studies conducted among Chinese children in Taiwan, ROC, and Singapore (Chang et al., 1992; Lee, Chang, Tzeng, Hung, & Wee, 1991; Stevenson et al., 1982).

Just as English readers use various language-cuing systems, such as syntactic, semantic, sound, and graphic cues, to construct meaning from print, monolingual Chinese readers also use language-cuing systems (Chang et al., 1992; Goodman, Watson, & Burke, 1987). However, research conducted among monolingual Chinese beginning readers in Taiwan, ROC (Chang et al., 1992), found that the Chinese writing system imposes additional challenges to these readers. Specifically, graphically presented Chinese spoken words are often displayed without apparent word boundaries. This differs significantly from English words in print. For example, in an English sentence such as "Children like to read story books," each word is separated by a space in print, so we know that the word for "children" starts with the letter "c" and ends with "n." However, in a Chinese written sentence, " 兒童喜歡讀故事書 " each character within a string of multicharacter words is equally spaced and displayed with any other character used in forming a sentence. Unless readers are aware of the two or three characters that form a specific word, it is a challenge to parse among them to identify word boundaries. For beginning readers, Chinese textbooks adopted in Singapore underline word boundaries in written passages.

Identifying any Chinese word among seemingly disjoined characters within a statement can be a difficult task for many beginning readers or any reader who does not recognize many characters or words. Consequently, these readers are more likely to randomly parse or segment among equally spaced characters while identifying word boundaries, particularly when multicharacter words are involved. This is called " 斷詞 " /tuan-tz'u/ in Chinese. Such random parsing will lead the reader to omit, insert, or substitute character(s) to form other semantically related or unrelated words or nonwords (see Chang et al., 1992). Subsequently, many readers who have difficulty parsing are likely to produce different words that either disrupt their meaning construction or only make sense in the context of improvised and reconstructed story lines. Such a phenomenon can also be observed among adult fluent readers while attempting to parse unfamiliar words that were formed by a direct translation of modern television language, such as " 叩應 " (call in), or " 作秀 " (show). If readers are not familiar with the current language used in a particular cultural context, they may not understand the intended meaning by parsing incorrectly among a string of characters.

Findings from this reading research conducted among beginning readers also suggest that reading behaviors observed among fluent Chinese adult readers may not be generalized to beginning readers (Chang et al., 1992). In contrast to adult fluent readers, beginning readers may not yet have the support of essential factors to construct meaning effectively from print. These essential factors include, but may not be limited to:

- Numbers of known sight words.

- Orthographic knowledge of character formations.
- General information acquired from their daily experiences.
- Speed for visual word recognition.
- Knowledge of a set of possible Chinese compound words that are formed by the same one character.
- Knowledge of a variety of classifiers and functional words.
- Awareness of commonly used literary or book language, or genre in print.
- Exposure to print on a regular basis.
- Awareness of story concepts.

These factors suggest that adult and beginning readers differ in their metalinguistic abilities, level of general information, and levels of proficiency in spoken and written vocabulary as well as in literary language.

A summary of observations made regarding language and literacy practices within an inner-city Chinese American community is provided next. The following section is intended to heighten teachers' awareness of the ways they may incorporate home and community literacy practices into their classroom literacy instruction to actively bridge the gap between school and home languages and cultures.

A SOCIOCULTURAL PERSPECTIVE OF THE HOME– COMMUNITY–SCHOOL-BASED LEARNING ENVIRONMENT OF INNER-CITY CHINESE AMERICAN STUDENTS

Society and literature often depict Asian American students as high-achievers; however, there are Asian American students who do not excel academically. The following discussion on selected issues is based on research findings obtained from a group of Chinese students who were poor, LEP, and mildly learning disabled (LD) or LEP + LD. It is important for all teachers to be keenly aware of all students' educational needs and workable methods available in generating optimal learning opportunities, particularly for Chinese/Asian American students who were poor, LEP, and mildly LD or LEP + LD. Furthermore, most of the contents presented in this section can be extended to a broad group of Chinese/Asian American students who are at risk of academic failure in inner-city schools.

Not all Asian American students are high-achievers, nor do they all have the home support necessary to succeed academically (Chang, 1995c; Suzuki, 1989). Moreover, the misconception and overgeneralization of all Asians being "model minority students" may ultimately mask teachers' responsibility of being aware of these students' needs and being prepared to address the needs of those who are not model students. A sociocultural perspective of the optimal learning environments of these students across home, community, and school as observed in one group of inner-city Chinese students (see Table 7.3) and a description of the incongruence observed between inner-city home practices and school expectations (see Table 7.4) may provide teachers with another view from which to examine their own beliefs, expectation, and common practices in teaching.

For inner-city Chinese American students, as with most students, their community is an integral part of their learning environment. The importance of multiple sites of learning (Chang, 1993) and the role these literacy learning contexts play in sustaining Chinese American students' school learning were the findings of a longitudinal study of a group of Chinese American students in northern California (Chang, 1995a). The conclusions were validated in another study involving Chinese American students at risk of academic failure in New York City (Chang, Fung, & Shimizu, 1996). The research findings suggested that Chinese LEP + LD children who had social and literacy support from at least two of three components, home, school, and community, tended to accomplish their school learning (Chang, 1993, 1995a). Thus, the term *multiple sites of learning* was further understood (Chang et al., 1996) to include any site where these children engaged in types of activities that:

1. Enhanced their ability to complete teacher-assigned homework.
2. Provided opportunities for them to borrow books or read newspapers and magazines and to listen to stories.
3. Helped them acquire the English language.
4. Engaged them in field trips to expand their social and learning experiences.
5. Involved them in discussions of experiences and events.
6. Allowed them to acquire information from hands-on activities.
7. Introduced them to different genres of Chinese children's literature, such as rhymes, folktales, stories, and narratives, as well as culture, value, and the Chinese written language. (p. 11)

The findings also indicated that literacy learning beyond school in various community-based sites enhanced LEP + LD children's maintenance of academic skills when their LEP parents were unable to assist them in completing their homework assignments.

Table 7.3 presents a composite of an optimal learning environment that facilitated the language and literacy development of inner-city Chinese American students as observed from research findings. The intent

TABLE 7.3

**A Brief Description of an Optimal Learning Environment
Related to Inner-City Chinese American Students**

Home	*Community*	*School*
• Parent(s) sustained their Chinese culture while respecting teachers and value school education	• Various social organizations provided after-school and weekend programs to support school learning.	• School personnel were sensitive to and addressed issues of diversity and provided bilingual services, such as parent liaisons or interpreters, to encourage and assist parents in attending school functions.
• Parents were willing to sacrifice their personal lives in order to pay the expenses related to children's language and literacy development by sending their child to after-school programs.	• The newly arrived immigrants had opportunities to work. • The volunteers and/or instructional staff members extended support to the newly arrived students and families.	• Chinese bilingual education programs were an option for LEP students.
• Parents were able to work with a teacher, specialist, or community instructional staff to reinforce concepts acquired by their child for school learning.	• Agencies or other organizations, ethnic Chinese magazines, newspapers, and/or TV programs provided information related to school practices and noncommercial related instructional materials and activities.	• Teachers assigned homework utilizing home language and resources and parents are encouraged and assisted in becoming involved. • Teachers and/or resource specialists reached out to LEP families by forging partnerships directly with parents or through a community instructional staff.
• Parents monitored or assisted with their child's homework completion and school attendance.		
• Parents engaged their children in daily conversations regularly in their native language.	• Agencies or organizations provided social activities and encouraged parents to allow their child to participate in order to help children broaden their knowledge about their surroundings.	• Teachers, LD and/or language specialists collaborated regularly to support children with LEP + LD within their classrooms.

TABLE 7.4
Inner-City Home Practices That Are Incongruent
With Expected School Behavior

Home Practices	School Practices
1. Children are oriented to be humble, quiet, obedient, respectful, and to passively follow adults/teachers' advice. In general, parents do not carry on extensive conversations with their children.	1. Students are expected to actively participate in and contribute to class discussions, voice their views/opinions, and demonstrate independence in decision-making process.
2. Children are expected to do homework each night following teachers' assignments. Many parents do not know how to utilize daily routines to generate opportunities for ideas/concepts.	2. Students are not mandated to have major homework each night. The types of homework assigned by teachers may or may not (a) tap into the child's home language or resources, and (b) have a clear guideline or direction for parents.
3. It is common for some inner-city ethnic Chinese parents to reject bilingual education fearing interference with learning English language. Children are expected to master English language proficiency in school. Parents do not, in general, understand the role of home language in English language and literacy development. Most of them, however, will send their child to attend community-based Chinese-language school or program in their attempt to maintain Chinese culture and identity. However, once a child is identified as LEP + LD, he or she is withdrawn from such an activity.	3. Students may or may not have an option to enroll in a Chinese bilingual classroom. It is still common for teachers, specialists, and school administrators to inform parents to use English at home with their child even though the parents may not be proficient in English. Within the school sites that have Chinese bilingual education programs, seeking administrative and/or collegial support for Chinese bilingual teachers is still a challenge. The quality of bilingual education programs is often affected by multiple factors, such as a shortage of teachers and/or instructional materials, and the lack of a clearly defined curriculum.
4. Children are oriented to learn academic skills through rote memory, and their learning centers around the school curriculum and textbooks.	4. Students are expected to adapt to various learning strategies and literacy material beyond schools.
5. Children are not encouraged to participate in nonacademically oriented social activities or events outside of school. Parents may not understand the value of such activities with respect to developing general information that forms the basis for reading comprehension and literacy learning.	5. Students are expected to have age-appropriate levels of general information as demonstrated among children from middle-class environments.
	6. School placement of students with LEP + LD do not often reflect sensitivity to the unique needs of

6. Children are expected to follow the teachers' guidance because teachers are the experts in school learning. Most of these parents felt ill-equipped or uncomfortable providing suggestions or recommendations that might assist their child's learning.

7. Parents respect schools as authorities in making the best decision for their child.

8. Parents are discouraged from attending school events or classroom activities due to a lack of an interpreter and time; many of the parents held two or three jobs to support the family. Many of them were unfamiliar with American school culture and practice.

individual students. Being LEP, LD, quiet, and cooperative in school often leads many of these students to have missed learning opportunities in their typical school days due to fragmented language and/or academic interventions.

7. Students with LEP + LD are often placed in ESL classes on entering middle school with little or no language and academic support. Many of them receive final grades of B by attending classes each day and turning in homework assignments. Furthermore, it is common for them to remain as LEP with little English reading comprehension skills and little or no home-language proficiency when reaching eighth grade.

8. With or without interpreters, parents are expected to be an integral part of home–school partnership to participate in school events, conferences, and classroom activities. Indicators for parental involvement were generally based on middle-class home practices.

---

of Table 7.3 is to help teachers gain insights into generating an optimal learning environment across home, school, and community to promote school learning for the benefit of these inner-city students.

Table 7.4 reveals the incongruence between home and school practices. Items presented here are likely to create misunderstandings between parents and teachers/administrators, with no fault on either side. These parents, for example, trusted teachers and school administrators because they are experts in providing the best instructional programs and practices for their children, whereas in reality, many of these inner-city students may easily fall through the cracks due to missed learning opportunities (Chang, 1995b). In addition, Chinese families usually overemphasize academic learning, and some may overlook the social growth of their children, particularly in attending nonacademically related events or field trips. This is particularly detrimental to these inner-city children who have less opportunities to acquire general information when compared with their English-speaking peers.

Open communication between inner-city parents and school personnel is also likely to be affected by a lack of a common language or cultural context to mediate differences. The findings from a home–community–school-based case study of inner-city Chinese American students with LEP + LD (Chang, 1993, 1995a) suggested that children's opportunities to learn were primarily generated through teachers, LD resource specialists, or parents who were able to take the initiative in collaborating across home, community, and school to meet the needs of the child. The general characteristics of such collaboration can be identified as follows:

- Teachers, LD resource specialists, and parents demonstrated a positive belief and attitude about the target student's ability to learn.
- Teachers or LD resource specialists demonstrated an ability to utilize more interactive or experiential approaches in one-to-one or small-group instruction in which academic skills were introduced within meaningful contexts. This particular approach prevents many Chinese American children's inevitable destiny to be word-callers with little or no reading comprehension or math reasoning ability.
- An LD resource specialist demonstrated an ability to team with a homeroom teacher (bilingual, English-language development, or regular education) and/or with a speech language specialist to provide more connected rather than disjoined social or academic interventions. This approach provides additional support, such as peer resources for these children who desperately need connected services, rather than a classroom experience disrupted by various pull-out based remedial services.
- Teachers, LD resource specialists, or parents demonstrated an ability to contact instructional personnel across the Chinese student's multiple literacy learning sites (e.g., community-based Chinese language schools, or after-school programs sponsored by the YMCA or public libraries).
- Teachers and LD resource specialists demonstrated an ability to involve Chinese LEP parents in using home language or resources. This approach openly acknowledged the LEP parents as resources and their culture and language as an integral part of school learning. In addition, multiple literacy was accepted as a valid base or practice to support school learning.

The characteristics of teachers and LD resource specialists who were effective in serving inner-city Chinese American students may be summarized as those who (a) basically believed that all children can learn, (b) utilized parents, the student's home language, and home resources and made them an integral part of school learning, and (c) incorporated multiple literacy in student's formal school curriculum whenever possible. In addition, Chinese children who maintained the academic progress were those who had opportunities to engage in hands-on activities with meaningful instructional dialogues, to experience field trips to acquire general information about their world, and to listen to a variety of genres in both languages at a level they could enjoy.

SUMMARY

The research conducted among inner-city Chinese American students who were considered at risk or identified as learning disabled has been scarce, particularly when conceptualized from a sociocultural perspective to examine their overall language and literacy environment across home, school, and community. The current studies conducted among these inner-city children reveal the incongruence between home and school practices and their missed learning opportunities. The findings heighten our awareness of these children's undesirable educational reality in our schools. However, the studies also suggest that teachers, resource specialists, and instructional staff members can all be resourceful and successful in reaching out to culturally and linguistically diverse students to generate an optimal learning environment for the inner-city poor.

To reiterate, teachers are highly valued and respected within the Chinese culture, both in the home and in the community. The field observations suggest that Chinese students, in general, are well behaved, eager to learn, and diligent about schoolwork (Chang, 1995b). In addition, parents show their support by closely monitoring their children's homework completion and school attendance. Inner-city Chinese American students and their families face unique challenges that are influenced by socioeconomic as well as language factors. Parents of these students believe strongly that their children need to master the English language, and they are willing to make sacrifices to support their children's school education. Language differences for many Chinese American students and families need not be a barrier for communication or learning. When utilized and connected properly, they are an important resource to support these students' school learning. Even though the Chinese language may influence certain learners' reading and writing performance, in general the academic concepts acquired through the Chinese language are transferable to school learning.

Community support is evident in forms that are conducive to school learning; moreover, various forms of literacy learning sites are available to inner-city students. In cases where Chinese American students received optimal support from home, community, and school, it was revealed that both general- and special-education teachers and parents recognized and fully utilized resources available in three interrelated home–school–community learning environments.

■ ACTIVITIES

1. To learn about the multiple sites of literacy learning among your inner-city, urban, or other Chinese/Chinese American students, you might conduct a survey of their typical day. For example, what do they do before and after school, during holidays and weekends, and so on?
2. To observe a child's attempt to identify Chinese word boundaries, you might tape the oral reading from a meaningful story slightly above his or her current reading level, analyze how the child deciphers the characters and words, and then study his or her reading patterns by recording how the child adds, deletes, omits, or substitutes characters in an attempt to make sense from reading while identifying Chinese word boundaries.
3. To examine the thought patterns in expository writing, you might conduct written discourse analysis of different groups of Chinese children, such as native Chinese versus English speakers, to reveal how, collectively, each group uses the English language to express ideas and thoughts.

SUGGESTED READINGS

Chang, J. M. (2003). Multilevel collaboration for English learners: An Asian American Perspective. In G. G. Garcia (Ed.), *English Learners: Reaching the highest level of English literacy* (pp. 259–285). Neward, DE: International Reading Association.

Cheng, L. L. (1995). *Integrating language and learning for inclusion: An Asian Pacific focus.* San Diego: Singular.

DeFrancis, J. (1984). *The Chinese language: Fact and fantasy.* Honolulu: University of Hawaii Press.

Li, W., Gaffney, J. S. , & Packard,, J. L. (Eds.). (2002). *Chinese children's reading acquisition: Theoretical and pedagogical issues.* Boston: Kluwer Academic.

Wang, S. Y. (1973, February). Chinese language. *Scientific American*, pp. 50–60.

REFERENCES

Boodberg, P. A. (1937). Some proleptical remarks on the evolution of archaic Chinese. *Harvard Journal of Asiatic Studies*, 2, 329–372.

Buckley, M. H., & Boyle, O. (1981). *Mapping the writing journey* (Curriculum Publication No. 15). Berkeley: University of California, Bay Area Writing Project.

Chang, J. M. (1993). A home-school-community-based conceptualization of LEP students with learning disabilities: Implications from a Chinese-American study. In J. Gomez & O. Shabak (Eds.), *The Proceedings of the Third National Research Symposium on Limited English Proficient Students; Issues: Focus on middle and high school issues* (Vol. 2, pp. 713–736). Washington, DC: U.S. Department of Education, Office of Bilingual Education and Language Minority Affairs.

Chang, J. M. (1995a). Asian students in special education: A need for multidimensional collaboration. In S. Walker, K. A. Turner, M. Haile-Michael, A. Vincent, & M. D. Miles (Eds.), *Disability and diversity: New leadership for a new era* (pp. 81–88). Washington, DC: President's Committee on Employment of People with Disabilities in collaboration with the Howard University Research and Training Center.

Chang, J. M. (1995b). LEP, LD, poor, and missed learning opportunities: A case of inner-city Chinese-American children. In L. L. Cheng (Ed.), *Integrating language and learning: An Asian Pacific Focus* (pp. 31–59). San Diego: Singular.

Chang, J. M. (1995c). When they are not Asian American model students ... *Focus on Diversity*, 5(3), 5–7.

Chang, J. M., Fung, G., & Shimizu, W. (1996). Literacy support across multiple sites: Experiences of Chinese American LEP children in inner cities. *NABE News*, 19(7), 11–13.

Chang, J. M., Hung, D. L., & Tzeng, O. J. L. (1992). Miscue analysis of Chinese children's reading behaviors at the entry level. *Journal of Chinese Linguistics*, 20(1), 120–158.

Chang, J. M., Lai, A., & Shimizu, W. (1995). LEP parents as resources: Generating opportunity-to-learn beyond schools through parental involvement. In L. L. Cheng (Ed.), *Integrating language and learning for inclusion: An Asian Pacific focus*. San Diego: Singular.

Chao, Y. R. (1968). *A grammar of spoken Chinese*. Berkeley: University of California Press.

Chen, C. C. (1977). *Interesting Chinese characters*. Taipei, Taiwan: Student Press.

Cheng, L. R. L. (1987). *Assessing Asian language performance: Guidelines for evaluating Limited-English Proficient students*. Rockville, MD: Aspen.

Comrie, B. (1976). *Aspect*. Cambridge, MA: Harvard University Press.

Connor, U., & Kaplan, R. B. (Eds.). (1987). *Writing across languages: Analysis of L2 texts*. Reading, MA: Addison-Wesley.

DeFrancis, J. (1984). *The Chinese language: Fact and fantasy*. Honolulu: University of Hawaii Press.

DeFrancis, J. (1989). *Visible speech: The diverse oneness of writing systems*. Honolulu: University of Hawaii Press.

Gelman, R., & Gallistel, C. R. (1978). *The child's understanding of number*. Cambridge, MA: Harvard University Press.

Goodman, Y., Watson, D. J., & Burke, C. (1987). *Reading miscue inventory: Alternative procedures*. New York: Richard C. Owen.

Grimes, B. F. (1992). *Ethnologue language of the world* (12th ed.). Dallas, TX: Summer Institute of Linguistics.

Guthrie, G. P. (1985). *A school divided: An ethnography of bilingual education in a Chinese community*. Hillsdale, NJ: Lawrence Erlbaum Associates.

Heimlich, J. E., & Pittelman, S. D. (1986). *Semantic mapping: Classroom applications*. Newark, DE: International Reading Association.

Herman, J. L., Aschbacher, P. R., & Winters, L. (1992). *A practical guide to alternative assessment*. Alexandria, VA: Association for Supervision and Curriculum Development.

Hoosain, R. (1986). Perceptual processes of the Chinese. In M. H. Bond (Ed.), *The psychology of the Chinese people* (pp. 38–72). Hong Kong: Oxford University Press.

Kaplan, R. B. (1996). Cultural thought patterns in intercultural education. *Language Learning, 16*(1 & 2), 1–20.

Lee, W. L., Chang, J. M., Tzeng, O. J. L., Hung, D. L., & Wee, G. C. (1991, November). *Phonemic awareness and learning to read a logographic script*. Paper presented at the 42nd Annual Conference of the Orton Dyslexia Society, Portland, OR.

Leki, I. (1991). Twenty-five years of constrastive rhetoric: Text analysis and writing pedagogies. *TESOL Quarterly, 25*(1), 123–143.

Li, C. N., & Thompson, S. A. (1976). Subject and topic: A new typology of language. In C. N. Li (Ed.), *Subject and topic* (pp. 457–489). New York: Academic Press.

Li, C. N., & Thompson, S. A. (1981). *Mandarin Chinese: A functional reference grammar*. Berkeley: University of California Press.

Miller, K. F., Smith, C. M., Zhu, J., & Zhang, H. (1995). Preschool origins of cross-national differences in mathematical competence: The role of number-naming systems. *Psychological Science, 79*, 79–82.

Miura, I. T. (1987). Mathematics achievement as a function of language. *Journal of Educational Psychology, 79*, 79–82.

Miura, I. T., Kim, C. C., Chang, C.-M., & Okamoto, Y. (1988). Effects of language characteristics on children's cognitive representation of number: Cross-national comparisons. *Child Development, 59*, 1445–1450.

Miura, I. T., & Okamoto, Y. (1995). The influence of number language characteristics on mathematics understanding and performance. *NABE News, 18*(8), 17–18, 20.

National Council of Teachers of Mathematics. (1989). *Curriculum and evaluation standards for school mathematics*. Reston, VA: Author.

Sheridan, E. M. (1983). *Ideographs, syllabaries, and alphabets: Reading as information processing in different writing systems*. South Bend: Indiana University, Division of Education. (ERIC Document Reproduction Service No. ED 192 263)

Stevenson, H. W., Stigler, J. W., Lucker, G. W., Lee, S. Y., Hsu, C. C., & Kitamura, S. (1982). Reading disabilities: The case of Chinese, Japanese, and English. *Child Development, 53*, 1164–1181.

Sun, C. (1996). Writing styles, technologies and their implications. In J. M. Chang & D. Lin (Eds.), *The fourth annual conference proceedings: Balancing academic achievement & social growth* (p. 18). Rockville, MD: Chinese American Educational Research & Development Association.

Suzuki, B. H. (1989). Asian Americans as the "model minority": Outdoing Whites? Or media hype? *Change, 24*, 12–19.

Tsao, F. F. (1980). *Sentences in English and Chinese: An exploration of some basic syntactic differences*. Paper in honor of Professor Lin Yu-K'eng on her 70th birthday. Taipei: National Taiwan Normal University.

Tzeng, O. J. L. (1983). Cognitive processing of various orthographies. In M. Chu-Chang (Ed.), *Asian and Pacific-American perspectives in bilingual education: Comparative research* (pp. 73–96). New York: Teachers College Press.

Tzeng, O. J. L., Hung, D. L., & Wang, W. S. Y. (1977). Speech recoding in reading Chinese characters. *Journal of Experimental Psychology: Human Learning and Memory, 3*(6), 621–630.

U.S. Bureau of the Census. (1994). *Statistical abstract of the United States*: 1994 (114th ed.). Washington, DC: Author.

Wang, S. Y. (1973, February). Chinese language. *Scientific American*, pp. 50–60.

Wong, S. C. (1988). The language situation of Chinese Americans. In S. L. McKay & S. C. Wong (Eds.), *Language diversity: Problem or resource? A social and educational perspective on language minorities in the United States* (pp. 193–228). New York: Newbury House.

Yang. G. (1996). Issues on Chinese language education in North America. In J. M. Chang & D. Lin (Eds.), *The fourth annual conference proceedings: Balancing academic achievement & social growth* (pp. 35–38). Rockville, MD: Chinese American Educational Research & Development Association.

8

Literacy and Instruction in African American Communities: Shall We Overcome?

Howard L. Smith

> I began by saying that one of the paradoxes of education was that precisely at the point when you begin to develop a conscience, you must find yourself at war with your society. It is your responsibility to change society if you think of yourself as an educated person. (Baldwin, 1963/1988, p. 11)

With these words, James Baldwin addressed a group of teachers regarding the education of African American children—*Negro* children, as he called them. Baldwin knew that for members of marginalized groups in American society, education was a means for liberation because it developed one's consciousness about American society. When he made his address in the 1960s there existed such social, economic, and political hegemony that only White males really enjoyed all the fruits of education within the United States. For Baldwin and his contemporaries, truly enlightened individuals (teachers) would see the inequities that pervaded the educational system and be moved to effect change. Nearly 40 years after Baldwin's message was first published, researchers (e.g., Kozol, 1991; Oakes, 1985) continue to report systemic inequities as well as bias in all subject areas including math (Zucker, 1991) and science (Blake, 1993; Brownstein & Destino, 1995). Nowhere are these inequities more noticeable than in literacy instruction (G. Garcia & Pearson, 1991; Shannon, 1989).

This chapter presents some of the realities of language and literacy development in African American communities. Because neither language nor literacy develops in a void, I trace literacy development for African Americans from the 1600s to the present day. A historical perspective of the social, economic, and cultural constraints experienced by African Americans explains many behaviors and beliefs that persist within and about the community. I later discuss some of the opposing and often combative views regarding educational practices most appropriate for the literacy development of African American children. My aim is to provide educators with a review of current literacy research with African American populations so that they can make informed decisions regarding their practices in the classroom. I conclude the chapter by offering some guiding principles and suggestions for instruction that are products of both the research and the sociohistorical experiences of African American communities.

The reader should note the use of the plural—African American *communities*. African Americans are not a monolithic assembly in thought, behavior, or language variety. Group distinctions can be perceived among those from Northern states and those of Southern states. Within these regions, one must distinguish between the experiences of those from urban communities and those from rural communities (Heath, 1983). Moreover, those with advanced formal education possess knowledge about language and culture that are unknown to those without it. Their shared experiences help create unique African American communities with distinctive customs, traditions, and dialects.

We should also recognize that people of African descent live in all parts of the world (e.g., Europe, the Caribbean, Central America, South America, Canada), and many of these people subsequently migrate to the United States. Students of African descent who are native speakers of Arabic (e.g., Algeria), Dutch (e.g., Surinam), French (e.g., Senegal, Guadalupe), Portuguese (e.g., Cape Verde, Brazil), Spanish (e.g., Panama, Cuba), and a host of other languages enter the U.S. school system every day. Their experiences are beyond the scope of the present work. I limit this discussion to those who can trace their history to the slave period of the United States by referring to them as African Americans, except in direct quotations.

My interest in this topic comes from many directions. I am a university professor of language and literacy with professional interest in literacy development in multicultural contexts. I am an African American educated in public schools and have personal experiences with literacy instruction in the school system. I am the product of a long line of public school teachers who spoke to me frankly about the importance of reading and writing for "our people" and the institutionalized barriers to prevent success. I am also a new parent and therefore have great concerns about the kinds of language and literacy instruction my daughter will experience in school.

LANGUAGE AND LITERACY FROM A HISTORICAL PERSPECTIVE

> We have, as far as possible, closed every avenue by which light may enter their minds. If we could extinguish their capacity to see the light, our work would be completed; they would then be on a level with the beasts of the field and we should be safe! I am not certain that we would not do it, if we could find out the process, and that on the plea of necessity. (Virginia House delegate upon the passage of an anti-educational bill, quoted in Salvino, 1989, p. 147)

Of the innumerable rights denied African Americans during slavery, none was more valued than education. Until the close of the 19th century, over 90% of them were unable to read and write (Foner, 1990). Slave owners, with rare exception, wanted their "human chattel" to remain illiterate to justify their state of servitude (Cornelius, 1991; Foner, 1988; McManus, 1973).[1] The very few who could read and write were part of a "slave aristocracy" (Watkins, 1993). These individuals "engaged in record-keeping, skilled labor, artisanship, household management, the purchase of insurance, and other commercial activities" (Watkins, 1993, p. 323).

Every Southern state except Tennessee had laws expressly forbidding instruction for African Americans until the reconstruction period (Foner, 1988; McCall, 1989). The church took exception to such laws (see Fig. 8.1). Although members of the clergy and laity commonly professed a belief in the inherent inferiority of African Americans, they also professed a belief that African Americans were human and had souls to be saved from fire and brimstone (Cornelius, 1991). According to McManus (1973):

> Although the darker pigmentation of their skin excluded Negroes from the mainstream of colonial life, it raised no barriers to them in the hereafter.

---

[1]Reverend Richard Fuller, a slaveholder and plantation owner, insisted on teaching his slaves to read even after the South Carolina legislature of 1850 refused his petition to that effect (Cornelius, 1991).

> The religious leaders of every colony saw no reason why slaves could not be converted into conventional Christians. (p. 99)

Throughout this period, the Quakers went beyond proselytizing and worked diligently for the emancipation and the education of slaves.[2] An exemplar was Prudence Crandall. In 1833, she opened a school for *Colored* young ladies in Connecticut that attracted African American women from Providence, Boston, and New York. Though her graduates would be among the first African American educators, townspeople objected to the existence of Crandall's school. Her neighbors smeared her home with feces and set it on fire, while storekeepers refused to sell her provisions. She was arrested, tried, and convicted twice but kept her school running for as long as possible (McCall, 1989, p. 5).

Betty Underwood (1971) wrote a children's book entitled *The Tamarack Tree* based, in part, on what occurred at the Crandall school. This is the story (historical fiction) of a 14-year-old White orphan who witnesses her town's anger at the opening of a local school for African American girls 1833. In 1996 Alan Schroeder, a children's author pub-

FIG. 8.1.   "The Church and African American Education." Sea Island School, established 1862, St. Helena Island (picture by Van-Ingen-Snyder), part of the American Freedman's Union Commission flyer. Reprinted by permission of Sophia Smith Collection, Smith College.

---

[2]According to McManus (1973, p. 19), the *Minutes of the Philadelphia Monthly Meeting (1682–1714)* indicate that initially "Even Quakers had no apparent qualms about selling slaves openly in the public marketplaces of Philadelphia."

lished *Minta: A Story of Young Harriet Tubman*. In this fictionalized version of Tubman's youth, Schroeder depicts the oppression that denied Tubman and others access to formal education or "book learning." He then goes on to describe how Tubman's father taught his daughter life skills that through which she extricate herself, and others, from slavery's bonds. *The Bondwoman's Narrative* (Crafts, 1855/2002) will be of special interest to adolescent and high school readers for several reasons. Noted scholar Henry Gates authenticated this first-person narrative as the autobiography of an educated slave woman. The modern printing includes facsimiles of the original handwritten manuscript.

Both historical documents and fictionalized accounts make it apparent that despite of the religious conviction of church leaders and kind-hearted souls, literacy instruction for African Americans was circumscribed and permeated with struggle. An African American who obtained even a minimal education had performed a monumental feat. They battled against illiteracy and the vicious mobs that assaulted their schools and churches engaged in instruction long into the 20th century (see Fig. 8.2).

Literacy and Liberation

By the mid-1800s, reading was no longer uniquely connected to the church. African Americans understood literacy to be the key to participation in the democratic process (Salvino, 1989) long before the theories of "critical pedagogy" (Freire, 1970) and "emancipatory literacy" (Freire & Macedo, 1987) of the 20th century. "When African-Americans fought to gain literacy, they expressed a desire for freedom and

FIG. 8.2. "Schools accepting black children." From L. Hughes, M. Meltzer, and C. E. Lincoln, 1970, *A Pictorial History of the Negro in America* (3rd ed.). New York: Crown Publishers. Reprinted with permission.

self-determination which had deep roots in modern culture" (Cornelius, 1991, p. 2).

For the slave and free person alike, literacy was a statement of one's humaneness. Literacy was another tool for enslaving African Americans. According to Salvino (1989), they had been "legislated into illiteracy [and] ... were held chattel by the power of words in the form of laws legalizing their bondage and tracts confirming their inherent inferiority to whites" (p. 147). For that reason, each person who learned was exalted as an example in direct opposition to the White oppressors' claim that the "dark savage" was too brutish to learn. "Stories of literate slaves traveled quickly from plantation to plantation and were a source of great satisfaction within the quarters" (Salvino, 1989, p. 149).

Those so schooled became cultural mediators and translators of the written word for those who could not read. They facilitated group expression and interaction around texts (Graff, 1979). The origin of their role can be traced to the *griots* of West Africa. These skilled orators helped to sustain the knowledge of the culture through songs, stories, and other oral events (Edwards & Sienkewics, 1990). In so doing, they demonstrated how knowledge and (spoken) text were socially constructed.

Sweet Clara and the Freedom Quilt (Hopkinson, 1993) is an excellent example in children's literature of the social construction of knowledge and alternative forms of literacy used by slaves. In the story, a young slave girl plans her escape to Canada with the help of a map that she crafts into a quilt. Fellow slaves, without acknowledging the quilt's purpose, would visit briefly with Clara and offer information about land masses, distances, or landmarks. Hopkinson (2000) later expanded upon this theme in *Under the Quilt of Night,* in which slaves follow the stars and a quilted map to freedom in the North.

African Americans viewed literacy as the core of freedom itself because it permitted the creation of a new consciousness within their community. Thus, for African Americans, literacy became transformative (Freire, 1970) and transactive (Rosenblatt, 1989, 1993). It refuted the claim that one group of humans was intellectually more capable than another. It permitted the transmission of a literate, creative culture and documentation of their history. Most important, it hastened the self-actualization of an ethnic community by pointing the way to freedom (Cornelius, 1991, p. 61).

Literacy for a New Era

In the decades after the Civil War, "education" became the rallying cry of those seeking to improve the lot of former slaves whose prospects were limited usually to hard labor in the fields or to domestic work in white people's homes. Black people during this era would be lucky to have had the chance to learn to read and write well enough to sign their own names. (Delany & Delany, 1993, p. 39)

With the demise of slavery and the advent of reconstruction, African Americans pursued education, in particular reading and writing, as if it were life itself. At that time and into the late 1900s, three fourths of the African American population lived in Southern states. The desire for learning led parents to migrate to towns and cities in search of education for their children and also led plantation workers to make the establishment of a schoolhouse "an absolute condition" of signing labor contracts. Those newly emancipated sought every opportunity for advancement and self-improvement through literacy learning.

Perhaps the most striking illustration of the freedmen's quest for self-improvement was their seemingly unquenchable thirst for education .... Access to education for themselves and their children was, for blacks, central to the meaning of freedom, and white contemporaries were astonished by their "avidity for learning." (Foner, 1988, p. 43)

The educational accomplishments of African Americans of that time were Herculean. Instruction came at a cost of great physical, emotional, and economic sacrifice. The following is a powerful example. In 1865, African Americans in the South raised money to purchase land, build schools, and pay teachers. By 1870, these former slaves had amassed and spent over $1,000,000 on education (Foner, 1990, p. 44). In many towns and cities, their educational structures were the first public schools.

African Americans knew from painful experience that government-run schools for their children would continue to be few and impoverished. "The colored schools were far inferior to the white schools. Oftentimes, 'school' was held at a church and the children would kneel on the floor and use the pews as desks" (Delany & Delany, 1993, p. 79). Writing materials were scarce and books were usually outdated. African American schools into the *1960s* received yellowed grammar books, coverless dictionaries, outdated history texts, tattered spellers, and incomplete sets of encyclopedias from White schools. For that reason, those in the African American community relied on the only resource that had proven consistently effective—themselves. Teachers and school directors petitioned parents and community members for the needed materials. Parents raised monies for books, furniture, and blackboards, as well as subsidizing the pay and housing of the teachers (Delany & Delany, 1993; Holt, 1990). Families were known to contribute even when they would be without clothing or food (Holt, 1990).

Although America produced notable poets, playwrights, essayists, and novelists of African descent,[3] most African Americans of this era received little more instruction than the rudiments of literacy. Student–teacher ratios were commonly 1 to 50, 60, or 70 (Holt, 1990). In order to instruct their large groups of pupils under such deplorable conditions, teachers used drills, repetition, and rote memorization. We show later how this instructional approach, born of necessity, would later be interpreted as the ideal mode of instruction for African Americans. Problems of scant materials, outdated texts, poorly equipped buildings, classroom overcrowding, low teacher salaries, reduced school terms, and overt racism would handicap literacy development for African American children, and their children's children, for several generations (Fishback & Baskin, 1991).

Literacy and Aspirations

No longer shackled by slavery, African Americans were bound by racially based social stratification that permeated their schools (Jones-Wilson, 1991). Schools into the *1950s* commonly utilized a curriculum that emphasized vocational training, physical and manual labor, and "the acceptance of racial subservience for Negroes" (Watkins, 1993, p. 324). Popularized by Booker T. Washington, this "Hampton–Tuskegee" model was transposed and implemented in African American grammar schools (Lane, 1986).

Children educated under this model read from the Bible, memorized rules of civic responsibility, and developed circumscribed literacy skills needed for manual or industrial labor (Watkins, 1993). Implied here was the belief that African American children were mentally incapable of learning the academic curriculum offered White students even at the age of 6 (Lane, 1986). Creativity was not a concern. Language arts were little more than inane repetition of basic skills. An elementary school principal who used the Hampton–Tuskegee model explained the goals: "Every boy will eventually become a first class cook, with the ability to make his own shirt" (Lane, 1986, p. 71). Naturally, those who continued to attend school did become functionally literate. But their instruction, far from liberating, was a deliberate attempt to develop low levels of literacy in order to control masses of people.

Children's author Robert San Souci (1989a) offered a glimpse of the Tuskegee–Hampton philosophy in his delightful *The Boy and the Ghost*. In a note to the reader, San Souci (1989a, p. 30) revealed that

---

[3]For further reference, see Magill (1992).

the idea for his story originated, in part, from a folktale first printed in the *Southern Workman and Hampton School Record* in March 1898. Although sharing many features of the "ghost story" genre, the Tuskegee–Hampton slant becomes apparent early in the story. Thomas, the son of hard-working but poor parents, decides to seek his fortune. As he prepares to leave, his parents admonish him to be polite, generous, and brave. It would be these virtues that provide him access to success at the tale's end. Not every student received Hampton–Tuskegee schooling. However, graduates from other programs likewise received second-class citizenship. The trend does not appear to have changed. Even today, children in working-class schools are taught to be submissive to authority. According to Shannon (1985), research shows that working-class schools (to which a large part of African Americans are assigned) appear preoccupied with controlling the behavior of students. More reading instruction time is spent on management and nonacademic activities in schools located in poor communities, whereas upper-class schools encourage social interactions even during academic activities (Shannon, 1985).

Literacy Instruction: Separate–but Equal?

> The visitor watched the teacher pass out two half sheets of paper to each pupil, saying, "It's got to do you all day, so be careful with it." She looked at one observer and said: "We don't have no pencils; we don't have no books; we don't have anything." (Cuban, 1993, p. 127)

The Great Depression exacerbated educational inequities. Towns and cities that had available monies for education channeled them toward their White schools (Meier, Stewart, & England, 1989). Districts would not repair *Negro* schools, let alone build new ones. Scores of children spanning seven grade levels were regularly assigned to one classroom. Those fortunate students with pencils practiced their "writing skills," which amounted to little more than penmanship exercises. With the pain of fingers frozen by drafts seeping through the walls, floors, and ceiling, students wrote sentences dictated by the teacher or another student, copied from a chalkboard or from an infrequent "store-bought" text (Cuban, 1993). Some states instituted a 10-year adoption of textbooks (Tyack, Lowe, & Hansot, 1984); other districts did not purchase materials at all.

In some cases, "no supplies, except a broom, were furnished to the school by the district during the year" (Tyack et al., 1984, p. 182). School terms were shortened. In Arkansas, several hundred schools used an academic calendar of less than 60 days (Tyack et al., 1984). Having fewer materials and greater numbers of students than before, teachers relied on drills, rote memorization, and repetition even more. In 1931 President Hoover's National Advisory Committee on Education described the state of affairs for African American children at this time:

> In hundreds of rural schools there are just four blank unpainted walls, a few rickety benches, an old stove propped up on brickbats, and two or three boards nailed together and painted black for a blackboard. In many cases, this constitutes the sum total of the furniture and teaching equipment. (National Advisory Committee on Education, 1931, quoted in Tyack et al., 1984, p. 32)

Another point of weakness in African American schooling was the academic preparation of the teachers. A national study of African American teachers in 1930 indicated that 12% were college graduates, 32% had 2 years of college training, 19% had less than 2 years of college training, and 37% had not graduated high school (McCuistion, 1932). As late as 1940, those with an eighth-grade diploma were instructing African American students (Cornelius, 1991; Foner, 1990; Holt, 1990). "Many teachers in Arkansas Negro schools had only that diploma and were licensed to impart wisdom" (Angelou, 1993, p. 144). The reasons for their lack of training are well known—African Americans were systemically barred from secondary and tertiary institutions. When admitted, they often received racially motivated abuse that prompted their leaving. Those who remained became personae non gratae and suffered in silence. My mother related the situation in the 1940s in our home town in the North:

> All of us [African Americans] went to Douglas Junior High School. In fact when our [older cousins] attended, it went through 10th grade. They made all the Colored go there. Then you went to old Chester High School. They [school administration] wanted to add two more grades—make Douglas a high school for the Colored. Have you ever heard of such a thing? A junior high school going all the way to 12th grade?! Well, the Colored families protested and picketed and got us in the high school, but they (the White teachers and administration) really didn't want you over there.

In spite of starting so far behind, within 12 years, the average academic level of African American teachers in the Southern states would surpass that of their White counterparts. The teachers of Georgia serve as one example. In 1940, approximately 50% of the African American educators in the state had less than 2 years of college training. By 1952, less than 2% were in this category (Pierce, Kincheloe, Moore, Drewry, & Carmichael, 1955, p. 200).

Because so few African Americans lived in the North, White teachers were assigned to teach in the institutional atrocities known as "proscribed schools." Record indicates that the least qualified teachers received these placements:

> The "proscribed schools" were the worst assignment in the system and drew its worst people. There could be no improvement until they were broken up or until the pupils were no longer humiliated by the prejudiced instructors, "poor white girls and white men who couldn't find employment at anything else." (Lane, 1986, p. 69)

There is an axiom that says students can learn with the teacher, without the teacher, and in spite of the teacher. Surely this defined what occurred in African American communities throughout the United States in the middle decades of this century. Even segregated schooling in the South did not prevent literacy development. Ravitch (1983) detailed the process:

> The very schools meant to contain Negroes produced not only a demand for graduate education (which was rarely available in segregated states) but trained the black leaders who conducted the fight against the segregated system. To maintain the fiction of "separate equality," the South had to provide literacy, and literacy proved to be subversive of segregation, for it provided access to new information and ideas which could not be controlled by the segregationists. The technological expansion of the national media meant that ideas hostile to racism would regularly enter the South via magazines, radio, television, movies, and books; the rising level of black literacy meant that blacks could not be isolated from the national culture. (p. 118)

During the 1930s, the National Association for the Advancement of Colored People (NAACP) and other organizations began a long series of battles against school segregation. In 1954, *Brown v. The Board of Education* would make separate accommodations illegal. Throughout the 1950s, 1960s, and 1970s, many battles were fought to give African Americans access to decent facilities, qualified teachers, sufficient matrials, and curricula designed to educate them beyond subservience.[4] Throughout this period, literacy development, in particular learning to read environmental print, became a means of survival. All African Americans learned to read the word and the world (Freire & Macedo, 1987). This included the social and physical context, nonverbal behaviors, and the hidden meanings (Fig. 8.3).

Perhaps the earliest children's book have been written about this important period of U.S. history was *The Empty Schoolhouse*

---

[4]See Willie, Garibaldi, and Reed (1991) for an in-depth discussion.

FIG. 8.3. "We wash for Whites only." From L. Hughes, M. Meltzer, & C.
E. Lincoln, 1970, *A Pictorial History of the Negro in America* (3rd ed.),
p. 299. New York: Crown Publishers, Inc. Reprinted with permission.

(Carlson, 1965). The story describes the bomb threats, brick throw-
ing, and the mob mentality of those who oppose integration. The
young protagonist, Lullah Royall, is an African American girl who is
one of the first to integrate a previously all-White school. *Bella Teal*, a
poor White girl, witnesses the hatred in the faces of the picketers outside her newly integrated school.

Although these first two children's books might be classified as
historical fiction, another book for older readers deserves a different
classification. *Little Rock: The Desegregation of Central High Spotlight on American History* (O'Neil, 1994) uses photographs and images from the newspapers of the time to reconstruct the events of the
highly publicized school desegregation case. In addition to the key
figures (e.g., Clarence Darrow, Orval Faubus), who are portrayed
with historical accuracy, the author also described the violence and
the military enforcement required to oversee the integration of the
high school.

In sum, education for African Americans can be characterized as a
struggle for access, full participation, and meaningful, authentic experiences. In spite of the efforts of religious groups like the Quakers, African Americans still faced the hurdle of laws that forbid their
instruction. Literacy was sought as if it were freedom itself. Those who
learned to read and write were respected and admired much as the
griots of West Africa. When laws against their education were repealed, African Americans, children and adults alike, invested their
time, money, and labor in education. For African Americans, learning,
and literacy especially, have always been accomplished through group
effort. However, in spite of such efforts, research finds strong evidence that the restrictions placed on earlier generations of African

Americans decreases the likelihood of success of the generations that followed (Fishback & Baskin, 1991).

LITERACY AND ORACY

Have I told you about my son Brian? His teacher at the nursery school told me that he preached his first sermon on Friday. He got all the little kids to sit in a circle, he made them say a prayer and then he preached to them. His topic? The potty! *"What you should and shouldn't do on the potty."* (Terrell, personal communication, October 6, 1996)

The Oral Traditions

It may seem inconceivable that in spite of oppressive social forces, African Americans created strong literary traditions that influenced the reading development of their children. "To say that blacks were denied written literacy is not to say that they were *il*literate" (Salvino, 1989, p. 148). The first and perhaps most important of these were the oral traditions. Because African Americans were denied access to printed media, they developed a highly structured system of oral communication that has grown and prospered "in the white literate society's blind spot, communicating messages in ways that whites could not begin to understand, especially music—its rhythms, tones, and lyrics" (Salvino, 1989, p. 148).

The oral traditions had their roots in various oral performances found in Africa. Among the many oral forms there existed the *apae* or praise songs, the *kabary* or formal speech, the epics sung in Zaire, stories from the Mende in Sierra Leone, and the *Sunjata* performed throughout West Africa (Edwards & Sienkewics, 1990, p. 4). Researchers of the oral traditions note how they were transformed and integrated into the contemporary African American speech. Often misunderstood and discounted by outsiders of the discourse communities, these modes of speaking involve highly structured, meaning-laden patterns of communication. For Edwards and Sienkewics (1990), "oral performance often creates a web of praising, blaming, boasting, and abusing" (p. 133).

When discussing the oral tradition of African Americans, it is helpful to remember that these experiences exist along a *sacred–secular* continuum (Smitherman, 1995) and an *oral–literate* continuum (Fig. 8.4) (Edwards & Sienkewics, 1990).[5] The former is because

---

[5]See Smitherman (1995) and Edwards and Sienkewicz (1990) for a complete discussion.

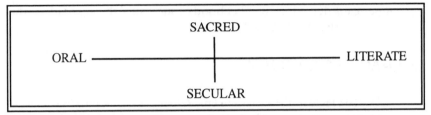

FIG. 8.4. Literacy and instruction in African American communities.

much of the uniqueness and lyrical color of African American *secular* oratory is tied to religious doctrine and *sacred* works of the church. The Rev. Martin Luther King is often cited as an example of this tradition at its finest. The second, the *oral–literate* continuum, is based on the observation that in this century in America, one form cannot exist in total isolation from the other. Even those ministers with the poorest education base their sermons on the written verses of the Bible. The lyrics to the latest rap song are included in the jewel case of the compact disc. Occupations and activities that had no such requirements in the past (e.g., the tire mechanic at Wal-Mart, banking services) demand print and computer literacy. A catchy phrase repeated in a high school cafeteria today can appear on a T-shirt tomorrow. As a more sacred example, many *Negro* spirituals, passed down orally (vocally) through generations, have been transcribed and reproduced for scholars and choirs. As such "the written word does not divide so much as the spoken word unites the alliterate and the literate" (Edwards & Sienkewcs, 1990, p. 6). All written literary concepts (e.g., genre, plot, time, space, characters, point of view) are found within the oral traditions of African Americans.

Smitherman (1995) suggested that within the continua, there are four modes of discourse or categories: call-response, signification (the "Dozens"), tonal semantics, and narrative sequencing (e.g., "Toasts," plantation tales). Call-response has been defined as "spontaneous verbal and nonverbal interaction between speaker and listener in which all of the speaker's statements ('calls') are punctuated by expressions ('responses') from the listener" (Smitherman, 1995, p. 316). During worship service, the minister says (gives the call) "Jesus is the light of the world!" to which a parishioner might respond with "Hallelujah!" or "Amen!"[6]

The original stanzas of the "Dozens" were 12 rhyming couplets that referred to sexual activity. In its present form the Dozens can range

---

[6]The reader is encouraged to see Angelou (1993, pp. 100–111) for an outstanding example.

from mild teasing to vicious slander, depending on the intention and skill of the speaker. Children often target a victim's mother as the object of derision:

First person: Your mother is so fat, she has her own zip code!

Second person: Oh, yea? Well, your mother's so fat, if she ever had to haul butt, she'd need to make two trips!

Given that many West African languages are linguistically described as *tone languages*, it should come as no surprise that African Americans use rhythm and vocal inflection to convey special meaning or to enliven their speech. Included in this category of tonal semantics are instances of talk-singing, alliterative word-play, repetition, and word stress. Jesse Jackson uses various forms of tonal semantics to punctuate his speeches, as do rap "artists" for entertaining. Muhammad Ali ("floats like a butterfly, stings like a bee"), of boxing fame, is another fine example.

Narrative sequencing, the final discourse mode, is the essence of the strong storytelling tradition in African American culture. Storytelling is a more secular example of oratory. Originally, *griots*, the revered tribal orators, were responsible for maintaining the history of a tribe. More than chroniclers, the griots offered composite views of the culture, beliefs, ethics, and values of a community. Considered living museums, "as part of their training for this sacred position, the storytellers took oaths never to alter the history, customs, and truths of their people" (Smitherman, 1995, p. 324). Within the African American community, stories have been used for entertaining, educating, working through problems, sharing history, and recording community events. Listeners participate and acknowledge especially well-spoken passages by repeating key phrases, shouting affirmations or other words of encouragement. Heath (1983) compared the storytelling styles of a White and an African American working-class community:

People in both Trackton and Roadville spend a lot of time telling stories. Yet the form, occasions, content, and functions of their stories differ greatly. They structure their stories differently; they hold different scales of features on which stories are recognized as *stories* and judged as good or bad …. [The White] community allows only stories which are factual and have little exaggeration: the other uses reality only as the germ of a highly creative fictionalized account. (p. 184)

The tonal quality of a story is apparent in *The Talking Eggs* by Robert San Souci (1989b). In some ways a variation of *Cinderella*, this tale describes how a poor girl, who lives with a cruel mother and vain sister, is befriended by an elderly woman. In addition to the vivid illustrations by Jerry Pinkney, the story features a *fête* of dancing rabbits playing banjos and square dancing, much in the style of the old South.

Those who know the community of their students understand the social, cultural, and linguistic realities of its children. Most (although not all) African American teachers are familiar with and respect the oral traditions of their African American students because they use it themselves. They "listen carefully to what country people call mother wit. That in those homely sayings [is] couched the collective wisdom of generations" (Angelou, 1993, p. 83). Storytelling, double-entendre, exaggeration, and religious-based phrases are part of their shared everyday life. I once asked my mother, upon her arrival from church, "Mom, was it a good sermon?" To which she replied, "Son, by the time the minister finished preaching, the men were crying and the women had passed out on the floor." On another occasion, my uncle conveyed his great displeasure over the workmanship at a local garage: "I asked to speak with the manager and when he got there I preached his funeral!"

Varieties of English and Educability

Another area of research is the speech patterns or dialects of African American children. There is a long history of myth and misinformation about African American Vernacular English (AAVE) and Black English Vernacular (BEV) (Heath, 1983; Smitherman, 1994) and those who speak it. In the late 1700s essayist de Crèvecoeur, like his contemporaries, erroneously described the language of the slaves as "crude jargon" and "uncouth dialect" (1904). Quaker Anthony Boneset (cited in Brooks, 1937, p. 48) complained about the educators of the 1700s he recruited to his school for Negroes:

> To find qualified teachers for the unhappy blacks was almost impossible. The Negro knew nothing and could learn nothing, so people said. In view of the universal prejudice, to teach Negro children was painfully humiliating, irksome, and monotonous, and one discouraged teacher succeeded another.

Throughout the 1800s, scholars, educators, and the noneducated alike continued to claim that people of color lacked the linguistic, cognitive, and physiological ability to speak a standardized language. Harrison's 1884 study of "Negro English" (cited in Smitherman, 1997) found clear indications that the former slaves had incorporated elements of various African languages systematically into their English speech. However, those same people, in his opinion, lacked the "linguistic resources" to reproduce specific elements of speech.

Tired of the spurious theories leveled against their language varieties, more African American scholars in the mid-1960s began the study of the African influence on the varieties of English used in the Caribbean and the United States. These linguists began to analyze the phonological (sound system), etymological (word origin), and morphological (word structure) and syntactical (grammar and structure) differences between and among these speech communities and Euro-American speakers of English. Soon linguists of European descent would come to contribute to the body of research that affirmed AAVE.

Turner (1949) had already documented African elements in Gullah spoken in the South. His work is especially important because he is credited as being the first African American linguist. Moreover, he was one of very few scholars of the time to master several African languages and to record them onto phonograph records for data collection (Smitherman, 1997). Bailey (1965) later described African traits in Jamaican Creole English of the Caribbean. In the 1970s, researchers such as Smitherman (1995) and Labov (1993), working with the language of inner-city African American youth, described the depth and breadth of the language spoken in those communities. This research helped to establish that some African American communities use a version of English that is heavily influenced by their African roots. Other researchers who verified the systematicity of AAVE include Baugh (1983, 1999, 2000), Dillard (1972, 1997), Taylor (1991), and Wolfram (1970), among the many. In contrast to earlier publications, their empirically based research demonstrated that AAVE was indeed a viable medium of communication—and not a substandard dialect or limited code. Their data showed that speakers of AAVE convey meaning and nuance as well as those who speak a standard English. Arguing against the prevailing theories of the period, this work demonstrated the logic, abstraction, and eloquence of AAVE.[7]

Heath (1983), in her research, found that African American communities use highly complex and systematic forms of communication to mediate events that occur in their world. She examined the oral and literate behaviors of three neighboring but culturally distinct communities. By studying and comparing the language use of "Roadville" (White working class), "Trackton" (working-class African American), and the townspeople (multiethnic middle class), she found that people of these groups had specific discourse patterns as a product of their historic experiences in the region. They were members of different *speech communities*; they belonged to groups that "shared rules for the conduct and interpretation of speech, and rules for the interpretation of at least one linguistic variety" (Hymes, 1972, p. 54). All

---

[7]For a detailed description of Black English Vernacular, see Smitherman (1995).

three sets of children came to school with knowledge and skills from their respective communities, but only the children from "in town" belonged to the speech community of the teachers. Until their teachers were guided through the code, the African American students were considered language deficient. Among her data, Heath (1983, pp. 270–271) recorded a teacher's reflection:

> The thing that none of us realized was that these children were almost like foreigners to us. True, they lived within our communities; we have all associated with and talked with Blacks in our homes all our lives, so we thought we understood them. We knew that their spoken language was different, but we always assumed these differences were from ignorance and lack of education.

Although not universally viewed as a positive, African American communication styles have been the object of study for many decades. Dillard (1972) studied the patterns within African American language varieties. Collier (1998) examined their conversational management styles, whereas Rogan and Hammer (1998) compared the degree of language intensity of African Americans with Anglo Americans. As is true of all cultural groups, African Americans employ varieties of speech and apply them within ritualized (predictable) dimensions of their personal interactions in ways that differ from other groups (Abrahams, 1993). A child's way of learning and *ways with words* (Heath, 1983) can challenge educators to look at their belief system about language, literacy, and learning. Although some teachers—past and present—have considered African Americans' dialects and variations as a handicap, those who know the community understand that a child's dialect is not an indication of intellect. Research shows that the incorporation of the language variations and modalities common to the African American community facilitates written language development (Smitherman, 1995). Those who engage in "hyper" correction of the speech of African American students hinder the growth desired (Smitherman, 1995). Indeed, one important component of good teaching for any group is acceptance of the students for who they are. A group of White schoolteachers wrote a play about language and cultural difference wherein an African American adolescent addresses her teacher:

> You must bring yourself to understand that there is a systematic basis for Black cultures. Your schools have been operating on the theory that everyone is the same beneath the skin .... I'm only asking you to look a little deeper—me as I am: I'm one of you but yet, I'm still me. My way of communicating may be different from yours but it fills my adaptive and emotional needs as I perform it. Why should my "at home" way of talking be "wrong"

> and your standard version be "right"? ... Show me ... that by adding a fluency in standard dialect, you are adding something to my language and not taking something away from me. Help me retain my identity and self-respect while learning to talk "your" way. (Heath, 1983, p. 271)

The focus of this discussion has been on the social, cultural, and historic origin of African American language variations and oral traditions. The disciplines of linguistics, anthropology, and sociology have demonstrated the depth and breath of communications rendered using the various African American dialects subsumed under the term BEV. Unfortunately, many times African American students sense the school's disrespect for their ways of speaking, ways of knowing, and ways of learning. Rather than encouraging students, most schooling experiences for African Americans reinforce feelings of inferiority, separateness, and eminent failure. Edwards (1982) offered the following explanation:

> I perceived that establishing "whose language counts" for purposes of schooling reflected and reinforced the balance of power and prestige between social groups .... To "sound disadvantaged" is to be disadvantaged in contexts where "correct" speech is "naturally" associated with social competence and credibility, and the danger of rejecting *what* is said because of *how* it is said is one against which teachers must be constantly on their guard. Pupils' use of socially-stigmatized forms of speech may shape teachers' judgments of their ability or ambition to an extent far beyond any evidence which such differences could provide. (p. 516)

In spite of the linguistic evidence to the contrary, African American dialects are regarded as deficient and substandard (Fairchild & Edwards-Evans, 1990). Students who use such language variations are often stigmatized by the education system (Smith & Heckman, 1995). Researchers (e.g., Fairchild & Edwards-Evans, 1990) continue to document that teachers have lower scholastic expectations for those who spoke AAVE.

LITERACY, INSTRUCTION, AND SOCIAL STRATIFICATION

> The Supreme Court decision in *Brown v. The Board of Education* 37 years ago, in which the court had found that segregated education was unconstitutional because it was "inherently unequal," did not seem to have changed very much for children in the schools I saw. Moreover, in most cities, influential people that I met showed little inclination to address this matter and were sometimes even puzzled when I brought it up. Many peo-

ple seemed to view the segregation issue as "a past injustice." ... [T]he nation ... has turned its back upon ... the *Brown* decision .... In public
schooling, social policy has been turned back almost one hundred years.
(Kozol, 1991, pp. 3–4)

Paradigm Shifts: Progression and Regression

The hard-earned victories of the Civil Rights era were many. Over time,
most blatantly racist or discriminatory practices were curbed in
schools throughout the United States. Yet numerous studies show
that covert and overt inequalities persist in the educational system
(Kozol, 1991; Oakes, 1985; Welner & Oakes, 1996) and are directly related to historic oppression. The institutionalized racism that oppressed African Americans centuries before (e.g., antiliteracy laws,
legalized school segregation) has had pernicious effects on those generations that followed *long after such laws had been repealed.* We
should acknowledge the great strides the United States has made toward equalizing educational opportunities for all of its students.
However, it would be ludicrous to believe that 300 years of oppression could be ameliorated in 30 years of desegregation and civil rights
legislation.

Cultural Deprivation and Interventionist Programs

During the Civil Rights era, America began to examine the damag-
ing effects of poverty, racism, and alienation on children (Bruner,
1996). It was reasoned that minorities and other disenfranchised
groups lived in impoverished environments. Their homes lacked the
needed stimuli for mental development of their children. They
should not be expected to do well in school because the curriculum
was based on mainstream values. Those living in such squalor were
limited to a substandard *Weltanschauung.* Such children needed help
to adopt the mainstream worldview and "the standard culture" for improved outcomes on standardized tests. These beliefs were the core
of the *cultural deprivation hypothesis* of the 1960s and 1970s.

In spite of the fact that the notion of a "standard culture" was based
on mythical childrearing practices—a middle-class, stay-at-home wife
and homemaker who could wax floors, decorate cookies, and read to
her preschool child while wearing high heels—it was never called into
question. The feeling was that the problem was the child's culture (or
the lack thereof). It was postulated that African American children
could not read and write well because they came from homes in which
literacy events were not commonplace. According to this belief system,

the stories teachers read in school were foreign to African American students because they lacked sufficient experience with worldly events that would allow them to understand what was depicted in the story.

In some ways, the Head Start programs were modeled after the polio vaccine campaigns of an earlier period (Sarason, 1990). Young children, marshaled in great numbers to a central location (Head Start centers), were administered a vaccine (literacy and other experiences based on White, mainstream culture) to inoculate them against the virus (of ignorance) found in their homes and communities that was inimical to their development (Sarason, 1990). These disadvantaged children would survive and thrive (academically) despite the contagions in their home environment. Twenty-five years of research show that Head Start programs have made a difference when compared to groups of children who went straight from the home environment to a mainstream curriculum (Bruner, 1996; Sarason, 1990). Head Start alumni were more likely to have greater academic success, to stay longer in school, to maintain steady employment, and to stay out of jail and commit fewer crimes (Bruner, 1996).

The major flaw in Head Start and similar educational models is the notion that the child's background is defective.[8] The programs did nothing to examine the institutionalized racism that privileged certain ethnic groups while oppressing others. With rare exception, the programs celebrated all that was "right and White" in the world, while intentionally avoiding the issues that perpetuated social stratification and poverty in the first place. Bruner (1996) stated that Head Start "was dedicated to stopping not the broader culture's system of racial discrimination, but one of its flawed cultures from depriving its children through faulty child rearing" (p. 73). In a phrase—it blamed the victim.

Approaches to Reading Instruction

Today, when African American children enter first grade they usually experience literacy instruction that undermines their self-worth and aspirations. There are three basic approaches to reading instruction in the elementary grades. The first two are based on publisher-produced materials and are usually skills driven. Whole language, the third approach, is based on a wide variety of texts and literacy experiences.

Basal Reader Programs.[9] At the turn of the century, findings from scientific management and business management were ap-

---

[8]One notable exception was the High Scope preschool program developed in Michigan in the 1980s. The cultural capital of the students was an integral part of the curriculum.

[9]The *Report Card on Basal Readers* (Goodman, Shannon, Freeman, & Murphy, 1988) offers a detailed account of the development of basal readers.

plied to reading instruction. Vast numbers of elementary school-teachers were poorly educated, and few knowledgeable supervisors were available to provide in-service training. Given the teachers' heavy reliance on textbooks, it was reasoned that a sequenced set of reading texts, accompanied by detailed instructions in a teacher's manual, would improve and standardize reading instruction throughout the United States (Goodman, Shannon, Freeman, & Murphy, 1988). Such a move seemed logical, given the social context of the period. In light of current research, and improved preservice education for teachers, logic would now dictate that such prescribed instruction would have been discontinued. However, few substantive changes have occurred in basal publications since their appearance in the United States.

The basal reader is an artificially generated text that is tightly focused on decoding skills and controlled vocabulary. "The central premise of the basal reader is that a sequential, all-inclusive set of instructional materials can teach all children to read regardless of teacher competence and regardless of learner differences" (Goodman et al., 1988, p. 1). Because most basal contributors are White, with limited awareness of the cultural heritage of African Americans, the reams of workbooks, worksheets, and skill/vocabulary-based anthologies are culturally irrelevant (J. Garcia & Florez-Tighe, 1986; J. Garcia & Sadoski, 1986). The language and activities found in basals marginalize students (Bloome & Nieto, 1989). The rich and vital prior knowledge that all students should blend into the act of reading is all but ignored in this "one-size-fits-all" approach to literacy development (Harste & Short, 1988).

In spite of these limitations, there are teachers who have used basal readers successfully with African American students. Theorists (Delpit, 1986, 1988; Ellsworth, 1989; Mosenthal, 1988) who advocate skills-based approaches such as those found in basal readers for African American students feel that they provide the knowledge necessary to "harmonize with the rest of the world" (Delpit, 1986, p. 384). This group of educators espouses the primacy of reading skills and writing mechanics as the key for African Americans to access middle-class society and economic benefit. Taken in this light, literacy becomes a means for assimilation. Once African Americans adopt certain literacy (and other) behaviors or literate discourses (Delpit, 1993; Pérez, chap. 2, this volume) they are granted admission into the larger society, which is controlled primarily by White Americans and White middle-class discourse.

Direct Instruction. The direct instructional models (e.g., *Direct Instructional System for Teaching Arithmetic and Reading—DISTAR*) are perhaps the most controversial of the approaches.

DISTAR, for example, incorporates "hand signals for student response, tightly sequenced scripts, massed practice in choral chant, and modified alphabet for easy access to the skill" (Shannon, 1989, p. 98). DISTAR and other direct methods use a theoretical framework that suggest that disadvantaged children (i.e., African American children) inherently lack basic linguistic, cognitive, and behavioral abilities that prevent them from mastering literacy and other skills (Ogletree, 1977). Advocates assert that regimented instruction implemented through scripts provide explicit information needed to decode words for reading development (Shannon, 1989). They feel that the mastery of essential skills is the object of literacy instruction not the discovery of a literate "voice" (Delpit, 1993).

Accompanying direct instructional approaches is the practice of homogeneous ability grouping. African American students are overly represented in the lower reading groups for reasons other than ability. Rist (1970) studied how classroom teachers assigned students to reading groups according to their perceptions of the students' cleanliness or lack of ethnic dialect. Shannon (1985) found that during reading instruction the teacher's perception of social class affected academic outcomes. Specifically, in addition to lower expectations, those students of low socioeconomic status (who are most often minorities): (a) are subjected to more interruptions when reading, (b) do more reading aloud, and (c) receive larger quantities of material beyond their difficulty level. Moreover, the kinds of tasks they receive during reading instruction in reality are not reading at all. In contrast, those in the highest ability groups read about three times as much per day as those in lower reading groups (Allington, 1977).

Critics of DISTAR, and similar approaches, object to the programs' view that African American children are cognitively deficient. Literacy experts criticize direct approaches for their "unapologetic advocacy of the need for total control over teachers and students during reading instruction—teachers read from scripts and students respond only when signaled" (Shannon, 1989, p. 99). Supporters of direct methods believe that they orient and prepare the student for the world awaiting them. This belief is far from original. A similar philosophic stance existed during the period of slavery. Literacy was closely connected to a slave's servitude (e.g., household management) or survival (e.g., forging a travel pass for escape). "Learning occurred through imitation, recitation, memorization, and demonstration. A functionalist curriculum shuns abstractions. It is tied to the practical, the useful, and the demonstrable" (Watkins, 1993, p. 324).

Today, some African American teachers feel that their primary responsibility during literacy instruction is to help students master the codes and skills of mainstream English. "They are anxious to move to the next step, the step vital to success in America—the appropriation of the oral and written forms demanded by the mainstream .... Yes, they are *eager* to teach 'skills' " (Delpit, 1986, p. 383). Such models, far from advancing the instructional practices for African American students, are a quantum leap backward to the period of the Tuskegee–Hampton model of education. Although the days of cotton picking are gone, 20th-century manual labor still awaits those who have only basic literacy skills. With an accommodationist curriculum, as exemplified in the Hampton–Tuskegee model and echoed, in part, by contemporary interventionist programs (e.g., Head Start), the problems with literacy learning are not within the instructional practices but rather in the children:

> Various policies have been promoted over the years to address this "problem." The first of these—assimilation—emphasized the incorporation of minority groups into the dominant culture and language. Minority languages and cultures were thought to be the cause of minority children's educational difficulties .... [C]hildren were encouraged to (and, in some cases, coerced into) leaving their own culture(s) and language(s) "at the school gate.".... However, assimilation failed to deliver for minority children because, many now think, it demeaned and excluded minority languages and cultures. (S. May, 1993, p. 364)

Whole Language.   The preceding approaches that emphasize decoding contrast with more holistic approaches to literacy instruction, commonly called "whole language." Whole language is based on the premise that children acquire the ability to read and write as naturally as they learned to walk and talk (Goodman, 1986). Literacy acquisition occurs when students are provided numerous learning situations in which they are actively engaged in authentic, meaningful communication that has a connection with their lives (Cummins, Lapkin, & Swain, 1991). In lieu of subskills instruction and rote memorization, students are encouraged to become active participants in their literacy experiences through reading centers, listening centers, writing centers, trade books, oral readings, and other varieties of literacy explorations. Literacy events are contextualized and meaning laden. Often, the texts are created from the child's home language and personal experience. Learning strategies (e.g., graphemic–phonemic relationships) are contextualized and offered to students as needed (Reed & Ward, 1982).

After years of "The Reading Wars" (see Cassidy & Wenrich, 1998), program administrators stumbled upon a term that seems to please everyone—Balanced Literacy. Simplistically thought of as a combination of phonics instruction and whole language, a balanced approach is much more:

> The balance offered ... [addresses] issues of environment design, assessment, modeling, guidance, interactivity, independence, practice, oral language acquisition, writing and reading processes, community building, and motivation .... Rather than this versus that, it ... [is] a comprehensive, seamless blend of factors related to reading success, coupled with a solid cadre of reading instructional approaches: reading aloud, language experience, shared reading, guided reading, interactive writing, independent writing, and independent reading. (Reutzel, 1998/1999, p. 323)

This approach, although conceivably offering détente among factionists, is no less subject to problems when implemented in classrooms. A few critical areas include (a) the use of grouping strategies for reading that promote growth and do not perpetuate tracking; (b) selection of titles for guided reading that have experiential or cultural relevance to the learners; and (c) selection of topics for guided writing or language experience that are culturally and socially relevant to the learner. As in all instances of instruction, success depends on the knowledge—linguistic, cultural, and cognitive—of the teacher.

Instructional Controversies. School districts serving a multicultural student population now adopt "literature-based" basal series that contain contemporary stories as well as the canons of children's literature. More teachers are moving toward a whole-language approach for reading and writing. As such, more trade books and "real" stories will find their way into the hands of African American children (Giroux, 1987). Teachers should not view authentic children's literature as a panacea for equitable reading instruction. Research on trade books and other authentic stories for and about African American children shows that an increase in quantity does not necessarily create a corresponding increase in quality.

For over 30 years, researchers have analyzed the poor representation of African Americans in children's literature—both the number of instances in which they appear and the kind of images ascribed to African Americans (Sadker & Sadker, 1985). Schwartz (1972), in his review of several award-winning children's books during the 1970s, found instances of blatant racism. Larrick's (1972) study of 5,206 children's books published between 1962 and 1964 located less than 7% (6.7) that included a single instance of an African American child, in text or illustrations. Of those having such representation, one third received unfavorable reviews or were ignored by the major journals in the field of juvenile literature (Larrick, 1972). Chall, Radwin, French, and Hall (1979) published a similar study 14 years later. Their analysis of 4,775 trade books for children found that about 14% (689) acknowledged the existence of African Americans, without a great increase in the quality of the images suggested. Although more titles appear every year, even books that have been lauded and awarded by mainstream society have been judged unacceptable by those who share concern for African American children (Schwartz, 1972).

In light of the limited change of the institutionalized goals of schooling for members of the underclass, it can be argued that lack of literacy skills per se is not the main barrier to the acquisition of social or economic power in the United States for African Americans. Highly skilled minorities and women are regularly denied access to jobs and are denied promotions and increasing levels of responsibility (Shannon, 1990). Ogbu (1987) argued that it is precisely the false promises of preparation for a job when the economy does not produce enough employment for African Americans that will lead youth to assume a stance of resistance to White literacy practices. As Bruner (1996) and other scholars noted, the 1960s was the decade in which the United States initiated public policy and educational reform to address the effects of institutionalized racism in its public schools. In spite of school desegregation, many of the efforts to reform U.S. schools have had poor results for African Americans. Regarding literacy instruction, experts argue for practices that are quite opposite—skills based versus culturally based. Government and private agencies spend millions of dollars each year to publish studies and opinion papers that essentially say the following: "The African American child cannot be taught."

Such negativism notwithstanding, there are success stories. There are individual classrooms and schools that produce literate, well-educated African American children. Teachers, administrators, and parents in these situations accomplish seemingly impossible goals with their students in spite of difficult conditions. How is that so?

In the following section we review studies of successful programs, exploring the features or characteristics that make them successful. We then analyze guiding principles that explain why varying teaching styles can achieve outstanding results with African American students.

LITERACY INSTRUCTION: SOCIAL RECONSTRUCTION AND GUIDING PRINCIPLES

> One will notice in the autobiographies of these extraordinary "underprivileged" persons who have had an extraordinary academic success ... almost always a reference to an extraordinary mother; or father; or grandparents; to an extraordinary adult who provided early information or advice; a minister; or a teacher; or to a school above the ordinary, meaning extraordinary teachers. (Bond, 1972, p. 120)

In the previous three sections, I presented the social, cultural, and historical influences on literacy instruction in African American communities. We reviewed laws that prohibited their instruction and those that legalized their access to equal educational opportunities. We saw how the oral tradition, perpetuated through *griots*, storytellers, and preachers, connects African American listeners, and all who listen, to their community, their culture, and their literacies. At this point, you may wonder how one might use all this knowledge to create new possibilities for success for African American students, especially around literacy. Like all good teaching, it is a long, involved, and evolving process.

First Principle: You've Got to Believe

Bond (1972) studied the lives of African Americans who had earned a doctorate by 1960. At that time, of the 10,000 Americans who had been awarded a doctorate, there were only 160 African Americans living, less than 2%, who held the degree. He wanted to discover the factors that contributed to the academic achievement of "underprivileged populations." He created 16 case studies of scholars who had beaten the odds. Among the contributing factors to their success, he found that the kinds of experiences they had as children in elementary and secondary school were pivotal in their long-term academic achievement. His research showed that there existed "demonstrable ecological distribution of high academic attainment ... closely related to the tangibles of superior elementary and secondary schools, and to the intangibles of high expectancy of high aspiration, motivation, and attainment among teachers, and in families" (Bond, 1972, p. 121). Bond acknowledged the social and economic hardships that African American children faced daily. For that reason he recommended that teachers working with African American students "have the capacity, first, to have faith in the potentialities of the student; and, second, to infuse the student with confidence in himself" (Bond, 1972, p. 124).

Twenty-two years later, Ladson-Billings (1994) analyzed the instructional practices of eight elementary school teachers who were known for their success with African American students. Her highly informative and readable book is entitled *The Dreamkeepers: Successful Teachers of African American Children.* In her discussion of literacy development, she presents two teachers with distinct approaches to literacy instruction.

Ann Lewis is White and trained in holistic approaches to literacy instruction. She grew up in the African American community where she now teaches, and she attributes much of her success to her in-service literacy training. She was observed engaging her students in a wide variety of reading and writing activities around core pieces of literature.

She also groomed her students, especially African American males, to assume increasingly more important leadership roles, despite setbacks or labels from previous years. Ladson-Billings (1994) described the classroom as a special place for all the children:

> The work was challenging and exciting. The students were presume to have some level of literacy, which formed the foundation for increased competency. Reading, writing, and speaking were community activities that Lewis believed all students could participate in—and they did. (pp. 111–112)

Julia Devereaux, the other teacher highlighted for her literacy teaching, is an African American, also from the community, but firmly believes in the product approach. Ladson-Billings (1994) described what would appear to be the "classic" basal lesson:

> Devereaux's reading lessons seem almost scripted. She begins with a phonics drill. A student goes to the front of the room, takes the pointer, and begins the drill by pointing to the chart above the chalkboard. The student points to the letter *b*. "Beating drum, beating drum, ba, ba, ba," she says. The class repeats in unison. She continues, "B sounds, 'bound.' What does 'bound' mean?" One student raises his hand and says, "Bound means to leap." The drill leader continues the drill throughout the consonants. Although this is a fourth-grade class, the words and terms they are asked to define seem sophisticated; they include "justice," "kinsman," "fatigue," "depositor," "lay waste," "preserve," "reunion," and "veranda." There is a high degree of participation in the drill. (p. 113)

In her analysis Ladson-Billings (1994) indicated that superficial differences (e.g., race, teaching methods) merely camouflage strong and important ideological similarities. "Both teachers want their students to become literate. Both believe that their students are capable of high levels of literacy" (p. 116). Like Bond (1972), her work contributes to a set of guiding principles or tenets for literacy instruction.

Fifteen teachers from a Midwestern suburb of Missouri explored their own teaching practices and beliefs about language, literacy, and culture of African Americans in *Mirror Images: Teaching Writing in Black and White* (Krater, Zeni, & Cason, 1994). Until the summer of 1987, they had attributed the lack of success to the children's language and culture, until they completed a study of their school community. Confusion came when they realized that some assumptions they had made about their students had been quite wrong:

> Reflecting on the text analysis and the community, we were more baffled than ever. If neither dialect nor social class explained why African American students were failing to thrive in our classrooms, where was the prob-

lem? Obviously, in that summer of 1987, we could not yet see our own roles with much clarity. (p. 24)

For 6 years they systematically examined the issue of literacy instruction for their African American students, engaging in action research (W. May, 1993). As they tested their beliefs, new beliefs developed about teaching and language. Like Ladson-Billings (1994), they discovered a teacher core belief system necessary for success for African American students, which they summarized in their chapter "Build on Strengths" (Krater et al., 1994, p. 71).

Second Principle: Build on Oral Language

The teachers described in the previous studies saw oral traditions in African American students as a strength. They understood that oral performances were more than just "talk." Teachers developed literacy lessons about genre, persuasive writing, and writing plays, because they utilized verbal skills that children brought from home (Edwards & Sienkewicz, 1990). Even the example Ladson-Billings (1994) offered of the phonics drill was true to the call-and-response oral performance widely known in African American communities.

In 1996, BEV entered public debate once more in the form of *ebonics,* a term that combines "ebony" and "phonics." A school district in California approved a policy statement recognizing BEV as another language, much the same as Spanish or Vietnamese. Noted leaders such as the Rev. Jesse Jackson and author Maya Angelou vehemently opposed the measure. Angelou stated on national television that she was "incensed" because it communicated to African American children that they were incapable of learning standard English (Angelou, CNN News, Sunday, December 22, 1996).

Students can and do learn a standard English, oral and written. They tend to acquire it with *less resistance* when it is presented as an additional communicative register or modality. It is best taught as a way to enrich their oral repertoire and not to supplant their means of communicating with people of their community (Strickland, 1994). African American students so schooled understand that learning standard English provides them a wider audience for their writings and increases the likelihood of being heard by mainstream society (Delpit, 1986).

Third Principle: Build on the Cultures of the Community and the Students

Give your students opportunities to discover their world—physical, social, and emotional (Guthrie, 1996). One way is to help students articulate problems and issues that effect them and their community, using the issues as the bases for inquiry-based learning (Ladson-Billings, 1994). As students pursue their "research agendas," they learn to organize thoughts, locate resources, test hypotheses, analyze data, interpret results, and organize information for presentation. Do not deny your students the concepts of the general curriculum. However, students will show more commitment when engaged in reading and writing activities based on experiences that have meaning to them.

Another way is to invite members of the community into the classroom to share their knowledge and skills. Have parents or cousins who are known for singing or storytelling share stories or songs that have been passed down for generations, like *Abiyoyo* (Seeger, 1986), the African lullabye and folktale. As parents share, have children transcribe stories. These can become classroom-community books (Pérez, chap. 12, this volume). Invite grandmothers to demonstrate quilting, as in *The Patchwork Quilt* (Flourney, 1985), or ask great-aunts who bake for holidays and community parties to invite you and your students to their kitchen to view the preparation of a masterpiece. Interview these people. Find out how they learned their craft and ask them to share recipes for children to write down and learn. Do an ethnography of your students' community.

Skill-based approaches address only part of the literacy equation. Even Delpit (1986) recognized the need for more: "I certainly do not suggest that ... a completely skills-oriented program is right" (p. 384). If you must use a basal-based curriculum, incorporate authentic reading and writing experiences that relate to the children's culture and life at every possible opportunity. Incorporate writing activities that allow students the opportunity to explore ideas and issues that are important to them. Ask your librarian to locate books that present aspects of your students' culture.

When using trade books, review their content for literary and cultural value and authenticity. Although the situation has improved in books for children, many negative images and stereotyping of African Americans that began at the inception of these United States exist today. There are many researchers of children's literature (e.g., Bishop, 1982; Harris, 1993; Sims, 1982) who offer suggestions for selection criteria, as well as effective use of texts and themes.

Fourth Principle: Create a Learning Community

Language and literacy development are social phenomena (Bruner, 1996; Krashen, 1989; Vygotsky, 1978; Wells, 1987). Create experiences that allow your students to collaborate as they engage in literate behaviors. Cooperative learning is an ideal way to achieve this. A word of caution: Paired and group work are good, but they *do not* constitute cooperative learning by themselves. Read literature that describes what it is (e.g., Johnson, Johnson, & Holubec, 1994) and how it can support the literacy development of all students (e.g., Krater et al., 1994; Routman, 1994).

Actively involve your students in instructional planning. Ask them for topics of interest, problems they would like to explore, or books they would like to read. As suggested by Routman (1994), when planning units, brainstorm and web ideas with your students. Reflect on the major concepts or "essential elements" that can be developed through the suggested activities, then have students suggest sequencing and procedures. To increase their sense of ownership, allow your students to recommend projects to their mastery of the concepts.

Fifth Principle: Connect With Your Students

In recounting her experiences as a student during America's period of de jure segregation, author Maya Angelou (1993) reminded us of the connection African American teachers of her time had with their students:

> In Stamps, teachers were much friendlier, but that was because they were imported from the Arkansas Negro colleges, and since we had no hotels or rooming houses in town, they had to live with private families. If a lady teacher took company, or didn't receive any mail or cried alone in her room at night, by the week's end even the children discussed her morality, her loneliness and her other failings generally. It would have been near impossible to maintain formality under a small town's invasions of privacy. (p. 53)

Although they were not always from the communities in which they taught, African American teachers were indeed products of a larger cultural experience shared by their students. Teachers were active members of civic and social organizations, church group leaders, and community activists. Most saw their students at school Monday through Friday, at the market on Saturday, and at church on Sunday. Because they shared a common community culture with their students and parents, they related better, increasing the likelihood of academic success (Foster, 1990; King, 1993).

In today's classroom, students of color are being taught by people far removed from their communities and the social-cultural experiences they bring to the classroom. Learn about the communities and the cultures of your students (Heath, 1983) to avoid making sweeping (and often erroneous) generalizations. Even African American teachers can be out of touch with the lives of African American students. Openly engage in the process of inquiry about the culture and the community to which the students' belong. Do *your* homework on the people you work with every day. Interview your students and their relatives. Go to the library. Find out how the community has changed.

These activities help you connect schooling and home experiences (Pérez, 1994), demonstrate your respect for the knowledge and skills within the community (Moll, 1992), and strengthen the students' self-image by providing a positive sense of cultural identity (Ladson-Billings, 1994). Then go the extra mile. Share your inquiry with your students; show them *your* outlines and rough drafts. Show them *your* struggle with writing and *your* tenacity to the process and the joy of discovery about them and their world. Krater et al. (1994) put it succinctly: "Value African American culture all year" (p. 71).

Help Students Understand How Literacy Is a Political Tool

Help your students understand that at times literacy itself is a political activity (Freire & Macedo, 1987). For African Americans and other minorities, reading the word is not enough. African American students must be taught to read the *world* (Freire & Macedo, 1995).

Encourage them to analyze the local newspaper and any other materials that land on their desks. Help them articulate their frustrations in writing. Engage your students in a discussion about the newspaper articles that ignore the positive things that occur in their community. Have them send letters of complaint (or praise) to merchants and other businesses so that they can see the power of the written word. Encourage them to write to their state representatives. Give them photocopies of the laws that denied their ancestors access to the written word. Ask them why they risked so much to learn how to read and write.

In lieu of subskills instruction and rote memorization, encourage students to become active participants in their literacy experiences and to relate literacy learning to their everyday lives. Provide them with literacy events that are contextualized and meaning laden. Create texts based on the child's home language and personal experience. African American students—all students—will be engaged when learning is connected to the child's life. Know that your students will use their prior knowledge and experience as filters to understand what they read. Help them broaden their knowledge base through authentic activities.

Understand that with holistic approaches to reading, cultural schemata are important. All readers will have greater recall of a text when it originates from their cultural frame of reference. Should a text not specify an intrinsic element in its prose, a person who is from the culture depicted (knowledgeable of it) will not only be able to supply the missing features but will do so automatically. African American students who are taught this way are not asked to leave their language and culture at the school door, but are encouraged to invite it into their learning experiences.

SUMMARY

A final thought: Based on observations of literacy instruction and other practices in America's schools, one can say that there are three categories, broken into groups of 70%, 25%, and 5%. The first group, composed of mostly poor and minorities, are taught through mindless drills and disconnected activities. These students are being groomed to occupy the ranks of the working poor and blue-collar jobs or what is currently called the "permanent underclass." The second group receives enough instruction to obtain slightly higher levels of literacy. They are being groomed to occupy white-collar jobs and midlevel management positions. They will be employed to enforce laws and maintain the social, political, and economic status quo. African Americans, and other minorities, are slowly entering this group. The final group, a select 5%, receive literacy instruction that develops true critical literacy. They will join the ruling class and create policy. They will become the new elite. For which of these groups are your preparing your students?

If schools are to challenge these social, political, and economic structural inequities, teaching practices must change. We must educate all students—African Americans, women, and other minorities—to develop a literate and a critical conscience. We must examine our own practices and challenge erroneous beliefs and harmful stereotypes. As reflective educators, we must prepare our students and ourselves for the struggle that awaits us outside the classroom door. To conclude, I offer the quote by James Baldwin (1963/1988) from my introduction:

> I began by saying that one of the paradoxes of education was that precisely at the point when you begin to develop a conscience, you must find yourself at war with your society. It is your responsibility to change society if your think of yourself as an educated person. (p. 11)

■ ACTIVITIES

1. Create a text set to explore social or historical experiences of African American communities. Examples: the Underground Railroad, the Civil Rights Movement, African American Astronauts.

2. Invite community members to discuss their oral and literacy traditions. Do they share experiences comparable to those described in this chapter? In what ways do they differ?
3. Interview older members of an African American community about their schooling experiences, especially about literacy issues.
4. Survey five teachers, five parents, and five students to elicit their definitions and understanding of ebonics or BEV. Ask them what role it should have in classroom instruction, if any. Based on the data from these interviews and the reading of this chapter, develop (write) a "professional position statement" that acknowledges the community's voices as well as the research on the best practices from the professional literature.

SUGGESTED READINGS

Cornelius, J. D. (1991). *When I can read my title clear: Literacy, slavery, and religion in the antebellum south*. Columbia: University of South Carolina Press.
Heath, S. (1984). *Ways with words: Language, life, and work in communities and classrooms*. Cambridge, England: Cambridge University Press.
Hughs, L., & Meltzer, M. (1963). *A pictorial history of the Negro in America*. New York: Crown.
Ladson-Billings, G. (1994). *The dreamkeepers: Successful teachers of African American children*. San Francisco: Jossey-Bass.
Lippi-Green, R. (2000). That's not my language: The struggle to (re)define African American English. In R. Dueñas González & I. Melis (Eds.), *Language ideologies: Critical perspectives on the official English movement: Vol. 1. Education and the social implications of official language* (pp. 230–247). Mahwah, NJ: Lawrence Erlbaum Associates.
Smitherman, G. (1995). The forms of things unknown: Black modes of discourse. In D. B. Durkin (Ed.), *Language issues: Readings for teachers* (pp. 314–330). Los Angeles: Longman.
Taylor, D., & Dorsey-Gaines, C. (1988). *Growing up literate: Learning from inner-city families*. Portsmouth, NH: Heinemann.
Willie, C., Garibaldi, A., & Reed, W. (Eds.). (1991). *The education of African-Americans*. New York: Auburn House.

REFERENCES

Abrahams, R. (1993). Black talking on the streets. In L. M. Cleary & M. D. Linn (Eds.), *Linguistics for teachers* (pp. 173–198). New York: McGraw-Hill.
Allington, R. (1977). If they don't read much, how they ever gonna get good? *Journal of Reading, 21*, 57–61.
Angelou, M. (1993). *I know why the caged bird sings*. New York: Bantam.
Bailey, B. (1965). *Jamaican creole syntax*. Cambridge, England: Cambridge University Press.
Baldwin, J. (1988). A talk to teachers. In R. Simonson & S. Walker (Eds.), *Multicultural literacy: Opening the American mind* (pp. 3–12). Saint Paul, MN: Graywolf Press. (Original work published 1963)

Baugh, J. (1983). *Black street speech: Its history, structure, and survival.* Austin: University of Texas Press.

Baugh, J. (1999). *Out of the mouths of slaves: African American language and educational malpractice.* Austin: University of Texas Press.

Baugh, J. (2000). *Beyond Ebonics: Linguistic pride and racial prejudice.* New York: Oxford University Press.

Bishop, R. (1982). *Shadow and substance: Afro-American experience in contemporary children's fiction.* Urbana, Il: National Council of Teachers of English.

Blake, S. (1993). Are you turning female and minority students away from science? *Science & Children, 30*(4), 32–35.

Bloome, D., & Nieto, S. (1989). Children's understandings of basal readers. *Theory Into Practice, 28*(4), 258–264.

Bond, H. M. (1972). *Black American scholars. A study of their beginnings.* Detroit, MI: Balamp.

Brooks, F. D. (1937). *The use of background in the interpretation of educational issues.* Chicago: University of Chicago Press.

Brown v. The Board of Education of Topeka, 347 U.S. 483 (1954).

Brownstein, E., & Destino, T. (1995). Science enrichment outreach. *Science Teacher, 62*(2), 28–33.

Bruner, J. (1996). *The culture of education.* Cambridge, MA: Harvard University Press.

Carlson, N. (1965). *The empty schoolhouse.* New York: Harper & Row.

Cassidy, J., & Wenrich, J. K. (1998). What's hot, what's not for 1998. *Reading Today, 15*(4), 1, 28.

Chall, J., Radwin, E., French, V., & Hall, C. (1979). Blacks in the world of children's books. *Reading Teacher, 32*, 527–533.

Collier, V. P. (1998). *The effect of age on acquisition of a second language for school.* Wheaton, MD: National Clearinghouse for Bilingual Education.

Cornelius, J. D. (1991). *When I can read my title clear: Literacy, slavery, and religion in the antebellum south.* Columbia: University of South Carolina Press.

Crafts, H. (2002). *The bondwoman's narrative.* New York: Warner Books. (Original work published 1855)

Cuban, L. (1993). *How teachers taught: Constancy and change in American classrooms, 1880–1990.* New York: Teachers College Press.

Cummins, J., Lapkin, S., & Swain, M. (1991). *Whole language strategies for ESL students.* San Diego: Dominie Press.

de Crèvecoeur, H. (1904). *Letters from an American farmer.* New York: Fox, Duffield & Company.

Delany, S., & Delany, A. (1993). *Having our say: The Delany sisters' first 100 years.* New York: Kodansha.

Delpit, L. (1986). Skills and other dilemmas of a progressive black educator. *Harvard Educational Review, 56*(4), 379–385.

Delpit, L. (1988). The silenced dialogue: Power and pedagogy in educating other people's children. *Harvard Educational Review, 58*(3), 280–298.

Delpit, L. (1993). The politics of teaching literate discourse. In T. Perry & J. Fraser (Eds.), *Freedom's plow: Teaching in the multicultural classroom* (pp. 285–295). New York: Routledge.

Dillard, J. L. (1972). *Black English: Its history and usage in the United States.* New York: Random House.

Dillard, J. L. (1997). *Lexicon of Black English.* New York: Seabury Press.

Edwards, A. (1982). Perspectives: Language difference and educational failure. *Language Arts, 59*(5), 513–551.

Edwards, V., & Sienkewics, T. (1990). *Oral cultures past and present: Rappin' and Homer.* Oxford: Basil Blackwell.

Ellsworth, E. (1989). Why doesn't this feel empowering? Working through the repressive myths of critical pedagogy. *Harvard Educational Review, 59,* 297–324.

Fairchild, H., & Edwards-Evans, S. (1990). African American dialects: A review. In A. Padilla, H. Fairchild, & C. Valadez (Eds.), *Bilingual education: Issues and strategies* (pp. 75–86). London: Sage.

Fishback, P., & Baskin, J. (1991). Narrowing the black-white gap in child literacy in 1910: The roles of school inputs and family inputs. *Review of Economics & Statistics, 73*(4), 725–728.

Flourney, V. (1985). *The patchwork quilt.* New York: Dial.

Foner, E. (1988). *Reconstruction: America's unfinished revolution.* New York: Harper & Row.

Foner, E. (1990). *A short history of reconstruction.* New York: Harper & Row.

Foster, M. (1990). The politics of race: Through the eyes of African-American teachers. *Journal of Education, 172*(3), 123–141.

Freire, P. (1970). *Pedagogy of the oppressed.* New York: Seabury Press.

Freire, P., & Macedo, D. (1987). *Literacy: Reading the word & the world.* South Hadley, MA: Bergin & Garvey.

Freire, P., & Macedo, D. (1995). A dialogue: Culture, language, and race. *Harvard Educational Review, 65*(3), 377–402.

Garcia, G., & Pearson, P. D. (1991). Modifying reading instruction to maximize its effectiveness for "all" students. In M. S. Knapp & P. M. Shields (Eds.), *Better schooling for the children of poverty* (pp. 31–60). Berkeley, CA: McCutchan.

Garcia, J., & Florez-Tighe, V. (1986). The portrayal of Blacks, Hispanics, and Native Americans in basal series. *Equity and Excellence, 22,* 72–76.

Garcia, J., & Sadoski, M. (1986). *The treatment of minorities in nine recently published basal series.* (ERIC Document Reproduction Service No. ED 268 501)

Giroux, H. (1987). Critical literacy and student experience. Donald Graves' approach to literacy. *Language Arts, 64,* 175–181.

Goodman, K. (1986). *What's whole in whole language?* Portsmouth, NH: Heinemann.

Goodman, K., Shannon, P., Freeman, Y., & Murphy, S. (1988). *Report card on basal readers.* Katonah, NY: Richard C. Owen.

Graff, H. (1979). *The literacy myth: Literacy and social structure in the nineteenth-century city.* New York: Academic Press.

Guthrie, J. (1996). Educational contexts for engagement in literacy. *Reading Teacher, 49*(6), 432–445.

Harris, V. (Ed.). (1993). *Teaching multicultural literature in grades K–8.* Norwood, MA: Christopher-Gordon.

Harste, J., & Short, K. (1988). *Creating classrooms for authors: The reading writing connection.* Portsmouth, NH: Heinemann.

Heath, S. B. (1983). *Ways with words: Language, life, and work in communities and classrooms.* Cambridge, England: Cambridge University Press.

Holt, T. (1990). "Knowledge is power": The Black struggle for literacy. In A. Lunsford, H. Moglen, & J. Slevin (Eds.), *The right to literacy* (pp. 91–102). New York: Modern Language Association of America.

Hopkinson, D. (1993). *Sweet Clara and the freedom quilt.* New York: Knopf.

Hopkinson, D. (2000). *Under the Quilt of Night.* New York: Atheneum.

Hughes, L., Meltzer, M., & Lincoln, C. E. (1970). *A pictorial history of the Negro in America* (3rd ed.). New York: Crown.

Hymes, D. (1972). Models of the interaction of language and social life. In J. Gumperz & D. Hymes (Eds.), *Directions in sociolinguistics* (pp. 35–71). New York: Holt, Rinehart & Winston.

Johnson, D., Johnson, R., & Holubec, E. (1994). *The new circles of learning: Cooperation in the classroom and school.* Alexandria, VA: Association for Supervision and Curriculum Development.

Jones-Wilson, F. (1991). School improvement among Blacks: Implications for excellence and equity. In C. Willis, A. Garibaldi, & W. Reed (Eds.), *The education of African-Americans* (pp. 72–78). New York: Auburn House.

King, S. (1993). The limited presence of African-American teachers. *Review of Educational Research, 63*(2), 115–149.

Kozol, J. (1991). *Savage inequalities: Children in America's schools.* New York: Crown.

Krashen, S. (1989). Bilingual education and second language acquisition theory. In *Schooling and language minority students: A theoretical framework* (pp. 51–79). Los Angeles: Evaluation, Dissemination and Assessment Center, California State University.

Krater, J., Zeni, J., & Cason, N. (1994). *Mirror images: Teaching writing in black and white.* Portsmouth, NH: Heinemann.

Labov, W. (1993). Recognizing Black English in the classroom. In L. M. Cleary & M. D. Linn (Eds.), *Linguistics for teachers* (pp. 149–173). New York: McGraw-Hill.

Ladson-Billings, G. (1994). *The dreamkeepers: Successful teachers of African American children.* San Francisco: Jossey-Bass.

Lane, R. (1986). *Roots of violence in Black Philadelphia: 1860–1900.* Cambridge, MA: Harvard University Press.

Larrick, N. (1972). The all-White world of children's books. *Saturday Review, 11,* 63–65, 84–85.

Magill, F. (Ed.). (1992). *Masterpieces of African-American literature: Descriptions, analyses, characters, plots, themes, critical evaluations, and significance of major works of fiction, nonfiction, drama, and poetry.* New York: HarperCollins.

May, S. (1993). Redeeming multicultural education. *Language Arts, 70,* 364–372.

May, W. (1993). "Teachers-as-researchers" or action research: What is it, and what good is it for art education? *Studies in Art Education: A Journal of Issues And Research, 34*(2), 114–126.

McCall, C. (1989). A historical quest for literacy. *Interracial Books for Children Bulletin, 19*(3/4), 3–6.

McCuistion, F. (1932). The South's Negro teaching force. *Journal of Negro Education, 1*(1), 17–23.

McManus, E. (1973). *Black bondage in the North.* New York: Syracuse University Press.

Meier, K., Stewart, J., & England, R. (1989). *Race, class, and education: The politics of second-generation discrimination.* Madison: University of Wisconsin Press.

Moll, L. C. (1992). Bilingual classroom studies and community analysis: Some recent trends. *Educational Researcher, 21*(2), 20–24.

Mosenthal, P. (1988). Understanding the histories of reading. *Reading Teacher, 42,* 64–65.

National Advisory Committee on Education. (1931). *Federal Relations to Education: Committee findings and recommendations.* Washington, DC: National Capitol Press.

Oakes, J. (1985). *Keeping track: How schools structure inequality:* New Haven, CT: Yale University Press.

Ogbu, J. (1987). Variability in minority school performance: A problem in search of an explanation. *Anthropology and Education Quarterly, 18*(4), 312–334.

Ogletree, E. (1977). *Does DISTAR meet the reading needs of inner-city kindergarten pupils?* (ERIC Document Reproduction Service No. ED 146 303)

O'Neil, L. (1994). *Little Rock: The desegregation of Central High spotlight on American history.* Brookfield, CT: Millbrook Press.

Pérez, B. (1994). Biliteracy development in Latino communities. In R. Rodríguez, N. Ramos, & J. Ruiz-Escalante (Eds.), *Compendium of readings in bilingual education: Issues and practices* (pp. 119–123). San Antonio: Texas Association for Bilingual Education.

Pierce, T., Kincheloe, J., Moore, R. E., Drewry, G., & Carmichael, B. (1955). *White and Negro schools in the South: An analysis of biracial education.* Englewood Cliffs, NJ: Prentice Hall.

Ravitch, D. (1983). *The troubled crusade.* New York: Basic Books.

Reed, L., & Ward, S. (1982). *Basic skills issues and choices, Vols. I & II.* St. Louis, MO: CEMREL.

Reutzel, D. (1998/1999). On balanced reading. *Reading Teacher, 52*(4), 322–324.

Rist, R. (1970). Student social class and teacher expectations. *Harvard Educational Review, 40,* 411–451.

Rogan, R. G., & Hamner, M. R. (1998). An exploratory study of message affect behavior: A comparison between African Americans and Euro-Americans. *Journal of Language and Social Psychology, 17*(4), 449–460.

Rosenblatt, L. (1989). Writing and reading: The transactional theory. In J. M. Mason (Ed.), *Reading and writing connections* (pp. 153–176). Boston: Allyn & Bacon.

Rosenblatt, L. (1993). The transactional theory: Against dualisms. *College English, 55,* 377–386.

Routman, R. (1994). *Invitations: Changing as teachers and learners, K–12.* Portsmouth, NH: Heinemann.

Sadker, D., & Sadker, M. (1985). Is the O.K. classroom O.K.? *Phi Delta Kappan, 66*(5), 358–361.

Salvino, D. (1989). The word in black and white: Ideologies of race and literacy in antebellum America. In C. Davidson (Ed.), *Reading in America: Literature and social history* (pp. 140–156). Baltimore: Johns Hopkins University Press.

San Souci, R. (1989a). *The boy and the ghost.* New York: Simon & Schuster.

San Souci, R. (1989b). *The talking eggs.* New York: Scholastic.

Sarason, S. (1990). *The predictable failure of educational reform: Can we change course before it's too late?* San Francisco: Jossey-Bass.

Schroeder, A. (1996). *Minta: A story of young Harriet Tubman.* New York: Dial Books.

Schwartz, A. (1972). Sounder: A black or white tale? In D. MacCann & G. Woodard (Eds.), *The Black American in books for children: Readings in racism* (pp. 89–93). Metuchen, NJ: Scarecrow Press.

Seeger, P. (1986). *Abiyoyo.* New York: Macmillan.

Shannon, P. (1985). Reading instruction and social class. *Language Arts, 62*(6), 604–613.

Shannon, P. (1989). *Broken promises: Reading instruction in twentieth-century America.* New York: Bergin & Garvey.

Shannon, P. (1990). *The struggle to continue: Progressive reading instruction in the United States.* Portsmouth, NH: Heinemann.

Sims, R. (1982). *Shadow and substance: Afro-American experience in contemporary children's fiction* (p. 346). Urbana, IL: National Council of Teachers of English.

Smith, H. L., & Heckman, P. (1995). The Mexican-American War: The next generation. In E. García (Ed.), *Yearbook in early childhood education* (pp. 64–84). New York: Teachers College Press.

Smitherman, G. (1994). "The blacker the berry, the sweeter the juice": African American student writers. In A. Dyson & C. Genishi (Eds.), *The need for story: Cultural diversity in classroom and community* (pp. 80–101). Urbana, IL: National Council of Teachers of English.

Smitherman, G. (1995). The forms of things unknown: Black modes of discourse. In D. B. Durkin (Ed.), *Language issues: Readings for teachers* (pp. 314–330). Los Angeles: Longman.

Smitherman, G. (1997). Black language and the education of Black children: One mo once. *Black Scholar, 27*(1), 28–35.

Strickland, D. (1994). Educating African American learners at risk: Finding a better way. *Language Arts, 71*, 328–336.

Taylor, H. (1991). *Standard English, Black English, and bidialectalism—A controversy*. New York: Peter Lang.

Turner, L. (1949). *Africanisms in the Gullah dialect*. Chicago: University of Chicago Press.

Tyack, D., Lowe, R., & Hansot, E. (1984). *Public schools in hard times: The great depression and recent years*. Cambridge, MA: Harvard University Press.

Underwood, B. (1971). *The tamarack tree*. Boston: Houghton Mifflin.

Vygotsky, L. S. (1978). *Mind and society: The development of higher psychological processes*. Cambridge, MA: Harvard University Press.

Watkins, W. (1993). Black curriculum orientations: A preliminary inquiry. *Harvard Educational Review, 63*(3), 321–338.

Wells, G. (1987). The learning of literacy. In B. Fillion, C. Hedley, & E. DiMartino (Eds.), *Home and school: Early language and reading* (pp. 69–93). Norwood, NJ: Ablex.

Welner, K., & Oakes, J. (1996). (Li)ability grouping: The new susceptibility of school tracking systems to legal challenges. *Harvard Educational Review, 66*(3), 451–470.

Willie, C., Garibaldi, A., & Reed, W. (Eds.). (1991). *The education of African Americans*. New York: Auburn House.

Wolfram, W. (1970). *A sociolinguistic description of Detroit Negro speech*. Washington, DC: Center for Applied Linguistics.

Zucker, A. (1991). Review of research on effective curriculum and instruction in mathematics. In M. S. Knapp & P. M. Shields (Eds.), *Better schooling for the children of poverty* (pp. 189–208). Berkeley, CA: McCutchan.

9

Emergent Spanish Writing of a Second Grader in a Whole-Language Classroom

Aurelia Dávila de Silva

Research examining the beginning writing of native English speakers has been increasing significantly. Some of the most exciting and best known studies of young native English-speaking children learning to write have been done by Bissex (1980), Dyson (1982, 1983, 1985, 1993), Y. Goodman and Altwerger (1981), Harste, Woodward, and Burke (1984), Schickendanz (1990), and Wilde (1986, 1992). However, few of these studies have examined the writing of students whose native language was Spanish and who are learning English as a second language. An important study examining the writing of Mexican American Spanish speakers enrolled in a bilingual program in Arizona was done by Edelsky (1982, 1986). The first-, second-, and third-grade children's written productions were analyzed for a number of aspects and overall quality of content in order to note changes over time as well as to make cross-sectional comparisons (Edelsky, 1986). Other important studies examining the writing of young native Spanish speakers who were developing literacy in bilingual contexts have been done by Flores and García (1984), K. S. Goodman, Y. Goodman, and Flores (1979), K. Goodman and Y. Goodman (1978), Gutierrez (1992), Hudelson (1984), Moll and Díaz (1987), Pérez (1994a, 1994b), Reyes

247

and Laliberty (1992), Silva (1992), and Silva and Menchaca (1992). Understanding the process by which children develop writing in a first and second language is critical in light of the tremendous challenge schools face in developing innovative ways to literacy instruction that are linguistically, developmentally, and culturally compatible. For many Mexican American Spanish-speaking children, there remains a growing unjust pressure to quickly develop English literacy and be competitive with English-speaking peers. This pressure is based on an old assumption that the language development process is instantaneous and that the native language should be abandoned for the new one. In the last 25 years, bilingual and second-language education have advanced the position that our educational goal should be the lifetime promotion and valuing of the native language and culture (Cummins, 1989). Some recent studies demonstrate how this can be done and thereby reduce the conflict between the language and culture of the school and the one found in the home and community (Moll, 1990).

This chapter examines research studies of literacy development in selected Mexican American communities; use of the case study as a tool for learning about literacy in classrooms; data from an extensive case study of Yolanda learning Spanish literacy in a whole-language bilingual classroom; and implications from the case study for literacy development and classroom practices.

LITERACY STUDIES IN MEXICAN AMERICAN COMMUNITIES

The following studies are of particular interest because they examine literacy in the broader arena of the students' social world, family, and community. Moll and González (1994) reported on a number of studies that examined the use of social and cultural resources from the students' home for instruction. They examined the learning conditions in the classroom and the "funds of knowledge" found in homes and communities, and they suggested strategies that incorporate the knowledge found in the community and that children brought to school into the school's literacy lessons. Studies conducted over a number of years in the Mexican American and African American homes and communities in Tucson, Arizona, have been reported in González et al. (1993), Moll and Greenberg (1990), and Moll, Amanti, Neff, and González (1992). These research studies used a sociocultural perspective and showed the complexity of schooling, and demonstrated how school literacy practices were different from home literacy practices. In addition, these studies suggested that we can no longer accept school literacy as the only true way of learning reading and writing. These results indicated how students' social and cultural resources of the home and the community can provide important relevant information for the development of literacy in the classroom.

Likewise, the importance of the sociocultural context of families and communities emerged in studies conducted by Delgado-Gaitan (1987, 1990). She studied the function and meaning of literacy in four Mexican American immigrant families. She found that despite the parents' limited formal schooling, text and print materials in both English and Spanish were a part of their everyday lives. Although the parents did not view themselves as readers, they read letters from their families, reviewed newspapers, and supported their children with their schoolwork. The study indicated that families supported each other emotionally and physically in many different ways.

Code-switching has been a much studied phenomenon in Mexican American communities. Code-switching is the alternation or switching of languages in bilingual speech. Aguirre (1992) and Valdés Fallis (1976) studied the general features of code-switching in Latino communities. These studies concluded that code-switching is an integral aspect of bilingual discourse, symbolizing a person's social identity. It is not merely the product of cooccurring social and linguistic variables, but it is an abstract entity with its own sociolinguistic grammar. Huerta-Macías (1977) and Huerta-Macías and Quintero (1992) studied code-switching of young children and their families and described the sociolinguistic functions of code-switching in Mexican American communities. Edelsky (1986) found that although the Mexican American children she studied used code-switching extensively in their speech, code-switching in the written productions was used very deliberately and judiciously.

The reviewed literature suggested that by addressing community, individual, and family issues, school can become relevant for the student. Social issues that are relevant to the student become the catalyst for writing and learning when they are introduced into the classroom. Further, these studies also suggested that teachers, in particular, need to be aware of the sociocultural context of the families and communities they serve. Teachers' knowledge of the cultural background of the students that includes their histories, educational experiences, social structures, conditions within the family, and parents' values can enable instruction based on the child's social world. Lastly, when the social world of students is considered, curriculum development will move from the home to the school instead of the traditional movement from school to home. Building curriculum that incorporates home literacy development processes can involve the parents' strengths and encourage critical thinking relevant to the students' social world. The students' cultural knowledge thereby contributes to rather than conflicts with school learning, and we can begin to understand the child's complex language, social life, and use of all cultural resources. In sum, learning to read and write involves reconceptualizing linkages between and within the world of home and the world of school.

THE CONTEXT OF SCHOOLING FOR SPANISH-SPEAKING STUDENTS

Embedded in the curriculum used to teach a second language are major assumptions or beliefs about second-language learning and literacy. These are referred to as assumptions because they do not arise from specific research but rather from a misunderstanding and underestimation of how children communicate and develop literacy (Flores, Cousin, & Díaz, 1991). A critical examination of materials published by major publishing companies and of other documents responding to regulations mandated by "authority" agencies, such as state boards of education, school boards, and local school systems, unveils the assumptions held by these policymakers and educators. Some of the most common erroneous assumptions are:

1. Learning English takes a year or two to develop native-language-like proficiency. Therefore, schools should suspend native-language instruction after 1 or 2 years. This assumption does not consider the role of the native language and culture in all of learning.

2. The time students spend learning the native language is a waste of time that could be better spent learning English as a second language.

3. Spanish is a phonetic language with sound–symbol correspondence, and Spanish literacy can be best taught by skill and drill.

4. Children learn language sequentially: listening, speaking, reading, and writing. Therefore, a particular English oral language proficiency level must be reached before students are allowed to read and they must read before they are allowed to write. Knowledge of grammar rules and conventional spelling has to be learned before writing can proceed.

5. Children who speak Spanish lack experiences. Their culture and language is deficient. These deficits cause learning problems that make it difficult for them to read and write in English.

6. The complexity of learning can be captured and measured by state-mandated tests.

Historically, school systems have viewed Spanish-speaking children as different from the mainstream and have applied numerous labels to them throughout the decades. For example, *retarded* was the label of the 1960s; *culturally and linguistically disadvantaged* was the label of the 1970s; *limited English speaking, alingual* (having no language), and *semilingual* (having some language) were the major labels of the 1980s (Flores, 1982). These labels carry particular assumptions about students' learning. In the 1990s the label *at risk* has been used to predict and rationalize failure. Often, Spanish-speaking, low-socioeconomic-background children are labeled under two categories, *linguistic minority* and *special education* (Cummins, 1984; Flores et al., 1991; Oakes, 1985; Ortiz & Yates, 1983).

CASE-STUDY RESEARCH

Case studies provide rich insights about a specific situation and add nuance and subtlety to the perspective of theory. The case study as a research tool has been traced back to Hippocrates by neurologist Oliver Sacks (1985). Hippocrates used patients telling their stories to doctors as case studies and as a powerful way of learning in the field of medicine. Case studies are prevalent in many fields and have a long tradition as a major way of knowing and of teaching in a number of disciplines and professions (Bettelheim, 1950; Freud, 1956; Luria, 1960; Piaget, 1955). A case study is a way of learning, not a method of proving. Practitioners in the field of education concerned with and for the individual can use case studies to examine questions about meaning construction and perspective that are central and ongoing to the teaching/learning process. Case studies provide rich contextualization for the particular phenomena and subjects under study. Studies of children's language acquisition and development have classically proceeded as case studies. Parents have studied their own children's literacy and language development, as in Bissex (1980), Baghban (1984), Weir (1970), and Yaden (1988). The utility of single case studies can also be documented in the field of bilingual education. Teacher researchers (Flores et al., 1985; Hudelson, 1984; Urzua, 1987) have studied Spanish-speaking students in classrooms and from their case studies have developed practical and effective pedagogy for facilitating children's first- and second-language and literacy learning, development, and evolution.

A case-study process is an important tool in the classroom to discover the strategies and theories children are using in learning language and literacy. If teachers want to move in the direction of incorporating parents and learning from the students' cultural experiences, case studies can assist in informing us of the rich cultural resources of parents and communities. Case studies can also help teachers who want to inform themselves about their students' social worlds in order to modify classroom social structures and curricular practices.

PLAN OF THE CASE STUDY

This case study describes biliteracy development and illustrates how insights can be discovered not only about bilingual but also monolingual readers and writers. With data from bilingual learners, a host of questions can be asked, such as about the relationship between first and second language, the relationship between reading and writing, the relationship between instruction and the acquisition of writing, the influence of home/community literacy and school literacy use, and the implications for bilingual and monolingual education.

The following study explores how a child learned and used a variety of linguistic information found in the writing systems of Spanish and English. Insights are revealed into the reading and writing of this second grader whose native language was Spanish and who was on her way to leaning English as a second language. This study is intended to encourage the reader to examine and question different alternatives for helping second-language learners gain access to literacy.

Yolanda's case study examines a second grader's native-language writing in Spanish. Yolanda's parents immigrated to the United States from Mexico. They traveled to Chicago and later settled in a small, South Texas town. Because of the immigration and traveling, Yolanda did not begin school until the age of 7, when she was placed in the second grade. Thus, Yolanda began the second grade with no schooling background (in either Spanish or English) and minimal English-language skills. Yolanda learned Spanish at home and continued her Spanish learning while she began English learning at school.

Other pertinent information is offered to help clarify and explain literacy development in Yolanda's classroom. The study discusses how Yolanda used linguistic information found in the writing systems of each of her developing languages and used cultural background knowledge to create text.

Collection of Data

Yolanda was observed in her second-grade bilingual classroom. The children and teacher were interviewed to obtain a picture of literacy events in this classroom. Observational data collected over the year were part of a larger study reported elsewhere; this chapter focuses on Yolanda's writing sessions during the last 2 months of the school year. Context and time span were important because one piece of writing cannot tell the entire story of what a child can do. Case studies must be conducted over time. It was also important to focus on an individual child in the class in order to document and understand individual learning. The writing sessions, which included writing independently and with peers, teachers, and the observer, demonstrated some ways in which this child developed her writing. Yolanda wrote a total of 21 stories in Spanish and 2 stories in English during the 2 months.

During this time, as part of the teacher's decision to conduct end-of-year assessments, the teacher helped all her students collect, appreciate, and assess their own work and development. The teacher reported that as a result, the students took greater interest in their own learning during these last 2 months. In addition to observation and writing sample data, other teachers, the principal, parents, and students were interviewed to gain insights into the teaching practices, materials, and theoretical beliefs of the elementary school and the classroom.

Community and Classroom Settings

This case study was conducted in a second-grade elementary classroom in South Texas. The school was in a community of about 11,000 residents composed of about 70% Mexican American and 30% Anglo residents. This agricultural community included many immigrants who worked in the fields following the crops to other states during much of the year. The majority of businesses in this community were owned by Anglos, many of whom had some knowledge of Spanish. Spanish and English were spoken at home by most of the Mexican American population. In addition, code-switching was a common form of communication among the Mexican American parents and children. It was possible for adults to function in this community without knowledge of English; they satisfied most of their social, medical, and other needs using the Spanish language. Although printed signs, directions, or legal documents were available only in English, it was common practice for the bilingual speakers to assist those who needed help with English.

The children in the classroom studied were all Mexican American and relatively dark skinned. The majority of the children in this particular group had been detained by various teachers for different reasons. School records showed that most of the children in this class were from low-income families and their parents had limited formal education. Parents were not involved in school affairs, perhaps because of their inability to speak English. According to the teachers in this elementary school, the parents were illiterate and disinterested. However, when interviewed, parents revealed that they had high hopes for their children. Studies by Delgado-Gaitan (1987, 1990) of Mexican American parents found similar high hopes and expectations for the education of their children.

The class was formed after the beginning of the academic year with overflow from the other classrooms. With the consensus of all teachers, children who were less likely to learn were placed in this classroom. The teacher, Chris, hired by the district to teach in this bilingual classroom, had secondary teaching credentials but did not have elementary or bilingual education credentials. She reported that "although she had taught 17 years in secondary schools in different communities, she knew nothing of how to teach young children to read and that was frightening to her." She recounted how she taught her own children and grandchildren to read as they were growing up and drew on what she remembered from this experience. Chris also reported that when the children were assigned to her classroom, they were individually described by other teachers as "low-achievers, possessing learning disabilities, not knowing English, and having behavioral problems." She felt that other teachers' descriptions of these children were based on either knowing the child or knowing (having taught) another member of their family, such as a brother or sister. Because brothers and sisters had been classified as failures, younger brothers and sisters were also classified as failures. In addition, Chris was instructed by other teachers that although this was supposed to be a bilingual class, she should teach the children in English because that was the language they had to learn. However, Chris felt that the students needed to learn content in Spanish while they learned English. She felt that it was important to place equal status on both Spanish and English if children were going to feel good about who they were and what they were going to learn—that children needed to learn to read and write and demonstrate their knowledge in both languages.

A first impression of her classroom might have been that the children and the teacher were disorganized and wandering around aimlessly. Chris had never heard of "whole language," yet her classroom practices reflected that philosophy. As the year progressed, Chris had many curious visitors trying to verify if the children in this classroom indeed were learning how to read and write in both languages. She recruited parents, and parental involvement became a significant aspect of classroom learning. Parents checked out books from the class library. Students were encouraged to help younger children in their families. Parents reported that they were happy with the progress of their children. Other teachers interviewed reported being surprised at the learning achieved by these children.

Observational data contained numerous examples where Chris encouraged children to ask questions and prompted them to answer their own questions. She read to them from a variety of materials and books. Children were eager to obtain more reading materials. They enjoyed funny books, picture books, informational books, poetry, and other printed materials. The teacher expressed high expectations for all the children. Children eagerly demonstrated what they had learned, for example, about the planets, science experiments, world events, and their written stories.

When students initiated conversations and questioned the teacher over various topics, Chris did not stop the questions but rather continued and expanded the conversations. The children often gathered in groups to explore a topic of their particular interest. They would gather information and then gladly share the information with other students who were interested. They moved around the room with facility to accomplish their work and explore questions whether with a globe, book, or other materials. After careful study, one could see that the teacher was a careful observer of children and encouraged them to discover and draw their own conclusions. The children did not sit in their chairs all day; rather, they spent a great deal of time talking purposefully as they endeavored to achieve goals they had internalized (such as writing a story).

In contrast, when I observed in other classrooms in the same elementary school, I saw children grouped by ability. On several occasions, teachers mentioned that a particular child was in a "slow group" even when the child was within hearing distance. In these classrooms, children routinely sat in rows and were ability grouped for language arts. Writing consisted of copying letters from the blackboard rather than the writing of stories. Reading was dependent on basal textbooks to ensure that skills in the teacher's manual were covered. Worksheets were plentiful and children sat in their chairs quietly working on them. The language of instruction was English, although many children spoke both languages and some classrooms were designated as bilingual. The content areas were taught in blocks of time rather than in the interdisciplinary approach that Chris used. Examination of these classrooms showed that most of the children assigned to the "lower groups" were from lower-income parents and were dark skinned.

In Chris's classroom, on any given day, children huddled around her while she read a story or demonstrated a science lesson. She often asked children to write about their experiences, about what they learned at school and home, and, most important, about what deeply interested them. Gradually the children asserted themselves, and their questions indicated the thinkers that they were becoming. Children appreciated books, and they developed a great desire for reading and writing. Students' writing was displayed everywhere in the classroom. Children wrote books, lists, recipes, community maps, and many other "authentic" or real materials with a specific, real-life purpose.

At one point, this observer mentioned to a group of children that a set of Bill Martin's books such as *Sounds of a Distant Drum* (Martin & Brogen, 1972) was located in the book room. Because the students had already been exposed to Martin's poetry, they asked the principal if these books could be brought to their classroom and were ecstatic when the box of Martin's books arrived. That was a turning point for the students and the observer. Although before the observer had been seen as a visitor who was interested in their reading and writing, at this point she became a friend with whom they shared their writing and other daily concerns.

The teacher reported that she respected all children and viewed teaching as a privilege because she had the opportunity to help children learn. She outlined her teaching philosophy as follows:

1. Teaching reading and writing should not depend on the adopted basals.
2. Oral and written language was learned through meaningful and authentic reading and writing in the child's native language.
3. Children had a logic of their own that could be developed by observing, talking, and questioning, empowering them to become independent and self-confident thinkers.
4. Children, regardless of their socioeconomic level and native language, were capable of learning.
5. Spanish reading and writing could be applied to English literacy when children were ready and chose to do so.
6. The classroom's physical and social organization influenced student's learning.
7. Her role was to help students connect their language and culture to classroom activities and to demonstrate content and linguistic knowledge.

TEXT FEATURES OF WRITING SAMPLES

Of the 21 stories in Spanish and 2 in English written by Yolanda during this 2-month period, 4 were in the form of books; 2 books were written in Spanish and 1 in English. The written samples collected were analyzed from multiple perspectives and data were organized into the following categories: lexical, syntactical, and semantic choices; themes of content of writing; use of dialect and code-switching; cultural understanding; story grammars; spellings and word approximations; and word boundaries, segmentation, and punctuation.

Lexical, Syntactical, and Semantic Choices

At the semantic level, Yolanda's stories reflected personal experiences. She relied heavily on her knowledge of everyday spoken language to write her stories. For example, as shown in Fig. 9.1, Yolanda titled a story "*el perro mañoso*" [the naughty dog] and started with "*avia, una, ves*" [once upon a time], continuing to tell how a naughty dog constantly got into the garbage and scattered it. Here, we discuss semantic and syntactic elements of this story; later, we discuss the invented spelling, segmentation, and punctuation. Her choice of words —*mañoso* [naughty] and *basura* [trash]—was not likely to have come from her learning in school or reading of books. These words came from her everyday language experiences. In Spanish, the phrase "*Habia una vez*" [Once upon a time] is a syntactic signal for the begin-

FIG. 9.1.   Name: Yolanda Montes [4/18/19]. es, la istoria, de, un pero [it is the story of a dog]. el, pero, mañosa, avia, una, ves, un pero, qe, todo, el tiento, tirava, la basura, i yo, no, savia, y, un, dia, pe, sali, para, huera, bi, a ese, pero, mañoso [the naughty dog, once upon a time, a dog who all the time threw the trash, and I did not know, and one day I went outside, I saw that naughty dog].

ning of an oral or written story. However, from a different perspective, the English phrase "Once upon a time" is considered a syntactic signal for the beginning of a fairy tale in written text (Harste et al., 1984). One often hears the notion that children have been read to at home because they start their written stories with the phrase "once upon a time." This is an interesting oversight and reflects a narrow world perspective that does not recognize that fairy tales were part of an oral traditional literature.

Themes of Content of Writing

Yolanda used her everyday experiences as themes for her writing. Her personal narratives reflected different understandings of the world. In several stories she wrote about health themes: a girl who did not eat because she was sick, a young boy's face that had broken out with bumps, about falling in the middle of weeds and getting a rash. In still another story (see Fig. 9.2), she fainted while at a family gathering and was taken to the hospital. Yolanda's personal writing reflected not only knowledge of the world, such as cause-and-effect relationships, but also judgments, such as liking the state of Texas where she lived. She occasionally wrote expository (informational) text. In one such text she explained that the President of the United States lived in Washington, DC. Other expository text reflected classroom lessons about her drawing of a map of several states with the appropriate names for each state. Three of the 21 Spanish texts were expository. Texts that were strictly expository were not as common as personal narratives, which included her developing knowledge of the world intertwined with her personal accounts.

Use of Dialect and Code-Switching

Another aspect of Yolanda's writings reflected her home and community experience with the use of dialect. All languages consist of different dialects that are geographically based. People in different parts of the United States speak the same language yet speak in ways that differ from each other in the way they pronounce words, use vocabulary, and combine words. Dialect differences are also related to social and ethnic groups (K. Goodman, 1993; Lindfors, 1987). In Texas we say "you all," yet in other parts of the country this expression is not socially acceptable. Further, we can say that dialect is related to gender and age. And the Spanish spoken by Mexican American children in San Antonio and South Texas is not the same as the Spanish spoken by children in Spain or Mexico.

FIG. 9.2. Name: Yolanda Montes [4/16/19]. mi familia [my family]. una. ves. estaba. toda. la. Familia. en. mi. casa. en. la. mesa. y. yolanda. se. desmallo. y. se la llevaron. pal. ospital *el Fin* [one time, there was the whole family at my house at the table and Yolanda fainted, and they took her to the hospital].

Yolanda's dialect was captured in her written stories and her dialect reflects that of the community. Words such as *muncho* for *mucho* [much], *jalar* for *trabajar* [work], *pa* for *para* [for], *juimos* for *fuimos* [we went], and *troca* for *camión* [truck] were examples of Yolanda's dialect. Clearly, *muncho* for *mucho, juimos* for *fuimos,* and *pa* for *para* are examples of dialect differences at the pronunciation or phonemic level. The lexical item *troca* for *camión* is an example of a dialect difference at the word level. Because the word *jalar* can be conjugated and *el jale* is used to denote work, *jalar* may be considered a dialect difference at a syntactical level. Figure 9.3 gives an example of her usage of *balar* for *jalar* and *troca.*

Code-switching is the alternate use of languages in the same utterance or conversation. The phenomenon of code-switching has been described as an important aspect of bilingualism (di Pietro, 1977; Huerta-

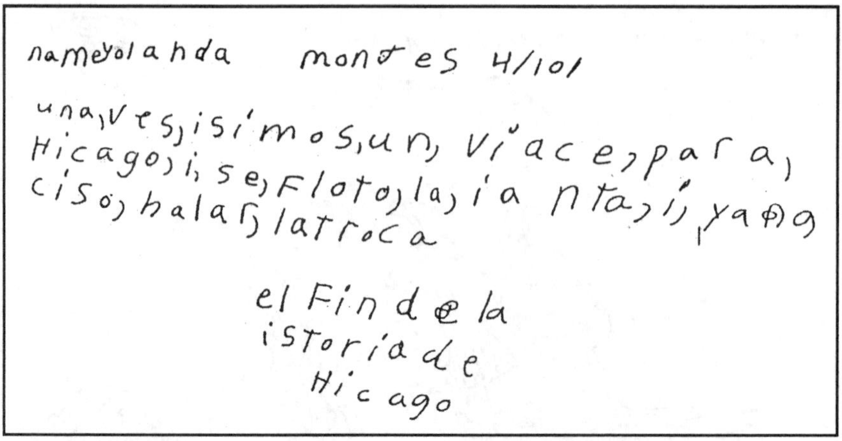

FIG. 9.3.   Name: Yolanda Montes [4/10]. una, ves, isimos, un, viace, para, Hicago, i, se, floto, la, ianta, i yano, ciso, halar, la troca el Fin de la istoria de Hicago [one time, we made a trip to Chicago, and the tire went flat, and the truck did not want to work, the end of the story about Chicago].

Macías, 1977; Quintero & Huerta-Macías, 1990; Valdés Fallis, 1976). Code-switching of bilingual students in the classroom has been viewed as enhancing learning and communication (Aguirre, 1992; Quintero & Huerta-Macías, 1992). In a recent study of a preschool-age child, Silva (1994) found that code-switching played a significant role in the development of narratives in the child's first and second language. These studies suggest that code-switching is an important tool in the demonstration of understanding of complex sociocultural relationships.

In this case study, Yolanda used code-switching orally as a tool to move her from one language to the other. While she spoke Spanish, she would interject English words. The number of interjected oral words in English appeared to increase throughout the observation time. A possible explanation for this was the fact that code-switching was a part of the adult's and children's social functions throughout her community. Although she used proper nouns such as "Chicago" in her Spanish writing and occasionally would write "name" in the header of some Spanish stories, as in Fig. 9.3, she did not use code-switching in the body of her Spanish texts. Edelsky (1986) reported similar findings with the first and second graders she studied. They code-switched orally between sentences and within sentences, but rarely code-switched in writing English texts. Within Spanish texts, she described the exceptions in code-switching with nouns, adjectives, verbs, and address terms. Edelsky observed that the first- and second-grade students used code-switching in Spanish text deliberately for meaningful purposes, such as to convey a specific meaning. However, code-switching in English text, although rare, seemed accidental. Edelsky speculated that children had figured out that English reflected power (or official language of school) and that code-switching in English text was unacceptable.

Cultural Understandings

Yolanda's stories in Spanish reflected not only her interests and understandings but also her culture. For example, Yolanda wrote of her grandmother telling stories. Oral stories are a strong aspect of Yolanda's cultural tradition. The traditional religious beliefs of the culture were also demonstrated in one story. In addition, Yolanda wrote some of the stories so that other children in the classroom could enjoy them. The setting of her stories reflected her experiences, neighborhood, and cultural understandings. For example, she fell in the middle of a patch of weeds, not in a playground. She had limited experiences with playgrounds and numerous experiences with weeds and agricultural fields. She wrote a story about a little orphan girl who lived in the street and did not have enough to eat. Yolanda mentioned a dog as an adversary in a story about the scattering of trash. Pets, cats and dogs living inside one's home, were not a cultural phenomenon in Yolanda's community. Other than this one time, Yolanda never mentioned animals in her Spanish stories. However, when she wrote her first book in English, it was about a boy and a rabbit. The theme of boy and animal relationship in her English story appeared to reflect her experience with an English basal story. Although the English basal was not a structured instructional activity in the classroom, the books were available to students for their perusal.

When Yolanda wrote books in Spanish, the teacher praised her accomplishments as a reader and writer. However, when interviewed, Yolanda described being a reader and writer as being able to read and write in English. Yolanda had internalized that outside of her classroom, in the school and larger community, her reading and writing was not valued unless she used English. Unfortunately, the school climate clearly reinforced her perceptions by publicly valuing English literacy.

Story Grammars

Yolanda had knowledge of story grammar; she had a sense of beginning, middle, and end of a story. Yolanda utilized formulaic beginnings and endings. She began written stories with *"Habia una vez"*

[Once upon a time] or "*una vez*" [one time] and ended them with "*El Fin*" [The End] (see Figs. 9.2 and 9.3). Additionally, in her story settings, characters were introduced and problems were usually posed. These problems or situations were described but not always resolved at the end of the story. All of Yolanda's stories included the reality element; thus, none involved fantasy. In this aspect, Yolanda's stories were similar to the stories of children that Heath described from Roadville. Heath (1983) noted that stories told orally by the Trackton working-class Black community involved fantasy whereas those of the working-class White community involved nonfiction formulaic stories. Yolanda's choice of topics was important because in this classroom children were encouraged to choose their own topics and they determined how long to stay with a topic. Children in Yolanda's class wrote on their own as they investigated topics and styles of their interest.

Spellings and Word Approximations

Yolanda's spellings demonstrated how Spanish, like English, can be encoded in invented spellings. On further analysis, the spellings made sense and show how more than one spelling for a word in Spanish can exist. This speaks to the myth of perfect phoneme/grapheme correspondences in Spanish. A simple predetermined phoneme/grapheme relationship did not exist for Yolanda; she explored phonemic and visual strategies and invented spellings as her writing developed. Table 9.1 contains conventional spellings from 21 stories, illustrating the number of words used in a story, the percentage of the total words that were conventionally spelled, and the percentage that were invented spellings. At times, the number of conventional words fell but the total number of words used in a story increased. In Spanish, 54% of the words were conventional spellings whereas 46% were invented spellings. Table 9.2 shows that in English, 39% of the words were conventional spellings and 61% of the spellings were invented.

Yolanda had a word that she had probably seen frequently—*que* [what]—but that she consistently spelled as *qeu*. She appeared to be focusing on the letters present in the word and the way it looked visually and not necessarily trying to produce a phoneme/grapheme match. More examples of the same phenomenon are *nanho* for *rancho* [ranch], *dihco* for *dicho* [saying], *hicago* for Chicago, and *Hoco* for *Choco* [person's nickname]. We can only speculate that she was using a visual memory strategy from having seen these words in her environment and other printed texts.

TABLE 9.1

Conventional and Invented Spellings in Spanish Stories ($n = 21$)

Writing Entry	Total Words per Story in Spanish	Conventionally Spelled Words in Spanish	Percentage of Conventions	Percentage of Invented Spellings
1	26	4	15.4	84.6
2	43	12	27.9	72.1
3	25	13	52	48
4	23	9	29.3	70.7
5	7	5	71.4	28.6
6	10	4	40	60
7	6	2	33.3	66.7
8	8	7	87.5	12.5
9	37	27	72.9	27.1
10	26	23	88.4	11.6
11	30	25	83.4	36.6
12	29	10	34.5	65.5
13	30	25	83.4	16.7
14	15	9	60	40
15	14	7	50	50
16	16	10	62.5	37.5
17	42	28	66.7	33.3
18	53	37	69.8	30.2
19	10	6	60	40
20	32	20	62.5	37.7
21	14	9	64.3	35.7
Totals	496	267	54	46

TABLE 9.2

Invented and Conventional Spelling in English Stories ($n = 2$)

Number of Words	Words Spelled Conventionally	Percent of Conventions	Percent of Inventions
18	3	17%	83%
15	10	67%	33%

Word Boundaries, Segmentation, and Punctuation

Segmentation, the separation of linguistic units or words, was an element that Yolanda, like other emergent writers (Harste et al., 1984), explored thoroughly. Sometimes Yolanda used either commas or periods to segment words, while occasionally mixing conventional segmentation with period segmentation. However, Yolanda's most frequent form for segmentation was the use of periods. Figure 9.2 shows how she used periods for segmentation as well as punctuation at the end of sentences in her stories. She primarily used commas for word segmentation, only twice using commas as conventional punctuation. Yolanda, like many children learning to write in Spanish, segmented some words syllabically (Edelsky, 1986; Ferreiro & Teberosky, 1982). For example, for "*queria*" [I wanted], she wrote "*que*" and went to the second line to write "*ria*," even though there was enough space for more words on the first line. She also segmented syntactically; for example, she wrote "*el fin de, todas, las, ystorias*" [the end of all stories] where "*el fin de*" is segmented as a phrase. Forty-three percent of the segmentations in Spanish were conventional. This 43% does not count the segmentation done by placing a comma or period after each word. She rarely mixed periods with commas to denote segmentation within any given story. We get a picture that Yolanda knows word units or word boundaries and that she is exploring with commas, spaces, and periods as ways of denoting these word boundaries. The picture is different in her two writing samples in English, where words are not segmented with commas or periods. She begins segmenting with spaces. She apparently used her knowledge and experimentation of writing in Spanish when she later wrote in English.

Specific formal lessons in punctuation were not a part of classroom instruction, however, Chris felt that if children encountered reading and writing in a variety of text formats, then they would be exposed to a variety of punctuation types and purposes. The teacher made a point of answering any questions that children had about punctuation. Table 9.3 shows the conventional use of punctuation as well as the number of omissions and nonconventional insertions. Periods, commas, accents (e.g., á), and tildes (e.g., ñ) were common in Yolanda's Spanish writing. In her two English stories, she used only periods and they are used in a conventional manner.

Yolanda did not reinvent her theories about writing in English; she progressed using the knowledge gained in Spanish in her English writing (Edelsky, 1986). She explored and reconstructed the writing system for herself based on her developing theories (Ferriero & Teberosky, 1982). This child, like the children studied by Harste et al. (1984), reconstructed writing because she was working with the whole system (pragmatics, semantics, syntax) instead of with individual parts.

TABLE 9.3
Frequency of Use of Spanish Punctuation ($n = 21$)

Punctuation	Conventional Use	Omissions	Insertions
Periods	7	20	52
Tildes	15	1	0
Accents	5	54	10
Commas	2	0	82[a]

[a]The number of commas used to segment words.

DISCUSSION

It would be erroneous to describe Yolanda's writing as full of mistakes. Rather, she was beginning to understand the writing system of the languages she knew. For example, while writing a grocery list with nonconventional spellings, she discovered basic principles about encoding the writing system. Yolanda eliminated spelling irregularities and developed a system for word segmentation. The lack of punctuation, the lack of separation of words, and elimination of spelling irregularities all demonstrate a natural phenomenon in young children. Similarly, Ferreiro (1986) found native Spanish-speaking children who did not segment words conventionally. Like other children, Yolanda explored the complex concepts of writing by formulating hypotheses and testing those hypotheses. She did not appear to use the letter name spelling strategy often used by English-speaking children learning to write in English in any of the works collected. The letter name strategy is the use of the name of a letter to represent a sound unit, such as the letter "u" for "you" (Harste et al., 1984). As Yolanda developed as a writer, she began to understand the organization of a written text. She explored the language and formed hypotheses in order to discover rules and relationships and to organize the discrete elements into an ordered whole system. Yolanda's writing in Spanish is testimony of a strong logic in children. As she moved into English print, she continued to be a remarkable hypothesizer with the English language as well.

COGNITIVE AND SOCIAL STRATEGIES

What strategies did Yolanda use to move from Spanish to English literacy? Initially, although Yolanda enjoyed reading and writing in Spanish, she did not perceive herself as a reader and writer because she did not read and write in English. When interviewed, she reported that you had to read and write in English to be considered a reader and writer. She had already learned that Spanish was not valued in her school and had built her paradigm for reading and writing on this perception.

Yolanda determined the time when she began to explore English print. She joined others and listened to stories in English from Bill Martin's *Sounds* books, although she did not always understand the entire story. She enjoyed listening to books that were considered beyond her comprehension. Although she requested specific English stories to be read aloud by the teacher, she also perused English books on her own. Yolanda was able to retell, in Spanish, stories read to her in English. By the end of the school year, she read and wrote in a language she could not yet speak fluently as she wrote her first English book. English reading and writing were important to her, and she enjoyed print as she patiently started her English-language literacy development. Yolanda learned by having major decision-making power over the literacy activities. Having the opportunity to speak, read, and write in Spanish allowed her to fully participate in the classroom. She learned many concepts about print and reading and writing in Spanish. If English had been the only language of instruction, Yolanda would not have been able to participate in many of the everyday classroom activities. The native language helped Yolanda to know what to do in the everyday context of school and classroom, and she used this knowledge as a reference in learning English.

Reexamination of Assumptions

Certainly, the length of this study was not sufficient time to conduct a systematic and thorough examination of a child's literacy development. Nevertheless, let us return to the starting point and examine the findings of this case study in juxtaposition to the beliefs (described in the section titled The Context of Schooling for Spanish-Speaking Students) held by educators regarding second-language learners.

1. For Yolanda, becoming literate in a first language centered on becoming involved in her own literacy development. She did this through social interaction, watching others' activities and reasons for reading and writing, and doing things for her own purposes. She trusted and cooperated in learning from and among friends who were accepting and supportive of her efforts. Therefore, the social functions of language in this classroom, as in other studies by

Edelsky (1986), Flores (1982), and Pérez (1994a), were an important part of her learning to read and write in Spanish.

2. For Yolanda, learning a second language, like learning a first language, will be a lifetime process. At the end of the second grade, remarkable progress was noted in the use of both languages. More important, she was motivated and eager to learn. Clearly, Yolanda understood that language learning is a cumulative task demanding time and planning. The use of Yolanda's native language and the absence of ability groups gave her the opportunity to participate in the everyday happenings of the classroom. She also recognized the powerful messages (Edelsky, 1991) she received concerning the relationship of her native language to learning English. She clearly verbalized that in order to gain access to literacy events in future classrooms, she needed to learn English. At the end of the second grade, Yolanda started to gain control of the English language, and her progress will continue if the school culture cares about her interests and achievements.

3. Yolanda learned to read in her native language first, and she started to use this knowledge base as a tool to learn her second language. She used what she understood of the written system in Spanish to write stories in English. She was able to read English print and talk about it in Spanish to confirm what she read. Similar findings were reported by K. Goodman and Y. Goodman (1978) and Hudelson (1984). They reported that children were aware of English print and could write in their second language long before they were orally fluent in that language. A focus on sequential skills and drills or an all English curriculum would not have allowed Yolanda to capitalize on her knowledge in the way encouraged by the creative opportunities and outlets presented in her classroom.

4. Yolanda determined the different aspects of language that were meaningful to her. Therefore, she had a powerful role in directing her own literacy development. She fully understood the function of texts in her native language; in addition, she began to read and write in a language she did not yet speak fluently. The fact that Yolanda could read a language before she spoke it disproves the common claim that language learning is sequential; first you listen, speak, read, and finally write. It would have been fruitless to assign her particular levels of reading material for different levels of language proficiency.

Yolanda spelled unconventionally in Spanish in order to write her stories. The emerging invented spellings were valued in this classroom. Yolanda's conventions of first- and second-language spelling surfaced in similar fashion through exposure to a variety of written text in both languages. Urzua (1987) and Edelsky (1982,

1986) reported similar findings with second-language learners in bilingual and English-as-second-language classrooms, where many of the same kinds of invented spellings as those used by native English-speaking children were used.

Yolanda was becoming literate in both languages by building hypotheses and having plenty of opportunities to test these hypotheses. Yolanda did this in a classroom where she was allowed to try out different possibilities in different languages and to make mistakes without negative consequences. Yolanda was experimenting with the grammar rules of both languages—such experimentation would not have been encouraged in a traditional classroom.

5. Yolanda's stories reflected the cultural experiences that she brought to a classroom where the teacher permitted or welcomed her language and culture. A study by Reyes and Laliberty (1992) reported that when the mainstream curricula and methods were devoid of the students' personal meaning and cultural relevance, the attention of children from diverse backgrounds could not be held for any length of time. In this classroom, Chris' convictions, high expectations, and her belief that language and culture were not obstacles to learning contributed to a respect for diversity and a positive learning environment. In this case study, the teacher's decision to use the children's native language although she was under tremendous pressure to teach in English demonstrated her conviction that linguistic and cultural diversity must be valued.

Yolanda also reflected the community linguistic knowledge. When she spoke Spanish, she code-switched with English words and used her own dialect. She also used her own dialect when writing in Spanish. These two language strategies, the use of code-switching and the use of local dialects, could have been misunderstood, and the child might have been labeled as having deficient language development and lacking cultural experiences.

6. The richness of Yolanda's language development and cultural knowledge evidenced by this study could not be measured with a standardized test. A standardized test would not capture Yolanda's use of linguistic, social, and cultural strengths to create her own texts. Gutierrez (1992) reported that we must give greater attention to the classroom contexts in which Mexican American students acquire writing, including who is present in the writing activity, the goals that drive the writing event, what is learned, and what knowledge is transmitted in our assessment processes. Careful observation not only can be used to assess student progress but also can give teachers valuable information about students' strengths and developing strategies.

EDUCATION IMPLICATIONS

In this case study, the teacher redefined what counted for reading and writing. The definition appeared to have a positive impact on the learner. The traditional view of perfect oral reading and conventional spelling was set aside. Instead, children and teacher viewed miscues and invented spelling as necessary for growth. Important in learning a second language is the establishment of a classroom culture that is concerned with what is meaningful to the learner and is conducive to meaningful communication. If the native language is Spanish, then it may be used as background knowledge and experience to build a second language. Conditions for learning a first language are important and apply to learning a second language.

The following guidelines for effective literacy instruction in a classroom setting are appropriate based on this case study and other studies cited:

- Create social situations where children can use oral and written language for a variety of their own purposes and interests.
- Accept children's oral and written miscues and provide opportunities for self-correction. This means that we do not have to demand that students read perfectly and write conventionally. Involving students in self-correction will encourage them to move to standard conventions on their own.
- Build and organize learning situations based on children's strengths, prior knowledge, interests, need to know, experience, and culture.
- Provide students with reading and writing experiences that give them success. For the second-language learners, this may include reading in a second language and having students retell (orally or written) in their native language. Reading an abundance of real texts, expository, and narrative can encourage writing for a variety of purposes.
- Explore the social/cultural context of literacy by examining community practices as the basis for informing school curriculum.
- To assess student literacy development, observe what students can and are doing and collect and analyze students products over time. Conducting case studies of selected children will provide valuable insights into the strategies and theories children are using in their literacy development.

SUMMARY

The discussion of Yolanda presented in this chapter illustrates her learning to read and write in Spanish and the beginning of English literacy in a supportive classroom. Some general conclusions emerge from this case study.

First, for this child who was learning English as a second language, the cognitive, linguistic, and social aspects of literacy developed similarly to those of English-speaking children developing literacy in their first language. Children can further their learning by reading and writing in a language they do not speak by drawing on their understandings of an oral and written language in the native language.

Second, teachers have come to better understand the process by which young native English speakers' literacy takes place. Teachers also need to rethink notions about second-language learners' reading and writing and stay current of literacy development research for native English speakers and second-language learners. New insights can provide better understanding and support literacy development in a classroom. The relationship between reading and writing is complex. One must assume that the relationship is not sequential. That is, one process did not occur and then the other process set in. Rather, both processes occurred simultaneously and supplemented each other.

Third, consider using holistic evaluation, such as this case study of Yolanda's reading and writing. One would not have surmised the whole picture of Yolanda's literacy understandings until what she was doing in her native language as well as in her second language was examined.

Lastly, the case study suggests the need for additional examination of existing paradigms or views held about second-language learning. Research that is longitudinal in nature is needed to add to the knowledge about the nature of learning in a first and second language. The research needs to be in the social context of school and home with the teacher's, child's, and parent's perceptions described. Studies must include the role of culture in literacy development. The opportunities afforded to the child during the everyday schooling contexts constitute a student's history as a learner and as a literate being, and we need to study and better understand this phenomenon. A more refined understanding of the nature of literacy learning in a second language would lead to more effective instruction for students whose native language is not English. The successful and unsuccessful learning of second-language learners described in the social and cultural settings of the classroom can provide educators with understandings about why so many students do not gain access to literacy.

■ ACTIVITIES

1. Observe a classroom and determine the teacher's paradigm of learning and teaching and how the model relates to literacy. For example, determine what counts as literacy in Spanish and literacy in

English. Compare your literacy paradigm with the teacher's. Interview the teacher and share your ideas. Ask the teacher how literacy practices in the everyday world are similar to or different from literacy in the classroom.

2. Carefully observe individual children's reading and writing efforts in the classroom. Study a child's use of writing conventions by collecting samples of work over a period of a semester in order to understand their meaning-making efforts. Read the student's work aloud to colleagues to ensure a focus on meaning. Respond to the student's work and describe it in great detail. Refer to specific pieces of writing and address patterns of change and topics discussed.

3. Individuals bring linguistic, social, cultural, and contextual presuppositions to a literacy situation that they use as resources to read, interpret, and participate in literacy events. Observe a classroom; then collect, read, and study the written works of several children to better understand the linguistic, social, cultural, and contextual writing life of individual children. Do the students bring their home experiences, language, and culture to the school setting? Do they code-switch orally and not in their school writing? Do particular themes surface in their writing?

SUGGESTED READINGS

Gutierrez, C. (1992). A comparison of instructional contexts in writing process classrooms with Latino children. *Education and Urban Society, 24*, 244–262.

Pérez, B. (1994). Spanish literacy development: A descriptive study of four bilingual whole-language classrooms. *Journal of Reading Behavior, 26*, 75–93.

Reyes, M., & Laliberty, E. (1992). A teacher's "pied piper" effect on young authors. *Education and Urban Society, 24*, 263–278.

REFERENCES

Aguirre, A. (1992). The sociolinguistic basis for code switching in bilingual discourse and in bilingual instruction. In R. V. Padilla & A. H. Benavides (Eds.), *Critical perspectives on bilingual education research* (pp. 70–92). Tempe, AZ: Bilingual Press/Editorial Bilingüe.

Baghban, M. S. M. (1984). *Our daughter learns to read and write: A case study from birth to three.* Newark, DE: International Reading Association.

Bettelheim, B. (1950). *Love is not enough: The treatment of emotionally disturbed children.* Glencoe, IL: The Free Press.

Bissex, G. L. (1980). *Gnys at wrk: A child learns to write and read.* Cambridge, MA: Harvard University Press.

Cummins, J. (1984). *Bilingualism and special education: Issues in assessment and pedagogy.* London: Multilingual Matters.

Cummins, J. (1989). *Empowering minority students*. Sacramento: California Association for Bilingual Education.

Delgado-Gaitan, C. (1987). Mexican adult literacy: New directions for immigrants. In S. R. Goldman & H. Trueba (Eds.), *Becoming literate in English as a second language: Advances in research and theory* (pp. 9–32). Norwood, NJ: Ablex.

Delgado-Gaitan, C. (1990). *Literacy for empowerment: The role of parents in children's education*. London: Falmer Press.

di Pietro, R. (1977). Code-switching as a verbal strategy among bilinguals. In F. Eckman (Ed.), *Current themes in linguistics: Bilingualism, experimental linguistics and language typologies* (pp. 3–13). Washington, DC: Hemisphere.

Dyson, A. H. (1982). The emergence of visible language: Interrelationships between drawing and early writing. *Visible Language, 16*, 360–381.

Dyson, A. H. (1983). The role of oral language in early writing. *Research in the Teaching of English, 17*, 1–30.

Dyson, A. H. (1985). Individual differences in emerging writing. In M. Farr (Ed.), *Advances in writing research: Children's early writing development* (pp. 59–125). Norwood, NJ: Ablex.

Dyson, A. H. (1993). *Social worlds of children learning to write in an urban primary school*. New York: Teachers College Press.

Edelsky, C. (1982). Writing in a bilingual program: The relationship of L1 and L2 texts. *TESOL Quarterly, 16*, 211–228.

Edelsky, C. (1986). *Writing in a bilingual program: Había una vez*. Norwood, NJ: Ablex.

Edelsky, C. (1991). *With literacy and justice for all: Rethinking the social in language and education*. New York: Falmer Press.

Ferreiro, E. (1986). La complejidad conceptual de la escritura. In L. F. Lara & F. Garrido (Eds.), *Escritura y alfabetización* (pp. 60–81). Mexíco, DF: Ediciones del Ermitano.

Ferreiro, E., & Teberosky, A. (1982). *Literacy before schooling*. Exeter, NH: Heinemann.

Flores, B. (1982). *Language interference or influence: Toward a theory of Hispanic bilingualism*. Unpublished doctoral dissertation, University of Arizona, Tucson.

Flores, B., Cousin, P. T., & Díaz, E. (1991). Transforming deficit myths about learning, language and culture. *Language Arts, 68*, 369–379.

Flores, B., & García, E. A. (1984). Collaborative learning and teaching experience using journal writing. *Journal of the National Association of Bilingual Education, 6*, 67–83.

Flores, B., García, E., González, S., Hidalgo, G., Kaczmarek, K., & Romero, T. (1985). *Bilingual holistic instruction strategies*. Tempe, AZ: Exito.

Freud, S. (1956). The relationship of the poet to day-dreaming and Leonardo da Vinci and a memory of his childhood. *Collected papers*. New York: Basic Books.

González, N., Moll, L. C., Floyd-Tenery, M., Rivera, A., Rendon, P., Gonzáles, R., & Amanti, C. (1993). *Learning from households: Teacher research on funds of knowledge. Educational Practice Report*. Santa Cruz: Center for the Study of Cultural Diversity and Second Language Learning, University of California.

Goodman, K. (1993). *Phonics phacts*. Portsmouth, NH: Heinemann.

Goodman, K., & Goodman, Y. (1978). *Reading of American children whose language is a stable rural dialect of English or a language other than English* (Final Report, Project NIE C-00-3-0087, University of Arizona).

Goodman, K. S., Goodman, Y., & Flores, B. (1979). *Reading in bilingual classroom: literacy and biliteracy*. Arlington, VA: National Clearinghouse for Bilingual Education.

Goodman, Y., & Altwerger, B. (1981). *Print awareness in preschool children: A study of the development of literacy in preschool children (Occasional Paper)*. Tucson: Program in Language and Literacy, Arizona Center for Research and Development.

Gutierrez, C. (1992). A comparison of instructional contexts in writing process classrooms with Latino children. *Education and Urban Society, 24*, 244–262.

Harste, J., Woodward, V., & Burke, C. (1984). *Language stories and literacy lessons*. Portsmouth, NH: Heinemann.

Heath, S. (1983). *Ways with words*. New York: Cambridge University Press.

Hudelson, S. (1984). Kan yu ret and rayt en inglés: Children become literate in English as a second language. *TESOL Quarterly, 18*, 221–238.

Huerta-Macías, A. G. (1977). The acquisition of bilingualism: A code-switching approach. *Working papers in sociolinguistics*. Austin, TX: Southwest Educational Development Laboratory.

Huerta-Macías, A., & Quintero, E. (1992). Code switching, bilingualism, and biliteracy: A case study. *Bilingual Research Journal, 16*, 69–90.

Lindfors, J. (1987). *Children's language and learning*. Englewood Cliffs, NJ: Prentice Hall.

Luria, A. R. (1960). *The mind of a mnemonist: A little book about a vast memory* (L. Solortaroff, Trans.). New York: Basic Books.

Martin, B., & Brogan, P. (1972). *Sounds of a distant drum*. New York: Holt, Rinehart & Winston.

Moll, L. C. (1990). *Community knowledge and classroom practice: Combining resources for literacy instruction*. Arlington, VA: Development Associates.

Moll, L. C., Amanti, C., Neff, D., & González, N. (1992). Funds of knowledge for teaching: Using a qualitative approach to connect homes and classrooms. *Theory Into Practice, 31*, 132–141.

Moll, L. C., & Díaz, S. (1987). Teaching writing as communication: The use of ethnographic findings in classroom practice. In D. Bloome (Ed.), *Literacy and schooling* (pp. 55–65). Norwood, NJ: Ablex.

Moll, L. C., & González, N. (1994). Lesson from research with language minority children. *Journal of Reading Behavior, 26*, 439–456.

Moll, L., C., & Greenberg, J. (1990). Creating zones of possibilities: Combining social contexts for instruction. In L. C. Moll (Ed.), *Vygotsky and education* (pp. 319–348). Cambridge, England: Cambridge University Press.

Oakes, J. (1985). *Keeping track: How schools structure inequality*. New Haven, CT: Yale University Press.

Ortiz, A., & Yates, J. (1983). Incidence of exceptionality among Hispanics: Implications for manpower training. *NABE Journal, 7*, 41–54.

Pérez, B. (1994a). Biliteracy development in Latino communities. In R. Rodríguez, N. J. Ramos, & J. Ruiz-Escalante (Eds.), *Compendium of readings in bilingual education: Issues and practices* (pp. 119–123). San Antonio: Texas Association for Bilingual Education.

Pérez, B. (1994b). Spanish literacy development: A descriptive study of four bilingual whole-language classrooms. *Journal of Reading Behavior, 26*, 75–93.

Piaget, J. (1955). *The language and thought of the child*. New York: Meridian.

Quintero, E., & Huerta-Macías, A. (1990). All in the family: Bilingualism and biliteracy. *Reading Teacher, 44*, 306–312.

Quintero, E., & Huerta-Macías, A. (1992). Learning together: Issues for language minority parents and their children. *Journal of Education Issues of Language Minority Students, 10*, 41–56.

Reyes, M., & Laliberty, E. (1992). A teacher's "pied piper" effect on young authors. *Education and Urban Society, 24*, 263–278.

Sacks, O. (1985). *The man who mistook his wife for a hat.* New York: Simon & Schuster.

Schickendanz, J. (1990). *Adam's righting revolutions: One child's literacy development from infancy through grade one.* Portsmouth, NH: Heinemann.

Silva, A. (1992). Some glimpses into the biliteracy history of a five-year-old child: At home and at school. In P. Swicegood (Ed.), *Reading in education in Texas, A yearbook of the Texas State Reading Association, 8,* 53–60.

Silva, A. (1994). The development of narratives in Spanish and English: A case study of a four-year-old. *State of Reading, 1,* 27–35.

Silva, A., & Menchaca, R. (1992). The writings of a bilingual kindergarten child. *The whole language catalog supplement on authentic assessment: Teaching as inquiry.* Santa Rosa, CA: American School Publishers.

Urzua, C. (1987). Second language children composing and revising. *TESOL Quarterly, 21,* 279–297.

Valdés Fallis, G. (1976). Social interaction and codeswitching patterns: A case study of Spanish/English alternation. In G. Keller, R. Teschner, & S. Viera (Eds.), *Bilingualism in the bicentennial and beyond* (pp. 53–85). New York: Bilingual Press/Editorial Bilingüe.

Weir, R. (1970). *Language in the crib.* The Hague, Netherlands: Mouton.

Wilde, S. (1986). *Spelling and punctuation development in selected third and fourth grade children (Occasional Paper).* Tucson: Program in Language and Literacy, Arizona Center for Research and Development.

Wilde, S. (1992). *You kan red this.* Portsmouth, NH: Heinemann.

Yaden, D. (1988). Understanding stories through repeated read-abouts: How many does it take. *Reading Teacher, 41,* 554–560.

III

LITERACY DEVELOPMENT IN MULTILINGUAL, MULTICULTURAL CLASSROOMS

10

Making Decisions About Literacy Instructional Practices

Bertha Pérez
Amy Nordlander

The subtle and seemingly inconsequential decisions that teachers make daily can profoundly affect the learning of culturally diverse children. Understanding the home literacy environments of children from diverse cultural and linguistic groups can help teachers understand how the everyday lessons, environment, and activities they create for children contribute to or impede literacy development. The starting point for making decisions about literacy must be for teachers to assume a *stance of inquiry* (Edelsky, 1991), which recognizes that the school's way of knowing may not be the way of knowing for culturally and linguistically diverse students. Rodriguez and Berryman (2002) argued that teachers may be resistant and opposed to "student-centered, inquiry-based, or social constructivist pedagogical strategies" because they may be opposed to "teaching as a vehicle for establishing social justice in our society; that is, teaching as a vehicle for students to use knowledge for self-empowerment and transformative action" (p. 1018) The task, then, for teachers is to understand their commitment to culturally sensitive teaching, to listen to students, to find out about their lives and culture, and to make space for their literacy practices. The single most important aspect of culturally sensitive teaching is for teachers to learn about the educational resources the children bring with them as well as the literacy practices of their cultures (Moll, 1992; Weinstein-Shr, 1995).

Each of the previous chapters sought to analyze literacy studies and practices found in distinct cultural communities and classrooms. However, it would be a mistake to assume that the home experiences of all children within a sociocultural group are comparable; a great deal of variability in the opportunities available to children for learning about literacy exists. Understanding home experiences and understanding parents' perspectives on literacy are important prerequisite factors to building connections between the culture of the home and the culture of the school.

CONSTRUCTING THE CONTEXT OF LITERACY

To construct the context of literacy for your classroom, you will have to make decisions in a number of areas. First, you will have to consider the role of the native-language literacy. McCarty and Watahomigie, Smith, and Torres-Guzmán (chaps. 4, 5, and 8, this volume) discuss the notion of a literacy continuum that would allow for students to make progress toward English literacy without sacrificing their native literacies. For many students, the goal of full biliteracy is attainable. Second, you will have to decide how to attend to and create the classroom cultural context for each literacy task. Within the classroom cultural context, how will you provide for your students to learn the majority culture? What role will your students' distinct cultures play in their English literacy development? How will you connect to the students' culture? Third, you will need to consider how you will socially mediate the literacy tasks for your students. A major consideration within the social context of literacy will be making decisions related to interactions with parents, some of whom will defer to the teacher as the authority. Fourth, you will have to consider the degree to which you will accept, value, and reinforce the student's voice and discourse, and to what degree you will insist that students develop the dominant literate discourses. Included in this decision about discourses are issues of learning the necessary skills versus focusing on voice, fluency, and processes. How will you lead your students to use literacy and literate discourse and critical stances? Finally, you will be expected to work toward the national, state, and locally established literacy standards by which the students will also be assessed. You will have to articulate your goals in conjunction with these standards and make assessment decisions based on your goals.

Teachers are the policymakers in the classrooms (Green & Dixon, 1996) making the decisions that most directly affect the lives of children. The teacher's set of purposes, goals, values, and relationships will guide the literacy practices enacted in the classroom.

Cultural Respect and Cultural Repertoire

Within a sociocultural perspective, literacy is a set of cultural practices, and a product of cultural activity (Heath, 1983; Vygotsky, 1986). Thus, what counts as literacy depends on the cultural perspective of the teacher who is identifying, understanding, and evaluating the cultural practices. To thi Dien (chap. 6, this volume) describes how Vietnamese students felt "conflicting demands of two cultures" within their classrooms. Bruner (1996) suggested that to provide access to school curriculum we must recognize "human groups and human culture and the needs human beings have for guarding a sense of their own identity and tradition" and that we must "appreciate the enabling nature of human culture as a toolkit for active, questing children seeking greater mastery over their worlds" (pp. 80–81). Attending to student home culture is important; however, one must also proceed with caution, for although membership in a cultural group plays a pivotal role in shaping identity, membership does not determine identity (Greene, 1993). It may well create differences and styles that must be honored and understood. McCarty and Watahomigie (chap. 4, this volume) describe the immense cultural differences between American Indian communities and recognize that many have evolved "these new cultural forms, along with elements of traditional cultures, [that] are in many places directly incorporated into children's socialization and have taken on new meaning as representative of ethnic identities" (p. 89). Thus specific traits cannot be attributed to any group but a cultural context must be created where students can evolve and incorporate new cultural behaviors without sacrificing them their native or traditional cultures.

School literacy practices are cultural practices that are supported or assailed by the sociopolitical tensions of the larger society (Nieto, 2002). Giroux (1983) argued that language and literacy practices "represent one feature of the dominant culture that schools legitimate in varying degrees" (p. 214). There is a persistent view that individuals who practice the more narrowly defined and socially valued school-based literacy are somehow considered cultured and able to think more logically (H. Bloom, 1994; Scribner, 1984). This narrow view of school-based literacy and issues of national cultural identity have formed the framework for many attempts to "fix" or reform minority education. Ferdman (1991) argued that "the ongoing debate over cultural literacy (Hirsch, 1987) ... is about the issue of what should constitute cultural identity at the national level and what should be the nature of the relationship of minority and dominant groups in the society" (p. 365). Hirsch and others (W. Bennett, 1993; H. Bloom, 1994) argued that cultural literacy can be attained only through the reading of the canon, the traditional Western literary texts. Hirsch defines cultural literacy as "the background information, stored in their minds, that enables them to take up a newspaper and read it with an adequate level of comprehension, getting the point, grasping the implications, relating what they read to the unstated context which alone gives meaning to what they read" (p. 2). Within this debate, culture is composed of a common set of concepts, institutions, and exchange systems that specify what roles people play and what status and respect these roles are accorded. It argues for a control by someone, usually majority group members or majority institutions, of the particular cultural concepts and their symbolism within the society. For example, the meaning and value attached to concepts as "westward movement" or "market forces" must have a uniform or one version of knowledge in order to unify us as a nation. Historically, this role of cultural control and transmission has been a function of education; that is, schools were to reproduce the culture that supports it—not only reproduce it, but further its economic, political, and cultural ends. However, Garrison (1995) argues that "if cultures are to progress productively as well as persist reproductively, they must continuously be retooling—that is, reconstructing entrenched social structures and functions. Progressive societies must permit newcomers to introduce new purposes to which cultural tools may be put" (p. 733).

In the 1980s, many advocates (W. J. Bennett, 1984; A. Bloom, 1987; Finn, 1989; Hirsch, 1987) called for a core curriculum (a required set of common courses) as a way of bringing culturally and linguistically diverse students into the mainstream, improving educational outcomes, and making the U.S. economy more competitive. Ogbu (1992) argued that an assumption of the core curriculum movement (and related school reform movements) is that what goes on in schools is most important and that in order to improve minority school performance one need only fix what happens in schools. He suggested that although what goes on in schools is important, what the children bring to school—their communities' cultural models of understandings of "social realities" and the educational strategies that they, their families, and their communities use or do not use in seeking education—is as important as within-school factors (p. 5). According to Ferdman (1991), the drive to educate all students about a set of "cultural facts" in the name of literacy education may simply serve to allow the dominant group to maintain its position and can be seen by culturally diverse students and communities as the imposition of a particular type of cultural identity. This definition of cultural literacy marginalizes the segments of our pluralistic society by devaluing the language, contributions, and histories of some groups.

Many traditional school literacy programs reflect Hirsch's view of cultural literacy. For the linguistically diverse students, what is at stake in participating in traditional school literacy events is the relationship to their native culture and community. Successful participation in school literacy may require students to distance themselves from their cultural identity and cultural heritage (Ferdman, 1991; Ogbu, 1991), or to construct multiple parallel cultural identities across school and community contexts (Bloome & Green, 1992). Some people, communities, and families may reject literacy learning in school settings rather than lose their cultural identity and way of life (Ogbu, 1991; Phillips, 1983). However, it is possible for teachers and schools to help transform school literacy practices to enhance cultural and community identity (Delgado-Gaitan, 1990; Fox, 1990; McLaughlin, 1989). McLaren (1989) suggested that there are other approaches to cultural literacy that include "the language standards and cultural information students bring into the classroom as legitimate and important constituents of learning" (p. 214).

The challenge for teachers is to argue for change in literacy education to allow for children's ways of making meaning to inform their practices. Proactive teachers will know, accept, and celebrate the children's different. Teachers can acquire this knowledge and acceptance either through an insider's understanding of a particular culture from being a member of the groups, or through directed, thorough education and training in the cultural aspects of the different communities into which children are born, nurtured, and socialized; it is these communities that shape the self-identity and world perspectives of children. Au (1998) and Ferdman (1991) suggested that for teachers to be able to acknowledge their students' cultural identity, they must first turn inward: "Before helping others ... one must initially explore one's values and attitudes about ethnic diversity, as well as one's degree of awareness of the role culture plays in one's own formation. A teacher should feel comfortable with his or her own background before attempting to delve into that of others" (Ferdman, 1991, p. 366).

Building on the knowledge gained from the study of the cultures and of the children in the classroom, the teacher and students can make progress toward the attainment of the goal of developing cultural repertoires for children. Two specific strategies, cultural interventions and cultural authenticity, can assist the teacher. Igoa (1995) suggested that teachers may have to be proactive in conducting what she calls *cultural interventions.* When culturally diverse children are outwardly rejecting their own culture in order to fit in with classmates, it is necessary for the teacher not only to intervene with the offending students about cultural sensitivity but also to intervene with the culturally distinct child. She described an example of cultural intervention:

> I observed an Afghan boy wearing a baseball cap backwards, his hands on his hips, trying to talk like an American Kid. "What's goin' on, man?" he asked .... I asked the boy to come over. We spoke a little about his background .... I assured him that he didn't have to act in a way that didn't feel Afghan. He smiled. We both understood. He removed his cap, returned to his seat, and seemed more relaxed. This was the beginning of a cultural intervention that lasted for the remainder of the year and enabled him to accept both sides of himself, Afghan and American. (pp. 120–121)

The teacher's intervention was a purposeful way of assisting the child toward the development of cultural repertoires. The child did not feel that he had to reject his home ways and culture in order to fit in and develop the ways of the school or what he perceived as the American culture.

Another strategy for teachers to use to assist children in the development of cultural repertoires can be described as *cultural authenticity* of literacy practices (Harris, 1992). This can be attained by incorporating the community's ways in literacy and learning. McCarty and Watahomigie (chap. 4, this volume) suggest the use of a Ciulistet or teacher leaders who work collaboratively with teachers, teacher aides, and elders in articulating and integrating the indigenous knowledge base as they cocreate the literacy curriculum. Within Latino communities, the work conducted by Moll, Velez-Ibáñez, and Greenberg (1990) described how the cultural and literacy "funds of knowledge" of the parents and community could be used to develop classroom literacy practices that allow students to use their cultural and literacy knowledge. Smith (chap. 8, this volume) stresses the need for cultural authenticity in the selection of children's literature and other materials used in school literacy. Cultural authenticity in children's books requires either that the authors be members of the culture groups they are writing about or that the authors have an almost "insider" understanding of the culture that can come only from studying, learning, and inhabiting the world they write about (Harris, 1992; Temple, Martinez, Yokota, & Naylor, 1998). When children can read a text that is culturally authentic—for example, when a group of Mexican American children read, discuss, and write about a book like *Chato's Kitchen* by Gary Soto (1995) or when African American children do the same with a book like *Shimmershine Queens* by Camille Yarbrough (1982)—the children can use their cultural knowledge to make meaning from the text and the children can use their linguistic knowledge to interpret specific use of language, rhythm, code-switching, and other elements.

Implementing literacy education that enables and nurtures distinct cultural identities implies a change in the way we educate children, if not an actual realignment of the social structures and functions of schooling in the lives of culturally diverse people. Chang (chap. 7, this volume) not only addresses the need to view children's culture as "cultural capital" but also emphasizes the need for "multiple sites of learning." When children from culturally and linguistically diverse communities are engaged in English reading and writing activities in schools, they are not only learning a new language but also adopting a whole new set of cultural symbols, referents, and meanings. With culturally sensitive, culturally knowledgeable perspectives and practices, teachers will be much better equipped to assist children in the development of literacy. Children from all sociocultural and linguistic groups deserve such teachers. If the school literacy program explicitly incorporates a perspective that allows students to learn about their own culture as well as the majority culture, then students may discover how what they are learning in English relates to their culture and ethnic identity. A goal of literacy within a sociocultural theoretical framework would be to assist the students in using all their literacy abilities in various cultural contexts, or to develop cultural repertoires (Pérez & Torres-Guzmán, 1996).

Social Interactions and Social Power

The teacher plays a significant role in shaping the literacy environment by providing opportunities for literacy learning and deciding on the specific knowledge the children need to participate successfully in various classroom contexts. Based on the teacher's perspective of literacy and schooling, the teacher may share opportunities for literacy to be socially constructed through the situationally specific ways of using and valuing literacy in the classroom and the social patterns of talk (Cazden, 1988).

How children participate in the active construction of personal and social understandings of literacy will depend on the social group and the purposes created for literacy within this social group. In your classroom, you will have children from different cultural groups. Even when children are from the same ethnic background, they will make literacy meaningful in their lives in personal ways. Although a teacher's official agenda may be that all children will acquire the same knowledge, there is much evidence from classrooms that children's

personal and cultural perspectives play a role in shaping their learning experiences (Alton-Lee, Nuthall, & Patrick, 1993; Au & Mason,
1981; Cazden, 1988; Dyson, 1993, 1994; Purcell-Gates, 1995;
Solsken, 1993).

Elementary schoolchildren are aware of the role of social interaction in literacy. Myers (1993) reported that the children she studied
saw some of the literacy practices as serving them in the future, such
as high school, college, and workplaces. The children also saw literacy
practices as social constructions, which they learned to use, based on
their own desires, views, positions, and values. To thi Dien (chap. 6,
this volume) compares the social perspectives of Vietnamese and educational success: "Americans view success as their own, while the Vietnamese thinks about success for his family or primary group" (p. 71).
The social organization of the classroom needs to be flexible enough
to allow children to engage in literacy activities within diverse social
situations and for distinct social purposes.

Mulhern (1994) described how the social authority of teachers is
interpreted in some communities. In her study, Luis and his parents
are confused with the literacy instruction of the first-grade classroom, which did not match the instruction Luis had in the Head Start
program:

> Luis was upset that he had to continue practicing the same letters over and
> over. His mother was unsure how to help her son be more successful and
> she worried because he was no longer excited about school as he had been
> in Head Start. Despite her doubts about the efficacy of the homework as-
> signments, Sonia (the mother) did not feel she should question the au-
> thority of the teacher because she was unfamiliar with American school
> practices. (p. 25)

Among some culturally diverse groups, especially new immigrants,
parental deference to the social authority of the teacher is common.
This position stems from parents' lack of sociocultural knowledge
about schools in the United States and the respect for the authority of
teachers in their native or traditional cultures (Delgado-Gaitan, 1990;
Flores, Cousin, & Díaz, 1991). The potential for teachers to misguide
from this position of authority can lead to still further social conflict
for the child and parents. For example, teachers and schools stress the
need to practice English at home and encourage children to not
"think" or talk in their native language. Children in homes where little
English is spoken are placed in a position that discourages elaborate
communication and social interaction with parents. As this occurs,
parents begin to lose their ability to communicate, guide, and influence the development of their children's lives (Moll, 1992; Valdés,

1996; Wong Fillmore, 1991). On the other hand, parents who begin to understand the impact they can have on their children's education through at-home and in-school involvement have received support from teachers who have made extra efforts to understand and include their perspectives .

For many researchers and educators, the potential of literacy to empower, foster group advancement, create critical consciousness (Freire, 1970), and promote social change is part of the renewed focus on literacy. Recognizing that literacy is inextricably linked to cultural and power structures in society, many (Gowen, 1992; Stuckey, 1991) argued that the attainment of literacy is critical for individual and social-group advancement. Thus learning to read, write, and think is not just about good school performance or future job attainment; it is linked with more fundamental cognitive, economic, and social consequences for the individual and society. As individuals and groups develop literacy, either they will be empowered to affect the social, political, and economic structures of their community and society or they will be disempowered socially, politically, and economically (Freire & Macedo, 1987). For many, this *empowerment* view of literacy is at the center of the current debate over the development of distinct educational approaches for diverse cultural and linguistic communities.

How a school or teacher defines literacy strongly influences how literacy is taught and what difficulties linguistically and culturally diverse students may face in the school context. Reyes (1993) described how schools and teachers re-create and reinforce the larger societal political context that pressures and demands "quick" English-language literacy, rather than creating the literacy programs that are most appropriate for linguistically and culturally diverse students. Fitzgerald (1995) suggested that "there is strong evidence that, on average, the target language [English] and sociopolitical contexts of second-language learning" (p. 117) in the United States have contributed to the dismal literacy achievement rates of linguistically diverse students. An understanding of the role of English in our society and in the world as the language of commerce and political power (Skutnabb-Kangas, 2000) as well as the sociopolitical context of educating linguistically diverse learners (Valenzuela, 1999) is prerequisite to making significant changes in the literacy achievement of these students.

Voice, Community Discourse, and Classroom Discourse

For literacy instruction to make sense for culturally and linguistically diverse students, it must begin with each learner's language and the learner's world that is encoded by that language. The concept of *voice* includes the development and expression of thought and encompasses a sense of agency (Oldfather, 1993; Shor, 1987). The issue of voice in literacy goes to the heart of how language, especially written language, is used and "how differences in language inscribe different ways of building an argument, naming a world, and describing the processes and practices of those within the world" (Green & Dixon, 1996, p. 294). To allow access to literacy for all children, instruction must recognize and appreciate what the child knows and does not know about print in all dimensions. It must begin from the learner's primary discourse. Freire and Macedo (1987) clarified the notion of voice saying "critical mastery of the standard dialect can never be achieved fully without the development of one's voice, which is contained with the social dialect that shapes one's reality" (p. 129). Instruction must proceed by recognizing the students' voices and social dialects, so that it makes sense to the learner.

Willis (1995) described the struggle that her son Jake encountered in continuing to write in the third grade after having enjoyed writing in the earlier years. She expressed both her frustration and that of her son with the teacher's lack of understanding and sensitivity to issues of audience, cultural identity, and selfhood.

> A teacher's unintentional disregard for the cultural history, understanding, experiences, and voice of a student occurred when my oldest son struggled to meet the requirements of a national essay contest entitled, "What it means to be an American." One of the contest's restrictions was that students should not mention the concept of race. My son thought this was an unfair and impossible task to complete, since his African American identity is synonymous with his being American .... He is trying to come to grips with how he can express himself in a manner that is true to his "real self," and yet please his teacher and audience or readers who are, in effect, evaluating his culture, thinking, language, and reality. (pp. 32–33)

By not being able to refer to his sociocultural experiences and by knowing that his writing was evaluated by what he perceived to be a "White" audience and a narrow "mainstream lens," Jake's voice was being silenced.

Delpit described how some teachers who define themselves as progressive teachers of literacy remain true to their ideology (an ideology that defines their role as one who empowers and politicizes the most disenfranchised students) by refusing to teach the dominant discourses: "Believing themselves to be contributing to their students' liberation by deemphasizing dominant Discourses, they instead seek to develop literacy *solely* within the language and style of the students' home Discourse" (Delpit, 1993, p. 291). She argued that African American students as well as other culturally diverse students need to have access to many voices, and that acquiring the ability to function in a dominant Discourse

> need not mean that one must reject one's home identity and values, for Discourses are not static, but are shaped—however reluctantly—by those who participate within them and by the form of their participation. Many who have played significant roles in fighting for the liberation of people of color have done so through the language of dominant Discourses. (p. 292)

Literacy programs that encourage and accept the students' home discourse but also teach the dominant discourses would be addressing the fundamental issue of power, of "whose voice gets to be heard" (Delpit, 1991, p. 501), by giving linguistically and culturally diverse students and communities a place in setting the literacy goals and agenda of the school and society. This dual position of accepting and developing dual discourses allows for what Greene (1993) described as a conversation with different voices: "Old silences have been shattered; long repressed voices are making themselves heard ... [allowing] the notion of a conversation with different voices ... conditioned by different perspectives" (p. 186).

For some students, the issue of voice is one where teachers are in denial of the students' linguistic abilities. Students are described as alingual or semilingual (Skutnabb-Kangas, 2000) due to the prevalent code-switching that occurs in their homes and communities. Silva (chap. 9, this volume) describes how a teacher recognized and used the code-switching style of the community in literacy development. Chang (chap. 7, this volume) discusses the need to address the discourse differences between English academic prose and rhetoric and Chinese, especially assisting Asian students to cope with the difficulty of writing within the discourse style of school literacy tasks.

Delpit (1993) suggested several possibilities for how teachers can assist students to develop their voice, master the dominant discourses, and transform the dominant discourse.

> First, teachers must acknowledge and validate students' home language without using it to limit students' potential .... The point must not be to eliminate students' home languages, but rather to add other voices and Discourses to their repertoires .... Second, teachers must recognize the conflict Gee details between students' home Discourses and the Discourse of school .... The teacher ... can reduce the sense of choice, students choosing to reject schooling for maintain a sense of identity, by transforming the school Discourse to a new Discourse that contains within it a place for all students .... Teachers can ... acknowledge the unfair "Discourse-stacking" that our society engages in. They can discuss openly the injustices of allowing certain people to succeed, based not upon merit,

but upon which family they were born into, upon which Discourse they
had access to as children. (pp. 293–294)

Smith (chap. 8, this volume) suggests that teachers who are com-
mitted to teaching all students will struggle to understand the complexities of culture, language, and social identities and the role they
play in becoming literate as well as how the decisions they make every
day impact their students literacy access and attainment. Given the
opportunity, children will "compose a place for themselves" (Dyson,
1993); that is, they will negotiate a social status and a literacy identity
in relationship with others (Dyson, 1993; Solsken, 1993). When the
teacher demonstrates sensitivity to differences in the literacy contexts, the children too will learn to negotiate and construct understandings within the cultural and social context formed by the
members of the class culture.

APPROACHES TO LITERACY INSTRUCTION

Home–School Connections

The place to begin making decisions abut the instructional approaches
is with knowledge about what home language and literacy experiences
your diverse students bring from home. The disconnect between home
and school is a strategy that has been used historically in North America
both to resocialize groups of diverse students and to ensure that students succeed at different rates. Those students who enter the school
environment with cultural customs from the majority culture have had
greater success. According to Graff (1991), the disconnect between
home and school can be seen as an educational dance to ensure repeated patterns of family illiteracy and school failure.

Research has explored how to best match home and school approaches to literacy acquisition (K. Bennett, Weigel, & Martin, 2002;
Cairney & Ashton, 2002; Goldenberg, 1993; Osterling, 2001;
Sonnenschein & Munsterman, 2002; Taylor, 1997). The match of
home and school approaches is not about working with parents to
change their home practices; it is about working with parents to find
ways to enrich home practices while modifying school practices.
Mulhern (1994) argued that parents can adopt new ways of viewing
children's literacy development when teachers invest time to explain
their practices to parents and work with parents to find ways that they
can support both home and school literacy practices. Studies (Chang-
Wells & Wells, 1993; Rodriguez & Villarreal, 2002) examined how children whose parents attended to the development of more school-like

literacy skills, for example, storybook reading in the home, had greater ease in transition to school-based literacy. Moll et al. (1990) demonstrated how teachers can study the "funds of knowledge" found in the home and community that can be integrated in the instructional approaches implemented in schools. Other researchers (Delgado-Gaitan & Trueba, 1991) critiqued the line of inquiry that focuses on congruity between home and school literacy. Delgado-Gaitan and Trueba interpreted this as implying "that children are deficient and cannot learn unless taught in the familiar way of the home" (p. 147). They and others (Delpit, 1993; Valdés, 1996) argued that searching for congruity between middle-class classroom culture and the family literacy practices of culturally diverse homes ignores the complexity and the sociopolitical implications of what it means to learn English literacy in the United States. A number of studies examined those classrooms that successfully integrated both home and school literacy to enhance the language and literacy learning (Heath, 1982, 1983; Ochs & Taylor, 1992). A collaborative mix of environments will foster learning and a natural ebb and flow of shared information between home and school.

Skill-Based Versus Meaning-Based Instruction

Literacy instruction continues to be debated as educators weigh the merits of skill-based versus meaning-based approaches (Delpit, 1991; Freppon, 1995; Jiménez, 2000; McKenna, Stratton, & Reinking, 1994; Pérez, 1994; Serna & Hudelson, 1993). Some scholars claim that a skills-based approach has an autonomous view of literacy that defines reading as a set of skills easily broken into parts to be learned and tested (Barton, 1994; Larson, 1996; Street, 1995, 1998). Thus, teachers are pressured to teach children so that they will be successful on standardized assessments that still measure mastery of discrete skills. However, teachers are also pressured to provide children with more meaning-based, authentic reading, and with authentic writing experiences that will engage them in exploring identity, context, and cultural relevancy. According to Buckner (2002), "We have research which tells us that authentic learning situations and projects that matter in students' lives are crucial for long-term learning" (p. 214).

The effects of this debate create confusion in the types of literacy programs and practices that schools and teachers adopt and implement, often resulting in an eclectic approach that lacks a sound theoretical base. In the late 1990s, balanced literacy was proposed as a way for integrating skills with meaning-based authentic approaches (Pressley, 1998). Teachers' difficulties in establishing a literacy curric-

ulum that is meaningful and authentic are further augmented by limited opportunities for teachers to engage in professional dialogue and
planning required for more authentic instruction and by the impact of
the mandated textbooks.

In too many classrooms, children are challenged by a curriculum
that teaches skills in isolation yet expects children to apply those skills
in more open-ended text-based activities, demanding that children
separate the different expectations and learning contexts for themselves. A skill-based approach disconnects the set of skills from the
learning context. Some children can comply with the need for different strategies required by different contexts, but for other children
this creates a level of incongruence that is overwhelming.

Our knowledge about literacy development and literacy instruction,
how it is learned, and how it can be taught has changed; new theories
and instructional advances have been undertaken—for example,
whole language, writing process, and writing across the curriculum.

Some researchers and teachers (Edelsky, 1991; Goodman, 1992;
Shannon, 1993; Smith, 1992) combine the writing process and whole
language to form a holistic process and philosophy of literacy learning
that focuses on meaning and comprehending rather than discrete
skills. This shift appears especially in the move toward greater integration of reading, writing, and subject matter. Whole-language and writing-process approaches for literacy development have been
suggested as solutions in schools where large numbers of culturally
and linguistically diverse students are not performing at adequate levels of reading and writing proficiency (Applebee, Langer, & Mullis,
1986, 1988; Edelsky, Altwerger, & Flores, 1991; Fitzgerald, 1995).

Some research comparing skills-based and whole language or literature-based instruction found more favorable or equal outcomes
in the whole-language kind of instruction (Freppon, 1991, 1995;
Knapp, 1995; McIntyre & Freppon, 1994; Morrow, 1992; Pérez,
1994; Purcell-Gates, McIntyre, & Freppon, 1995). For example, Morrow found that minority children in a process/literature-based instruction in second-grade classrooms had an increase in reading
comprehension and motivation. Their behavior reflected new understandings of their roles as learners, of classroom expectations,
and of how they were to engage in literacy. Serna and Hudelson
(1993) found that instruction based on the whole-language philosophy, which encouraged individual learners' construction of knowledge as they interact in authentic activities, supported the emergent
literacy development of at-risk Spanish-speaking students (see also
Hudelson, 1992). Whole-language classrooms are more consistent
with a sociocultural constructivist perspective (Vygotsky, 1986) because they view children as active constructors of knowledge, re-

gardless of the child's prior knowledge or home situation (Edelsky et al., 1991).

Children in skill-based classrooms, where literacy learning is sequenced and teacher directed, also try to make sense of the skill-based literacy they are experiencing. However, they are likely to have fewer opportunities to construct their own texts or have their approximations celebrated than children in classrooms where literacy learning involves more social interaction, choice, and authentic reading and writing activities.

Meaning-Based Approaches: Issues and Complications.
Regardless of the theoretical approach a teacher uses, children have particular ways of seeing the world that will affect how they construct personal understandings of written language within different social contexts at school. Similarly, children who have different literacy experiences at home than do mainstream children should not be viewed as deficient or at risk when their home "funds of knowledge" (Moll et al., 1990) remain largely undiscovered and untapped by schools. By teachers ignoring sociocultural factors that children bring with them to school, the children are bound for frustration. Jiménez (2000) described this sense of disconnect: "Language minority students will succeed or fail to the extent that their language and culture are incorporated into the school program" (p. 973).

A fundamental assumption of meaning-based and process approaches is that teachers function primarily as creators of contexts and as facilitators of learning, not as the source and transmitter of knowledge. This role may create dissonance within a cultural group's expectations of teachers. Reyes (1991, 1992) reported that the Hispanic second-language learners she studied sought the teacher's help in selecting books, but the teacher chose not to impose her "expertise"; instead, the teacher encouraged students to select books of their liking. The teacher did not provide explicit assistance, which led to some students' failure to complete the task. Reyes reported that the "teacher was left with the impression that students lacked motivation to learn." Reyes concluded that incidents such as these led her to question the assumption that all students, including second-language learners, flourish in classrooms where there is ample freedom to choose activities and where the teacher's role is that of facilitator. Reyes went on to cite another example where the student's interpretation and the teacher's interpretation of a literature log activity were different and the teacher failed to make the expectations explicit. She reported, "They (the students) got in trouble for trying to socialize with the teacher by expressing affection, interjecting personal topics, and failing to view the literature log as a businesslike diary, which was the teacher's view of the task" (Reyes, 1991, p. 166).

Reyes (1991) referred to mini-lessons and conferences within the context of a process approach to literacy:

> These sessions paid little, if any, heed to adjustments that might need to be made for children as a function of language fluency and cultural background. The failure of these leaders (whole language advocates) to point out the need for linguistic and cultural modification when using these practices with second-language learners encouraged the notion that process instruction works equally well with all students regardless of backgrounds .... The result was that teachers did not provide the needed mediation and scaffolding of tasks for students. (p. 167)

Kucer (1995) concluded that a shift to a process-oriented curriculum does not guarantee that students will apply what they are being taught. Meaning-based and process approaches to literacy will succeed only to the extent that teachers understand and assume the role of mediators for literacy learning within the classroom culture as well as with the child's ethnic culture. Willis (1995), in an analysis of the literacy experiences of her young son, Jake, as he "struggles to affirm himself as both a literacy learner and an African American" (p. 30), described the literacy practices and materials of Jake's third grade, which the teacher referred to as a whole-language approach to literacy:

> [It] includes lots of reading and writing for meaning, working in cooperative groups, process writing, and having sustained time for reading and writing .... [The] teacher had selected the books she planned to use during the school year, ahead of time, and the children were allowed only to choose which of these books to read. All of the books were written by European American authors. Even the folk tales from other countries were rewritten by European Americans. Very few books by or about U.S. minorities have been read to students by the teacher, student teachers, or in the reading groups. (p. 42)

Theoretically, the whole-language philosophy of this classroom purported to be culturally neutral and not mediated by any dominant view of language or culture; in fact, this classroom reflected a mainstream cultural view. The teachers had narrowly defined the cultural perspective through which the children, especially the culturally and linguistically diverse students, were expected to develop and understand literacy.

Some studies (Fuller, 1990; Lucas, Henze, & Donato, 1990; Reyes, 1991; Valdés, 1991) suggest caution in extrapolating practices designed for mainstream schools and classrooms to schools and classrooms with second-language learners. The classroom-based research of Atwell (1987), among others, implies that exposure to correct models of conventional form helps students learn and apply correct form. Reyes (1991) did not find similar results with bilingual students. Despite extensive opportunities to write, the bilingual sixth-grade students in her study did not achieve the high levels of writing that Atwell and others described for mainstream students in writing-process classrooms. In fact, most traditional measures show no widespread effect of the meaning-based or process approaches on achievement (Applebee et al., 1988; Langer, Applebee, & Mullis, 1990).

Whole-language and writing-process approaches may also be misunderstood by children's parents as well as by the general public, as is evident by the often heated public discussions that took place in California during 1996 over whole language and reading and writing. Family members of culturally diverse students may be uninformed about the school methods of literacy instruction, and this may result in tension. For example, children's approximations of written language may be criticized by parents or older siblings; thus, children may attempt to minimize such remarks by avoiding tasks that reinforce their feelings of incompetence. The lack of communication between home and school about children's literacy learning efforts can create an environment that is less than supportive for the child.

The diversity among families within one community, defined by class and ethnicity, can be extensive. Yet some researchers continue to look for commonalities across families that can lead to generalizations about community literacy uses. In working-class Latino communities specifically, Goldenberg (1987) found similarities between home and school when parental support for skill learning matched skill-based activities in a first-grade classroom. Similarly, Goldenberg, Reese, and Gallimore (1992) compared the use of worksheets and repetitive little books by parents and children and found that both kinds of materials were used in school-like ways. This led these authors to suggest sending worksheets home with children in order to reduce home–school mismatches. Yet solutions that propose the continued precedence of isolated skill learning at home for children who may not have had multiple early experiences with texts (Delgado-Gaitan, 1990; Teale, 1986) are likely to limit both parents' and children's opportunities for perceiving literacy learning as meaning making. Research indicated that the common middle-class activity of shared book reading is infrequent in low-income Hispanic homes (Goldenberg & Gallimore, 1991; Teale, 1986). Parents who have been introduced to the practice by teachers and literacy program leaders welcomed information about assisting their children in literacy learning (Ada, 1988; Delgado-Gaitan, 1990; Eldridge-Hunter, 1992; Mulhern, 1994). Moreover, generalizations that point to community-wide literacy practices mask variability at the family and individual level. There are various intertwining forces affecting children's literacy learning, thereby precluding the search for simplistic solutions to home–school mismatches.

Although a growing body of research indicates that some culturally diverse families may have different and sometimes less frequent uses of written language than mainstream families, it also reveals that significant learning occurs at home that is often unacknowledged by the school (Delgado-Gaitan & Trueba, 1991; Moll & Greenberg, 1991: Purcell-Gates, 1995). These studies have made important contributions to our knowledge of the variability among families and the rich contexts for learning some families provide and children bring to the school literacy learning. At the center of a teacher's decision about appropriate instructional approaches should be community- and child-specific prior knowledge. A reasonable set of clear goals could focus the efforts of teachers and school personnel, and could help to focus the efforts of parents.

LITERACY CURRICULUM STANDARDS

Literacy education has long suffered from a lack of clear goals for student learning. Historically, most of the goal and standard setting was left to local school districts, but in the last decade we have seen a shift to state and national standardization of learner outcomes. The primary vehicles for standardization are textbooks and the standardized or state-mandated, often high-stakes tests. According to Kohn (2002), the push for common standards and high-stakes testing is built on "politically tendentious premises" that schools' differentiated student expectations—that is, higher expectations in schools serving affluent families than for schools with high numbers of poor or culturally diverse populations—will be fixed through the "current accountability fad" (p. 251). Kohn cautioned educators about exacerbating the inequity in the quality of instruction that such testing is leading to:

> High-stakes testing leads to a more systematic use of low-level, drill-and-skill teaching, often in the context of packaged programs purchased by school districts. Therefore, when someone emphasizes the important of "higher expectations" for minority children, it is vital the we reply, "Higher expectations to do what? Bubble in more ovals correctly on a bad test—or pursue engaging projects that promote sophisticated thinking?" ... The more that poor children fill in worksheets on command (in an effort to raise their test scores), the further they fall behind affluent kids who are more likely to get lessons that help them understand ideas. (p. 252)

On the other hand, Au (2000) argued that linguistically diverse students can meet high standards when given "extra teaching and time" and that their English achievement "can be improved through assessments based on standards, once high-quality instruction is in place" (p. 844).

National Literacy Standards

Since the mid-1980s through the passage of the *No Children Left Behind Act of 2001* (U.S. Department of Education, 2002), the educational reform movement has advocated systemic reform through the development of sets of standards for student learning, curriculum, and assessment. According to Salinger (1995–1996), this approach is based on two assumptions:

> First, the very process of striving toward consensus on what students should know and be able to do will itself initiate reform. Second, dialogue among educators about what they most value in their discipline—what they think is important—will strengthen the discipline and increase understanding of best practice. This dialogue will also raise public awareness and give the public a yardstick against which to measure student progress. (p. 292)

Although standards are supposed to be relevant for all students, the standards for literacy, like curriculum standards in general, are skewed toward an English-speaking, majority culture perspective, and thus the process of reform strives toward a consensus of what students should know from this perspective. The *No Child Left Behind Act of 2001*, also known as H.R. 1 (U.S. Department of Education, 2002), states that

> The new Act will focus on helping limited English proficient (LEP) students learn English through scientifically based teaching methods. Under H.R. 1, all LEP students will be tested for reading and language arts in English. (p. 3)

The standards and reform movement dialogue thus excludes understandings of literacy development in a second language or that of culturally diverse students. Beyond culture and language of instruction, many critics question the conceptualization schemes reflected in the magnitude of indicators or benchmarks that accompany each set of standards. Many seem overly prescriptive, which could result in further fragmentation of curriculum. At the same time, some broader standards have been critiqued as so vague that they are subject to diverse interpretation and are difficult to assess. Salinger (1995–1996) further criticized the discrete set of standards for each discipline and subdiscipline:

> In addition, the very idea of so many distinct standards documents, each touting its own vision of excellence, flies straight in the face of current belief in integration across curriculum areas. For example, the Department of Education funded three separate panels to develop standards in history, civics, and geography, a move questioned by those who pointed out that the three disciplines should be considered together. Further, the National Council of Social Studies has also published its own set of standards, developed without federal funding. To add to the stew, the American Forum in New York is developing standards for global education. (p. 294)

Attempts by bilingual and multicultural advocates to include indicators that are more inclusive have had limited success. When panels working on standards respond to issues of linguistic diversity, it is usually within the context of foreign-language education. For example, the National Education Goals Panel (1991) included the following statement with regard to its foreign-language achievement goals: "The native language skills of immigrant children constitute a potential resource to the nation; such children will more easily than others be able to meet the objective of showing competence in two languages …. Unless schools show overt evidence of valuing native languages, many children will refuse to continue using them" (p. 48). As a whole, the standards movement has ignored the changing diversity and the need for more opportunities for culturally and linguistically diverse students to build on their home language as they develop literacy in English. The fear of some educators is that the standards-based systemic reform movement represents attempts to nationalize educational decision making and will lead to the development of a national curriculum to be followed by national tests.

State Curriculum Frameworks

Some states (e.g., California, Texas, New York) and local school districts have responded to the national standards reform movement by developing curriculum frameworks that establish overall program goals and grade level objectives while encouraging teachers to construct instructional plans to meet these goals and objectives. During the early 1990s, many states' literacy frameworks (e.g., California, Michigan) used a constructivist perspective of reading that focused on meaning. According to Valencia and Wixson (2000), "Most recently, there has been a shift away from attention on comprehension, writing, and integrated lan-

guage arts to early reading, especially phonemic awareness and phonics" (p. 923). Many state curriculum frameworks reflect this shift to
skill-based reading. Teachers of culturally and linguistically diverse students in these states will need to evaluate their literacy curriculum not
only from the perspective of the state framework but also for the appropriateness of the goals and objectives as applied to the students in their
class for any given academic year.

Most of these state frameworks also suggest delivery systems (how
the teacher organizes the classroom context for the delivery of the curriculum) that will have to be examined with regard to the sociocultural
organizational experiences of the students in the class. Saravia-Shore
and Martínez (1992) quoted a teacher citing the benefits of individualized teaching as "the only possibility for the successful instruction of inner-city students. You can't just go through the curriculum, ... but
rather there needs to be constant clarification of concepts and building
on each student's knowledge" (p. 234). Au (2000) suggested that attention must also be given to state or district polices regarding the time al-
located for language arts in many frameworks. In a study conducted by
Au and Carroll (1997, as cited in Au, 2000), they found that successful
teachers of culturally diverse students "spent a minimum of 60 minutes
for reading plus 45 minutes for writing, four to five times per week"
(Au, 2000, p. 845).

Additionally, curricular frameworks must clearly model and articulate a philosophy of education, teaching, and learning that are inclusive and value diversity: what McCarthy and Hoffman (1995) called
the relationship "between teachers' epistemological orientations and
their assumptions about students as manifested in their beliefs about
reading and classroom practices" (p. 74).

Textbooks and Curriculum Frameworks

The political arguments over reading, or "reading wars" (Piluski, 1997),
have greatly influenced what counts as literacy in schools today. The policy actions taken by the federal and state government, especially with
funding research and textbooks, have shaped a national curriculum for
literacy. The standards reform movement and state frameworks for literacy have necessitated changes by publishers of basal reading programs
(Hoffman, Sailors, & Patterson, 2002; McCarthey & Hoffman, 1995). Although most publishers describe their basal reading programs as integrated and literature based, most of their reading textbooks continue to
assume a perspective that is reductionist, a skill-based instructional
methodology. Most basal reading series include isolated skill development, vocabulary-regulated reading passages, topically organized sto-

ries, informational selections, and limited writing opportunities. Most basal series have been revised to include "universal" themes and include illustrations of characters from various racial/ethnic groups; however, rarely do they make reference to the culture of the people. Most texts will include token "ethnic" stories, but often these have been abridged or edited versions of original works, and in some instances, such as folktales, legends, and fairy tales, are translations or a retelling of the original, in many cases by European Americans (Willis, 1995).

The textbooks reduce or segment the content to be learned into parts that must be taught and learned to some level of mastery before advancing to new content. The teachers guides that accompany the textbooks contain goals and learning objectives; predetermined content, prescribed methods, and teaching strategies to be used and specified evaluation procedures. Most of the lesson content is predetermined through some task analysis undertaken by publishers, with little attention paid to the experiences that students who will be using these materials might have or not have had with the specific content. When the task is to teach a strategy, according to Palincsar and David (1991), "there is segmentation of the strategy into steps and emphasis on students' following procedural steps in utilizing the strategies" (p. 124). Textbooks and other curriculum materials reinforce this segmentation and procedural bias, making the development of an inclusive diverse curriculum even more difficult. Willis (1995) argued that the use of this type of material reflects and reinforces a "narrow ethnocentric view of school literacy" (p. 43).

Constructivist Framework for Diversity

Curricular frameworks are most useful when developed locally, by teachers, parents, support staff, and community through a collaborative process among multigrade levels or through school wide discussions that include all the stakeholders of the school's diverse community. Through this discussion process, values, perspectives, and assumptions can be clarified and goals for curriculum established. The notion of a constructivist curriculum is not new. Dewey first proposed in it at the turn of the 20th century. Dewey envisioned curriculum and instruction as a relationship between the individual students, community, and world mediated by socially constructed ideas (Dewey, 1992; Prawat, 1995). A curriculum framework that incorporates a constructivist perspective, that is, engages children in reorganizing and reconstructing the experiences of their physical and social environment, and that values diversity can be most responsive to the needs of all students. When a constructivist curriculum framework is adopted, a literacy curriculum will emerge that supports student's growth on a continuum of culture, language, and cognition.

A constructivist framework is also responsive to the new demands and literacy practices of the world being created in the 21st century, one in which the world itself and the types of knowledge, literacies, and experiences required in this world will change. In order to develop the literacies needed for the future, we will need to examine school practices in terms of the emerging cultural and social world.

In order to teach literacy to culturally and linguistically diverse students, teachers must have a background that goes beyond the most frequently required introduction to developmental reading courses. An understanding of reading theory and research alone does not sufficiently prepare the prospective teacher to teach reading, writing, and thinking to children who come to school speaking a language other than English, or children whose social and cultural experiences are other than of the historically European American origin, middle-class, mainstream culture. Bernhardt (1994) examined how linguistically diverse students were "portrayed in reading and language arts methods textbooks and in practice-oriented reading and language arts journals" (p. 159). She found that only a few texts mentioned that linguistically diverse students may already be literate in their native language, and even fewer discussed the implications of native literacy for English reading instruction. Most texts discussed linguistic diversity as a "second-language problem" or linked in the context of discussing learners with disabilities. Bernhardt found that "teachers have been given little direction regarding instructional strategies that build on the differences between and among languages in their various syntactic, phonological and social dimensions" (p. 177).

Without an understanding of the learning/teaching processes that linguistically and culturally diverse students have experienced in learning their native language, teachers are unprepared to assess and assist these students in literacy development. Teachers need to know about first- and second-language literacy development, and they need to develop strategies for working with the different literacy instruction needs of culturally diverse students. Additionally, prospective teachers must be able to articulate and show leadership in the implementation of the approaches derived from recent research and learned in their professional training. The well-entrenched traditional methods that are all too often practiced in classrooms must be changed, for many are no longer appropriate and may be considered counterproductive. Teachers must be at the core of the school reform, for they are the ones on whom we must rely to solve instructional problems. Unless teachers become more knowledgeable and skillful in constructing new strategies and approaches to literacy instruction, most culturally and linguistically diverse students' literacy learning will not improve (Cohen, 1995).

SUMMARY

Teachers make daily decisions about instruction that impact the lives of the children in their classrooms. The starting place for decisions about literacy is with the literacy knowledge and experiences the students bring to the classroom. Teachers can learn about their students' prior experiences within their cultural and linguistic communities by assuming a stance of inquiry. The attainment of literacy for culturally and linguistically diverse students will require that teachers act respectfully of the students' culture and cultural identity while assisting students in the development of cultural repertoire. This includes attending to issues of voice, discourse style, and social interactions.

Teachers have numerous sources of guidance for making instructional decisions. National standards, state frameworks, textbooks, and professional dialogues (such as the debate between skill-based and process approaches) attempt to inform and sometimes mandate instructional practice; however, it is the teacher who must be the "policy" decision maker and implementer for any particular classroom. Recognizing that the school's way of knowing may not be the way of knowing for culturally and linguistically diverse students may require that teachers redefine the purpose and function of literacy. As teachers view literacy as a social, political, and ideological act, their expectation of what counts as literacy in the broad sense and their understanding of literacy learning and teaching more specifically will be recontextualized. Many teachers and advocates of linguistically and culturally diverse students see "literacy as empowerment" as the true goal of a responsive literacy or biliteracy program.

■ ACTIVITIES

1. Interview a teacher to determine the assumptions on which she or he bases the selection of literacy goals, objectives, tasks, and materials. Compare the similarities and differences with interviews conducted by your classmates.
2. Interview a parent or parents of a culturally or linguistically diverse child about their aspirations and assumptions of school literacy for their children. Discuss your answers with other classmates.

3. Examine a basal reading series and analyze the literacy perspective described or implied. Compare the similarities and differences to the characteristics described in this chapter.

SUGGESTED READINGS

Au, K. H., & Scheu, J. A. (1996). Journey toward holistic instruction: Supporting teachers' growth. *Reading Teacher, 49*(6), 468–477.
Buckner, A. (2002). Teaching in a world focused on testing. *Language Arts, 79*(3), 212–213.
Kohn, A. (2002). Poor teaching for poor kids. *Language Arts, 79*(3), 251–255.
Reyes, M. de la L. (1992). Challenging venerable assumptions: Literacy instruction for linguistically different students. *Harvard Educational Review, 62*(4), 427–446.
Willis, A. I. (1995). Reading the world of school literacy: Contextualizing the experience of a young African American male. *Harvard Educational Review, 65*(1), 30–49.
Yau, J., & Jiménez, R. (2003). Fostering the literacy strengths of struggling Asian American readers. *Language Arts, 80*(3), 196–205.

CHILDREN'S LITERATURE CITED

Soto, G. (1995). *Chato's kitchen.* New York: Putnam's Sons.
Yarbrough, C. (1982). *The shimmershine queens.* New York: Scholastic.

REFERENCES

Ada, A. F. (1988). The Pajaro Valley experience: Working with Spanish-speaking parents to develop children's reading and writing skills in the home through use of children's literature. In T. Skutnabb-Kangas & J. Cummins (Eds.), *Minority education: From shame to struggle* (pp. 223–238). Clevedon, England: Multilingual Matters.
Alton-Lee, A., Nuthall, G., & Patrick, J. (1993). Reframing classroom research: A lesson from the private world of children. *Harvard Educational Review, 63,* 50–84.
Applebee, A. N., Langer, J. A., & Mullis, I. V. S. (1986). *The writing report card: Writing achievement in American schools.* Princeton, NJ: Educational Testing Service.
Applebee, A. N., Langer, J. A., & Mullis, I. V. S. (1988). *Who reads best? Factors related to reading achievement in grades 3, 7, and 11.* Princeton, NJ: Educational Testing Service.
Atwell, N. (1987). *In the middle: Writing, reading, and learning with adolescents.* Portsmouth, NH: Boynton/Cook.
Au, K. H. (1998). Social constructivism and the school literacy learning of students of diverse cultural background. *Journal of Literacy Research, 30,* 297–319.
Au, K. H. (2000). A multicultural perspective on policies for improving literacy achievement equity and excellence. In M. L. Kamil, P. B. Mosenthal, P. C. Pearson, & R. Barr (Eds.), *Handbook of reading research* (Vol. III, pp. 835–851). Mahwah, NJ: Lawrence Erlbaum Associates.

Au, K. H., & Carroll, J. H. (1997). Improving literacy achievement through a constructivist approach: The KEEP demonstration classroom project. *Elementary School Journal, 97,* 203–221.

Au, K. H., & Mason, J. (1981). Social organizational factors in learning to read: The balance of rights hypothesis. *Reading Research Quarterly, 17,* 115–152.

Barton, D. (1994). *Literacy: An introduction to the ecology of written language.* Oxford: Blackwell.

Bennett, K., Weiger, D., & Martin, S. (2002). Children's acquisition of early literacy skills: Examining family contributions. *Early Childhood Research Quarterly, 17,* 295–317.

Bennett, W. (1993). *The book of virtues.* New York: Simon & Schuster.

Bennett, W. J. (1984). *To reclaim a legacy: A report on the humanities in higher education.* Washington, DC: National Endowment for the Humanities.

Bernhardt, E. B. (1994). A content analysis of reading methods texts: What are we told about the nonnative speaker of English? *Journal of Reading Behavior, 26,* 159–189.

Bloom, A. (1987). *The closing of the American mind: How higher education has failed democracy and impoverished the souls of today's students.* New York: Simon & Schuster.

Bloom, H. (1994). *The Western canon.* New York: Harcourt, Brace.

Bloome, D., & Green, J. (1992). Educational contexts of literacy. *Annual Review of Applied Linguistics, 12,* 71–85.

Bruner, J. (1996). *The culture of education.* Cambridge, MA: Harvard University Press.

Buckner, A. (2002). Teaching in a world focused on testing. *Language Arts, 79*(3), 212–213.

Cairney, T., & Ashton, J. (2002). Three families, multiple discourses: Parental roles, constructions of literacy and diversity of pedagogic practice. *Linguistics and Education, 13*(3), 303–345.

Cazden, C. B. (1988). *Classroom discourse: The language of teaching and learning.* Portsmouth, NH: Heinemann.

Chang-Wells, G., & Wells, G. (1993). *Dynamics of discourse: literacy and the construction of knowledge contexts for learning: Sociocultural dynamics in children's development.* New York: Oxford University Press.

Cohen, D. K. (1995). What is the system in systemic reform? *Educational Researcher, 24,* 11–17, 31.

Delgado-Gaitan, C. (1990). *Literacy for empowerment: The role of parents in children's education.* London: Falmer Press.

Delgado-Gaitan, C., & Trueba, H. (1991). *Crossing cultural borders.* Bristol, PA: Falmer Press.

Delpit, L. D. (1991). The silenced dialogue: Power and pedagogy in education other people's children. In M. Minami & B. P. Kennedy (Eds.), *Language issues in literacy and bilingual/multicultural education* (pp. 483–502). Cambridge, MA: Harvard Educational Review.

Delpit, L. D. (1993). The politics of teaching literate discourse. In T. Perry & J. W. Fraser (Eds.), *Freedom's plow* (pp. 285–295). New York: Routledge.

Dewey, J. (1992). *The child and the curriculum.* Chicago: University of Chicago Press.

Dyson, A. H. (1993). *Social worlds of children learning to write in an urban primary school.* New York: Teachers College Press.

Dyson, A. H. (1994). "I'm gonna express myself": The politics of story in the children's worlds. In A. H. Dyson & C. Genishi, *The need for story: Cultural diver-*

sity in classroom and community (pp. 155–171). Urbana, IL: National Council of Teachers of English.

Edelsky, C. (1991). *With literacy and justice for all: Rethinking the social in language and education.* London: Falmer Press.

Edelsky, C., Altwerger, B., & Flores, B. (1991). *Whole language: What's the difference?* Portsmouth, NH: Heinemann.

Eldridge-Hunter, D. (1992). Intergenerational literacy: Impact on the development of the storybook reading behaviors of Hispanic mothers. In C. K. Kinzer & D. J. Leu (Eds.), *Literacy research, theory and practice: Views from many perspectives* (pp. 101–110). 41st Yearbook of the National Reading Conference. Chicago: National Reading Conference.

Ferdman, B. M. (1991). Literacy and cultural identity. In M. Minami & B. P. Kennedy, *Language issues in literacy and bilingual/multicultural education* (pp. 347–390). Cambridge, MA: Harvard Educational Review.

Finn, C. E. (1989, July 16). Norms for the nation's schools. *Washington Post*, p. B7.

Fitzgerald, J. (1995). English-as-a-second-language reading instruction in the United States: A research review. *JRB: A Journal of Literacy, 27*, 115–152.

Flores, B., Cousin, P. T., & Díaz, E. (1991). Transforming deficit myths about learning, language and culture. *Language Arts, 68*, 369–379.

Fox, T. (1990). *The social uses of writing: Politics and pedagogy.* Norwood, NJ: Ablex.

Freire, P. (1970). *Pedagogy of the oppressed.* New York: Seabury Press.

Freire, P., & Macedo, D. (1987). *Reading the world and the world.* South Hadley, MA: Bergin & Garvey.

Freppon, P. A. (1991). An investigation of children's concepts of the purpose and nature of reading in different instructional settings. *Journal of Reading Behavior, 23*, 139–163.

Freppon, P. A. (1995). Low-income children's literacy interpretations in a skills-based and a whole-language classroom. *Journal of Reading Behavior, 27*, 505–534.

Fuller, L. M. (1990). *The relative effectiveness of a meaning emphasis approach and a phonics emphasis approach to teaching beginning reading in English to second- or third-grade bilingual Spanish readers.* Unpublished doctoral dissertation, Boston University.

Garrison, J. (1995). Deweyan pragmatism and the epistemology of contemporary social constructivism. *American Educational Research Journal, 32*, 716–740.

Giroux, H. A. (1983). *Theory and resistance in education: A pedagogy for the opposition.* South Hadley, MA: Bergin & Garvey.

Goldenberg, C. (1987). Low-income Hispanic parents' contributions to their first-grade children's word recognition skills. *Anthropology and Education Quarterly, 18*, 149–179.

Goldenberg, C. (1993). The home–school connection in bilingual education. In M. B. Arias & U. Casanova (Eds.), *Bilingual education: Politics, practice, and research* (pp. 225–250). Chicago: University of Chicago Press.

Goldenberg, C., & Gallimore, R. (1991). Local knowledge, research knowledge, and educational change: A case study of early Spanish reading improvement. *Educational Researcher, 20*, 2–14.

Goldenberg, C., Reese, L., & Gallimore, R. (1992). Effects of literacy materials from school on Latino children's home experiences and early reading achievement. *American Journal of Education, 100*, 497–536.

Goodman, K. S. (1992). Why whole language is today's agenda in education. *Language Arts, 69*, 188–199.

Gowen, S. G. (1992). *The politics of workplace literacy.* New York: Teachers College Press.

Graff, H. (1991). *The literacy myth: Cultural integration and social structure in the nineteenth century*. New Brunswick, NJ: Transaction.

Green, J., & Dixon, C. (1996). Language of literacy dialogues: Facing the future or reproducing the past. *Journal of Literacy Research, 28*, 290–301.

Greene, M. (1993). The passions of pluralism: Multiculturalism and the expanding community. In T. Perry & J. W. Fraser (Eds.), *Freedom's plow* (pp. 185–296). New York: Routledge.

Harris, V. J. (1992). *Teaching multicultural literature in grades K–8*. Norwood, MA: Christopher-Gordon.

Heath, S. B. (1982). What no bedtime story means: Narrative skills at home and at school. *Language and Society, 11*, 49–76.

Heath, S. B. (1983). *Ways with words*. Cambridge: Cambridge University Press.

Hirsch, E. D. (1987). *Cultural literacy: What every American needs to know*. Boston: Houghton Mifflin.

Hoffman, J. V., Sailors, M., & Patterson, E. U. (2002). Decodable texts for beginning reading instruction: The year 2000 basals. *Journal of Literacy Research, 34*(3), 269–298.

Hudelson, S. (1992). Reading in a bilingual program. *Canadian Children, 17*, 13–25.

Igoa, C. (1995). *The inner world of the immigrant child*. New York: St. Martin's Press.

Jiménez, R. T. (2000). Literacy and the identity development of Latina/o students. *American Educational Research Journal, 37*(4), pp. 971–1000.

Knapp, M. S. (1995). *Teaching for meaning in high poverty classrooms*. New York: Teachers College Press.

Kohn, A. (2002). Poor teaching for poor kids. *Language Arts, 79*(3), 251–255.

Kucer, S. B. (1995). Guiding bilingual students "through" the literacy process. *Language Arts, 72*, 20–29.

Langer, J. A., Applebee, A. N., & Mullis, I. V. S. (1990). *Learning to read in our nation's schools: Instruction and achievement in 1988 at grades 4, 8, and 12*. Princeton, NJ: Educational Testing Service.

Larson, J. (1996). Challenging autonomous models of literacy: Street's call to action. *Linguistics and Education, 8*, 439–445.

Lucas, T., Henze, R., & Donato, R. (1990). Promoting the success of Latino language-minority students: An exploratory study of six high schools. *Harvard Educational Review, 60*, 315–340.

McCarthey, S. J., & Hoffman, J. V. (1995). The new basals: How are they different? *Reading Teacher, 49*, 72–75.

McIntyre, E., & Freppon, P. A. (1994). Children's development of alphabetic knowledge in a skills-based classroom and a whole language classrooms. *Research in the Teaching of English, 28*, 391–417.

McKenna, M. C., Stratton, B. D., & Reinking, D. (1994). On research, politics, and whole language. *Journal of Reading Behavior, 26*, 211–233.

McLaren, P. (1989). *Life in schools*. New York: Longman.

McLaughlin, D. (1989). The sociolinguistics of Navajo literacy. *Anthropology and Education Quarterly, 20*, 275–290.

Moll, L. (1992). Literacy research in community and classrooms: A sociocultural approach. In R. Beach, J. L. Green, M. L. Kamil, & T. Shanahan (Eds.), *Multidisciplinary perspectives on literacy research* (pp. 211–244). Urbana, IL: National Council on Teachers of English.

Moll, L. C., & Greenberg, J. B. (1991). Creating zones of possibilities: Combining social contexts for instruction. In L. C. Moll (Ed.), *Vygotsky and education* (pp. 319–348). Cambridge, England: Cambridge University Press.

Moll, L., Vélez-Ibáñez, C., & Greenberg, J. (1990). *Community knowledge and classroom practice: Combining resources for literacy instruction.* Arlington, VA: Development Associates.

Morrow, L. M. (1992). The impact of a literature-based program on literacy achievement, uses of literature, and attitudes of children from minority backgrounds. *Reading Research Quarterly, 27,* 250–275.

Mulhern, M. M. (1994). *Webs of meaning: The literate lives of three Mexican-American kindergartners.* Unpublished doctoral dissertation, University of Illinois at Chicago.

Myers, J. (1993). The value-laden assumptions of our interpretive practices. *Reading Research Quarterly, 28,* 582–587.

National Education Goals Panel. (1991). *Measuring progress toward the national education goals: Potential indicators and measurement strategies.* Washington, DC: U.S. Department of Education.

Nieto, S. (Ed.). (2002). *Language, culture, and teaching: Critical perspectives for a new century.* Mahwah, NJ: Lawrence Erlbaum Associates.

Ochs, E., & Taylor, C. (1992). Family narrative as political activity. *Discourse and Society, 3*(3), 301–340.

Ogbu, J. (1991). Cultural diversity and school experience. In C. Walsh (Ed.), *Literacy as praxis: Culture, language, and pedagogy* (pp. 25–50). Norwood, NJ: Ablex.

Ogbu, J. U. (1992). Understanding cultural diversity and learning. *Educational Research, 21,* 5–14.

Oldfather, P. (1993). What students say about motivating experiences in a whole language classroom. *Reading Teacher, 46,* 672–681.

Osterling, J. P. (2001). Waking the sleeping giant: Engaging and capitalizing on the sociocultural strengths of the Latino community. *Bilingual Research Journal, 25,* 1–30.

Palincsar, A. S., & David, Y. M. (1991). Promoting literacy through classroom dialogue. In E. H. Hiebert (Ed.), *Literacy for a diverse society: Perspectives, practices, and policies* (pp. 122–140). New York: Teachers College Press.

Pérez, B. (1994). Spanish literacy development: A descriptive study of four bilingual whole-language classrooms. *Journal of Reading Behavior, 26,* 74–94.

Pérez, B., & Torres-Guzmán, M. E. (1996). *Learning in two worlds: An integrated Spanish/English biliteracy approach* (2nd ed.). New York: Longman.

Philips, S. (1983). *The invisible culture: Communication in classroom and community on the Warm Springs Indian reservation.* Prospect Heights, IL: Waveland Press.

Piluski, J. J. (1997). Beginning reading instruction: From the "great debate" to the reading wars. *Reading Today, 15,* 32.

Prawat, R. (1995). Misreading Dewey: Reform, projects, and the language game. *Educational Researcher, 24,* 13–22.

Pressley, M. (1998). *Reading instruction that works: The case for balanced teaching.* New York: Guilford Press.

Purcell-Gates, V. (1995). *Other people's words: The cycle of low literacy.* Cambridge, MA: Harvard University Press.

Purcell-Gates, V., McIntyre, E., & Freppon, P. A. (1995). Learning written storybook language in school: A comparison of low-SES children in skills-based and whole language classrooms. *American Educational Research Journal, 32,* 659–685.

Reyes, C. (1993). *The fabric of education in a Latino community: The social-political context of literacy development in a second language.* Unpublished doctoral dissertation, University of California, Berkeley.

Reyes, M. de la L. (1991). A process approach to literacy using dialogue journals and literature logs with second language learners. *Research in the Teaching of English, 25*, 291–313.

Reyes, M. de la L. (1992). Challenging venerable assumptions: Literacy instruction for linguistically different students. *Harvard Educational Review, 62*, 427–446.

Rodríguez, A. J., & Berryman, C. (2002). Using sociotransformative constructivism to teach for understanding in diverse classrooms: A beginning teacher's journey. *American Educational Research Journal, 39*(4), 1017–1045.

Rodríguez, R. G., & Villarreal, A. (2002). *Development through engagement: Valuing the "at-promise" community. IDRA Newsletter.* San Antonio, TX: Intercultural Development Research Association.

Salinger, T. (1995–1996). IRA, standards, and educational reform. *Reading Teacher, 49*, 290–298.

Saravia-Shore, M., & Martínez, H. (1992). An ethnographic study of home/school role conflicts of second-generation Puerto Rican adolescents. In M. Saravia-Shore & S. F. Arvizu (Eds.), *Cross-cultural literacy: Ethnographies of communication in multiethnic classrooms* (pp. 227–252). New York: Garland.

Scribner, S. (1984). Literacy in three metaphors. *American Journal of Education, 93*, 6–21.

Serna, I., & Hudelson, S. (1993). Emergent Spanish literacy in a whole language bilingual classroom. In R. Donmoyer & R. Kos (Eds.), *At-risk students: Portraits, policies, programs and practices* (pp. 291–321). Albany: State University of New York Press.

Shannon, P. (1993). Developing democratic voices. *Reading Teacher, 47*, 86–94.

Shor, I. (Ed.). (1987). *Freire for the classroom: A sourcebook for liberatory teaching.* Portsmouth, NH: Boynton/Cook, Heinemann.

Skutnabb-Kangas, T. (2000). *Linguistic genocide in education—Or worldwide diversity and human rights?* Mahwah, NJ: Lawrence Erlbaum Associates.

Smith, F. (1992). Learning to read: The never ending debate. *Phi Delta Kappan, 73*, 432–441.

Solsken, J. W. (1993). *Literacy, gender and work in families and in school.* Norwood, NJ: Ablex.

Sonnenschein, S., & Munsterman, K. (2002). The influence of home-based reading interactions on 5 year-old reading motivations and early literacy development. *Early Childhood Research Quarterly, 17*, 318–337.

Soto, G. (1995). *Chato's kitchen.* New York: Putnam's Sons.

Street, B. (1995). *Social literacies: Critical approaches to literacy in development, ethnography, and education.* London: Longman.

Street, B. (1998). New literacies in theory and practice: What are the implications for language in education? *Linguistics and Education, 10*(1), 1–24.

Stuckey, J. E. (1991). *The violence of literacy.* Portsmouth, NH: Boynton/Cook.

Taylor, D. (1997). *Many families, many literacies: An international declaration of principals.* Portsmouth, NH: Heinemann.

Teale, W. H. (1986). Home background and young children's literacy development. In W. H. Teale & E. Sulzby (Eds.), *Emergent literacy: Writing and reading* (pp. 173–206). Norwood, NJ: Ablex.

Temple, C., Martinez, M., Yokota, J., & Naylor, A. (1998). *Children's books in children's hands.* Boston: Allyn & Bacon.

U.S. Department of Education. (2002). *Fact Sheet: The No Child Left Behind Act of 2001.* Washington: Author. www.ed.gov/offices/OESE/ esea/factsheet

Valdés, G. (1991, April). *Background knowledge and minority students: Some implications for literacy-based instruction.* Paper presented at the American Educational Research Association Conference, Chicago.

Valdés, G. (1996). *Con respeto: Bridging the distances between culturally diverse families and schools: An ethnographic portrait.* New York: Teachers College Press.

Valencia, S. W., & Wixson, K. K. (2000). Policy-oriented research on literacy standards and assessment. In M. L. Kamil, P. B. Mosenthal, P. D. Pearson, & R. Barr (Eds.), *Handbook of reading research* (Vol. III, pp. 909–935). Mahwah, NJ: Lawrence Erlbaum Associates.

Valenzuela, A. (1999). *Subtractive schooling: U.S.-Mexican youth and politics of caring.* Albany: State University of New York Press.

Vygotsky, L. (1986). *Thought and language.* Cambridge, MA: MIT Press.

Weinstein-Shr, G. (1995). Learning from uprooted families. In G. Weinstein-Shr & E. Quintero (Eds.), *Immigrant learners and their families: Literacy to connect generations* (pp. 113–133). McHenry, IL: Center for Applied Linguistics & Delta Systems.

Willis, A. I. (1995). Reading the world of school literacy: Contextualizing the experience of a young African American male. *Harvard Educational Review, 65,* 30–49.

Wong Fillmore, L. (1991). Second-language learning in children: A model of language learning in social context. In E. Bialystok (Ed.), *Language processing in bilingual children* (pp. 49–69). Cambridge, England: Cambridge University Press.

Yarbrough, C. (1982). *The shimmershine queens.* New York: Scholastic.

11

Creating a Classroom Community for Literacy

Bertha Pérez

Because students from different cultural groups may have different expectations about schooling, teachers will not be able to anticipate a given culture for all classrooms. Teacher and students will have to negotiate and create the classroom culture and community for school literacy events. *Classroom culture* means the norms for social interaction and cooperation in the use of space and time, for the use of resources, and for valuing and behaving in a particular classroom. A classroom culture that values diversity and encourages repertoires of behaviors and that reflects the values of the students' homes will be more conducive to student-initiated learning. The classroom culture will also include the values of the school and mainstream society. The classroom community may be a composite culture where students can use home/community experiences and learn about the mainstream culture. In a classroom that values the students' home language and culture, the classroom culture and community are developed and realized in such a way that life in school is not so different from life out of school. Children can use and apply in school what they have learned at home, and what they are learning in school relates to their daily lives within their homes and communities.

How can such a classroom culture be realized? How can you establish norms for behavior in such a classroom community? How can teachers provide children the choices that foster true collaboration, negotiation, and authentic literacy learning? These are the concerns discussed in this chapter.

MEETING THE NEEDS OF INDIVIDUAL STUDENTS AND DIVERSITY IN THE CLASSROOM

Having a clear understanding of the number of different languages and cultures that are represented in the class is the place to start. Many teachers believe that by not noticing children's differences they will be just and fair to everyone. Some teachers have been known to say or write that "I don't notice who is Asian, or Black, or Latino. I just see children." However, the children may have received and internalized numerous messages about their differences and may interpret a teacher's lack of acknowledgment of their differences as lack of concern. Saravia-Shore and Martínez (1992) reported on a teacher's perceptions of culturally and linguistically diverse students: "After many years of involvement with the system, she feels that teachers' lack of concern is a real problem. 'This sickness has spread to the majority of teachers.' There are many reasons for this lack of concern, but they certainly reflect the system's inability to deal with 'different students' " (p. 234).

This lack of acknowledgment of the children's linguistic and cultural heritage denies the children's prior literacy and learning experiences, especially when the prior literacy experiences might be different from the expected middle-class experiences. Affirming everyone's unique linguistic, cultural, and school experiences can be done at the beginning of the year in small groups or in individual interviews. The information that children share can be captured in an individual student profile and combined to make a class profile of students prior to literacy and education experience.

The second step in dealing with diversity is to prepare a curriculum that includes all the cultures represented in the classroom so that children may find a place for themselves and may feel that their prior knowledge and experience are valid and useful within this new context.

The third step is reflective teaching practices that will help you assess your progress toward the characteristics of effective teachers of culturally and linguistically diverse students as described by Chang (chap. 7, this volume) and Nieto (2002). These are: basically believing that all children can learn; utilizing parents, the student's home language, and home resources, making them an integral part of school learning; and incorporating multiple literacies in the students' formal learning whenever possible.

A fourth and perhaps most important strategy is learning how to communicate with every child's parent(s) early in the school year. If the child's parents do not speak English and you do not speak the language of the parents, ask the school to provide you with assistance. If the school does not have a translator, such as a bilingual teaching assistant, you can ask the child to offer suggestions. Usually, within the family or community, an aunt, uncle, relative, or neighbor who speaks the native language and English can assist with this communication. The effort you make to assure communication with the parents will demonstrate that you respect and value their role in their child's life (G. R. López, Scribner, & Mahitivanichcha, 2001). You will also have gained parental trust and support.

Children's Social Networks

Children are an integral part of society within which there are many kinds of social networks and social relationships. Social relationships within social networks vary across cultures. Thus, to create social networks with children who come from diverse cultures will require the creation of a classroom culture within which social relationships can develop. McCarthey (1998) studied the multiple factors that influence student participation and found that group composition, task engagement, and gender, social class, and ethnicity were important factors in student participation. Teachers can assist children by attending to group composition and the social interactions within the classroom. The manner in which one person relates to another, the extent to which one helps or supports another, and the literacy expectations or demands that one holds for another are all characteristics of social relationships that can be made common across language groups within the classroom culture. Outside of the classroom, social networks for language-minority students may range from permanent to transient. Family relationships are permanent for many, but relationships for new immigrant children may be in a state of flux or transition. Many language-minority children who are also poor may experience a considerable amount of transiency in their living arrangements. For many children, the classroom becomes their important social network that offers a large degree of stability.

Children will need to be reassured that they can become fully literate in English without having to turn their backs on their native language and culture. Children will need strategies for dealing with feelings of inadequacy that may have been internalized by the child from exposure to subtle monolingual/monocultural attitudes that one language or culture is the only way, or the best way. The child will depend on teacher reassurance that the door is open to maintain his or her own language and culture even as he or she learns to live within this new environment. If children are not encouraged to resolve issues of language and culture loyalty, they may choose to abandon their native language and culture, thus breaking important ties with family and heritage; or children may develop resistance to the development of English literacy and begin a cycle of low school achievement. For example, To thi Dien (chap. 6, this volume) and Bankston and Zhou (1995) suggested that literacy and academic achievement for Vietnamese students are positively related to identification with the ethnic group, and that Vietnamese-language skills contribute to maintaining community-level social capital, as well as to individual-level psychological adaptation. An environment can be created, even by monolingual teachers, that sends a strong message to students that there is a richness in diversity and that there are rewards for becoming bilingual and bicultural.

Peer Bonding

Encouraging peer bonding is an important strategy for coping with diversity in the classroom. During the middle childhood years, peer bonding is a necessary stage of development. Children's sense of isolation, fear, and loss can be assuaged through peer friendships. Language-minority children who have achieved second-language literacy often emphasize the significance of friends helping them adjust and adapt to the teacher and classroom expectations. Friends help validate them, act as counselors, and stimulate learning and literacy use. For many culturally and linguistically diverse students, the friends they make during the early years help carry them in later years from class to class. Igoa (1995) described how difficult it can be in a culturally diverse classroom for children to make friends, because "when cultures are so different, it is difficult for a child to find that common ground." She quotes an 11-year-old boy from Afghanistan who stated:

> My family lived in Pakistan during the war with Russia, I found friends easily because we are similar peoples, but when I came here it was more difficult because the people are different.
>
> At first it was boring at school. At recess time everybody was playing. I was thinking I should go back to Pakistan because I have lots of friends there; I thought I would never get a friend in here. In Pakistan I made friends right away. (p. 139)

Teachers can assist with peer bonding by allowing children to choose partners in pair activities. These partners may be from their own cultural group, but some children will choose children from other cultural groups. The use of cooperative learning groups will also encourage the active interactions among students that are needed for friendships to develop. The themes/topics studied in the cooperative learning groups should be selected so that they provide each child from specific cultural groups the opportunity to be an expert. For example within a theme-based study on "exploration" or "heritage," ample opportunities exist for learning specific concepts from diverse points of view so that different children at different times have the cultural referents or cultural capital to take the leadership in the study (see chap. 12).

Within all communities, including classrooms, the social networks and the relationships that exist among their members will affect literacy development. Schmidt (1993), studying the literacy development of two kindergarten students from Southeast Asia, described how the students struggled in small- and large-group interactive work and play settings to make sense of the literacy tasks required in this classroom. She suggested that teachers will need to attend not only to the task of creating classrooms that encourage social interaction for literacy learning but also to mediating the social interactions for ethnic-minority children. The challenge for teachers in multilingual, multicultural classrooms is to understand how children's different social relationships promote literacy and how they contribute to the overall goal of literacy development.

LITERACY AS COLLABORATION

Literacy as a sociocultural phenomenon requires that attention be paid to the social context and social interactions among students and between students and teacher. Sociocultural groups have different patterns of preferred interaction. The patterns within the group may vary, and not all members of the group will assume similar patterns of behavior. Individuals can move beyond a collective way of behaving when they begin to explore and integrate other cultural ways. Children's willingness to collaborate and participate will depend on their sense of safety; according to Phelps and Weaver (1999), children will not speak up when they fear ridicule. However, through interaction and collaboration with others, individuals change by recombining and integrating new attitudes, patterns for behavior, and ways of knowing.

Vygotsky (1978) described learning as a fundamentally social process among adult or more knowledgeable group members and less capable novices. He theorized that this social process bridged the learner's "zone of proximal development," that is, "the distance between the actual developmental level as determined by independent problem solving and the level of potential development as determined through problem solving under adult guidance or in collaboration with more capable peers" (p. 86). Understanding the social nature of learning and the need for collaboration is significant for the success of culturally and linguistically diverse students. These students are novices in many of the mainstream classroom practices due to the notable differences between the norms and values of language and literacy use in the speech community at home, and those in the speech community at school. For example, the use of the initiation-response-evaluation (IRE) as the predominant mode of instruction, documented by Cazden (1988) and Mehan (1979), is often also found in homes of mainstream, middle-class, English-speaking families (Heath, 1983; Wells, 1986). However, the IRE mode of interaction is not found as frequently in homes of working-class Whites and rural African Americans (Heath, 1983), inner-city African Americans (Labov, 1972), Native Americans (Philips, 1972), native Hawaiians (Au et al., 1986), and Mexican Americans (García & Carrasco, 1981; M. E. López, 1999; Valdés, 1996). These different interactional patterns have consequences for the child when interacting at school, which impact success in the classroom. Students who have not learned the norms of school discourse may have difficulty interacting according to the teacher's expectations. This difficulty may lead to miscommunication and misunderstanding in the classroom. Teachers also interpret as misconduct the students' attempts to interact in a style different from the expected and preferred classroom norms (Hull, Rose, Fraser, & Castellano, 1991).

The diversity of languages and culture will require that many opportunities for collaboration be provided where children with different prior experiences and worldviews can come together to negotiate a new shared way of meaning making and naming of new experiences. Individual children have had varying experiences and therefore may possess very different knowledge schemes (Duran, 1985) on a particular topic or task. Thus, individual children offer different contributions to, and have different interpretations of, what is being studied or what the expectations of the teacher or the task might be. The cultural and linguistic diversity means that children also bring their own complex customs or styles of interaction to their activities or projects. Children from different cultural backgrounds have different rules for communication and for instructional conversations (Brown & Campione, 1994; Goldenberg, 1996; Pérez, 1996). Because their "ways with words" (Heath, 1983) may not be like those of the other children or of the teacher, collaboration is crucial.

Instructional Conversations

An important place for beginning any literacy activity is the instructional conversation that sets up the activity (Tharp, 1994; Wilkinson & Silliman, 2000). Instructional conversations can model aspects of typical conversations; that is, they should be a *collaborative activity* between participants, who take turns offering, modifying, extending, and sustaining a meaning that is coconstructed by all the participants. In these instructional conversations, the teacher may suggest the topic or task for the literacy activity, but it is through *negotiating* with the students as participants that the meaning of the topic and or task will be defined (Pérez, 1996).

In nonclassroom conversations with speakers who share the same language, these speakers negotiate meaning subconsciously; each person has different ideas and experiences, and each person has different purposes and expectations about what the conversation is to achieve. The speakers make constant adjustments to take account of the perspective of the other. This exchange between speakers (or speaker and listener) is what linguists and psycholinguists call *intersubjectivity* (Pappas, Kiefer, & Levstik, 1995). It means that the speaker and listener know that the other knows what meaning has been coconstructed. The speaker and the listeners have to be sure that they are talking about the same thing, referring to the same meanings.

Negotiation is the only means by which classroom participants—children and teacher alike—can deal with their various ways of participating or interacting. This is how intersubjectivity is achieved and understanding is accomplished.

Children collaborate and hold instructional conversations with peers and teacher about their learning activities, reading, writing, and projects. For example, several children in a small group may collaborate with their group members in creating meaning from a shared text that they may be reading. Other children may be collaborating at a computer as they construct a story for a writing activity. Or children may be collaborating on the construction of a survey for a community inquiry project.

The diversity within classrooms that creates the sociocultural context for literacy learning in school can develop to capitalize on children's needs for social networks, conversations, and collaboration.

Cooperative Learning Groups

One way for collaboration to be systematically and democratically integrated into the literacy curriculum is through the use of cooperative learning groups. Cooperative learning in the United States can be described as learning that is organized so that small groups of students (up to six) interact in face-to-face discourse while learning and assume responsibility for the learning of all members of the group. Most cooperative learning models assign learning tasks to the group, but individual group members assume individual roles. The structured group process maximizes the social nature of learning while holding individual students accountable (Johnson & Johnson, 1991; Slavin, 1990). When groups work successfully at accomplishing a task, a positive interdependence develops among group members. Smith (chap. 8, this volume) suggested that for culturally and linguistically diverse students, the opportunity to build on each other's background knowledge, the face-to-face interaction and contextualization of the task, and the social nature of the groups make cooperative learning an important strategy for literacy learning.

Cohen, Kepner, and Swanson (1995) cautioned us about status hierarchies in the classroom that appear to transfer to cooperative learning groups. In an analysis of laboratory studies, they found that

> race and ethnicity are also status characteristics that will affect interaction ... whites and Anglos were more active and influential than African-Americans and were also more active than Mexican-Americans who looked different. Although girls are less active and influential than boys in cooperative groups of adolescents, gender does not appear to act as a status characteristic in the early elementary years. (p. 20)

Unless the teacher is aware of the hierarchies within the class and constructs the cooperative groups and the tasks in ways to challenge the existing status hierarchies and the set of cultural beliefs, cooperative groups will not meet the goal of equal-status interaction in the classroom.

When using cooperative groups, your classroom will look and sound very active. Children will work together, consult with one another, check for understanding, and teach one another while using literacy and being creative. The room arrangement signals the teacher's intention and expectations regarding the talk and flow of activity in the classroom. If possible, exchange desks for tables, or rearrange desks into table groupings. These types of arrangements focus attention toward sharing materials, spreading out projects, and cooperating with peers. An alternative arrangement might be to use a table or some grouped desks as centers where children can work on and leave out ongoing cooperative projects. Teacher and students will need to explore and think about ways in which the physical classroom environment fosters peer interactions, collaboration, and cooperative group work.

You will want to consider two major types of cooperative groups. The first type is short-term and more informal in nature; the second is more structured and long-term. Informal, short-term groups can be used when students work together on approaches to solving problems, buddy or paired reading, brainstorming, character/story mapping, peer conferencing, and sharing around writing. In short-term cooperative groups, students may have a preferred partner or group but the group membership may frequently change and the group activities are of short duration. Thus, membership in this type of cooperative group is usually created spontaneously by students or simply determined by adjacent seating when a particular activity is initiated.

In the second type of cooperative learning, the groups are more formally constituted and work together over a period of time on a given project or unit. Students in these groups could work together for whole thematic cycles or for a large portion of one. An important factor for teachers to consider in organizing cooperative groups that will work together over a period of time is the diversity of the group. Teachers should try to make sure that the group includes both genders, is academically and socially diverse, and is culturally and linguistically mixed. For students who have very limited English literacy, it is helpful to have another student from their native language (if another child is available) to assist each student in fully participating in the group's work.

In these longer term cooperative groups, students can assign and reassign roles to each other as they progress through the project. For example, a fourth-grade cooperative group, investigating the social services provided by an agency adjacent to their school, identified and assigned the following roles to group members: *team leader*—was responsible for facilitating the groups discussion, leading the group to decisions, initiating next steps, and making appointments; *interviewers*—two students were assigned, one to conduct interviews in English, the other in Spanish, as they would be interviewing some community members who might speak only Spanish; *media person*—was responsible for reserving and planning for the use of school tape recorders, still cameras, and video cameras, as well as gaining releases from persons recorded or photographed; *recorder/documenter*—was responsible for assuring that all work was documented in notes or on audio/videotape; and *designer*—was responsible for the ongoing thinking, planning, and organizing of the final products (a book and a multimedia presentation in this case). The students worked over a period of 2 months, and all students participated in developing surveys, interview questions, notetaking, collecting and analyzing data and documents, writing, and preparing materials for the final products. Students took their roles very seriously, often defending or redesigning their duties when tasks came up that were not clearly in the domain of the assigned roles.

Hertz-Lazarowitz (1992) described how cooperative groups that include students with wide ranges of native and English linguistic skills have helped all students make progress in language and literacy development. As students strive to understand and be understood, they push their developing language and literacy skills. When students are encouraged to use their native languages to make sense of the learning tasks, the students participate actively and construct more meaning. Tinajero, Calderón, and Hertz-Lazarowitz (1993) pointed to the social and academic benefits of cooperative groups:

> The fact that students use both languages in their discussions about the reading selections [or learning tasks] and then phrase their discussions as a final group product in one language contributes a great deal to the social self-esteem and academic competence of all students. (p. 151)

Personal Narratives

The sharing and writing of personal stories is also important in creating a classroom community that values collaboration and diversity. Narratives help us make sense of the world and may be a fundamental process of the mind (Bruner, 1996). Stories are a basic narrative form; however, personal narratives may use patterns of expression and topics that are different from culture to culture. All children have stories to share, and through the sharing, diverse children can come to understand and appreciate each other. The cultural stories from children's homes as well as personal narratives about everyday life can provide a way for children to express their identity, pride, concerns, and accomplishments. As children feel that their personal narratives are accepted and valued, they will explore with recombining and integrating new themes and attitudes as they explore other possible identities.

Sluys (2003) studied the writing of a recent immigrant from Poland in the second–third grade. She described how Wera reconciled the differences in language, culture, and social worlds through her writing. She concluded that when culturally diverse children like Wera are given the opportunity to negotiate their identities between cultures, they will write "from the life that surrounds them, construct significant texts, and tell stories that invoke history, culture, and difference. And in telling the stories of their 'trew lives' they explore not only who they are but also who they might become" (p. 183).

One way to help children with the writing of personal narratives is through Writer's Workshop (Calkins, 1986). The Writer's Workshop allows for teacher modeling and student collaboration. You can begin to incorporate the use of the workshop by (a) encouraging children to generate stories on topics of importance to them, (b) allowing children time to draft and rewrite, (c) organizing small-group sharing and conferencing where children share their writing and give each other suggestions, (d) assisting children in rewriting while being true to their developing voice, and (e) finding venues for public sharing or publishing that will require that children edit their stories to a culturally and developmentally appropriate standard. This process assists children to develop literacy in socioculturally authentic ways. It can value children's cultural knowledge, allows for cross-cultural sharing, and encourages collaboration.

THE TEACHER'S ROLE IN BILITERACY

Within a sociocultural constructivist perspective, teachers and students become learners; and the roles of learners, language, literacy, and knowledge are constantly being challenged and are evolving. The teachers have certain roles; however, the daily life of the classroom community considers and negotiates the teacher's and children's interests and priorities. When teaching and learning are viewed as a constructivist collaborative enterprise, teachers will need to take a collaborative style of teaching that involves sharing power and authority with children. This view is counter to the traditional classroom stance about power and control as it relates to teaching and learning because instead of the teacher being in control of what is to be learned, when, and how, the children provide input and share the power and control. Children are viewed as having their own theories, prior knowledge, or schemes about what they are learning and choices about how to learn and use literacy. Literacy events and classroom discourse in these classrooms reflect the shared power and control.

Many schools will have specific programs designed to handle language and cultural groups that have significant numbers; however, most schools find it difficult to address the needs of students from *low-incidence populations*. This term is used to refer to students who speak a particular language for which there may not be sufficient speakers within a school to provide a specific program such as bilingual education or English as a second language (ESL). Whether your school has a specific program such as bilingual education or an ESL program (discussed in chap. 1, this volume), you, as a classroom teacher, will receive students for whom there is no specific program or who have been transitioned out of these programs. Thus, you must be prepared with some second-language strategies in order to help children make meaning of the higher learning demands and expectations placed on their developing language (Meed & Whitmore, 2001). All teachers will sometime in their careers encounter culturally and linguistically diverse students and must be prepared to teach in a culturally sensitive manner.

Your first step to culturally sensitive teaching is to find out about your students. After getting acquainted with the entire class, prepare quiet, productive activities on which children can work individually or in pairs without the need of direct participation of an adult. You can prepare two to four students to respond to student needs, so that if questions need answering or directions need clarification, these students can act as monitors. You can then use these quiet times to meet with each student for a one-on-one dialogue. These dialogues are an important methodology in working with diverse children. The teacher must find a way to connect with the child as a unique individual, and to validate the child's cultural history and establish a trusting, respectful, and warm relationship. If the child is in a silent stage or if he or she resists, you can respect the silence and wait for the child to come forth with oral production, but you can still have individual time with the child where you can share a poem or story from the child's culture; this will begin to establish trust and warmth. If resistances persist, speak very directly to the child and try to find out what you can do to make it safe for the child to speak and participate. If you can figure out what the child is feeling, you can understand his or her behavior.

Teacher as Literacy Expert and Gatekeeper

In traditional or skill-based reading/writing programs, the teacher shares or may even subsume the role of expert and gatekeeper with textbooks and tests, whereas within a constructivist framework the teacher assumes the major role of literacy expert and the potential exists for the teacher to become the literacy gatekeeper. The teacher must create a classroom context where children can take risks in reading, writing, and problem solving and offer their own ideas and theories about text. This requires that the classroom context be supportive of nonlinear thinking, be accepting of language approximations, and be open and reassuring. If the teacher encourages the students to demonstrate what they know, then they are, in a sense, treated as coexperts who are expected to refine their knowledge bases with the new content and strategies required in classroom literacy. Auerbach (1989) examined the changing role that teachers need to assume, stating, "Literacy is meaningful to students to the extent that it relates to daily realities .... The teachers' role is to connect what happens inside the classroom to what happens outside so that literacy can become a meaningful tool for addressing the issues in students' lives" (p. 166). The teacher is constantly assessing what students bring to the literacy event, what they need to know, and how to provide for successful learning. O'Malley and Chamot (1990) suggested how teachers can assume this role with second-language learners:

> This requires that teachers not only be good managers but also have an extensive knowledge base about their subject and about teaching learning strategies .... Teachers act as models and demonstrate mental processes and learning strategies by thinking aloud to their students. (p. 188)

For culturally and linguistically diverse students, the need for the teacher to assist or scaffold the literacy connections so that students can construct meaning is even more important (Wollman-Bonilla & Werchadlo, 1999).

Bruner (1996) argued that "if pedagogy is to empower human beings to go beyond their 'native' predispositions, it must transmit the 'toolkit' the culture has developed for doing so" (p. 17). *Metalinguistics* is the capacity to examine our language to transcend limits; that is, we can expand any limits imposed by the languages we use by increasing out "linguistic awareness." Thus, one function of leading children to literacy is to cultivate such awareness. We can also help improve the capacity for construing meanings and constructing realities by metacognitive strategies or "thinking about thinking." Both metalinguistic and metacognitive strategies have to be principal ingredients in instruction for the empowering potential they have on literacy development (Bruner, 1996).

Scaffolding Linguistic and Background Knowledge.
The teacher can *scaffold* (Bruner, 1983; Cazden, 1988) literacy by selecting tasks for which the children have background knowledge and experiences. For example, reading stories that relate to the child's culture and for which the child has cultural background knowledge will assist the child in comprehending the text. From a second-language perspective, literacy tasks that focus on common experiences of culturally diverse students, like reading and writing about translating, can also tap into children's background knowledge. The background knowledge and experiences that students bring to literacy tasks are perhaps the most important elements that influence children's ability to read with high levels of comprehension and to write coherent and cohesive texts (Salinger, 1993).

Teachers will also need to scaffold children's use of linguistic codes. Asking decontextualized questions will limit the linguistic support that students will need to demonstrate their knowledge and understanding. Asking open-ended questions (What do you think or what have you learned so far from this story? How did this make you feel? Did you learn anything new from reading this?) will allow children to draw on their own understandings and use their linguistic knowledge to respond and to demonstrate evidence of the strategies they are using. By scaffolding, the teacher adapts the participation and interactive activity to allow children to successfully participate, however minimally, while encouraging the child (Cazden, 1988).

Langer, Bartoleme, Vasquez, and Lucas (1990) described how researchers asked Mexican American bilingual fifth-grade students to use all their linguistic skills in meaning construction of literacy tasks. They reported that:

> The students' language competence in Spanish enriched their meaning making in both languages. Their knowledge of Spanish was a support to them both in developing understandings and in answering decontextualized questions. They [students] reported that they thought of words and ideas in Spanish when they read English texts, and thought in Spanish when they were "stuck." When reading Spanish texts, they did not rely on English to the same extent. Further, as a group, the students recalled more content, hypothesized more effectively, and provided more elaborated recalls when they read (and often responded) in Spanish, and answered decontextualized questions more successfully when they were asked in Spanish and they answered in Spanish. (p. 463)

Teachers can provide classroom materials (children's literature but especially children's dictionaries in the native languages where possible) and can encourage children to use these in reading and writing.

Setting Purpose for Literacy. Teachers can help students learn to determine appropriate purposes for reading and to include within their purpose active, critical thinking about the texts they are reading. Students' purposes for literacy can influence reading comprehension and writing. If students do not establish a purpose for reading or writing, they often find reading and writing to be difficult, inefficient, and possibly unsuccessful. Linguistically and culturally diverse students may not attend to important parts of text, may miss nuances of language, or may fail to comprehend.

When children are made aware of the purpose, audience, and appropriate form for their writing, their success at both reading and writing will improve. Children should have a clear purpose in mind both for their reading and for their communication of its results. What is this reading or writing for: to gain information, to explain, to persuade, to maintain relationships, or combinations of these? Children also need a sense of their audience. Who is this writing for: for self, for the teacher, for the class or school, for parents, or for the wider community? Discussing the purpose and audience with children before they begin their reading sets the stage, as they make decisions about what is important and what they will need to know in order to write. This is important for all children, but it is particularly important for culturally and linguistically diverse students. Students' metacognitive control over their own literacy is enhanced by making the basis for writing decisions explicit to students (Englert, 1992).

Meaning-Making Strategies. Strategies students develop to gain meaning from text rather than a student's English-language competence will affect reading comprehension. Raphael and Brock (1993) described how Mei, a third-grade Vietnamese student, participated in a literature-based reading instruction program called the Book Club, where diverse students with differing levels of literacy and oracy abilities came together to discuss the text and to construct meaning. Over the 3-year period of the study, Mei's command of the English language and public use of English in academic settings increased. The Book Club was found to be a valuable social context for Mei to have meaningful and authentic opportunities to learn to use academic discourse.

Langer et al. (1990) in their study of bilingual fifth graders found that "the use of good meaning-making strategies rather than degree of fluency in English, differentiated the better from the poorer reads ... despite their proficiency in the English language, their ability to make sense in English was limited" (p. 463). Bialystok (1991) described the reading strategies of bilingual children with reading difficulties:

> One group of children could sound out words correctly and appeared to be reading fluently, but they had poor comprehension of what they read .... They read ... by paying excessive attention to the forms and inadequate attention to the developing meanings. Another group of children did not have the necessary analyzed conceptions of language to even develop adequate decoding skills, and they read by focusing all their attention on the meanings, disregarding the forms. Most of the errors these children made were to substitute words that were roughly appropriate to the context but bore no formal similarity to the word written in the text. (p. 129)

Teachers can facilitate the process of making meaning of school literacy tasks by modeling *metacognitive* strategies, the processes of problem solving or thinking about what we know and how we came to know; and *metalinguistic* strategies, the processes of thinking about language use, discourse, genre, and other forms of language. Duran (1987) suggested that metacognition is especially relevant for second-language learners because "metacognition calls attention to the context of communication and to language form and modality—speaking, reading, writing, and oral comprehension—as well as to other problem solving activities not accompanied by overt language" (p. 49). For example, in reading in a second language, readers with high proficiency in a second language should be better able to concentrate their attention on the extraction of meaning from a text. They may be more capable of enacting automated, analytic word recognition and syntax recognition reading strategies, and thus may focus on extracting meaning and making inferences that will help them make additional interpretations of the text. On the other hand, less proficient second-language readers may allocate more attention to word decoding and word recognition, rather than to making meaning of the text as a whole. For second-language learners, the issues are the allocation of attention, depth of processing, and coordination of word level and meaning strategies.

Teachers can assist students to develop meaning-making strategies by maximizing what they know, encouraging them to use available prior knowledge to draw on, build, and relate meaning. This teacher modeling can use self-generated questioning (Muñiz-Swicegood, 1994), think-aloud procedures (Langer et al., 1990) to demonstrate how to reflect on and talk about metacognitive strategies. For example, the teacher might say, "This title, *Big Thunder Magic* [Strete, 1990], makes me think of a rainstorm. I can see in my mind a mental image of a dark night with thunder and rain. What do you think when you read this title?" To demonstrate metalinguistic strategies, the teacher can comment on the use of words or comment on various aspects of text structure. For example, Snow, Cancino, De Temple, and Schley (1991) described the metalinguistic strategies required for the common school literacy task of giving a definition:

> Young children very reasonably respond to a question like "What's a hat?" with "You wear it," and such a response is tolerated if the child is young enough. Older children, on the other hand, are expected to respond to such questions by giving "formal definitions," which conform to particular standards for form as well as for content, for example, "A hat is an article of clothing worn on the head." (p. 90)

> Children must first analyze the task situation in which they find themselves, decide that a formal definition is required, and recall the form peculiar to this particular genre; then they must reflect on the meaning of a target word, analyze what they know about that word in order to decide

> what is central to its meaning, and to organize that crucial information into the standard form for the definitional genre. At every stage of this process, analysis is crucial—analysis of the situation first, of the genre-specific demands second, and then of one's own lexical knowledge. (p. 104)

Kucer (1995) studied the instructional events and behaviors that significantly promoted as well as inhibited meaning-making strategy internalization for third-grade bilingual students. The teacher in the classroom studied had categorized the strategies into reading strategies, reader response strategies, writing strategies, and spelling strategies. Each category had between 7 and 10 strategies suggested; these were placed on wall charts as illustrated in Fig. 11.1 so that children could refer to it as needed. Figure 11.2 illustrates the instructional events and behaviors that significantly promoted as well as inhibited strategy internalization. Some frequently suggested strategies for second-language learners, such as "use of predictable story formats" and "retelling or writing about personal experiences," were not found to be very helpful with this particular group of students. Instead, motivation and engagement were found to have had the greatest effect on internalization of strategies. Over the course of the year, the teacher and research concluded that:

> The issue of "desire" appeared to be a constant factor in promoting strategy internalization .... The students, however, told us in very direct ways that they wanted to know *why* the strategies were to be learned and used .... When students found the texts interesting, engaging, or felt a degree of ownership, they were more willing to experiment with alternative strategies as they struggled with text meanings. (pp. 28–29)

Some second-language learners may approach English literacy tasks with a limited, rigid, and poorly understood set of strategies. They may think that reading is "saying the words," that comprehending is "word-for-word interpretation," and that writing is "spelling correctly." They may fail to understand that literacy tasks will require the conscious application of various meaning strategies. Helping diverse students learn how to think about reading and writing will give children control over their literacy behaviors. Task knowledge and self-monitoring are closely related metacognitive behaviors that when understood will assist readers and writers to plan and to make progress toward completing the literacy task. Students should have some sense that different tasks require different sets of behaviors and that they, as readers and writers, can select and control their behaviors. Students may require assistance in developing this "reading engagement" (Baker, Afflerbach, & Reinking, 1996) so that they will play an active role in developing their own literacy competencies.

When reading and you come to "something" that you do not recognize, know, or understand, you can:

Reading Strategies

1 Stop reading → think about it → make a guess → read on to see if the guess makes sense.

2 Stop reading → reread the previous sentence(s) or paragraph(s) → make a guess → continue reading to see if the guess makes sense.

3 Skip it → read on to get more information → return and make a guess → continue reading to see if the guess makes sense.

4 Skip it → read on to see if what you do not understand is important to know → return and make a guess if it fits with the rest of the text.

5 Put something in that makes sense → read on to see if it fits with the rest of the text.

6 Stop reading → look at the pictures, charts, graphs, etc. → make a guess → read on to see if the guess makes sense.

7 Sound it out (focus on initial and final letters, consonants, known words within the work, meaningful word parts) → read on to see if the guess makes sense.

8 Stop reading → talk with a friend about what you do not understand → return and continue reading.

9 Stop reading → talk with a friend about what you do not understand.

10 Read the text with a friend.

11 Stop reading.

When reading and you have a hard time "getting into" or engaging with what you are reading, you can ask yourself:

Reader Response Strategies

1 What is my purpose for reading this text?

2 What am I learning from reading this text?

3 Why did the author write this text? What was the author trying to teach me?

4 What parts do I like best; what parts are my favorite; why do I like these particular parts?

5 What parts do I like the least? Why do I dislike these parts?

6 Does this text remind me of other texts I have read? How is this text both similar and dissimilar to other texts?

7 What would I change in this text if I had written it? What might the author have done to have made this text better, more understandable, more interesting?

8 Are there things/parts in the text that I am not understanding? What can I do to better understand these things/parts?

326

When writing and you come to a place where you do not know what to write next or have difficulty expressing an idea, you can:	When writing and you come to a word that you do not know how to spell, you can:
Writing Strategies	*Spelling Strategies*
1 Brainstorm possible ideas and jot them down on paper.	1 Sound it out.
2 Reread what you have written so far.	2 Think of "small words" that are in the word and write these first.
3 Skip to a part that you know what you will write about. Come back to the problem later.	3 Write the word several different ways and choose the one that looks the best.
4 Write it as best you can; return later to make it better.	4 Write the letters that you know are in the word.
5 Write it several different ways and choose the one that you like the best.	5 Make a line for the word.
6 Write whatever comes into your mind.	6 Ask a friend.
7 Talk about it/conference with a friend.	7 Look in the dictionary.
8 Read other texts to get some new ideas.	
9 Stop writing for a while and come back to it later.	

FIG. 11.1. Strategy wall charts. From Kucer (1995). Guiding bilingual students "through" the literary process. *Language Arts, 72*, 20–29. Copyright 1995 by the National Council of Teachers of English. Reprinted with permission.

The teacher as literacy expert will have to model the metacognitive and metalinguistic strategies for culturally and linguistically diverse students. The modeling will facilitate meaning making during reading and writing and in discussions about the comprehension and interpretation of written texts. The teacher, as gatekeeper, must be reflective and vigilant of the valuing and reinforcing of what counts as meaningful literacy practices.

Teaching Styles, Facilitating, and Questioning

As a teacher, you will want to find strategies for literacy and biliteracy learning and use among your students. Finding a useful style that does

PROMOTING			
Reading Strategies	Reader Response Strategies	Spelling Strategies	Writing Strategies
Student's oral reading of their drafts to other students	Texts with numerous pictures	Teacher's refusal to provide correct spelling	Theme-related writing
Pair reading	Students responding to student drafts during writing conferences	Understanding the concept of drafts versus publishable texts	Internalization of spelling strategies
	Student response to stories orally read by the teacher		
	Filmstrips		
	Reading student-published texts during free reading		

INHIBITING
Use of predictable story formats
Retelling of stories, movies, and personal experiences
Completion of a text in one class period
Lack of engagement

FIG 11.2. Significant instructional events and behaviors that either promoted or inhibited strategy internalization. From Kucer (1995). Guiding bilingual students "through" the literary process. *Language Arts, 72,* 20–29. Copyright 1995 by the National Council of Teachers of English. Reprinted with permission.

not occupy center stage may be difficult at first. When teachers take center stage in a class, they easily slip into the position of dispenser of information and gatekeeper or arbiter of talk, and the traditional IRE classroom discourse pattern usually prevails (Cazden, 1988; Mehan, 1979). Explain your anticipated behaviors and the role or style you will assume to the students. Some culturally diverse students will be expecting very traditional teacher behaviors and will be looking for teacher feedback and direction.

At the beginning of the academic year, you may explain to students that the classroom will attempt to reflect the democratic principles of U.S. society. Model this democratic process by having children participate in establishing class rules and consequences. Set up a process for electing revolving management teams and conflict resolution teams. Turn over the classroom functions to a committee of students. Some of these functions may be lunch counts, attendance money collection, and writing invitations and thank-you notes. Working in pairs or committees will provide checks and support while still encouraging student responsibility and meaningful authentic literacy learning.

Much of the literature on literacy practices within sociocultural communities stresses the diverse use of questions within these communities. Therefore, it is important that, within the classroom discourse, teachers signal or explain to students their use of questions. A beginning rule of thumb is to not use questions when the intent is to give instructions or directions; for example, do not say, "Will you take out your math books?" when the intent is a direction for students to take out their math books. Say instead, "Take out your math books." A second rule of thumb is to ask many authentic questions (questions for which you do not have the answers and genuinely want to know) both about the content of literacy lessons and about students' interests and lives. This will stimulate students' use of oral language and literacy, as well as give the children the message that you are concerned for their learning.

Other questioning strategies, such as guiding discussion questions, comprehension questions, cognitive questions, and questions based on Bloom's taxonomy, will have to be monitored by the teacher to assure that the function of the questions is being understood by the students. Some students may not respond appropriately to a teacher-initiated question, not because they do not have the factual information to answer the question but because they do not understand the function or the reason the question is being asked.

Altering the teacher's role is not easy, not even for beginning teachers who are coming out of teacher education programs that have stressed the role of teacher as facilitator, observer, reflective thinker. Novice teachers tend to "revert to poor instructional practices used by their own teachers" (California Commission on Teacher Credentialing, 1992, p. 7) under pressure. But culturally sensitive teaching will require a change in teacher behaviors. Figure 11.3 lists some instructional practices that can help teachers facilitate the achievement of culturally and linguistically diverse students.

CREATING A MULTICULTURAL CLASSROOM COMMUNITY

Creating a learning community that is not only respectful of differences but values and sees differences as learning resources is the intentional goal of a multicultural classroom community. A multicultural learning community is built on values that reflect the fundamental belief that all people should be respected, regardless of age, race, gender, economic class, religion, or physical or mental ability. Establishing a classroom community that is democratic and inclusive creates a common experi-

- Introducing students to a challenging, thinking, doing curriculum
- Organizing the classroom for more effective instruction through the use of such techniques as cooperative learning and peer tutoring
- Giving clear instruction to second-language learners, and developing English language in the course of accomplishing academic tasks
- Diagnosing students' literacy and learning needs
- Organizing appropriate learning activities that engage students in productive literacy tasks
- Monitoring student progress and providing student feedback
- Reteaching individual students when necessary, making explicit strategies and skills
- Including student's experience through the use of relevant cultural topics
- Promoting self-esteem and positive social relations among students from diverse backgrounds
- Relating to parents from diverse backgrounds, to coordinate home and school learning

FIG. 11.3. Instructional practices and improved diverse student achievement. Adapted from California Commission on Teacher Credentialing (1992), with permission.

ence for all students and develops a core of shared values and social relationships.

By drawing all students into full citizenship in a classroom that embraces multiracial/multicultural democracy, students experience the need for learning to live and work in an interdependent world. Unfortunately, much of multicultural education has generally been superficial, celebrating holidays, heroes, and festivals but not integrating diverse perspectives and experiences in the whole educational process.

The multicultural community's core shared values should permeate everything we do in the classroom, from respect for personal to physical space, resolution of conflicts, curriculum content and process, classroom and interpersonal discourse, and so forth. The environment broadcasts powerful messages to children about their place in the classroom and the world. This means that the physical environment communicates the teacher's commitment to the goals of the multicultural learning community. The literacy/learning tasks, the room arrangement, selected resources and activities, bulletin and other displays, and books in the classroom library all reflect a valuing and an attention to diversity. As you reflect about ways in which diversity is represented in your classroom and plan for a more inclusive multicultural classroom community, consider the checklist suggested in Fig. 11.4 as a way to periodically evaluate the messages projected by the classroom environment.

Environment Indicators	Good Progress	Needs Attention

1. Does the classroom reflect the cultural diversity of the students?
    a. Displays
    b. Literature
    c. Films and videos
    d. Other learning materials		

2. Does the classroom reflect an acceptance and valuing of students' native languages, using multilingual print where possible?
    a. Displays
    b. Literature
    c. Other learning materials		

3. Are interaction and communication patterns sensitive to students' cultural preferences?		
4. Does the room arrangement encourage collaboration and cooperative group work?		
5. Do the activities and tasks engage a variety of learning styles?		
6. Are experiences, situations, and examples from a wide variety of cultures used in the learning opportunities?		
7. Are invited guest speakers and resource persons representative of students' cultures?		
8. Is there a place (physical, emotional, psychological) for culturally diverse parents to feel comfortable in the classroom?		

FIG. 11.4.   Multicultural classroom community checklist.

Finding culturally and linguistically relevant artifacts, print materials, and guest persons is not as difficult as it may seem at first. Start with the children themselves; ask them to write and illustrate personal stories and histories. Ask parents to collect cultural and print artifacts, for example, candy and food wrappers, coins from the country of origin, newspapers, and magazines in the native languages. Begin building a personal or class collection of children's multicultural literature and resource books; contact Reading Is Fundamental or other community organizations and request support. While you are building a personal or class collection, visit a local library and ask the librarian to assist you with identifying children's and adult books about the different cultures in your classroom. When attending regional, state, and national teacher conferences, ask exhibitors for samples of multicultural posters and book covers.

Multicultural Literature as Model Text

The cultures and languages represented by the students in the class should be at the heart of the literacy curriculum. To help students from a variety of cultures and languages learn more and feel comfortable about their place in the classroom and school, it is necessary to continuously seek ways to include content to which students can bring their personal and cultural experiences. Using literature that not only uses themes/topics for diverse cultures but also uses authentic discourse patterns that have resonance to children from the particular linguistic group will provide a *model text* for children with which they can identify and for which they have the cultural referents. The themes of stories, the qualities attributed to characters, the text discourse patterns, and the composition of illustrations will all give students messages about the authenticity of understandings about their unique culture. Authenticity can best be assured by finding multicultural children's literature that is written by members from the ethnic group, which might be a difficult but not impossible undertaking. Harris' (1992) *Teaching Multicultural Literature in Grades K–8* is a good reference for teachers to get to know about diverse authors and quality multicultural literature.

The cultures and languages of the children in the class should be the starting point; however, the final goal is the learning and valuing of all cultures. Multicultural understanding can be developed through literature that describes experiences that are common to all, by relating the uniqueness of each cultural group, and by exploring the effects of racism, linguicism, and poverty on people's lives. Through multicultural literature, children can share in the lives and feelings of characters from cultures with which they may have little contact. Enciso (1994) described how a literature discussion of *Maniac Magee* (Spinelli, 1990) stimulated student discussion about their own and others' cultural and social identities. She cited the response of Marisa, a fourth-grade student:

> This is weird. 'Cause you know how like [they] talk about it and there's a black part and a white part. Where would like Mexicans or Chinese or someone like that be? Could they be friends with one of them? (Enciso, 1994, p. 524)

Multicultural literature can also provide opportunities for children to explore issues of identity and ethnicity. Broughton (2002) studied the construction of subjectivities of four sixth-grade girls as they read and discussed *Lupita Mañana* (Beatty, 1981), a novel about two Mexican adolescents who immigrate illegally to the United States. Although the four girls were identified as Hispanic with each having at least one parent of Hispanic descent, one self-identified as Mexican American. According to Broughton,

> discussions of the novel led the girls to engage in a debate about what it means to be a typical Hispanic. Some of the characteristics noted by the

grils included short stature, dark hair, dark skin, black eyes. Hoever, for almost every characteristic that one girl identified, another girl refuted it,
and the conversation became quite argumentative ... Through the social
interactions with peers, the girls became more aware of the complexity of
the socially constructed subject position of ethnicity .... The girls began to
use the book club as a way of exploring the ways they had constructed
themselves. (pp. 28–30)

As demonstrated by Broughton (2002) and Langer (1995), through
literature study and discussions children have opportunities to explore
and analyze their views about themselves, their families, and others.
Chapter 12 (this volume) illustrates how multicultural literature that
capitalizes on diverse cultural experiences and text discourses can be
integrated in a theme-based collaborative inquiry curriculum.

CAPITALIZING ON STUDENTS' LANGUAGES TO CREATE A MULTILEVEL LITERATE COMMUNITY

Freire and Macedo (1987) discussed the need for literacy to be
contextualized: "The command of meaning and writing is achieved
beginning with words and themes meaningful to the common experience of those becoming literate, and not with words and themes
linked only to the experience of the educator" (p. 42). The significance of Freire's concept, of reading the world before reading the
word, has not pervaded classroom teachers' understanding of the social relationships of literacy. Community literacy necessitates reading
the world because children live the world. Within their communities,
children have learned to interpret print and literacy practices in the
context of their world. But many existing classroom literacy practices
often negate the importance of reading the world and the importance
of social relationships in the development of literacy. In too many
classrooms, literacy becomes an individualistic activity, with individual students interacting with individual texts, and each child is responsible for reading certain pages and writing papers while the
teacher plays the role of monitor and evaluator. From this perspective,
school literacy is useful only for "school purposes," and literacy is only
valued in English. The child's literacies in languages other than English and the child's ability to read the social and contextual meanings
of his or her world are not recognized.

In working with culturally and linguistically diverse children, an
awareness that each comes from a valuable cultural history and language will create a first level of context where everyone can learn from
each other. Take time to read and learn about each child's native lan-

guage and to locate multicultural literature that the children will find culturally and linguistically relevant. The more you show interest in who they are and what linguistic riches they have brought into the classroom, the more comfortable the children will feel to be curious, to ask questions, and to seek information about the new classroom environment and about each other.

A second level of context can be created when children are encouraged to use all of their linguistic skills to accomplish literacy tasks. This means that children can find learning materials in their native languages in the classroom and that when children need to or choose to, they can respond and write in their native languages. The teacher encourages the use of buddy translators to accomplish tasks or seeks community members who can assist the class in interpreting and enriching the classroom linguistic environment.

The third level of context can be created when important literacy tasks require the use of the children's native language and literacy. This creates a context for the development of biliteracy. Many linguistically diverse children bring to the class prior knowledge and experiences developed in ethnolinguistic communities. When children are expected to use all their linguistic and literacy skills to connect with resources outside the classroom, as in the theme-based collaborative inquiry described in the next chapter, children's native language and English will continue to develop. When literacy is limited to English literacy the possibilities of involvement by parents and others from the child's community is limited. Biliteracy, in contrast, can create the expanded possibility of accessing the lived experiences of not only one but two social worlds.

SUMMARY

Efforts to make literacy accessible to socioculturally diverse students will require what Dyson (1993) described as linking composing a text and composing a place in this social world, where literacy learning is viewed as a social process in a complex social world that extends far beyond the classroom. Linking literacy from home and community helps students to make sense of school literacy in a number of ways. Children have opportunities to apply their home literacy knowledge and their prior or world knowledge to develop additional concepts of the meaning and functions of literary. Children know that their involvement with literacy extends to and includes their family as well as other people and many goals. Literacy develops for the "sake of others rather than for the sake of developing literacy competency as a skill in itself" (Fagan, 1995, p. 261).

Teachers in culturally and linguistically diverse classrooms will need to develop a different view of what counts as literacy and knowledge. This view should include the knowledge that children use their home and community experiences, native language, and culture to construct school knowledge and literacy. Teachers can facilitate students' transition from home to school literacy by creating interaction structures that allow students to use their knowledge. Teachers can ease role changes for students by utilizing social networks, encouraging peer bonding, and organizing interaction patterns that encourage collaboration and cooperation. Use of collaborative and cooperative group structures will require that teachers develop classroom discourse structures that are student centered.

By capitalizing on the cultural and linguistic diversity the children bring to the classroom a multicultural, multilingual classroom community can be created. Children's literature that reflects the child's lived experiences and discourse as well as literature that opens new worlds and possibilities will enrich the school literacy learning. Supporting and building on the biliterate skills children bring to school will encourage and support the child's ability to read the word and the world.

■ ACTIVITIES

1. Observe an elementary classroom during literacy time (reading/writing/language arts) and describe (a) the teacher role(s) and interaction with students, (b) the student–student relationships and interactions, and (c) the degree of collaboration and cooperation.
2. Prepare a list of typical literacy tasks a learner could encounter in the following situations: bus/train stations, grocery store, city street, clinic or doctor's office, and restaurant.
3. Select a reading passage from a children's literature book. Describe the roles that background knowledge and cultural schemata play in comprehension of the text.

SUGGESTED READINGS

Enciso, P. E. (1994). Cultural identity and response to literature: Running lessons from *Maniac Magee, Language Arts, 71*(7), 524–533.

Igoa, C. (1995). *The inner world of the immigrant child.* New York: St. Martin's Press.

López, G. R., Scribner, J. D., & Mahitivanichcha, K. (2001). Redefining parental involvement: Lessons from high-performing migrant-impacted schools. *American Educational Research Journal, 38*(2), 253–288.

Pérez, B. (1996). Instructional conversations as opportunities for English language acquisition for culturally and linguistically diverse students. *Language Arts, 73*(3), 15–23.

CHILDREN'S LITERATURE CITED

Beatty, P. (1981). *Lupita Mañana*. New York: Beech Tree.
Spinelli, J. (1990). *Maniac Magee*. Boston: Little, Brown.
Strete, C. K. (1990). *Big thunder magic*. New York: Greenwillow.

REFERENCES

Au, K. H., Crowell, D., Jordan, C., Sloat, C., Speidel, F., Klein, T., & Tharp, R. G. (1986). Development and implementation of the KEEP reading program. In J. Orasanu (Ed.), *Reading comprehension: From research to practice* (pp. 235–252). Hillsdale, NJ: Lawrence Erlbaum Associates.

Auerbach, E. (1989). Toward a socio-contextual approach to family literacy. *Harvard Educational Review, 59*, 165–181.

Baker, L., Afflerbach, P., & Reinking, D. (Eds.). (1996). *Developing engaged readers in school and home communities*. Hillsdale, NJ: Lawrence Erlbaum Associates.

Bankston, C. L., & Zhou, M. (1995). Effects of minority-language literacy on the academic achievement of Vietnamese youths in New Orleans. *Sociology of Education, 68*, 1–17.

Bialystok, E. (1991). Metalinguistic dimensions of bilingual language proficiency. In E. Bialystok (Ed.), *Language processing in bilingual children* (pp. 113–140). Cambridge, England: Cambridge University Press.

Brown, A. L., & Campione, J. C. (1994). Guided discovery in a community of learners. In K. McGilly (Ed.), *Classroom lessons: Integrating cognitive theory and classroom practice* (pp. 229–270). Cambridge, MA: MIT Press.

Broughton, M. A. (2002). The performance and construction of subjectivities of early adolescent girls in book club discussion groups. *Journal of Literacy Research, 34*(1), 1–38.

Bruner, J. S. (1983). *Child's talk: Learning to use language*. New York: Norton.

Bruner, J. (1996). *The culture of education*. Cambridge, MA: Harvard University Press.

California Commission on Teacher Credentialing. (1992). *Success for beginning teachers: California new teacher project*. Sacramento: California Department of Education.

Calkins, L. M. (1986). *The art of teaching writing*. Portsmouth, NH: Heinemann.

Cazden, C. B. (1988). *Classroom discourse: The language of teaching and learning*. Portsmouth, NH: Heinemann.

Cohen, E. G., Kepner, D., & Swanson, P. (1995). Dismantling status hierarchies in heterogeneous classrooms. In J. Oakes & K. H. Quartz (Eds.), *Creating new educational communities* (pp. 16–31). Chicago: University of Chicago Press.

Duran, R. P. (1985). Discourse skills of bilingual children: Precursors of literacy. *International Journal of the Sociology of Language, 53*, 99–114.

Duran, R. P. (1987). Metacognition in second language behavior. In J. A. Langer (Ed.), *Language, literacy, and culture: Issues of society and schooling* (pp. 49–63). Norwood, NJ: Ablex.

Dyson, A. H. (1993). *Social worlds of children learning to write in an urban primary school*. New York: Teachers College Press.

Enciso, P. C. (1994). Cultural identity and response to literature: Running lessons from *Maniac Magee. Language Arts, 71*, 524–533.

Englert, C. S. (1992). Socially mediated instruction: Improving students' knowledge and talk about writing. *Elementary School Journal, 92*, 411–449.

Fagan, W. T. (1995). Social relationships of literacy. *Reading Teacher, 49*, 260–262.

Freire, P., & Macedo, D. (1987). *Reading the world and the word.* South Hadley, MA: Bergin & Garvey.

García, E. E., & Carrasco, R. L. (1981). An analysis of bilingual mother–child discourse. In R. P. Durán (Ed.), *Latino language and communicative behavior* (pp. 257–270). Norwood, NJ: Ablex.

Goldenberg, C. (1996). Latin American immigration and U.S. schools. *Social Policy Report of the Society for Research in Child Development, 10*(1), 1–29.

Harris, V. J. (1992). *Teaching multicultural literature in grades K–8.* Norwood, MA: Christopher-Gordon.

Heath, S. (1983). *Ways with words.* New York: Cambridge University Press.

Hertz-Lazarowitz, R. (1992). Understanding students interaction behavior: Looking at six mirrors of the classroom. In R. Hertz-Lazarowitz & N. Miller (Eds.), *Interaction in cooperative groups: Theoretical anatomy of group learning* (pp. 77–95). New York: Cambridge University Press.

Hull, G., Rose, M., Fraser, K. L., & Castellano, M. (1991). Remediation as a social construct: Perspectives from an analysis of classroom discourse. *College Composition and Communication, 43*, 299–329.

Igoa, C. (1995). *The inner world of the immigrant child.* New York: St. Martin's Press.

Johnson, D. W., & Johnson, F. (1991). *Joining together: Group theory and group skills* (4th ed.). Englewood Cliffs, NJ: Prentice Hall.

Kucer, S. B. (1995). Guiding bilingual students "through" the literacy process. *Language Arts, 72*, 20–29.

Labov, W. (1972). *Sociolinguistics patterns.* Philadelphia: University of Pennsylvania Press.

Langer, J. (1995). *Envisioning literature: Literary understanding and instruction.* New York: Teachers College Press.

Langer, J. A., Bartoleme, L., Vasquez, O., & Lucas, T. (1990). Meaning construction in school literacy tasks: A study of bilingual students. *American Educational Research Journal, 27*, 427–471.

López, G. R., Scribner, J. D., & Mahitivanichcha, K. (2001). Redefining parental involvement: Lessons from high-performing migrant-impacted schools. *American Educational Research Journal, 38*(2), 253–288.

López, M. E. (1999). *When discourses collide: An ethnography of migrant children at home and in school.* New York: Peter Lang.

McCarthey, S. J. (1998). Constructing multiple subjectivities in classroom literacy contexts. *Research in the Teaching of English, 32*, 126–160.

Meed, S., & Whitmore, K. F. (2001). What's in your backpack? Exchanging funds of knowledge in an ESL classroom. In P. G. Smith (Ed.), *Talking classrooms: shaping children's learning through oral langauge instruction* (pp. 42–56). Newark, DE: International Reading Association.

Mehan, H. (1979). *Learning lessons: Social organization in the classroom.* Cambridge, MA: Harvard University Press.

Muñiz-Swicegood, M. (1994). The effects of metacognitive reading strategy training on the reading performance and student reading analysis strategies of third grade bilingual students. *Bilingual Research Journal, 18*, 83–98.

Nieto, S. (Ed.). (2002). *Language, culture, and teaching: Critical perspectives for a new century*: Mahwah, NJ: Lawrence Erlbaum Associates.

O'Malley, J., & Chamot, A. U. (1990). *Learning strategies in second language acquisition.* New York: Cambridge University Press.

Pappas, C., Kiefer, B. Z., & Levstik, L. S. (1995). *An integrated language perspective in the elementary school* (2nd ed.). New York: Longman.

Pérez, B. (1996). Instructional conversations as opportunities for English language acquisition for culturally and linguistically diverse students. *Language Arts, 73,* 173–181.

Phelps, S., & Weaver, D. (1999). Public and personal voices in adolescents' classroom talk. *Journal of Literacy Research, 31,* 221–254.

Philips, S. (1972). Participant structures and communicative competence: Warm Springs Indian children in community and classrooms. In C. Cazden, V. John, & D. Hymes (Eds.), *Functions of language in the classroom* (pp. 370–394). New York: Teachers College Press.

Raphael, G. E., & Brock, C. H. (1993). Mei: Learning the literacy culture in an urban elementary school. In D. J. Len & C. K. Kinzer (Eds.), *Examining central issues in literacy research, theory, and practice* (pp. 179–188). Chicago: National Reading Conference.

Salinger, T. (1993). *Models of literacy instruction.* New York: Merrill.

Saravia-Shore, M., & Martínez, H. (1992). An ethnographic study of home/school role conflicts of second generation Puerto Rican adolescents. In M. Saravia-Shore & S. F. Arvizu (Eds.), *Cross-cultural literacy: Ethnographies of communication in multiethnic classrooms* (pp. 227–252). New York: Garland.

Schmidt, P. R. (1993). Literacy development of two bilingual, ethnic-minority children in a kindergarten program. *National Reading Conference Yearbook, 42,* 189–196.

Slavin, R. E. (1990). *Cooperative learning: Theory, research and practice.* Englewood Cliffs, NJ: Prentice Hall.

Sluys, K. V. (2003). Writing and identity construction: A young author's life in transition. *Language Arts, 80*(3), 176–184.

Snow, C. E., Cancino, H., De Temple, J., & Schley, S. (1991). Giving formal definitions: A linguistic or metalinguistic skill? In E. Bialystok (Ed.), *Language processing in bilingual children* (pp. 90–112). Cambridge, England: Cambridge University Press.

Spinelli, J. (1990). *Maniac Magee.* Boston: Little, Brown.

Strete, C. K. (1990). *Big thunder magic.* New York: Greenwillow.

Tharp, R. (1994). Research knowledge and policy issues in cultural diversity and education. In B. McLeod (Ed.). *Language and learning: Educating linguistically diverse students* (pp. 129–167). Albany: State University of New York Press.

Tinajero, J. V., Calderón, J. E., & Hertz-Lazarowitz, R. (1993). Cooperative learning strategies: Bilingual classroom applications. In J. V. Tinajero & A. F. Ada (Eds.), *The power of two languages: Literacy and biliteracy for Spanish-speaking students* (pp. 241–253). New York: Macmillan/McGraw-Hill.

Valdés, G. (1996). *Con respeto: Bridging the distance between culturally diverse families and schools.* New York: Teachers College Press.

Vygotsky, L. S. (1978). *Mind and society.* Cambridge, MA: Harvard University Press.

Wells, G. (1986). *The meaning makers.* Portsmouth, NH: Heinemann.

Wilkinson, L. C., & Silliman, E. R. (2000). Classroom language and literacy learning. In M. L. Kamil, P. B. Mosenthal, P. D. Pearson, & R. Barr (Eds.), *Handbook of reading research* (Vol. III, pp. 337–360). Mahwah, NJ: Lawrence Erlbaum Associates.

Wollman-Bonilla, J., & Werchadlo, B. (1999). Teacher and peer role in scaffolding first graders' responses to literature. *Reading Teacher, 52,* 598–607.

12

Literacy, Curriculum, and Language Diversity

Bertha Pérez

The literacy opportunities, materials, and projects that teachers provide for students give powerful messages to children about the role, importance, and nature of reading, writing, and thinking in everyday life. Teachers make many daily decisions about curriculum in classrooms. Even when using the state frameworks and adopted textbooks as the core of their literacy curriculum, teachers must necessarily select specific texts and activities. Teachers who are using a literature-based or interdisciplinary curriculum make decisions about themes, literature, time and space utilization, project publication format, and assessment. What the teacher values is reflected in the many decisions. Children, even very young children, interpret and, in many cases, internalize the messages transmitted by these decisions.

This chapter looks at curriculum standards and frameworks, with suggestions for designing a constructivist literacy curriculum; it contains curriculum examples that are theme-based inquiries that build on a student's interest, culture, and experience. A variety of assessment practices and the use of portfolios to evaluate children's multiple literacies are suggested.

DEVELOPING A LITERACY CURRICULUM

From a constructive perspective, the goal of the literacy curriculum is to help students set their own goals for literacy learning and to monitor their own progress in achieving these goals. In order for students to know the full range of possible goals, the teacher must develop settings that focus on challenging literacy opportunities for all students. Within this setting students can be in charge of setting goals for their own literacy learning. The starting point for the literacy curriculum should be the students' needs, interests, and goals. This means that teachers begin the process of planning for instruction by asking students to identify the goals they have for themselves. It is especially important for teachers to listen to students' ideas about their own literacy learning because students from diverse backgrounds may have literacy goals influenced by circumstances outside of school that are unfamiliar to teachers and to the standard school literacy curriculum.

Theme-Based Collaborative Inquiry

Within a constructivist framework, the literacy curriculum can be organized as *theme-based collaborative inquiry.* Collaborative inquiry requires dialectics, argumentation and mutual investigation, dialogues, clear communication between the collaborating partners, and most important, a shared purpose. Wasley, King, and Louth (1995) defined collaborative inquiry as "the process of engaging in inquiry on a topic of mutual interest, negotiating the conditions of the partnership, and once underway, communicating about the subject of inquiry" (p. 204). A curriculum based on inquiry can draw its overt content from the local community, and can use the pedagogical approach that reinforces "patterns of learning in natural situations outside the classroom" (McCarty, chap. 4, this volume). Inquiry can use the questions children have as the organizational focus and the disciplines and literacy provide *ways of* or *tools for* examining and constructing knowledge. With theme-based collaborative inquiry learning, no one, not even the teacher, has all the answers and the sociocultural perspectives are fluid. Thus, any kind of problem or question that comes up is an invitation to inquire, read, write, and learn. Within a constructivist framework curriculum, reading and writing are also seen as questions or solutions for inquiry—for example, what was the problem for which reading was the answer? Similarly, writing must be thought of as inquiry, or, what was the problem for which writing was the answer?

The theme-based collaborative inquiry does not focus on integrating the language arts into the content areas. Rather, it develops around a theme arising from students' questions, for which goals are developed and learning opportunities planned. The content-area skills that are planned as part of the inquiry are an integral part or natural extension of the theme. Likewise, the literacy skills incorporated are an integral part or a tool to be used in the theme-based collaborative inquiry.

The theme-based collaborative inquiry can also be different from a literature-based integrated curriculum that focuses on central pieces of literature. The theme-based collaborative inquiry focuses on literacy as a social and cognitive phenomenon. It emphasizes the use of language and literacy to conduct theme-based collaborative inquiry throughout the content areas including literature.

In theme-based collaborative inquiry, not only literacy but the total curriculum is viewed very differently from the past. Inquiry and constructing knowledge become a philosophical frame from which to view the whole of what happens in classrooms and schools. Children and teachers pose questions from interest and from living. Children are encouraged to wander and wonder about questions, themes, and topics of their choosing. The curriculum has an openness that encourages children to go off in directions that may not be predetermined and that reach conclusions that are unforeseen. When children follow their own questions, they become engaged in literacy and learning.

Preplanning for Collaborative Inquiry

In order to organize a curriculum that is constructivist and allows students to inquire, it is important that teachers plan to plan. That is, teachers from their living and experience might consider those themes that might be of importance or interest to students. They then consider how those themes might be viewed through the different disciplines and what important topics and concepts each discipline contributes to the themes. For example, for any particular theme, ask: What would a biologist want to know about this theme and what concepts would he or she want us to know? What would a writer, artist, or anthropologist want to know, or what generalizations would they want us to form? The themes must also be considered through the social and cultural knowledge shared by the group of students you are working with this year. Equally important to ask about a theme would be: What questions would Esperanza, Justin, or Lien pose about this theme and topics? Planning to plan allows the teacher to anticipate inquiry questions that interest the students and to explore ways to invite children to inquire about different themes. McCarty and Watahomigie (chap. 4, this volume) illustrate a Hualapai Bilingual/Bicultural Curriculum Framework that begins from the child's perspective. The starting point centers on the child as it moves outward to the home environment, the community and school environment, and the natural environment. This curriculum framework begins with the children's own life accounts and those passed down from elders in their community.

A literacy program that values and is respectful of diversity allows children and teachers to examine and contribute to the content and purpose of instruction. Teachers can begin to create a constructivist framework for literacy by asking about, observing, and assessing students' interest. Students and teacher can participate in identifying student interests; in some classrooms, this very process of interest identification becomes a most meaningful literacy event. Students may develop surveys or interview questions, collect data, analyze data, write reports, and lobby one another in the decision-making process for selecting themes and guiding questions for classroom study and inquiry.

Community Connections— A Sample Collaborative Inquiry

Let us look at an example from a classroom where a community collaborative inquiry project was implemented with inner-city predominantly minority students. This community collaborative inquiry project varied from a theme-based inquiry only in that the themes the children explored and were encouraged to select were from the immediate school community. It also used what Chang (chap. 7, this volume) and Schustack, King, Gallego, and Vasquez (1994) defined as *multiple sites of learning*, where the community became the learning environment.

At Brewer Elementary, fourth- and fifth-grade teachers asked students to brainstorm about things they might study that were in the immediate school community. Next to the school are housing projects that have colorful murals painted on them. Many topics were discussed, but students kept returning to questions about why the murals were painted. Who had painted them? Were the paintings any good (artistic quality)? Among other topics discussed were community practices based on herbal or folk medicine, the railroad, the produce market, and the clinic. After much discussion, the students decided to conduct a survey to ask all fourth- and fifth-grade students about their interests for the community collaborative inquiry theme. In the end, after teams of students collected, analyzed, charted, and reported the results of the survey, students voted to study two themes: the murals and folk medicine. Students from four classrooms and their four teachers organized their curriculum around the two themes. Students were allowed to select between the two community collaborative inquiry themes, murals and folk medicine. What resulted was two multigrade groups of fourth and fifth graders, with two teachers for each group studying each theme.

Figure 12.1 illustrates the planning and implementation of the community connections collaborative inquiry of the murals. Once the themes and general organizational structure for the inquiry were decided, the children's questions were categorized and children were asked to brainstorm topics that would help them investigate their questions. They worked in groups to pursue those particular topics and questions. Students made their own plans for conducting their collaborative inquiry from posing questions, identifying perspectives for the study, negotiating with each other about groups and tasks, making appointments, requesting teacher and other adult support, and so forth. An important product of the collaborative inquiry study was that students learned how to ask teachers to identify certain kinds of information, tasks, and experts that they needed in order for them to learn and lead their collaborative inquiry. For example, the group working on the murals early in the inquiry asked the teacher to suggest where they could find an artist to invite to the class that would help them frame questions about the quality of the murals. Students, in consultation with their teachers, decided to group into teams around areas of interest in which they wished to work. These included the history of the creation of the murals and the maintenance of the murals; the study of the artistic, social, cultural, and political themes expressed in the murals; the survey of community sentiment and interest in the murals; the study of the physical qualities, dimensions, and material needs of the murals; a technology design team; and a planning team whose job was to help other teams organize and document their work. Within these teams, students focused on conversation, collaboration, researching, and documenting. Students found important and authentic reasons for reading and writing; they were involved in interviewing specialists and community members. Students wrote questions and interviewed in English and Spanish, depending on the language skills of the interviewee. They sought differing opinions and explanations for their questions and consulted different sources of information. The students were challenged to keep thinking about questions from different perspectives or disciplines; for example, what might an artist, chemist, historian, or community member ask about their study? Their comprehension of materials that were read or information gained from interviews extended into new inquiry questions. During the weeks that followed, students planned to present their findings and document their in-

COMMUNITY CONNECTIONS INQUIRY—MURALS

Guiding Questions	Topics/Times	Texts/Research Materials	Participation Structures and Student Engagement	Products/Assessment
What is a mural? How is it different from other paintings?	Murals, fresco paintings, iconography, visual arts (begins study for all for 2-3 days; 1 team works for 2 weeks; design team together 3 weeks)	Diego: The Little Painter of Sabona Grande; Compton on CD-ROM	Whole group takes a walking tour of the murals followed by small-group & whole-class discussion. Children are paired for reading/researching basic theme/topics; whole group sharing; 1 team (5 students) continues research on muralist; 1 team designated as "technology design team."	Video of class walking tour. Hypercard button "What is a Mural?"; class composed/illustrated book on muralist. Portfolios: each student completes K-W-L charts; students select drafts to include.
Why were these murals painted? When? Who? How? Who painted them?	Artist/community motivated, public/private financing, multiple/one artist, time/materials, maintenance (begins on 4th day; 2 teams work for 2 weeks)	Interviews of community and housing authority members, & artists	One team contacts/interviews housing authority personnel; 1 team constructs a questionnaire for community interviews; 1 team works on identifying/inviting artist; all children participate in presentation & interview of guest artist; everyone has choice to interview community members.	Appointments; interview questions and transcriptions; questionnaire; Design/writing of Hypercard stacks: "How were murals made?" "Who were the artists?" "When were the murals started," and "Why were murals painted on the walls?" Portfolios: drafts/final products of interview questions and transcriptions; drafts for stacks. Teacher/team conferences.
What are the themes of the murals?	U.S./Mexican history, culture, religion, politics (begins on 4th day; 2 teams work 2 weeks)	Texas: In Words and Pictures; Social Studies: Texas, The U.S. and the World; Comptons	Two teams study the historical, cultural, political, and religious themes of the murals; all teams make presentations to whole group on their ongoing research.	Class composed and illustrated book on themes of the murals; Hypercard stack "Themes of murals." Teacher/student conferences with individual and teams.
Where are the murals?	Community map; map of selected murals, favorite/best/worst (begins 3rd week for all students for 3-4 days; 1 team continues work for 8 days)	Maps of the city; Exploring Mathematics	All children are paired to create a series of maps drawn to scale on the locations of 5 selected murals in relation to the city & school.	Hypercard stack "Where are the murals? Portfolios: New K-W-L charts will be completed; students will select drafts and sample products to include. Portfolio conferences with individual and teams.
What would it take for us to create a new mural today?	Estimate dimensions, materials, time/money (one team begins work during 2nd week; all students work for 3-4 days during 2nd week)	Housing authority, artists	All children are paired to (a) estimate/measure the dimensions of the murals, (b) estimate the quantity of paint for each/all murals, and (c) estimate average cost for painting each mural; 1 team continues work on drawings for class mural	Hypercard stacks "Time/Cost" and "What next?"; designs for class mural; Portfolios: Students write a self-assessment and include additional samples. Parents/community invited for multimedia presentation; books & portfolios are exhibited.

FIG. 12.1. Community connections inquiry—murals.

quiry by creating a multimedia presentation using Hyperstudio. They also made decisions about who to invite to view their presentation and when and how to extend invitations.

Implications of Community Collaborative Inquiry as Literacy

Through the community collaborative inquiry, students generated topics and questions that permeated the literacy program as well as the content learning. Once the students had identified the questions that interested them, they read, wrote, and problem solved as they went into the community to interview and conduct field work. Students explored the conceptual tools that people from different disciplines had used to reach conclusions and generalizations as they reached their own conclusions. The inquiry did not yield only one conclusion. In fact, the inquiry fostered a range of possible further study questions as well as new understandings and new perspectives. The starting point and the group's task were different, requiring students to share knowledge and become experts. Students came to very different levels of understanding about different aspects of the inquiry. However, because the curriculum, in terms of both literacy and content learning, was developed through inquiry rather than a predetermined body of knowledge that had to be mastered, students' school attendance improved and students were motivated and actively involved. A by-product of the inquiry was that parents and community members who had not been involved with the school took a new interest in school activities.

Implementing Theme-Based Collaborative Inquiry Curriculum

When you read about or even observe a classroom were children are using inquiry as they learn across the curriculum, you may wonder where to start. In the community connections collaborative inquiry, the teachers and students began by reading children's literature on the theme of community. This helped students and teachers think of ideas for possible themes.

Selecting a Theme. The first step is the identification of a theme or question. Brainstorm with students about their interests, questions, concerns, or their notions of what school and learning should be—for example, "What should third grade be like?" Themes should reflect student interests and be substantive enough to allow you to incorporate topics around which you might organize important ideas, processes, and skills that children need to know and be able to do. Remember, all of the learning activities that are taught should be natural extensions of the theme you select.

By focusing on the diversity of the group, a wide variety of dimensions can be brought to bear on the theme. By beginning with a theme and thinking through the various topics within that theme, the teacher can invite children to explore different dimensions of the theme and topics.

Collecting Resource Materials. When children are allowed to pick their own inquiry project, even within a common theme, the task of supporting students in the exploration of their topics becomes a difficult task for most teachers. However, in the pre-planning, teachers can identify possible resources, experts within the community, possible field sites, and so forth that might help students use disciplines and literacy as tools for gaining not only knowledge but a new perspective on the theme.

Begin by using the materials that you have in your classroom; textbooks can be a valuable resource as you and the students begin to develop plans for your theme-based collaborative inquiry. Expand your search for materials to include computer programs, videos, games, films, and music. The school librarian and the local branch of the public library are also great sources for information on the selected theme.

Organizing and Engaging Students and Collaborators. Determine the specific goals and objectives that you will want to accomplish based on the students' questions and the theme and topics selected. The next step is to design beginning activities that encourage conceptual learning and will foster accomplishment of major goals (Frank, 1999).

Now determine how each phase of the theme collaborative inquiry will be carried out. Preplan what portions will be done in whole-group instructional formats, in small groups, in pairs, or individually. Involve students in various grouping arrangements. Such arrangements provide you with opportunities for content-specific instruction and mini-lessons focusing on specific literacy tasks and skills.

Monitoring, Adjusting, and Expanding. Involve students in monitoring and adjusting of the theme-based study by holding class meetings or whole-group sharing sessions that will allow students to assess the progress of the study. These sessions can also identify ways for students to expand the theme. Topics or questions that have come up can be evaluated against the goals for the theme-based collaborative inquiry and decisions made about which of these to pursue. Additionally, students and teacher can use these sessions to evaluate the organizational structures and regroup if necessary.

Assessing Student Growth. Early in the inquiry, the teacher and students will also want to make decisions about what the goals of the inquiry will be, what the types of products will be, and for what purposes the students will be producing. For example, in the community connections inquiry of the murals (see products/assessment section of Fig. 12.1), the students prepared a multimedia Hypercard presentation to be made to parents, and they also prepared gallery exhibits for special invited guests (school board members, community members, or university students and faculty).

When you begin the planning for the theme-based collaborative inquiry, you should also begin planning on ways of assessing student growth. The assessment should allow you to determine how each student is making progress toward the instructional goals of the theme-based collaborative inquiry, as well as to assess how well the collaboration is functioning. The assessment tools you select should complement your designated goals and instructional activities. Later in this chapter there is a discussion of a variety of assessment forms that may be used.

Themes for Possible Collaborative Inquiry

Communication. We suggest an inquiry on the theme of "communication" for study by older children, third through sixth grade, depending on the literacy development of the children and the level of sophistication incorporated into the inquiry. A theme-based collaborative inquiry of "communication" that focuses on the languages and cultures of the children in the classroom will capitalize on the students' knowledge and ability to create a multilevel literate community. In such an inquiry, different students and parents, as well as the teacher, will have the opportunity to assume the role of expert and novice as they study "all you ever wanted to know and more" about communication. This theme inquiry also provides an opportunity for exploring the cultural experiences and meanings behind words such as *respect, educated, dignity,* and so on discussed by Torres-Guzmán (chap. 5, this volume).

Teacher and students can begin the theme-based inquiry by brainstorming around the theme, listing what they know, and what they would like to know. An especially useful graphic organizer that can be used to organize and capture ideas from the students' discussion is the "Know, Want to Know, Learn" or K–W–L strategy (Ogle, 1989). A three-column chart with K–W–L headings is used. As students brainstorm what they know about a topic, students write this information in the K column of the graphic organizer. Next, students are asked to anticipate what they would like to know about the theme and they record this in the second column. Later, as students begin organizing and studying the theme, the third column, what they have learned, is recorded. Using a graphic organizer, such as the K–W–L, can assist students to categorize what they expect from their study and to organize the collaborative work. It is also beneficial for the teacher to check students' assumptions or understandings and to correct as well as fill any conceptual gaps during the study.

Based on the K–W–L information, the teacher and students can continue brainstorming about the theme using a concept or semantic map. Semantic maps focus on relationships between ideas and concepts, thus they assist in depicting schemes—our mental models of our knowledge. As the students call out ideas, words, and questions related to communication, the teacher or another student can begin to jot down suggestions. The class can later refine the semantic map around general categories. Figure 12.2 illustrates the type of semantic map that can result. The semantic map is just the beginning; as children research, read, and discuss what they are finding they can enlarge and extend the original map. Based on the semantic map, the teacher and students can now generate some guiding questions that will guide their quest for information as illustrated in Fig. 12.3. Guiding questions should be "large picture" or major questions that will guide learning and instruction over a series of days. However, at the beginning of the process, some children may insist on listing very specific knowledge questions; these should be accepted and listed. The teacher can stimulate questions by posing questions of interest to him or her or by sharing information. For example, on the theme of communication, the teacher can share information such as suggested by Heath and Mangiola (1991):

> All sociocultural groups have some unique ways of transmitting to their children background knowledge about the world and of asking their children to display what they know. In some groups, adults will ask children many questions to which the adults already know the answer .... In some communities, by contrast, telling what one knows or competing overtly against another invites ridicule, censure, and even punishment from elders. (p. 14)

This might lead the children to pose a question like "How do different culture groups communicate?" or "Does everyone ask questions?"

The teacher and students can use the semantic map and the guiding questions to identify and gather resources such as children's literature

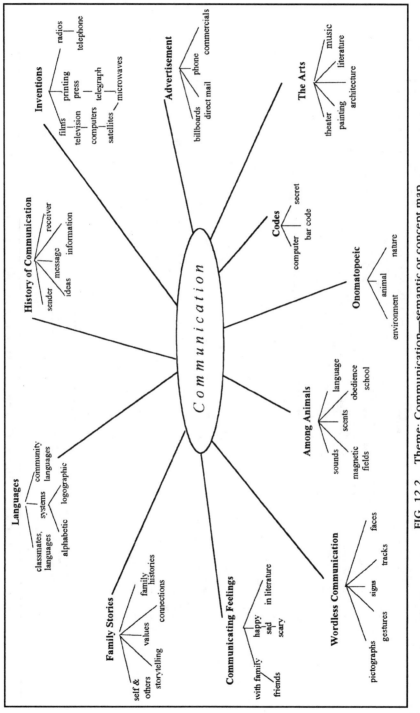

FIG. 12.2. Theme: Communication—semantic or concept map.

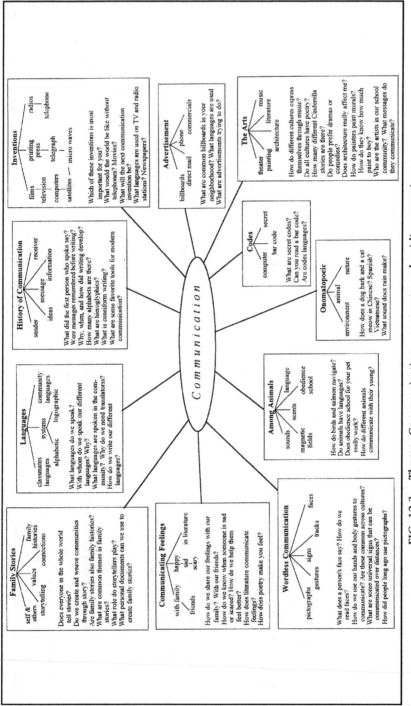

Family Stories

self & others
values
storytelling
family histories
connections

Does everyone in the whole world tell stories?
Do we create and weave communities through story?
Are family stories also family histories?
What are common themes in family stories?
What role do storytellers play?
What personal documents can we use to create family stories?

Communicating Feelings

with family
friends
happy
sad
scary
in literature

How do we share our feelings with our family? With our friends?
How do we know when someone is sad or scared? How do we help them feel better?
How does literature communicate feelings?
How does poetry make you feel?

Wordless Communication

pictographs
gestures
signs
tracks
faces

What does a person's face say? How do we read faces?
How do we use our hands and body gestures to communicate? Are these common across cultures?
What are some universal signs that can be communicated over distances?
How did people long ago use pictographs?

Languages

classmates languages
systems
alphabetic
logographic
community languages

What languages do we speak?
With whom do we speak our different languages? Why?
What languages are spoken in the community? Why do we need translators?
How do we write our different languages?

Among Animals

sounds
magnetic fields
scents
language
obedience school

How do birds and salmon navigate?
Do animals have languages?
Does obedience school for your pet really work?
How do different animals communicate with their young?

Onomatopoeic

environment
animal
nature

How does a dog bark and a cat meow in Chinese? Spanish? Vietnamese?
What sound does rain make?

Codes

computer
bar code
secret

What are secret codes?
Can you read a bar code?
Are codes languages?

History of Communication

sender
ideas
message
receiver
information

What did the first person who spoke say?
Were messages remembered before writing?
Why, when, and how did writing develop?
How many alphabets are there?
What are hieroglyphics?
What is cuneiform writing?
What are some favorite tools for modern communication?

Inventions

films
television
computers
satellites — micro waves
printing press
telegraph
radios
telephone

Which of these inventions is most important for you?
What would the world be like without telephones? Movies?
What will the next communication invention be?
What languages are used on TV and radio stations? Newspapers?

Advertisement

billboards
direct mail
phone
commercials

What are common billboards in your neighborhood? What languages are used in advertisements?
What are advertisements trying to do?

The Arts

theater
painting
music
literature
architecture

How do different cultures express themselves through music?
Do all cultures have poetry?
How many different Cinderella stories are there?
Do people prefer dramas or comedies?
Does architecture really affect me?
How do painters paint murals?
How do they know how much paint to buy?
Who are the artists in our school community? What messages do they communicate?

Communication

FIG. 12.3.   Theme: Communication—concepts and guiding questions.

and trade books, and to organize possible activities to conduct the research, reading, writing, learning, discussing, publishing, and so forth about the theme. Figure 12.4 suggests children's literature and learning activities for the theme of communication. Children's literature about native languages, like *Pepita Talks Twice/Pepita habla dos veces* (Lachtman, 1995), and children's attitudes about learning English, like *I Hate English* (Levine, 1989) or *Tea With Milk* (Say, 1999), and about translating, like *I Speak English for My Mom* (Stanek, 1989) or *Home at Last* (Elya, 2002) can also be read, discussed, and explored. Stories about children's names and what names tell about a person's langauge and culture can be discussed through such books as *The Name Jar* (Choi, 2001) or *My Name Is María Isabel* (Ada, 1993).

Because of differences in discourse styles, children may benefit from utilizing a variety of graphic organizers that will help them compare different genres of reading and writing. When reading and writing narrative texts, story mapping, character mapping, problem–solution outlines, and event–time sequences are but a few organizational tools that can be used. When working with descriptive, informative, or expository texts, graphic organizers such as compare–contrast charts and semantic features analysis will help students understand and make meaning.

Home and Neighborhood Theme-Based Collaborative Inquiry.

To begin a new school year, especially with younger children or new immigrant students, a theme-based collaborative inquiry of home and neighborhood will help make the connections between the community and the school (see Fig. 12.5). With guiding questions like How would you define a family?, How do we find our way around the neighborhood?, How do we get emergency help?, or Which is your favorite family celebration?, and others suggested in Fig. 12.6, students can make a transition from home to school and learn valuable information in the process. To explore ideas about mapping their neighborhood you could start by reading *Madlenka* (Sis, 2000), a young girl's description and mapmaking about her neighbors who come from different cultures all over the world. Figure 12.7 suggests children's literature and learning activities for this theme.

To facilitate the collection of information about families and community members, Igoa (1995) suggested that students can learn how to use tape recorders. The children can take turns taking the tape recorders home, with the assignment of working with their families to capture the sounds of their culture, their language, and its music. Reading about different cultural ways of doing things, such as Ada's (2002) *I Love Saturdays y Domingos* or Lijima's (2002) *The Way We Do It in Ja-*

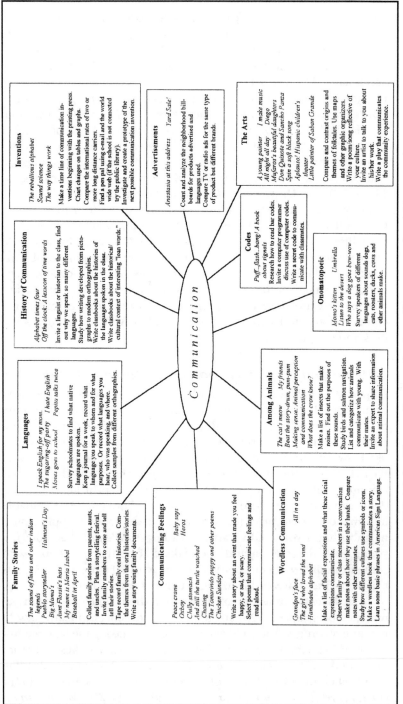

Family Stories

The sound of flutes and other indian legends   *Halmoni's Day*
Pueblo storyteller
Big Mama's
Aunt Flossie's hats
My name is Maria Isabel
Baseball in April

Collect family stories from parents, aunts, and uncles. Plan a storytelling festival. Invite family members to come and tell tell their stories.
Tape record family oral histories. Combine the themes from the oral histories/stories.
Write a story using family documents.

Languages

I speak English for my mom.   *I hate English*
The sugaring-off party   *Pepita talks twice*
Moses goes to school

Survey schoolmates to find out what native languages are spoken.
Keep a journal for a week, record what language you speak to whom and for what purposes. Or record what languages you hear, who was speaking, and where.
Collect samples from different orthographies.

History of Communication

Alphabet times four
Off the clock: A lexicon of time words

Invite a linguist or historian to the class, find out why we speak so many different languages.
Study how writing developed from pictographs to modern orthographies.
Write classbooks about the histories of the languages spoken in the class.
Write classbooks about the historical/cultural context of interesting "loan words."

Inventions

The rebellious alphabet
Sound science
The way things work

Make a time line of communication inventions beginning with the printing press. Chart changes on tables and graphs.
Compare the international rules of two or more long distance carriers.
Find a pen pal using e-mail and the world wide web (if the school is not connected try the public library).
Investigate and create a prototype of the next possible communication invention.

Communication

Wordless Communication

Grandpa's face   *All in a day*
The girl who loved the wind
Handmade alphabet

Make a list of facial expressions and what those facial expressions communicate.
Observe family or class members in a conversation make notes about how they use their hands. Compare notes with other classmates.
Study how different cultures use symbols or icons.
Make a wordless book that communicates a story.
Learn some basic phrases in American Sign Language.

Communicating Feelings

Peace crane   *Baby says*
Oxboy   *Heros*
Chilly stomach
And still the turtle watched
Cheating
The Tamorindo puppy and other poems
Chicken Sunday

Write a story about an event that made you feel happy, or sad, or scary.
Select poems that communicate feelings and read aloud.

Among Animals

The cat's meow   *My friends*
Beat the story-drum, pum-pum
Making sense: Animal perception and communication
What does the crow know?

Make a list of insects that make noises. Find out the purposes of these sounds.
Study birds and salmon navigation. List and categorize how animals communicate with young. With their mates.
Invite an expert to share information about animal communication.

Onomatopoeic

Momo's kitten   *Umbrella*
Listen to the desert
Who says a dog goes bow-wow

Survey speakers of different languages about sounds dogs, cats, roosters, ducks, cows and other animals make.

Codes

Puff...flash...bang! A book about signals

Research how to read bar codes.
Invite a computer programmer discuss use of computer codes.
Write a secret code to communicate with classmates.

Advertisements

Anastasia at this address   *Yard Sale!*

Count and analyze the neighborhood billboards for products advertised and languages used.
Compare TV or radio ads for the same type of product but different brands.

The Arts

A young painter   *I make music*
All night all day   *Diego*
Mufaro's beautiful daughters
Don Quixote and Sancho Panza
Spin a soft black song
Aplauso! Hispanic children's theater
Little painter of Sabon Grande

Compare and contrast origins and themes of folktales. Use maps and other graphic organizers.
Write a poem/song reflective of your culture.
Invite an artist to talk to you about his/her work.
Write a play that communicates the community experience.

FIG. 12.4.   Theme: Communication—literature and activities.

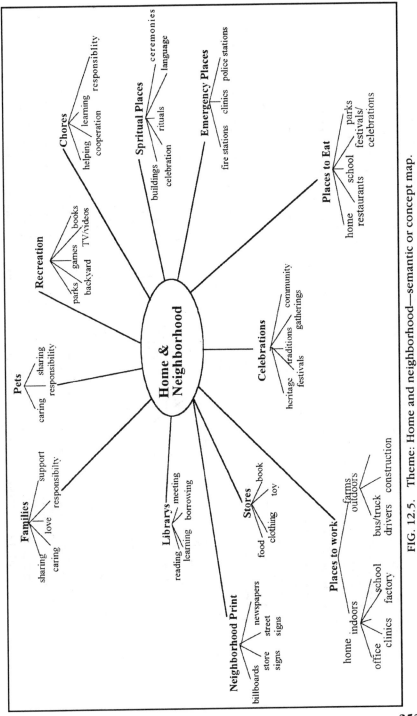

FIG. 12.5. Theme: Home and neighborhood—semantic or concept map.

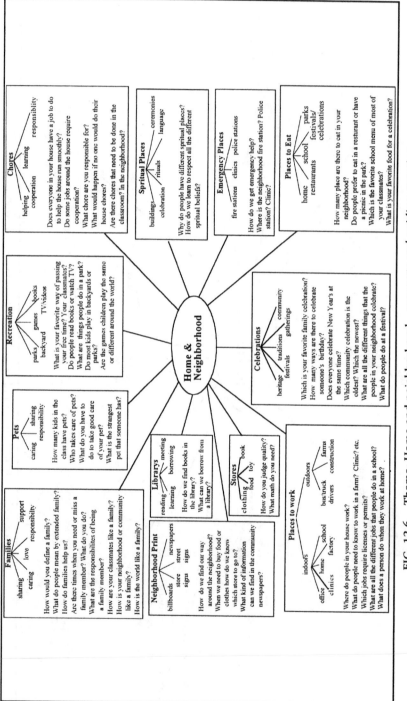

FIG. 12.6. Theme: Home and neighborhood—concepts and guiding questions.

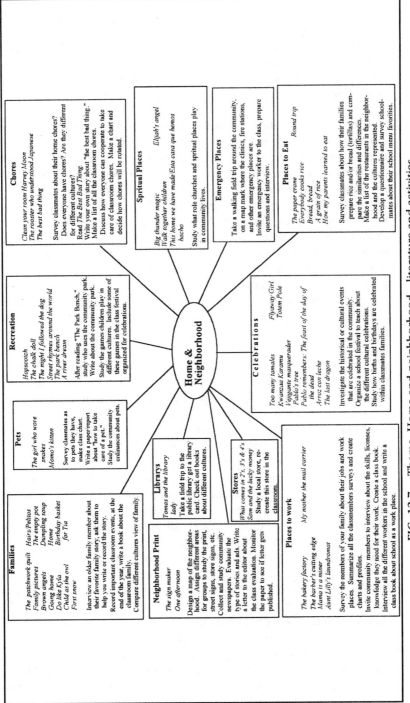

Families

The patchwork quilt   *Hairs/Pelitos*
Family pictures   *The empty pot*
Brown angels   *Dumpling soup*
Going home   *Home   Birthday basket*
Do like Kyla   *for Tia*
Child at the owl
First snow

Interview an older family member about
their favorite family story; ask them to
help you write or record the story.
Record important classroom events, at the
end of the year, write a book about the
classroom family.
Compare different cultures view of family.

Neighborhood Print

The sign maker   *My mother the mail carrier*
One afternoon

Design a map of the neighborhood. Assign different areas
for groups to study the print,
street signs, store signs, etc.
Collect and study community
newspapers. Evaluate the
type of stories and ads. Write
a letter to the editor about
the class evaluation. Monitor
the paper to see if letter gets
published.

Library's

Tomas and the library
lady

Take a field trip to the
public library get a library
card. Check out books
about different cultures.

Places to work

The bakery/factory
The barber's cutting edge
Mama is a miner
Aunt Lilly's laundromat

Survey the members of your family about their jobs and work
places. Summarize all the classmembers surveys and create
charts and profiles.
Invite community members to interview about the skills, licenses,
knowledge they need for their work. Create a class book.
Interview all the different workers in the school and write a
class book about school as a work place.

Pets

The girl who wore
snakes
Momo's kitten

Survey classmates as
to pets they have,
make class chart.
Write a paper-report
about "how to take
care of a pet."
Study the community
ordinances about pets.

Stores

If that comes in 2's, 3's & 4's
Sam and the lucky money

Study a local store, re-
create this store in the
classroom.

Recreation

Hopscotch
The chalk doll
The night I followed the dog
Street rhymes around the world
The park bench
A river dream

After reading "The Park Bench,"
study who uses the community park.
Write about the community park.
Study the games children play in
different cultures. Include some of
these games in the class festival
organized for celebrations.

Celebrations

Too many tamales   *Flyaway Girl*
Kwanzaa Karamu   *Totem Pole*
Vejigante masquerader
Pablo remembers: The feast of the day of
*   the dead*
Arroz con leche
The last dragon

Investigate the historical or cultural events
that are celebrated in the community.
Organize a school festival to teach about
the different cultural celebrations.
Study how births and birthdays are celebrated
within classmates families.

Chores

Clean your room   *Harvey Moon*
The rooster who understood Japanese
The best bad thing

Survey classmates about their home chores?
Does everyone have chores? Are they different
for different cultures?
Write your own story about "the best bad thing."
Read *The Best Bad Thing*
Make a list of all the classroom chores.
Discuss how everyone can cooperate to take
care of classroom chores. Make a chart and
decide how chores will be rotated.

Spiritual Places

Big thunder magic   *Elijah's angel*
Walk together children
This home we have made/Esta casa que hemos
*   hecho*

Study what role churches and spiritual places play
in community lives.

Emergency Places

Take a walking field trip around the community,
on a map mark where the clinics, fire stations,
and other emergency places are.
Invite an emergency worker to the class, prepare
questions and interview.

Places to Eat

The paper crane   *Round trip*
Everybody cooks rice
Bread, bread
A grain of rice
How my parents learned to eat

Survey classmates about how their families
prepare rice and/or bread (tortillas) and compare the similarities and differences.
Make a list of the restaurants in the neighborhood and the cultures represented.
Develop a questionnaire and survey schoolmates about their school menu favorites.

Home & Neighborhood

FIG. 12.7.   Theme: Home and neighborhood—literature and activities.

355

pan can help children plan for their family interviews. Engaging their families in this project is one more way of validating the culture and giving the child a sense of place within the school culture. For younger children, the products or exhibitions that culminate theme-based inquiries can be whole-class or individually published books, models of the community or neighborhood, or a gallery of celebrations.

Journeys Theme-Based Collaborative Inquiry. To begin a study of the theme of journeys, the students can look at a map and a globe to discover the distance they and their ancestors have come from their countries of origin to their present school. After pinpointing the locations on maps, the students can work in pairs or groups as they begin to find out about their countries of origin or the movements of their ancestors from place to place. For American Indian students the ancestral homes will not be another country but the relocation of Native Americans to reservations can be studied (see McCarty & Watahomigie, chap. 4, this volume). Older students can explore the theme of journey through the novel by Harrell (1999), *Longwalker's Journey: A Novel of the Choctaw Trail of Tears,* which not only recounts the historical journey of the resettlement of the Choctaw but also poignantly describes the personal and spiritual journeys of Minko Ushi and his family. To thi Dien (chap. 6, this volume) cautions that teachers should get to know their students before dealing with topics that may be too painful for some students. One way to begin the sensitive exploration of the topic of immigrant journeys, without children having to self-disclose, is through literature, such as Buss' (2002) *Journey of the Sparrows*, a story of a Salvadoran family's journey, or Surat's (1989) *Angel Child, Dragon Child,* the story of a young Vietnamese girl's longing for her mother. The general study of this theme may provide ways for children to learn about a variety of "journeys": for example, reading the poems of Naomi Shihab Nye (2000) in *Come with Me: Poems for a Journey* will encourage children to explore their thoughts and affirms personal journeys of the spirit. As children read and study, they will discover some of the common experiences of students from different culture groups.

Within these theme-based studies, students will have the freedom to make choices, to create personal meaning, to see curriculum as connected to something relevant in their lives, and to maintain control of their learning. The authentic nature of theme-based collaborative inquiry gives students real reasons to think like mathematicians, scientists, historians, artists, geographers, and authors. In the process, students learn to plan, to direct, and to assess their learning. Figure 12.8 illustrates a possible semantic map for the "journey" collaborative inquiry. Figures 12.9 and 12.10 suggest guiding questions, literature, and learning activities for this theme.

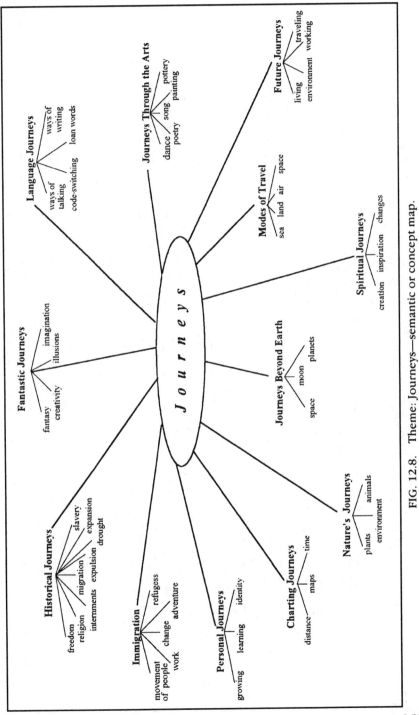

FIG. 12.8.   Theme: Journeys—semantic or concept map.

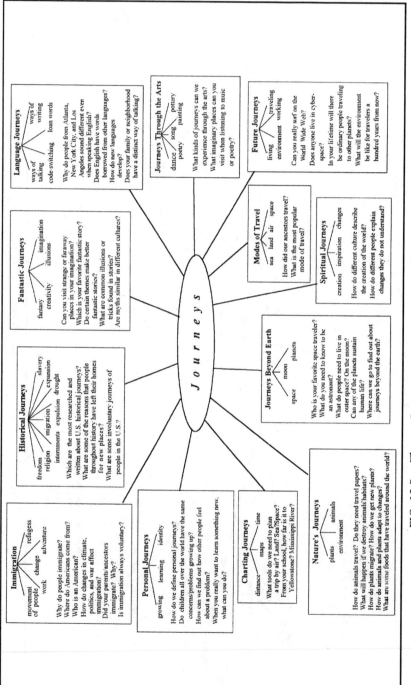

FIG. 12.9.   Theme: Journeys—concepts and guiding questions.

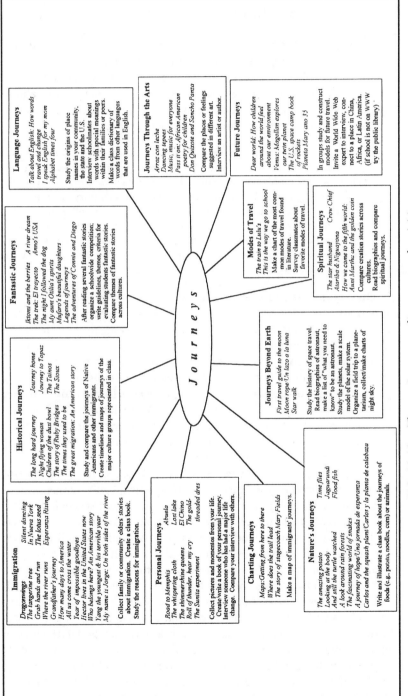

Immigration

Dragonwings   Silent dancing
The tangerine tree   In Nueva York
Grab hands and run   The lotus seed
Where the river runs   Esperanza Rising
Grandfather's journey
How many days to America
All us come cross the water
Year of impossible goodbyes
Hector lives in the United States now
Who belongs here? An American story
Yang the youngest & his terrible year
My name is Jorge: On both sides of the river

Collect family or community elders' stories
about immigration. Create a class book.
Study the reasons for immigration.

Personal Journeys

Road to Memphis   Abuela
The whispering cloth   Lost lake
The shimmershine queens   El Chino
Roll of thunder, hear my cry   The gold-
The Sunita experiment   threaded dress

Collect pictures and mementos from your life.
Create/write a book of your personal journey.
Interview someone who has had a major life
change. Compare your interview with others.

Charting Journeys

Maps: Getting from here to there
Where does the trail lead
The story of stagecoach Mary Fields

Make a map of immigrants' journeys.

Nature's Journeys

The amazing potato   Time flies
Looking at the body   Jaguarundi
And still the turtle watched   Flood fish
A look around rain forests
The fascinating world of snakes
A journey of hope: Una jornada de esperanza
Carlos and the squash plant: Carlos y la planta de calabaza

Write and illustrate a class book about the journeys of
foods (e.g. potato, noodles, corn) or animals.

Historical Journeys

The long hard journey   Journey home
Night flying woman   Journey to Topaz
Children of the dust bowl   The Tainos
The story of Ruby Bridges   The Sioux
The times they used to be
The great migration: An American story

Study and compare the journeys of Native
Americans and other immigrants.
Create timelines and maps of journeys of the
major culture groups represented in class.

Journeys Beyond Earth

First travel guide to the moon
Moon rope: Un lazo a la luna
Star walk

Study the history of space travel.
Read biographies of astronaut,
make a list of "what you need to
know" to be an astronaut.
Study the planets, make a scale
model of the solar system.
Organize a field trip to a plane-
tarium, collect/make charts of
night sky.

Fantastic Journeys

Iktomi and the berries   A river dream
The trek: El trayecto   Anno's USA
The night I followed the dog
My aunt Otilia's spirits
Mufaro's beautiful daughters
Legends of journeys
The adventures of Connie and Diego

After reading several fantastic stories
organize a schoolwide competition;
write guidelines, themes, criteria for
evaluating students fantastic stories.
Compare themes of fantastic stories
across cultures.

Modes of Travel

The train to Lulu's
This is the way we go to school
Make a chart of the most common modes of travel found
in literature.
Survey classmates about
favorite modes of travel.

Spiritual Journeys

The star husband   Crow Chief
Atariba & Niguayona
How we came to the fifth world:
Aunt Martha and the golden coin
Compare creation stories across
cultures.
Read biographies and compare
spiritual journeys.

Language Journeys

Talk about English: How words
travel and change
I speak English for my mom
Alphabet times four

Study the origins of place
names in your community,
the state and the U.S.
Interview schoolmates about
words with special meanings
within their families or peers.
Make a class dictionary of
words from other languages
that are used in English.

Journeys Through the Arts

Arroz con leche
Dancing teepees
Music, music for everyone
Pass it on: African American
poetry for children
Don Quixote and Sancho Panza

Compare the places or feelings
suggested in different art.
Interview an artist or author.

Future Journeys

Dear world: How children
around the world feel
about our environment
Venus: Magellan explores
our twin planet
The U.S. space camp book
of rockets
Planeta Mary ano 35

In groups study and construct
models for future travel.
Invite a World Wide Web
expert to interview, con-
nect to a place in China,
Africa, or Latin America.
(if school is not on WWW
try the public library)

Journeys

FIG. 12.10.   Theme: Journeys—literature and activities.

LITERACY ASSESSMENT

A constructivist literacy program demands knowledgeable teachers who know the disciplines they teach, know about the development of children, and know assessment. The assessment discussed here is not the high-stakes tests that are a part of state or national accountability system (No Child Left Behind Act of 2001). Buckner (2002), an elementary teacher, reflected on the focus on testing:

> School is becoming more about test and test scores. There is a tug of war between those who want school to be about learning and growing and those who want higher test scores. I am a teacher who tugs for learning and growing, and I work in a system, a state, and a country that tug at test scores .... Those of us with a lot of knowledge, a deep understanding for how children really learn, and a strong grasp on quality assessment need to stand strong in the face of the controversy. And that means not sacrificing our teaching, our devotion to children, or our standards of excellence for any high-stakes test. (pp. 212–215)

Quality assessment informs and is integrated with instruction. Assessment that informs instruction will assist teachers in evaluating their teaching, modifying strategies, identifying student learning needs, and adjusting the teaching–learning interactions and environments. Assessment that is integrated will be an essential part of every instructional interaction, activity, or lesson. Assessment is the way teachers know if students are making progress toward the learning goals that have been established (Hurley & Tinajero, 2001).

Teachers will have to design literacy assessment strategies that are congruent with their literacy goals. For example, a literacy goal should be for all students to demonstrate on grade-level reading and writing abilities in English; however, if we know that demonstrating second-language literacy may require 5 to 7 years (Cummins, 1989; Ramírez, Yuen, Ramey, & Pasta, 1991), interim goals and assessment strategies will be needed. Traditional literacy assessment has all too frequently reflected narrow cultural values; students with different cultural and linguistic backgrounds often have not been fairly assessed. If a goal of literacy in your classroom is for children to develop cultural repertoires, then literacy assessment strategies should elicit children's use of cultural knowledge in various settings. Rueda and García (1996) examined the beliefs of teachers with regard to literacy assessment of language-minority students and they found that teachers do not have clearly defined assessment strategies that are developmentally, culturally, and linguistically appropriate for gaining information about what children can do, say, read, and write within a variety of contexts. Johnston (1990) called for teachers to become "constructive evaluators," who are able both to establish a context where children engage in meaning making and to assess students' development within that context.

Teachers will have to develop observation and performance assessment skills to become constructive evaluators. First, they must hone their observation skills. Teachers must learn not only how to observe, but also how to qualitatively and quantitatively describe their observations against goals and criteria that are appropriate for their students' literacy development. They must be able to describe the quality of a child's attempts or responses, as well as to describe the frequency of the child's attempts or responses over time. This is an assessment strategy that looks for strengths and describes what students can do. For example, if a student is attempting to decode words using his or her native language, the teacher needs to be able to describe the specific word and the verbalization that the student is making, as well as make an assessment of whether the strategy is assisting or hindering in the making of meaning for this student with this text. Second, teachers will have to develop expertise in creating and scoring oral, written, and performance assessments. Teachers will need to maintain equitable assessment conditions within their classrooms where all children have opportunities to demonstrate what they know in their areas of strength as well as their areas of weakness. Teachers will need to support students as they develop products, exhibitions, and portfolios, while also appraising students against the established criteria.

Integrating Assessment and Instruction

In classrooms, as children are engaged in inquiries, teachers collaborate with children as they move around the room interacting with individuals or small groups. The teacher should be available for the children to consult, question, and relate their efforts and progress. Teachers will be continually assessing and teaching.

Meaningful assessment is ongoing, multidimensional, takes place in authentic contexts, and is an integral part of the ongoing processes of inquiry, learning, and teaching. Assessment, like instruction, is developmentally, culturally, and linguistically responsive and appropriate. The assessment tools that teachers use must document valued inquiries as well as learning outcomes. The tools must capture and reflect how children learn and think in context, how they connect what they have learned across disciplines, how they make progress over time, and how they grow in their ability to self-motivate, self-monitor, and self-evaluate. The assessment tools or processes will need to capture both the final products of student investigations—writing, exhibits, books, reports, presentations—and the processes of meaning making—student attempts, approximations, and risk taking.

Nelson (1994), a fifth-grade teacher, described the role of assessment within her literacy program: "Assessment of the learning becomes a daily, ongoing task. Students are involved in conferences and self-evaluation and I record anecdotal comments and observations throughout the process" (p. 555).

You want practical means to gather and record information that are part of everyday classroom activities. You want formative assessment that helps you and the students plan the learning opportunities and participation structures for the thematic inquiries. Formative assessment information can assist you to determine when to conduct minilessons. It can be used for student–teacher conferences and for parent–teacher conferences. Assessment must also be summative in that you will need to interpret students' achievement and progress over time.

Purposes and Goals of Assessment

The main purpose for assessment is to provide the student and the teacher with information to help make decisions about learning opportunities and to better understand individual students' learning. Therefore, when attempting to assess the literacy development of culturally and linguistically diverse students, any responsible assessment must engage the full complexity of situations faced by diverse children in developing a whole continuum of language and literacy skills (see McCarty & Watahomigie, chap. 4, this volume). This includes the general goals or standards specified by the state.

The goals of assessment are for the most part, the goals for instruction. Meaningful goals identified for the curriculum will be what are to be measured in assessment. Winograd (1994) cautioned:

> After meaningful goals are identified, we must still ensure that they actually drive assessment and instruction. If meaningful goals are included in curriculum documents but the district or school still relies heavily on traditional multiple-choice tests, the test makers' scope and sequence become the de facto goals of assessment and instruction. (p. 420)

The challenge for teachers is to articulate a stance about instructional methodologies and link these to meaningful assessment strategies. Wolf and Wolf (2002) described how six exemplary teachers in a state with high-stakes testing worked to maintain their commitment to the best instructional and assessment practices while ensuring that children were prepared for the state assessment. The students "had time to devote to their writing and opportunities for peer and teacher response as well as self-reflection. In addition, their teachers helped them understand the standards, rubrics, and genres involved in their day-to day writing as well as in assessments" (p. 239).

Assessment Techniques and Tools

Assessment processes that teachers can consider include performance assessments, developmental checklists, case studies, conferencing, portfolios, and other methods of alternative assessment. The following section .describes several assessment techniques and suggests how portfolios can be used to assist students to reflect on and conduct self-assessments of their developing literacy.

Student Schooling Profile. Because for some older culturally and linguistically diverse children literacy learning might have been compounded with benign but inappropriate classroom practices, you will find some fourth, fifth, and sixth graders who cannot express complex ideas orally, who read haltingly, and who have difficulty writing. For these children, the literacy learning task may no longer be developmental but will require specific assessment strategies and intervention by the teacher. The key here is to find out what the students perceive as reading, writing, and problem solving and to gather information about the students' literacy strategies. Igoa (1995) suggested that for new immigrant children this information gathering might begin by interviewing the students and asking the following questions:

> Were the children schooled or unschooled before they came into the country? Was their education fragmented?
>
> Was there clear communication between school and home? Are the children caught in the middle, where parents believe that acculturation is the school's responsibility but the school believes it is the parents' responsibility, so that the children play one against the other?
>
> Are the children dependent on the teacher for learning? Do they have any independent learning skills?
>
> Were they in a bilingual program? Was that process interrupted? Were they taught to transfer skills from one language to another? Did they learn any English abroad? [or in their home?] How much of their own language did they learn, orally and in writing, receptively and productively?
>
> Were the theories and methods recommended by the district misapplied or misinterpreted by those who came before me? Were they taken too literally? Was there a clear understanding of the cumulative aspect of language—native as well as second language? What is the status of the parents? (p. 148)

Information gleaned in response to these questions can be confirmed or verified with the parents. The answers to the foregoing questions can provide information about educational gaps and can also document valuable educational histories for students whose educational experiences are too often fragmented.

Observations Across Cultures.   Teacher observations and anecdotal records must be sensitive to the children's diversity in culture, language, prior experience, interest, and developing needs. Teachers must observe children, especially culturally diverse children, for what they are doing rather than with a preconceived notion of what third graders should be able to do. For example, when a teacher observes a child attempt to read a book from right to left, the teacher must ask: Does the child lack experiences with books? Does the child have experiences reading an orthography that is written from right to left? As teachers observe and make mental as well as written notations about the literacy accomplishments and ever-changing literacy needs of children, these must be situated within the child's cultural and social experience.

Davila de Silva (chap. 8, this volume) also suggests some guidelines to consider when observing culturally and linguistically diverse students. The skills involved in the conduct of a case study require keen observation over time and careful analysis of the information gathered to create an account of the child's literacy development.

Running Records.   Running records are a form of interactive assessment developed by Marie Clay (1979). A running record can provide a breadth of information about a child's reading strategies. This technique can be useful with young children or with older children who may not be making progress in their reading. The preparation of reading passages and the conduct of running records will require time to be set aside for reflection. In conducting a running record, the following steps are followed: (a) A passage is selected and the level (grade/reading) of the passage determined; (b) the student reads the passage orally while the teacher codes the miscues, that is, marks the substitutions, omissions, repetitions, insertions, or corrections the child makes while reading; (c) the child is asked to retell what was read, but the teacher may cue retelling if the child hesitates; (d) the child is asked to reflect on or self-evaluate the reading and retelling; and (e) the teacher analyzes the miscues noted and their effect on meaning and retelling. Running records can provide clues on the process or strategies that culturally and linguistically diverse students are using in creating meaning from text during reading.

Miscue analysis and informal reading inventories are other assessment techniques that can be used to assess students' oral reading strategies and progress.

Rubrics. Rubrics are guidelines that describe student work in reading, writing, mathematics, and other content areas. Rubrics are created by specifying the indicators that correspond to the established criteria for the set of learning opportunities being assessed. The indicators within the rubric are evaluated on a point-scale system that can range from the *highest quality* to the *minimal quality*. The teacher or scorer compares the individual student's work to the indicators in the rubric and assigns points. Rubrics can be useful to students teachers, parents, and others to understand and make explicit what is expected for high-quality work. Although many different rubrics for the assessment of writing and other content areas exist, the best rubrics are the ones developed by teachers and students in alignment with their curriculum or theme-based inquiries. The valuable outcome when children establish the indicators for the assessment of writing is that they will have a better idea of what is expected or judged as good writing.

Portfolios

An important part of assessment and evaluation is the keeping of "archives" or portfolios of children's work which provide a record of children's learning. Portfolios can serve as a management system for the collection of literacy and learning products to be assessed periodically by the student, teacher, and parent. The use of portfolios supports a systematic process for assessing students' growth and progress in relation to classroom literacy goals (Canales, 1993; Salinger & Chittenden, 1994). To be congruent with the constructive perspective, student and teacher must jointly determine what student work will be included in portfolios, how this evidence will be collected, and how the performance will be judged. Fourth-grade teacher Aimee Buckner (2002) cautioned teachers about using buzz words without understanding the practices, saying, "There is a difference between a teacher's file on a student and a student portfolio" (p. 214).

An important value of the use of portfolios is opportunity for students to reflect on their learning as they prepare their portfolios. Student–teacher conferences are the best ways to evaluate the portfolio material. However, some teachers choose to examine the portfolio first and then hold the student–teacher conferences. The evidence collected in portfolios can also be useful in the conduct of teacher–parent conferences. They can help ground parent–teacher discussions around concrete pieces of evidence of student's work, "instead of the teacher's reported impressions or summaries" (Salinger & Chittenden, 1994, p. 450). Portfolios can also be the products of a particular theme-based collaborative inquiry, which exhibits the student learning.

Organizing and Introducing Portfolios. Teachers and students must distinguish between work folders and a portfolio system. In a portfolio, it is preferable to include representative samples (plans, drafts, final products) of the students' work over a period of time or for the duration of a collaborative inquiry. Students should make decisions about what is included in the portfolio. If the portfolio is just a collection of teacher-initiated assignments, the students will not be motivated to exert the effort and reflection necessary to make portfolios authentic.

As students are brought into the planning and into the process for selecting materials to be included, they take ownership of the portfolio. Teachers and students can prepare a list of possible categories of work samples to be included in each student's portfolio at the beginning of a collaborative inquiry. The list delineates what data the teacher will collect and what samples students may themselves select. This list can be adjusted as the inquiry progresses. Performance evidence such as tapes of oral readings, writing drafts and final products, plans and charts for inquiry, illustrations and drawings, transcriptions of interviews and conferences, and other evidence of students' work can be included. Data for starting a portfolio system are adapted from Pérez and Torres-Guzmán (1996, p. 164).

SUGGESTED DATA OR EVIDENCE FOR STARTING A PORTFOLIO SYSTEM

Written Work

1. Examples of initial and final drafts of writing assignments or student-initiated writing.
2. Examples of students' literature response logs.
3. Plans, drafts, and products of thematic unit studies.
4. Other illustrations, graphic organizers, charts, graphs, and so on that may demonstrate students' planning and organization of learning.

Audio or Videotapes—For Performance Pieces

1. Examples of students' oral reading.

2. Retelling, discussions, or reflections of literature read.
3. Role playing, readers' theater, or other productions based on literature or classroom study themes.

Other Data and Evidence

1. Student self-analysis and reflection.
2. Teacher observations and running logs.
3. Running records or informal reading inventories (IRI) of oral reading.
4. Critiques of items from peers.
5. Parent's analysis and reflection.

Student Self-Evaluation and Reflection. The child should have responsibility for the maintenance of the portfolio. Systematic collection of portfolio data can be scheduled, so students select and organize items to be included in the portfolio. Students can also choose to put items in their portfolio at any time. As students choose the work to be included, they should have time for planning the reflection, organizing, and categorizing what they consider to be their best work, as well as drafts leading up to their best work. It can be helpful for students to work in pairs when they are organizing their portfolios. In pairs, they can discuss, compare, critique, and practice defending their individual choices.

For each theme-based collaborative inquiry or evaluation period, students can write a self-assessment reflective piece (explanation, letter, poem, etc.). This reflective piece should help the students gain insights as they explain why particular items in the portfolio demonstrate growth and understanding of their inquiry. Students can also write a few goals for themselves to accomplish.

Teacher–Student Conferences. The portfolio is evaluated during a teacher–student conference where teacher and student can each assess the items included against established criteria. The focus of the teacher–student portfolio conference is on constructing meaning from the items in the portfolio. Together they can analyze and come to understand the reading, writing, and thinking strategies the student is using successfully. Teacher and student can ask questions and express opinions about the literacy goals, learning opportunities, and the progress the student has made. The conference should also be open to questions for which there are no "right" answers—questions that lead the child and the teacher to an increased awareness of the literacy and learning process. The teacher and student can suggest how developing areas can be supported. Conferences can close with teacher and child setting goals for literacy and future inquiries.

Performance assessment tasks, exhibitions, and portfolios of student work can yield rich, individualistic data about each student. When teachers are willing to discuss observations and evidence about strengths and weaknesses and support these discussions with concrete suggestions for improvement in specific areas of development, students can make a lot of progress. When they are integrated in the assessment process, students can gain insights about their learning and assume more responsibility for the learning process. Teachers and students can judge how far each has progressed toward meeting the literacy goals and can seek clues within the assessment data to support improved student performance. When these evaluations are conducted in a respectful, constructive, positive atmosphere that allows students to provide valued input, the discussions may encourage students to take risks, assume responsibility, and generally become more independent.

SUMMARY

This chapter has discussed how the modeling of literacy must be authentic and how the social relationships required for literacy acquisition must be genuine. All students, but especially culturally and linguistically diverse students, should be encouraged to read and write when reading and writing are meaningful, enjoyable, and functional. Teachers must understand the importance of the world knowledge that often develops in the native language and culture; teachers must recognize the social relationships inherent in such knowledge. Social relationships for literacy will entail a broader social web than just interaction between child and teacher. Opportunities to bridge the home and community literacies while developing the second-language literacies will facilitate and maximize student learning.

When teachers facilitate the connections between literacy and content and between school and community, students will begin to see the connections and are able to reach a better understanding of themselves and their world. When students make the connections between learning and living, they see the authenticity of reading, writing, thinking, listening, speaking, and problem solving in everyday tasks. They will better see their need to become lifelong learners. Finally, the chapter has also described processes for literacy assessment and the use of portfolios as opportunities for students to reflect on their literacy development.

■ ACTIVITIES

1. Interview a group of elementary students from diverse cultures about their learning interests. Analyze what types of theme-based inquiries could be pursued from the student's interest viewpoint.
2. With your classmates, brainstorm around several themes creating concept maps. Select one theme and concept map to generate possible guiding questions. Find 10 multicultural literature books that could be used in a theme-based inquiry around your selected theme.
3. Find a class/school that is using theme-based collaborative inquiry. Ask the teacher to invite you and classmates to the next exhibition of their theme-based collaborative inquiry products. Write a reflective paper describing what you saw, what you think students learned, and how students were assessed.
4. Interview the teacher/students using portfolios. Ask them to compare the advantages and disadvantages of using portfolios versus traditional student testing and assessment. Ask the teacher/students to see copies of the class portfolios.

SUGGESTED READINGS

Heath, S. B., & Mangiola, L. (1991). *Children of promise: Literate activity in linguistically and culturally diverse classrooms.* Washington, DC: National Education Association.

Kohn, A. (2002). Poor teaching for poor kids. *Language Arts, 79*(3), 251–255.

Monahan, M. B. (2003). "On the lookout for language": Children as language detectives. *Language Arts, 80*(3), 206–214.

Moll, L. C., & González, N. (1994). Lessons from research with language minority children. *Journal of Reading Behavior, 26*(4), 439–436.

Smith, M. A., & Ylvisaker, M. (Eds.). (1993). *Teachers' voices: Portfolios in the classroom.* Berkeley, CA: National Writing Project.

West, K. (1998). Noticing and responding to learners: Literacy evaluation and instruction in the primary grades. *Reading Teacher, 51,* 550–561.

REFERENCES

Buckner, A. (2002). Teaching in a world focused on testing. *Language Arts, 79*(3), 212–216.

Canales, J. (1993). Innovative assessment in traditional settings. In J. V. Tinajero & A. F. Ada (Eds.), *The power of two languages: Literacy and biliteracy for Spanish-speaking students* (pp. 132–142). New York: Macmillan/McGraw-Hill.

Clay, M. M. (1979). *Reading: The patterning of complex behavior.* Portsmouth, NH: Heinemann.

Cummins, J. (1989). *Empowering minority students*. Sacramento: California Association for Bilingual Education.

Frank, C. (1999). *Ethnographic eyes*. Portsmouth, NH: Heinemann.

Harrell, B. O. (1999). *Longwalker's journey: A novel on the Choctaw trail of tears*. New York: Dial Books.

Heath, S., & Mangiola, L. (1991). *Children of promise: Literate activity in linguistically and culturally diverse classrooms*. Washington, DC: National Education Association.

Hurley, S. R., & Tinajero, J. V. (2001). *Literacy assessment of second language learners*. New York: Allyn & Bacon.

Igoa, C. (1995). *The inner world of the immigrant child*. New York: St. Martin's Press.

Johnston, P. (1990). Constructive evaluation and the improvement of teaching and learning. *Teachers College Record, 91*, 1–42.

Nelson, C. S. (1994). Historical literacy: A journey of discovery. *Reading Teacher, 47*, 552–556.

Ogle, D. M. (1989). The know, want to know, learn strategy. In K. D. Muth (Ed.), *Children's comprehension of text* (pp. 205–223). Newark, DE: International Reading Association.

Pérez, B., & Torres-Guzmán, M. E. (1996). *Learning in two worlds: An integrated Spanish/English biliteracy approach* (2nd ed.). New York: Longman.

Ramírez, J. D., Yuen, S. D., Ramey, D. R., & Pasta, D. (1991). *Final report: Longitudinal study of structured English immersion strategy, early exit and late-exit bilingual education programs for language-minority children, Vol. 1* (No. 300-87-0156). Washington, DC: U.S. Department of Education.

Rueda, R., & García, E. (1996). Teachers' perspectives on literacy assessment and instruction with language-minority students: A comparative study. *Elementary School Journal, 96*, 311–332.

Salinger, T., & Chittenden, E. (1994). Analysis of an early literacy portfolio: Consequences for instruction. *Language Arts, 71*, 446–452.

Schustack, M. W., King, C., Gallego, M. A., & Vasquez, O. A. (1994). A computer-oriented after-school activity: Children's learning in the fifth dimension and la clase magica. In F. A. Villarreal & R. M. Lerner (Eds.), *Promoting community-based programs for socialization and learning: New directions for child development* (pp. 35–50). San Francisco: Jossey-Bass.

Wasley, P. A., King, S. P., & Louth, C. (1995). Creating coalition schools through collaborative inquiry. In J. Oakes & K. H. Quartz (Eds.), *Creating new educational communities* (pp. 202–223). Chicago: University of Chicago Press.

Winograd, P. (1994). Developing alternative assessments: Six problems worth solving. *Reading Teacher, 47*, 420–423.

Wolf, S. A., & Wolf, K. P. (2002). Teaching *true* and *to* the test in writing. *Language Arts, 79*(3), 229–240.

CHILDREN'S LITERATURE CITED

Communication Theme

Ada, A. F. (1993). *My name is María Isabel*. New York: Atheneum.

Anno, M. (1986). *All in a day*. New York: Philomel.

Bercaw, E. C. (2000). *Halmoni's day*. New York: Dial Books.

Brooks, B. (1993). *Making sense: Animal perception and communication.* New York: Farrar, Straus & Giroux.

Brown, R. (1991). *Alphabet times four.* New York: Dutton.

Bryan, A. (1980). *Beat the story drum, pum-pum.* New York: Atheneum.

Bryan, A. (1991). *All night, all day: A child's first book of African-American spirituals.* New York: Atheneum.

Caines, J. (1986). *Chilly stomach.* New York: Harper & Row.

Choi, Y. (2001). *The name jar.* New York: Knopf.

Crews, D. (1991). *Big mama's.* New York: Greenwillow.

De Zutter, H. (1992). *Who says a dog goes bow wow?* New York: Doubleday.

Diaz, J. (1994). *The rebellious alphabet.* New York: Holt.

Elya, S. M. (2002). *Home at last.* New York: Lee & Low.

Erodoes, R. (1976). *The sound of flutes and other Indian legends told by Lame Deer, Jeeny Leading Cloud, Leonard Crow Dog and others.* New York: Pantheon.

Facklam, M. (1994). *What does the crow know? The mysteries of animal intelligence.* San Francisco: Sierra Club.

Fakih, K. O. (1995). *Off the clock: A lexicon of time words and expressions.* New York: Houghton Mifflin.

Fiovanni, N. (1987). *Spin a soft black song.* New York: Farrar, Straus & Giroux.

Gibbons, G. (1993). *Puff... flash... bang! A book about signals.* New York: Morrow.

Gomi, T. (1990). *My friends.* San Francisco: Chronicle.

Greenfield, E. (1988). *Grandpa's face.* New York: Philomel.

Greenfield, E. (1991). *I make music.* New York: Black Butterfly.

Hamanaka, S. (1995). *Peace crane.* New York: Orchard.

Hodges, M. (1992). *Don Quixote and Sancho Panza* (Adaptation from *Don Quixote of La Mancha* by Miguel de Cervantes Saavedra). New York: Scribner's Sons.

Howard, P. E. (1991). *Aunt Flossie's hats.* New York: Clarion Books.

Hoyt-Goldsmith, D. (1991). *Pueblo storyteller.* New York: Holiday House.

Hughes, S. (1994). *Chatting.* New York: Candlewick Press.

Kaner, E. (1991). *Sound science.* New York: Addison Wesley.

Lachtman, O. D. (1995). *Pepita talks twice/Pepita habla dos veces.* New York: Atheneum.

Levine, E. (1989). *I hate English.* New York: Scholastic.

London, J. (1995). *The sugaring-off party.* New York: Dutton.

Lowry, L. (1991). *Anastasia at this address.* Boston: Houghton Mifflin.

Macaulay, D. (1988). *The way things work.* New York: Houghton Mifflin.

MacGill-Callahan, S. (1991). *And still the turtle watched.* New York: Dial.

Markan, P. N. (1993). *The little painter of Saban Grande.* New York: Bradbury Press.

Mazer, A. (1993). *The oxboy.* New York: Knopf.

Millman, I. (2000). *Moses goes to school.* New York: Farrar.

Mochizuki, K. (1995). *Heros.* New York: Low Books.

Modarressi, M. (2000). *Yard sale!* New York: Dorling Kindersley.

Mora, P. (1994). *Listen to the desert/Oye al desierto.* New York: Houghton Mifflin.

Polocco, P. (1992). *Chicken Sunday.* New York: Putnam.

Pomeranz, C. (1993). *The Tamarindo puppy and other poems.* New York: Greenwillow.

Rankin, L. (1992). *The handmade alphabet.* New York: Dial.

Rosenberg, J. (1994). *¡Aplauso! Hispanic children's theater.* New York: Arcade.

Say, A. (1999). *Tea with milk.* Boston: Houghton Mifflin.

Soto, G. (1987). *The cat's meow.* San Francisco: Strawberry Hill Press.

Soto, G. (1990). *Baseball in April.* New York: Harcourt Brace.

Stanek, M. (1989). *I speak English for my mom.* Niles, IL: Albert Whitman.

Steptoe, J. (1987). *Mufaro's beautiful daughters.* New York: Lothrop Lee & Shepard.

Steptoe, J. (1988). *Baby says.* New York: Lothrop Lee & Shepard.

Winter, J., & Winter, J. (1991). *Diego.* New York: Random House.

Yashima, T., & Yashima, M. (1961). *Momo's kitten.* New York: Viking Press.

Yashima, T. (1958). *Umbrella.* New York: Viking Press.

Yolen, J. (1993). *The girl who loved the wind.* Katonah, NY: Richard C. Owen.

Zhensun, Z., & Low, A. (1991). *A young painter.* New York: Scholastic.

Home/Neighborhood Theme

Ada, A. F. (2002). *I love Saturdays y domingos.* New York: Atheneum.

Ancona, G. (1993). *Pablo remembers: The fiesta of the day of the dead.* New York: Morrow.

Aker, S. (1990). *What comes in 2's, 3's, and 4's.* New York: Simon & Schuster.

Bang, M. (1985). *The paper crane.* New York: Greenwillow.

Brady, A. (1995). *Kwanzaa Karamu.* Minneapolis, MN: Carolrhoda.

Bryan, A. (1981). *Walk together children.* New York: Aladdin.

Bunting, E. (1996). *Going home.* New York: HarperCollins.

Chinn, K. (1995). *Sam and the lucky money.* New York: Lee & Low.

Cisneros, S. (1994). *Hairs/Pelitos.* New York: Knopf.

Coutant, H., & Vo-Dinh, T. (1974). *First snow.* New York: Knopf.

Cumming, P. (1991). *Clean your room Harvey Moon.* New York: Bradbury Press.

Delacre, L. (1993). *Arroz con leche.* New York: Scholastic.

Delacre, L. (1993). *Vejigante masquerader.* New York: Scholastic.

Demi. (1991). *The empty pot.* New York: Holt.

Dooley, N. (1991). *Everybody cooks rice.* Minneapolis, MN: Carolrhoda.

Flournoy, V. (1985). *The patchwork quilt.* New York: Dial.

Friedman, I. (1984). *How my parents learned to eat.* New York: Houghton Mifflin.

Garza, C. L. (1990). *Family pictures/Cuadros de familia.* San Francisco: Children's Book Press.

Greenberg, M. H. (1994). *Aunt Lilly's laundromat.* New York: Dutton.

Hammond, A., & Matunis, J. (1993). *This home we have made: Esta casa que hemos hecho.* New York: Crowell.

Heo, Y. (1994). *One afternoon.* New York: Orchard.

Holbert, R. (1986). *The barber's cutting edge.* New York: Children's Book Press.

Hoyt-Goldsmith, D. (1990). *Totem pole.* New York: Holiday House.

Jenness, A. (1978). *The bakery factory.* New York: Crowell.

Johnson, A. (1990). *Do like Kyla.* New York: Orchard Books.

Johnson, A. (1993). *The girl who wore snakes.* New York: Orchard Books.

Jonas, A. (1983). *Round trip.* New York: Greenwillow.

Laden, N. (1994). *The night I followed the dog.* San Francisco: Chronicle.

Lankford, M. D. (1992). *Hopscotch around the world.* New York: Morrow Junior Books.

Lijima, G. C. (2002). *The way we do it in Japan.* New York: Whitman.

Lyon, G. E. (1994). *Mama is a miner.* New York: Orchard.

Maury, I. (1976). *My mother the mail carrier.* Old Westbury, NY: Feminist Press.

Mora, P. (1993). *A birthday basket for Tía.* New York: Macmillan.

Mora, P. (1993). *Tomás and the library lady.* New York: Knopf.

Mora, P. (1994). *Pablo's tree*. New York: Macmillan.
Morris, A. (1989). *Bread, bread, bread*. New York: Mulberry.
Myers, W. D. (1993). *Brown angels: An album of pictures and verse*. New York: HarperCollins.
Nunes, S. M. (1995). *The last dragon*. New York: Clarion.
Pittman, H. (1986). *A grain of rice*. New York: Hastings.
Pomerantz, C. (1989). *The chalk doll*. New York: Lippincott.
Rattigan, J. K. (1993). *Dumpling soup*. New York: Little Brown.
Rosen, M. (1992). *Elijah's angel*. New York: Harcourt Brace Jovanovich.
Rosen, M. J. (Ed.). (1992). *Home*. New York: HarperCollins.
Say. A. (1988). *A river dream*. Boston: Houghton Mifflin.
Sis, P. (2000). *Madlenka*. New York: Farrar.
Soto, G. (1993). *Too many tamales*. New York: Putnam's Sons.
Strete, C. K. (1990). *Big thunder magic*. New York: Greenwillow.
Takeshita, F. (1988). *The park bench*. New York: Kane/Miller.
Uchida, Y. (1976). *The rooster who understood Japanese*. New York: Scribners.
Uchida, Y. (1983). *The best bad thing*. New York: Atheneum.
Yashima, T., & Yashima, M. (1961). *Momo's kitten*. New York: Viking Press.
Yep, L. (1977). *Child of the owl*. New York: Harper & Row.
Yolen, J. (Ed.). (1992). *Street rhymes around the world*. Honesdale, PA: Wordsong.

Journey Theme

Albert, B. (1991). *Where does the trail lead?* New York: Simon & Schuster.
Anno, M. (1983). *Anno's USA*. New York: Philomel.
Baird, A. (1994). *The US space camp book of rockets*. New York: Morrow.
Baer, E. (1990). *This is the way we go to school*. New York: Scholastic.
Brown, R. (1991). *Alphabet times four*. New York: Dutton.
Blumberg, R. (1980). *First travel guide to the moon: What to pack, how to go, and what to see when you get there*. New York: Four Winds.
Branley, F. (1994). *Venus: Magellan explores our twin planet*. New York: HarperCollins.
Broker, I. (1983). *Night flying woman: An Ojibway narrative*. St. Pau: Minnesota Historical Society Press.
Bunting, E. (1988). *How many days to America?* New York: Clarion.
Buss, F. L. (2002). *Journey of the sparrows*. New York: Puffin.
Choi, N. (1991). *Year of impossible goodbys*. New York: Houghton Mifflin.
Clifton, L. (1973). *All us come cross the water*. New York: Holt, Rinehart & Winston.
Clifton, L. (1974). *The times they used to be*. New York: Holt, Rinehart & Winston.
Coles, R. (1995). *The story of Ruby Bridges*. New York: Scholastic.
Delacre, L. (1993). *Arroz con leche*. New York: Scholastic.
Dorros, A. (1991). *Abuela*. New York: Dutton.
Ehlert, L. (1992). *Moon rope/Un lazo a la luna*. New York: Harcourt Brace.
Garland, S. (1993). *The lotus seed*. New York: Harcourt Brace.
García, M. (1987). *The adventures of Connie and Diego/Las aventures de Connie y Diego*. San Francisco: Children's Book Press.
García, R. (1987). *My aunt Otilia's spirits* (rev. ed.). San Francisco: Children's Book Press.
Goble, P. (1989). *Iktomi and the berries*. New York: Orchard.
Goble, P. (1992). *Crow chief*. New York: Orchard.

Graff, N. (1993). *Where the river runs: A portrait of a refugee family.* New York: Little, Brown.

Greenberg, S. (1995). *Flood fish.* New York: Crown.

Hamilton, V. (1995). *Jaguarundi.* New York: Scholastic.

Hanson, R. (1995). *The tangerine tree.* New York: Clarion.

Harrell, B. O. (1999). *Longwalker's journey: A novel of the Choctaw trail of tears.* New York: Dial Books.

Harvey, D. K. (1991). *A journey of hope/Una jornada de esperanza.* New York: Bantam.

Hewett, J. (1990). *Hector lives in the United States now: The story of a Mexican-American child.* New York: J. B. Lippincott.

Hodges, M. (1992). *Don Quixote and Sancho Panza* (Adaptation from *Don Quixote of La Mancha* by Miguel de Cervantes Saavedra). New York: Scribner's Sons.

Howard, P. E. (1988). *The train to Lulu's.* New York: Bradbury Press.

Hudson, W. (Ed.). (1993). *Pass it on: African American poetry for children.* New York: Scholastic.

Jacobs, F. (1992). *The Tainos: The people who welcomed Columbus.* New York: Putnam's Sons.

Jacob, L. (1993). *The great migration: An American story.* New York: HarperCollins.

Jonas, A. (1991). *The trek: El trayecto.* New York: Greenwillow.

Julivert, M. A. (1993). *The fascinating world of snakes.* New York: Barron's.

Klausner, J. (1990). *Talk about English: How words travel and change.* New York: Crowell.

Knight, M. B. (1993). *Who belongs here? An American story.* New York: Tilbury House.

Laden, N. (1994). *The night I followed the dog.* San Francisco: Chronicle.

MacGill-Callahan, S. (1991). *And still the turtle watched.* New York: Dial.

Marsden, C. (2002). *The gold-threaded dress.* New York: Candlewick.

McKissack, P. (1989). *The long hard journey.* New York: Knopf.

Medina, J. (1999). *My name is Jorge: On both sides of the river.* Honesdale, PA: Boyds Mill.

Meltzer, M. (1992). *The amazing potato.* New York: HarperCollins.

Miller, R. (1995). *The story of stagecoach Mary Fields.* Morristown, NJ: Silver Press.

Mobley, J. (1979). *The star husband.* Garden City, NY: Doubleday.

Mohr, N. (1991). *In Nueva York* (rev. ed.). Houston, TX: Arte Publico Press.

Namiok, L. (1992). *Yang the youngest and his terrible year.* Boston: Little, Brown.

Norris, O. J. (1988). *Legends of journeys.* New York: Cambridge University Press.

Nye, N. S. (2000). *Come with me: Poems for a journey.* New York: Greenwillow.

Ortiz Cofer, J. (1990). *Silent dancing: A partial remembrance of a Puerto Rican childhood.* Houston, TX: Arte Publico Press.

Perkins, M. (1993). *The Sunita experiment.* New York: Little, Brown.

Pérez, E. (1993). *A look around rain forest.* St. Petersburg, FL: Willowsip.

Rodriguez, A. (1993). *Aunt Martha and the golden coin.* New York: Clarkson Potter.

Rohmann, E. (1994). *Time flies.* New York: Crown.

Rohmer, H. (1988). *Atariba & Niguayona.* San Francisco: Children's Book Press.

Rohmer, H. (1988). *How we came to the fifth world/Como vinimos al quinto mundo.* San Francisco: Children's Book Press.

Ryan, P. M. (2002). *Esperanza rising.* New York: Scholastic.

Say, A. (1988). *A river dream.* Boston: Houghton Mifflin.

Say, A. (1989). *Lost lake.* Boston: Houghton Mifflin.

Say, A. (1990). *El Chino.* Boston: Houghton Mifflin.

Say, A. (1993). *Grandfather's journey.* New York: Houghton Mifflin.

Shea, P. D. (1995). *The whispering cloth.* New York: Boyds Mills Press.

Simon, S. (Ed.). (1995). *Star walk.* New York: Morrow.

Sneve, V. D. H. (1993). *The Sioux.* New York: Holiday House.

Sneve, V. D. H. (Ed.). (1989). *Dancing tepees: Poems of American Indian youth.* New York: Holiday House.

Stanley, J. (1992). *Children of the dust bowl: The true story of the school at Weedpatch Camp.* New York: Crown.

Steptoe, J. (1987). *Mufaro's beautiful daughters.* New York: Lothrop Lee & Shepard.

Stevens, J. R. (1993). *Carlos y la planta de calabaza: Carlos and the squash plant.* New York: Northland.

Surat, J. (1989). *Angel child, dragon child.* New York: Scholastic.

Suzuki, D. (1987). *Looking at the body.* Toronto: Stoddart.

Taylor, M. (1975). *Roll of thunder, hear my cry.* New York: Dial.

Taylor, M. (1990). *The road to Memphis.* New York: Dial.

Temple, F. (1993). *Grab hands and run.* New York: Orchard.

Temple, L. (1993). *Dear world: How children around the world feel about our environment.* New York: Random House.

Turín, A. (1980). *Planeta Mary Año 35/Planet Mary Year 35.* Barcelona: Lumen.

Uchida, Y. (1976). *Journey to Topaz.* New York: Atheneum.

Uchida, Y. (1978). *Journey home.* New York: Atheneum.

Weiss, H. (1991). *Maps: Getting from here to there.* New York: Houghton Mifflin.

Williams, V. (1984). *Music, music for everyone.* New York: Greenwillow.

Yarbrough, C. (1982). *The shimmershine queens.* New York: Scholastic.

Yep, L. (1975). *Dragonwings.* New York: Harper & Row.

About the Authors

Bertha Pérez is Professor of Education and Bicultural Bilingual Studies at the University of Texas at San Antonio. She teaches courses on biliteracy, early literacy, multicultural children's literature, sociocultural issues in literacy, and Spanish reading in bilingual programs. Her research interests include biliteracy development of Spanish-speaking children, literacy instruction in bilingual contexts, and language-minority issues.

Teresa L. McCarty is a social-cultural anthropologist who lives and works in the U.S. Southwest. She is Professor of Language, Reading, and Culture at the University of Arizona. She also codirects the American Indian Language Development Institute, an international program for educators of Native American youth. She teaches courses on language and culture, anthropology and education, multicultural/American Indian education, and qualitative methods. Her research focuses on the relationship between federal policy and local educational practice in American Indian and other language-minority communities. She is especially interested in using ethnography and participatory action research to study American Indian children's biliteracy development as a means of informing and improving bilingual education programs.

Lucille J. Watahomigie is a member of the Hualapai Tribe of northern Arizona. She is currently Director of Federal Programs and Hualapai language teacher at Peach Springs School on the Hualapai reservation. In 1978, she founded the American Indian Language Development Institute, which is now an internationally known program in American Indian linguistics and bilingual/bicultural curriculum development serving indigenous and nonindigenous teachers from the United States, Canada, and Latin America. She has authored numerous scholarly articles, bilingual children's texts, and training models that have enabled other Indian schools and communities to replicate the bilingual education program at Peach Springs. As a faculty member in the AILDI, she teaches courses on bilingual methods and materials, bilingual curriculum development, and second-language acquisition and teaching.

María E. Torres-Guzmán is Associate Professor and Director of the Bilingual/Bicultural Education Program at Teachers College, Columbia University. Her research interests include parental and community involvement in education, classroom ethnography, and the relationship between language, culture, and instruction.

To thi Dien was an instructor in the Vietnamese teacher preparation program in the College of Education at San Jose State University. She taught courses in multicultural education, ESL methodologies, and dual language instruction. Her research included the cultural perception of educational reforms from the perspective of the students and their families and the sociocultural impact of American schooling on Vietnamese immigrants.

Ji-Mei Chang is a Professor in the Division of Special Education and Rehabilitative Services, College of Education, San Jose State University. She teaches both graduate and credential courses in the areas of developing authentic assessment and the integrated curriculum across social studies, math, science, and language arts for students with learning disabilities. She conducts school-based research to promote teachers' professional development in the areas of reading comprehension strategies for students with limited English proficiency and rubric development for Chinese language arts.

Howard L. Smith is Associate Professor of Bicultural Bilingual Studies at the University of Texas at San Antonio, where he teaches undergraduate and graduate courses in bilingual education theory, bilingual and ESL teaching methodology, multicultural children's literature, and biliteracy. His research interests include two-way bilingual schools and biliteracy development.

Aurelia Dávila de Silva is an educational consultant in San Antonio, Texas. She has been a classroom teacher and university professor. Her work has concentrated on biliteracy development of young children and literacy learning through literature. She is currently conducting case study research on Iseña's literacy development.

Amy Nordlander is a doctoral student in the Culture, Literacy, and Language Program at the University of Texas at San Antonio. She has studied sociocultural factors regarding literacy, language, and identity in Sweden and the United States.

Author Index

Subject Index

A

AAVE (African American Vernacular English), 222, 223
Abriendo Caminos program, 129–130
Ada, A. F., 40
Additive bilingualism, 13, 14
African American communities, and literacy
  cultural deprivation hypothesis, 226–227
  discourse style, 29
  family literacy, 37, 38, 40
  historical perspective
    Great Depression era, 215–216
    Hampton–Tuskegee model, 214–215, 230
    historical repression effects, 218–219
    mid-1800s, 211–212
    post-Civil War era, 212–214
    pre-liberation, 209–211
    proscribed school, 217
    school segregation, 217–218
    teacher preparation, 216–217
  literacy and oracy
    African roots, 219
    call-response, 220–221

    narrative sequencing, 221–221
    oral traditions, 212, 219–222
    sacred–secular/oral–literate continuum, 219–220 (fig)
    signification (the Dozens), 220–221
    tone semantics, 221–222
  literacy development at Trackton, 38
  sociocultural context of language learning, 12
  varieties of English/educability
    African American Vernacular English, 222, 223
    Black English Vernacular, 9–10, 46, 222, 225, 235
    educability, 224–225
    speech communities, 223–224
African American student
  Black English Vernacular use by, 9–10, 46
  Head Start program and, 227
  linguicism and, 227
  literacy instruction principle
    believe in student, 233–235
    build on community/student culture, 235–236

391